Contents

Acknowledgments

We all know the old cliché of a picture is worth a thousand words. My intention for this second book is to educate using illustrations that were sketched as I figured out who the Mammoth People were and what their folklore tales were about. This book is a companion to my first book *The Sentient Mammoth People; Pure Microlithic Abstract Art.*

I want to extend a very special thanks to my banker friends Steve Cleveland and Emily Rischling for their help in formatting my illustrations and the descriptions that went with them into this second book for self-publication and for doing the same for the e-pub version.

Preface

This is a book of line sketch illustrations that were created at the moment of inception of the sentient Mammoth People's folklore tales. They were drawn immediately after I finished interpreting the second or third microlithic abstract artwork that had scenes from one of the Mammoth People's repetitive themes or folklore tales. Upon completion of an interpretation I was left with the most permanent indelible image on my 'mind's eye' and I knew that the only way I could capture that snapshot image in Pleistocene time was to immediately pick up my black ink pen and sketch what I had just seen for the first time in at least thirteen millennia.

I never wadded up the paper to re-sketch the scene. If a mistake was made I just continued sketching right over it. My goal was to be as true as possible to the talented Stone Age microlithic abstract artist that planted that imagery in my 'mind's eye'. Consequently, I very seldom had to re-sketch that particular folklore tale on subsequent interpretations because the original line sketch of it was so accurate that I didn't think that I could improve on it. How could that be when I hadn't picked up a pen to sketch or draw anything for at least thirty years while I farmed, raised my family and rebuilt our hundred and seven year old house? The black line sketches flowed out of me as if my right hand was being guided by the incredibly talented Ice Age microlithic abstract artisans.

The line sketches are listed in chronological order by the dates that I sketched them which verifies the order that I was figuring out all of the folklore tales, most of which were constantly overlapping in my 'mind's eye'. That turned out to be a very lengthy and complex voyage of discovery filled with constant eureka moments. It was these simple line sketches that covered every square inch of the small research room of my home as if they were plastered all over the inside of my head. They aided me in identifying the microlithic abstract artwork that I would be currently interpreting because a picture is worth a thousand words. The beauty of these simple line sketches is that without ever having to actually read or follow one of the interpretations, anyone can have the Mammoth People hunter herder microlithic abstract artists folklore tales implanted in their own 'mind's eye'.... which is all I ever intended to do when I first figured out their unprecedented Stone Age microlithic abstract art figurative language...

REFLECTIONS FROM THE PLIESTOCENE

As you advance through this book of line sketch illustrations that were created upon completion of individual interpretations, keep in mind that scenes were addendums to each individual folklore tale until the complete folklore tale was achieved. This will appear obvious as you advance from the rougher appearance of the earliest sketches and their interpretations to the last ones that are a compilation of a seven year period of research. You will be seeing what I saw in my 'mind's eye' moments after I finished a particular interpretation and therefore, you will actually be able to follow along with my progression of discovery....

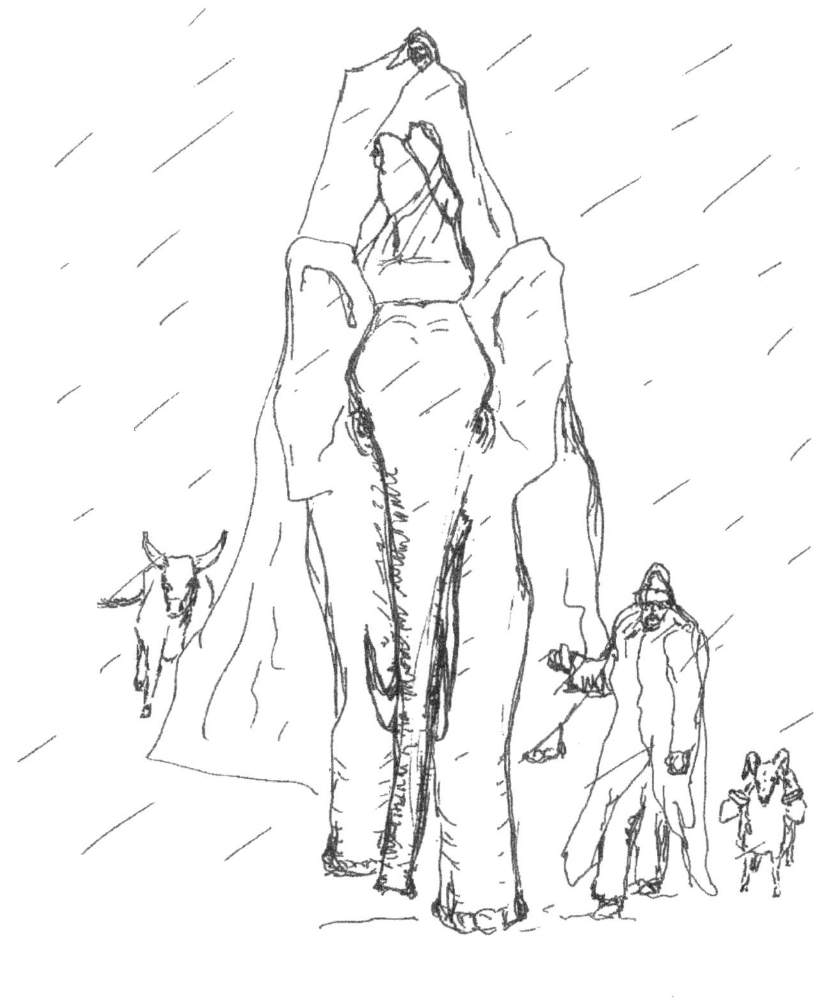

"ARE WE THERE YET?!...this BABIES FREEZING!"

1) This was sketched shortly after I figured out that the Caucasian Mammoth People rode atop their domesticated mammoth during their epic trek to 'here'.

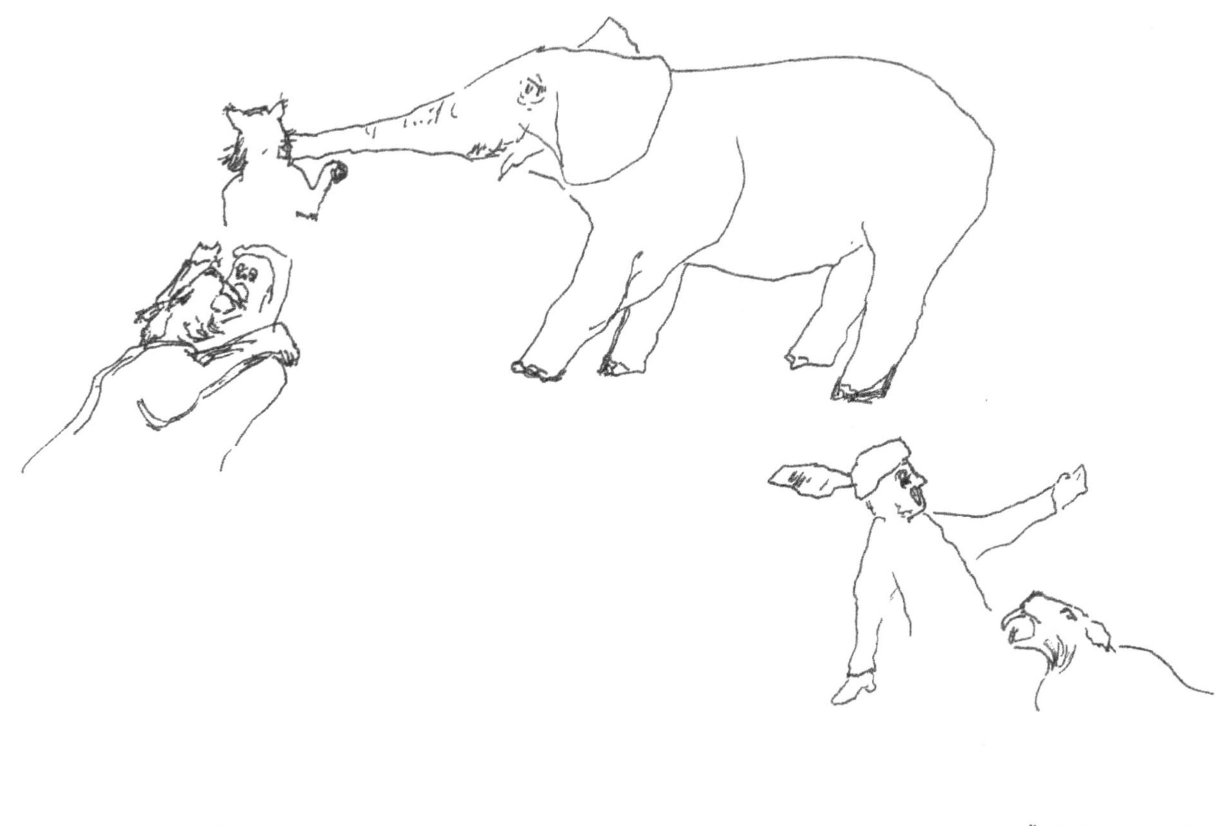

'...both of these Caucasian herders were... EATEN ALIVE!'

2) This piece shows the symbiotic relationship between saber-toothed cats and mammoth. They usually worked in groups of three to take down a running mammoth. One climbed up on its back and went to work slicing off the splayed out ears, the second went to work clawing at its eyes and the third jumped up and caught its raised trunk to slice it off with its two long saber fangs that were designed to do just that. Then they simply waited for the weakened mammoth to succumb.

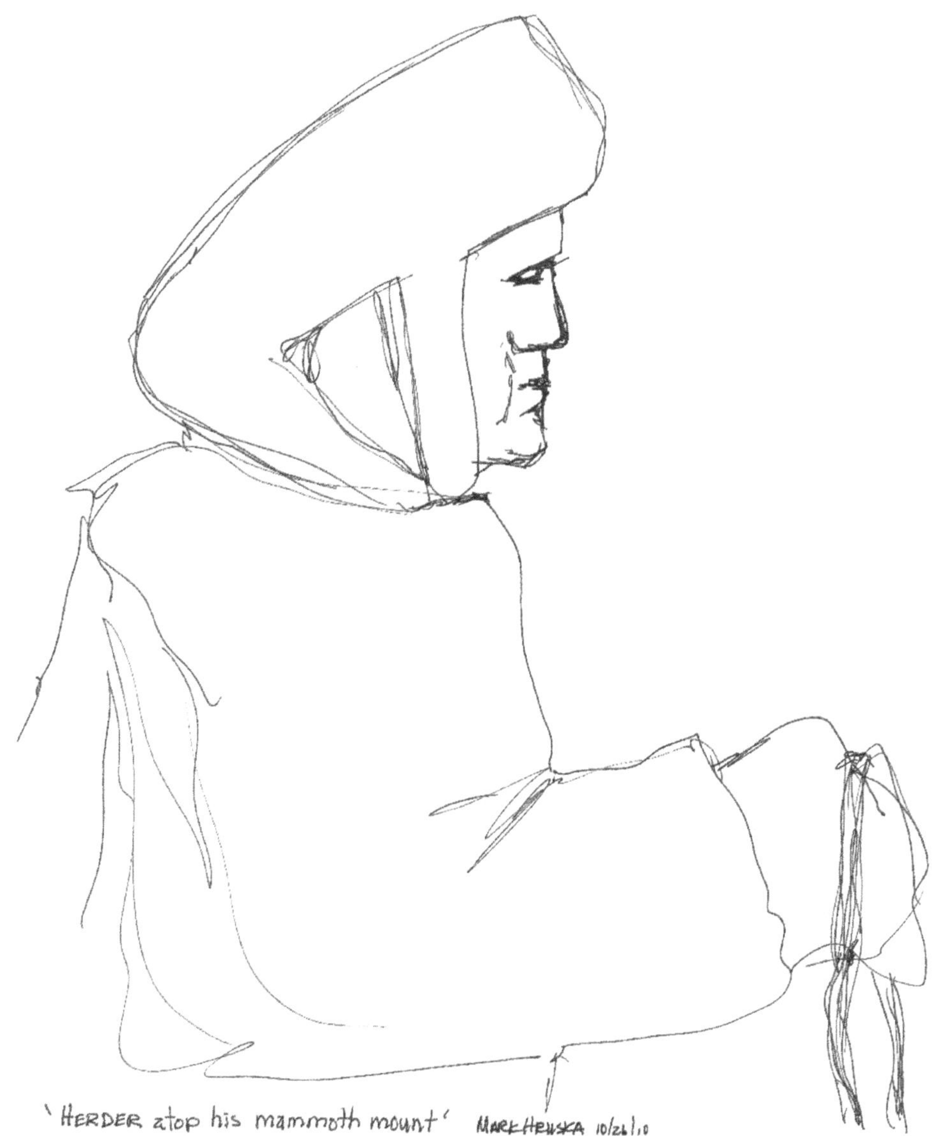

'HERDER atop his mammoth mount'

3) This is one of the earliest images that I got of the hunter herder and he happened to be riding atop a mammoth.

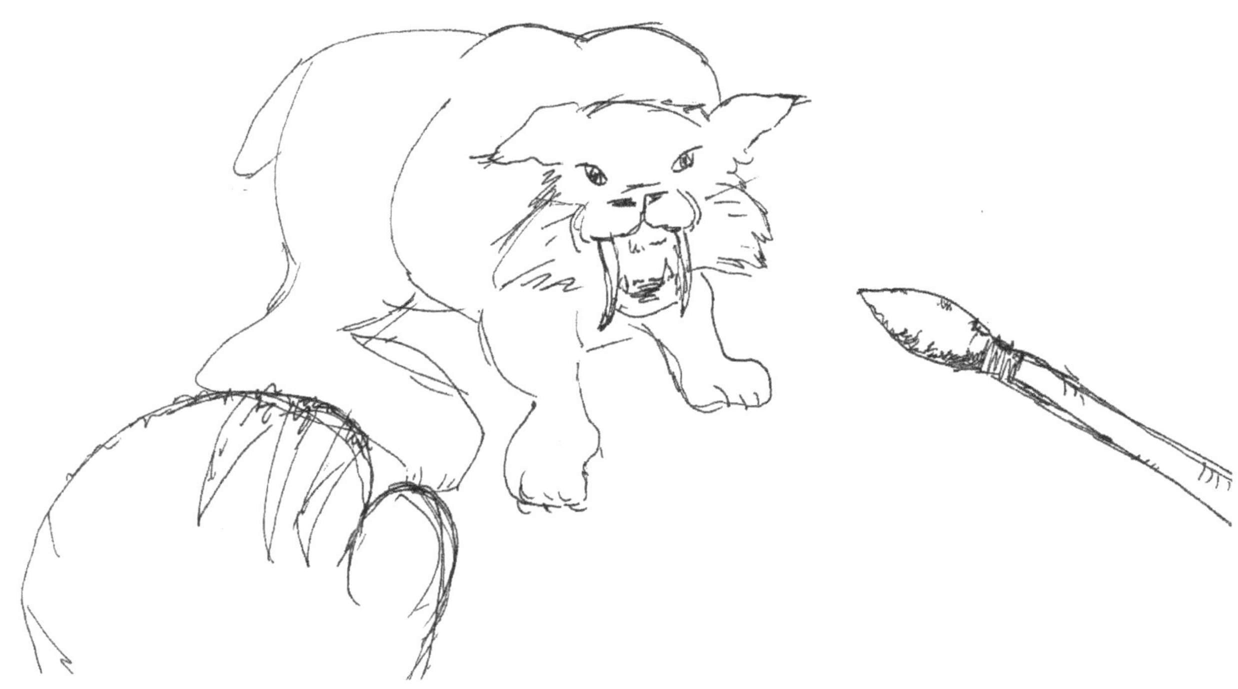

"I'M GOING FOR THE JUGULAR"... "THIS IS IT!"

4) When I first saw the cognitive illusion image of the saber-toothed cat in this piece of flint it left an indelible image in my 'mind's eye' because I knew that I was seeing him through the eyes of the hunter herder that was standing face to face with him with his spear tip the only thing between them.

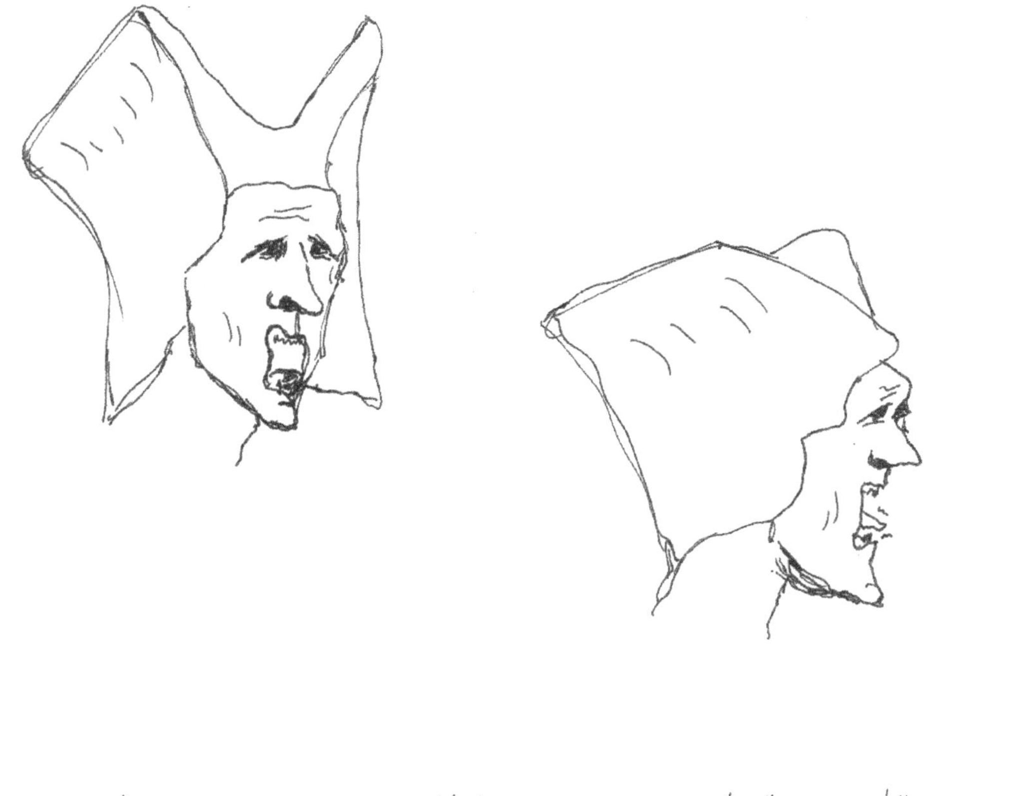

"CROTCHETY OLD QUEEN"... "Don't get in my way!"... "OR ELSE!"

5) When I first saw her all crotchety and all, I thought she was their queen, but further into my research I realized that she was crotchety grandma during their exodus from their violently erupting mountainous homeland. Even though she was sitting on her special armchair that was attached to a stretcher that her four porters were carrying on their shoulders, she was still being tormented by fiery hot cinder balls and all of the other drama that was playing out around her during that hellish Pleistocene night.

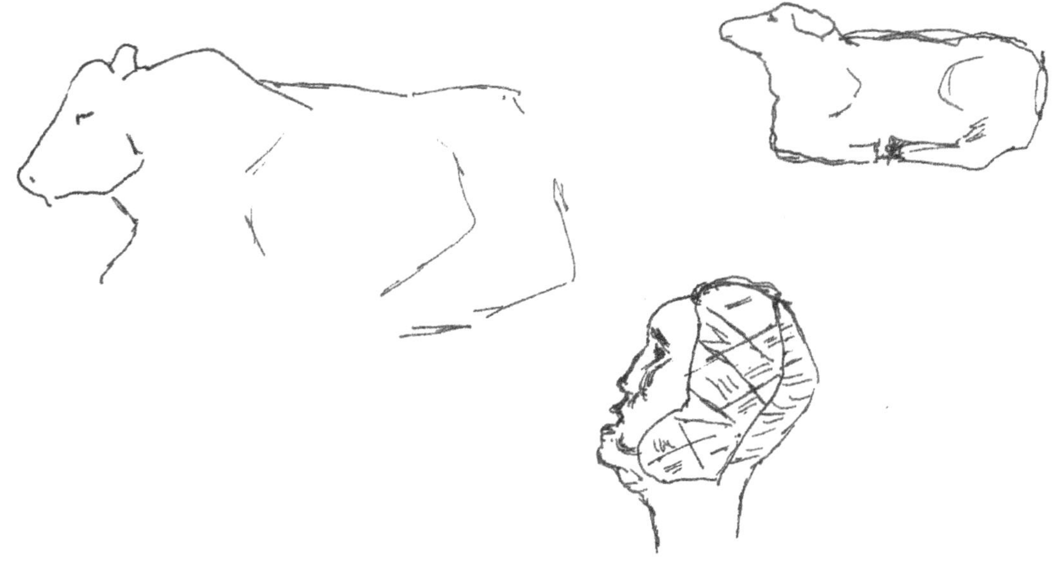

'pottery rim sherd...laying down, watchful ram, old bull...and... OLD WOMAN!'

6) This was undoubtedly scenes from the Mammoth People folklore tale of when kind loving grandma shepherdess was sitting out in the meadow tending her lulling sheep and cattle. I just hadn't tied it all together yet because somewhere else on that piece would surely be imagery of an attacking bear, lion or a pair of dire wolves.

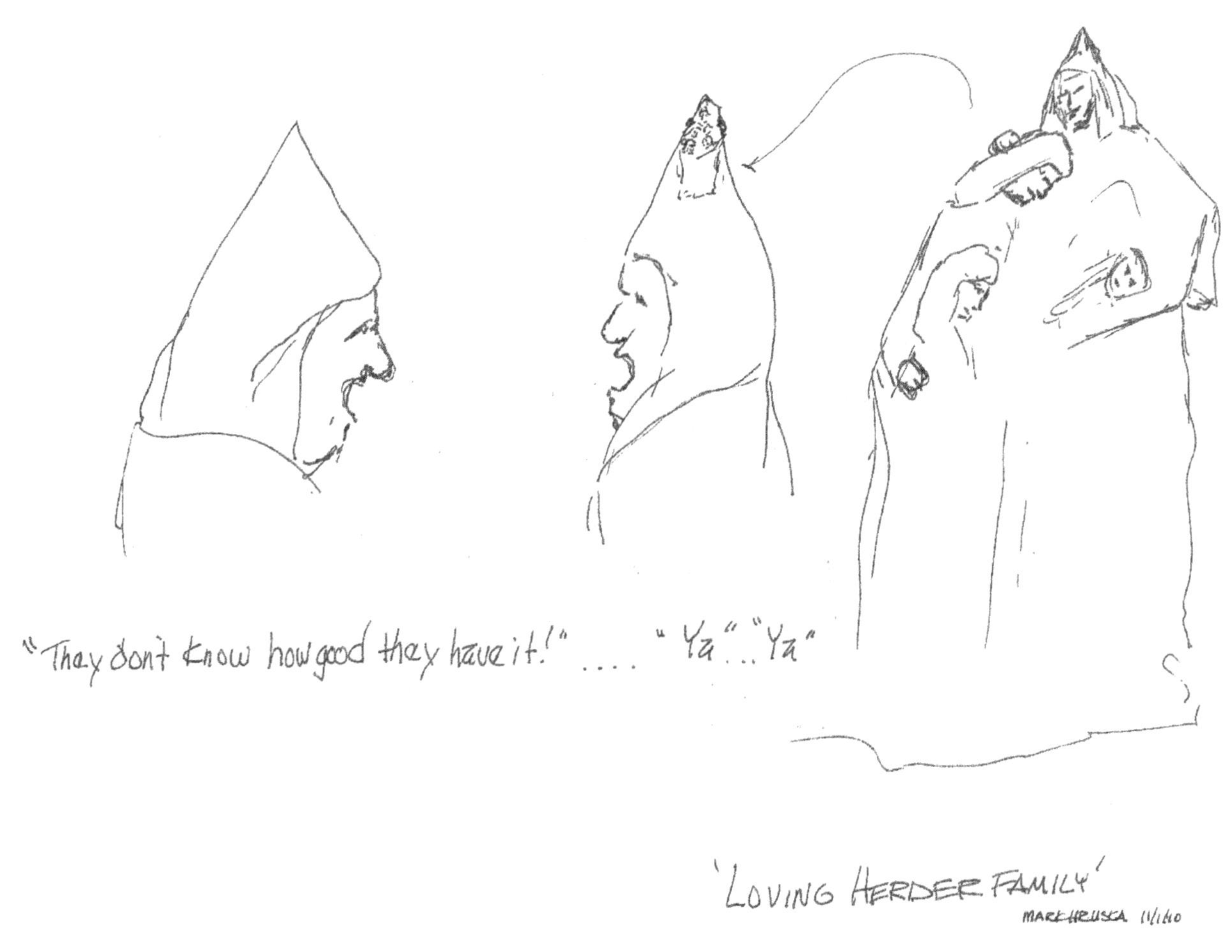

'LOVING HERDER FAMILY' "They don't know how good they have it!"

7) I distinctly remember this potshard piece when for the first time I saw the loving Mammoth People family subtly etched and rubbed out in the light grey inside slip of the potsherd, learning another one of their abstract art techniques.

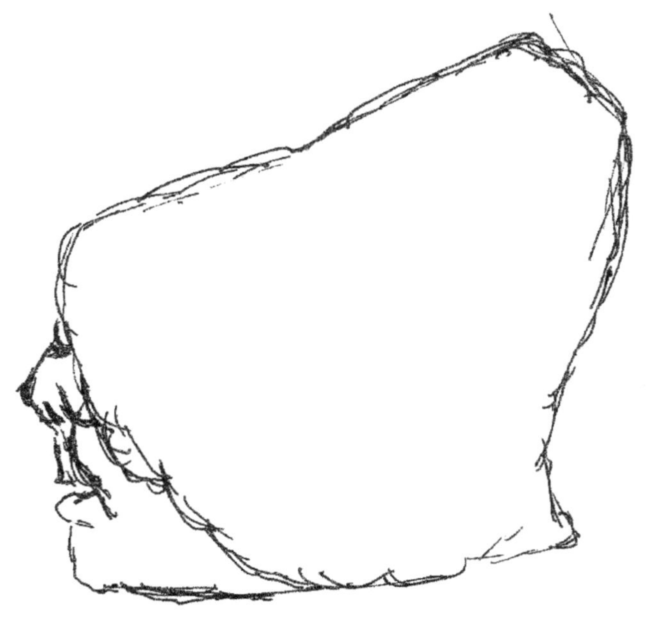

'Actual herders image from the 'pottery shard'...
'Distorted herders face...and the cat that's attacking!'

8) This piece is self-explanatory and without reading the interpretation I can't tell you if it's a saber-toothed cat or a lion that's attacking him.

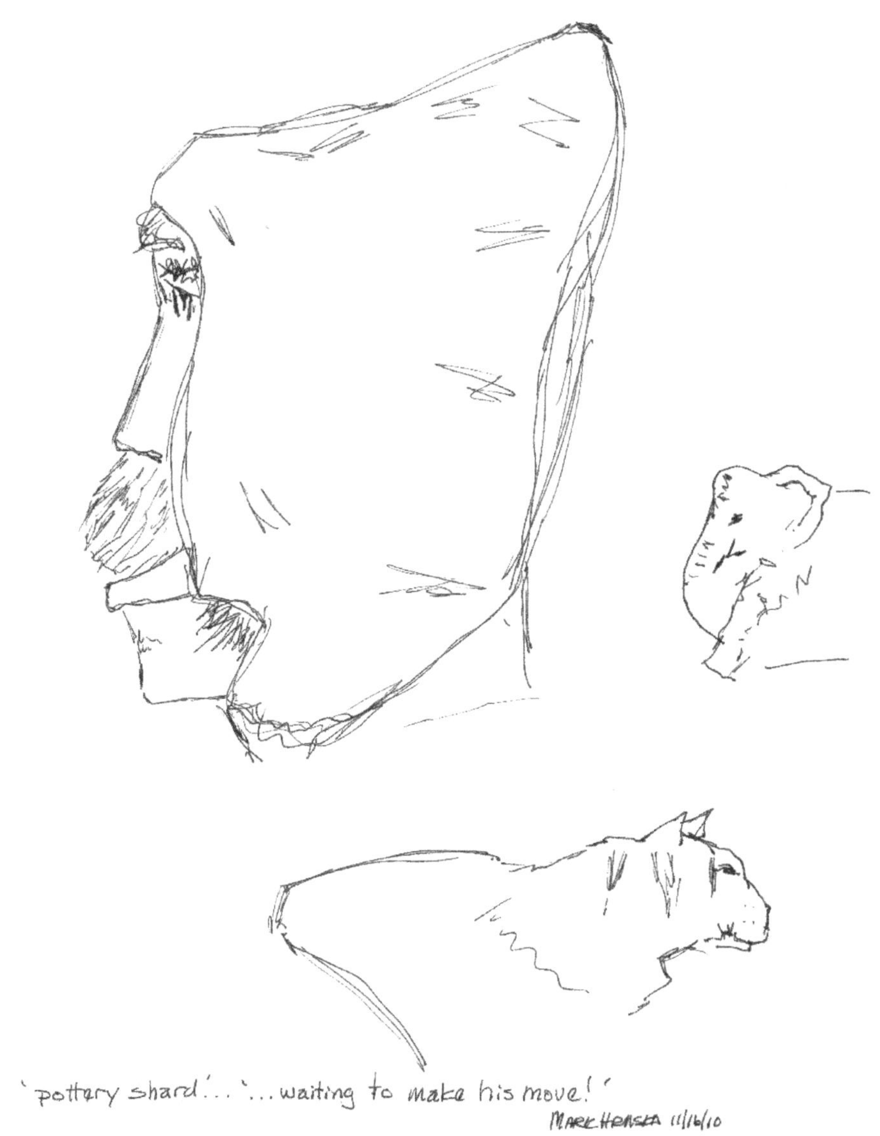

'pottery shard'... '...waiting to make his move!'
MARK HENSLA 11/16/10

'pottery shard'... '...waiting to make his move!'

9) This is another self-explanatory piece.

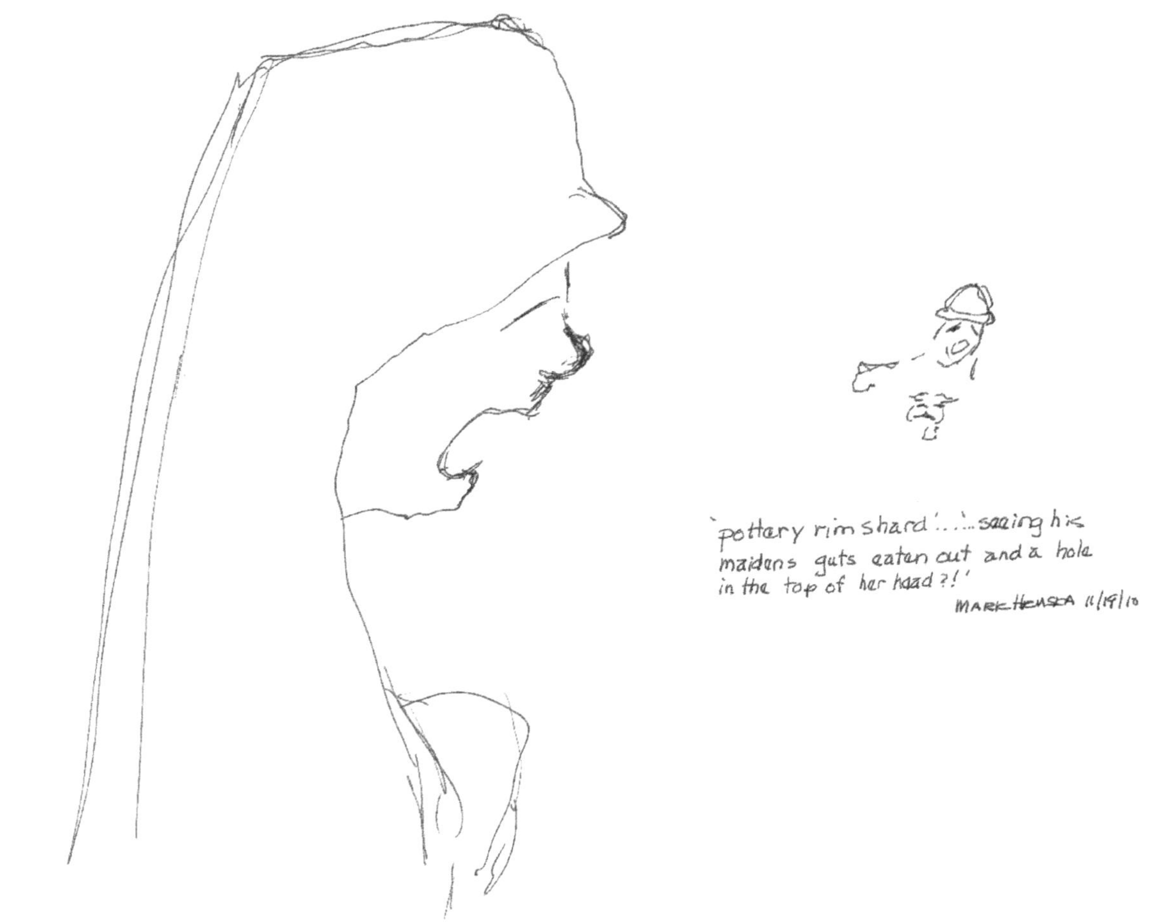

'pottery rim shard'.... '...seeing his maidens guts eaten out
and a hole in the top of her head?!'

10) This was undoubtedly one of those grizzly scenes when dad found his freshly eaten waist high young maiden or fair young maiden daughter. I have to relate that it took some getting used to when I first came across these images that were before I tied them into their popular folklore tales.

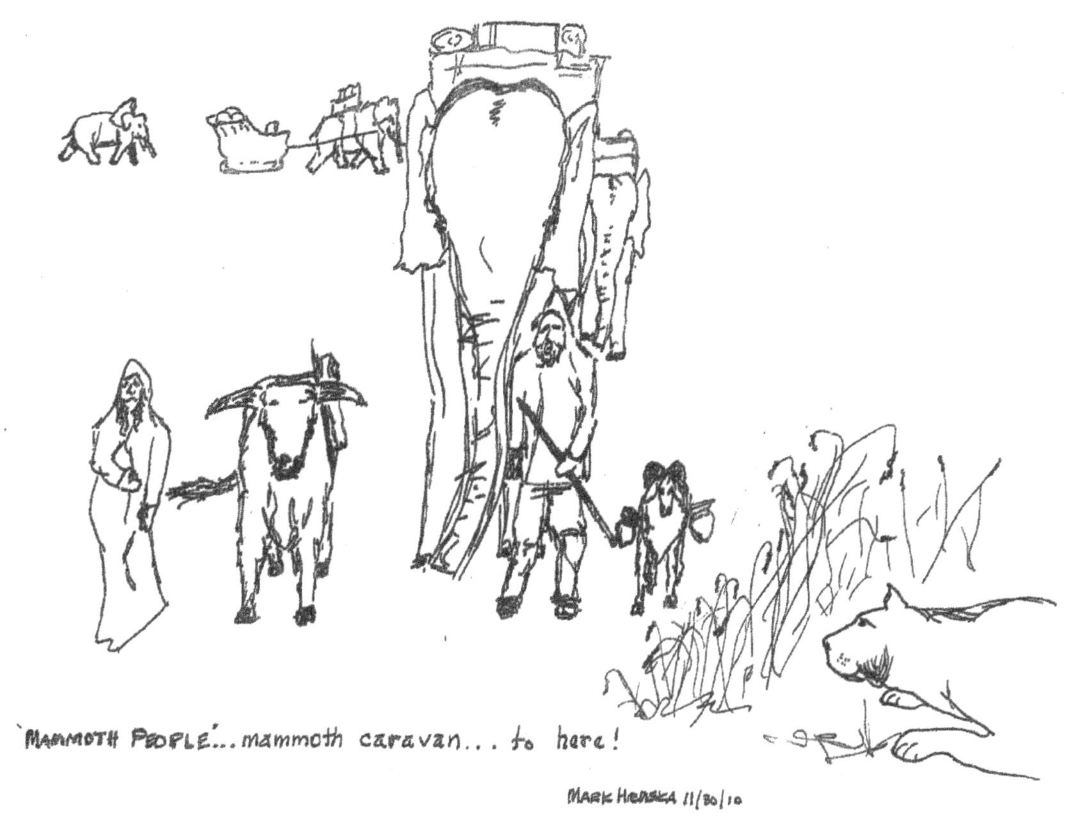

'MAMMOTH PEOPLE'...mammoth caravan to here!

11) This is how I was seeing the Mammoth People mammoth caravan at this time in my research. As you can see, irate grandma wasn't sitting atop the lead mammoth yet because she was sitting in a sled with her pregnant ewe and her lambs behind it which is part of the folklore tale of when the three cooperating saber-toothed cats usually attacked the caravan. She was usually the first in line because they came over the back wall of the sled first.

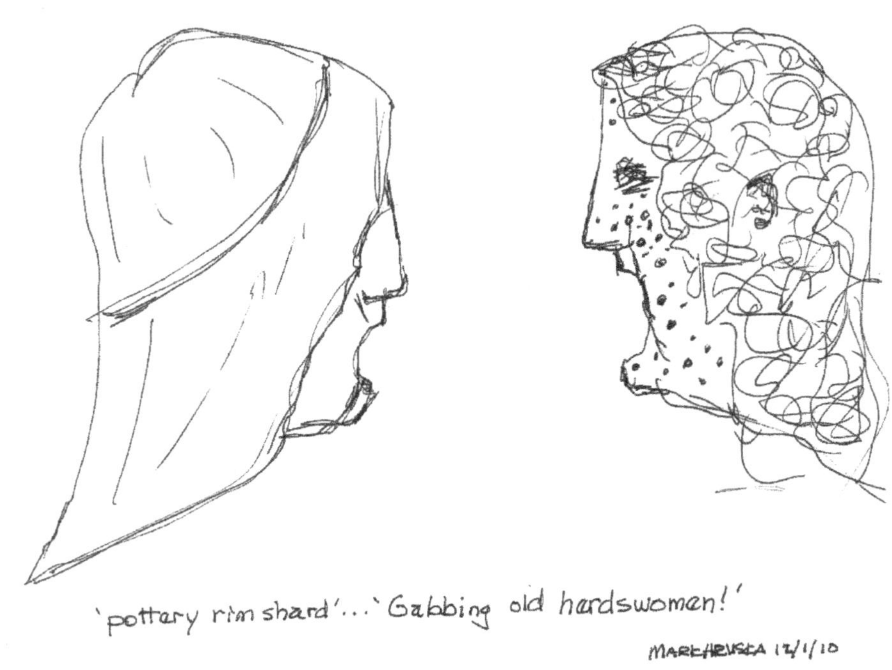

'Pottery rim shard'... 'Gabbing old herdswomen!'

12) I'm sure that I interpreted this piece just to show how the Mammoth People herdswomen looked. As I ventured further and further into my research I realized that the old herdswomen were often shown with distinctive moles on their faces as well as missing teeth and front buck-teeth.

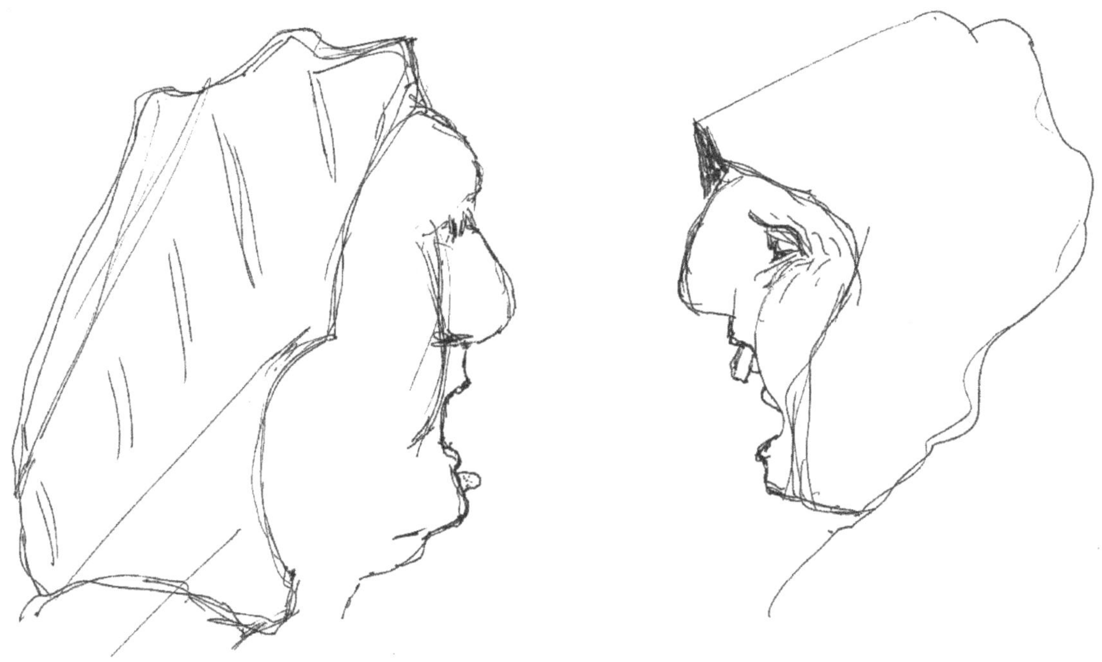

"HAAA!"... "HAA!"... "ha".... "HAAA!"... "HAAA!"...
"ha"... "...they'll never try that again!"

13) This is the interpretation of the opposing heads of a gossiping old herdswoman and a gossiping old herdsman.

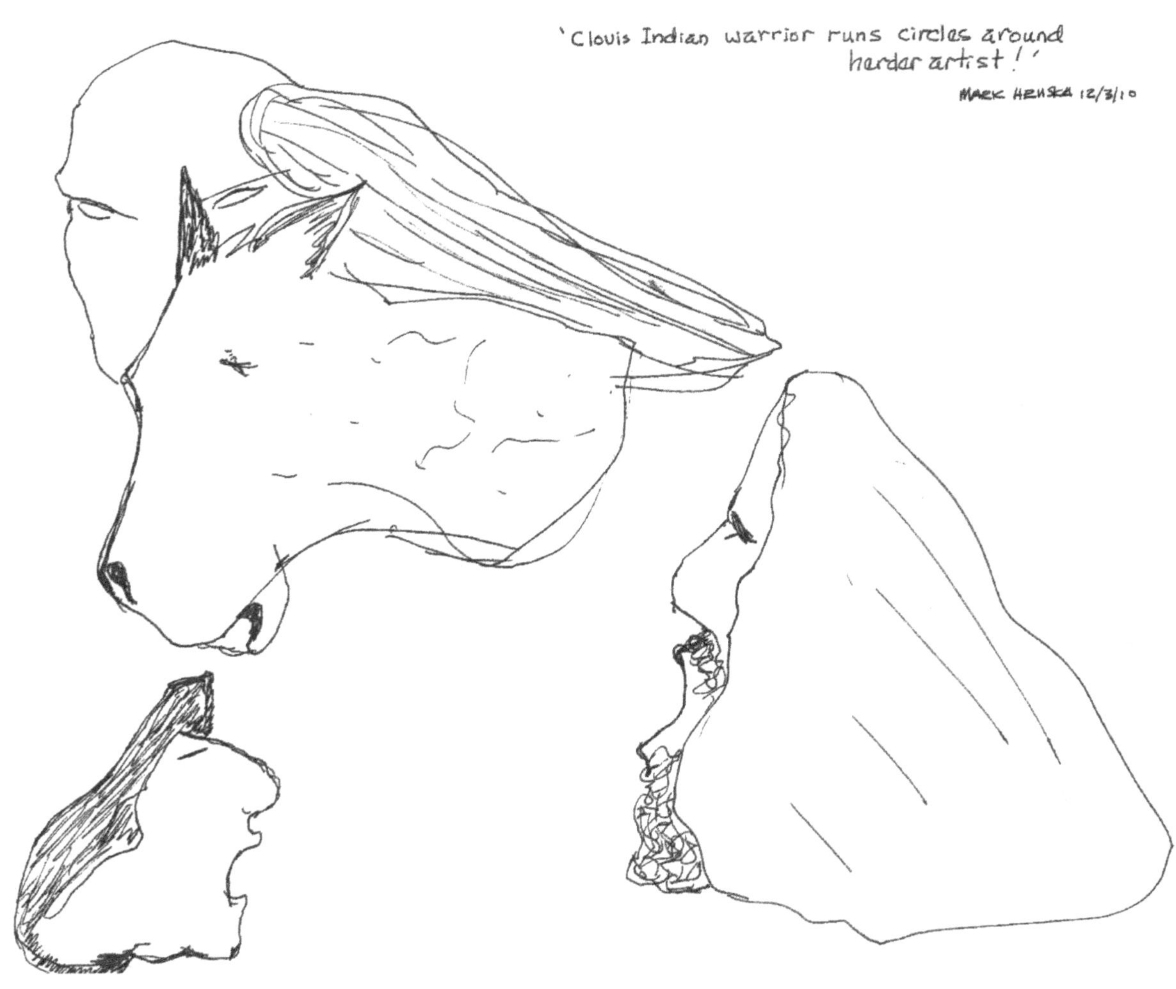

'Clovis Indian warrior runs circles around herder artist!'

14) This is one of the first times that I started to put together the 'powwow' repetitive theme or folklore tale. Notice how you can see the wicked looking warrior braves face on the other side of his galloping horses head and that the top of his head is shaved. Below is a second image of the right side view of his whooping and hollering face that's looking towards the hunter herder's face. They were undoubtedly viewed as opposing heads. This is also before I realized that the whooping and hollering warrior braves rode 'sulfur' or palomino horses, and is before I named them the Palomino Pony People.

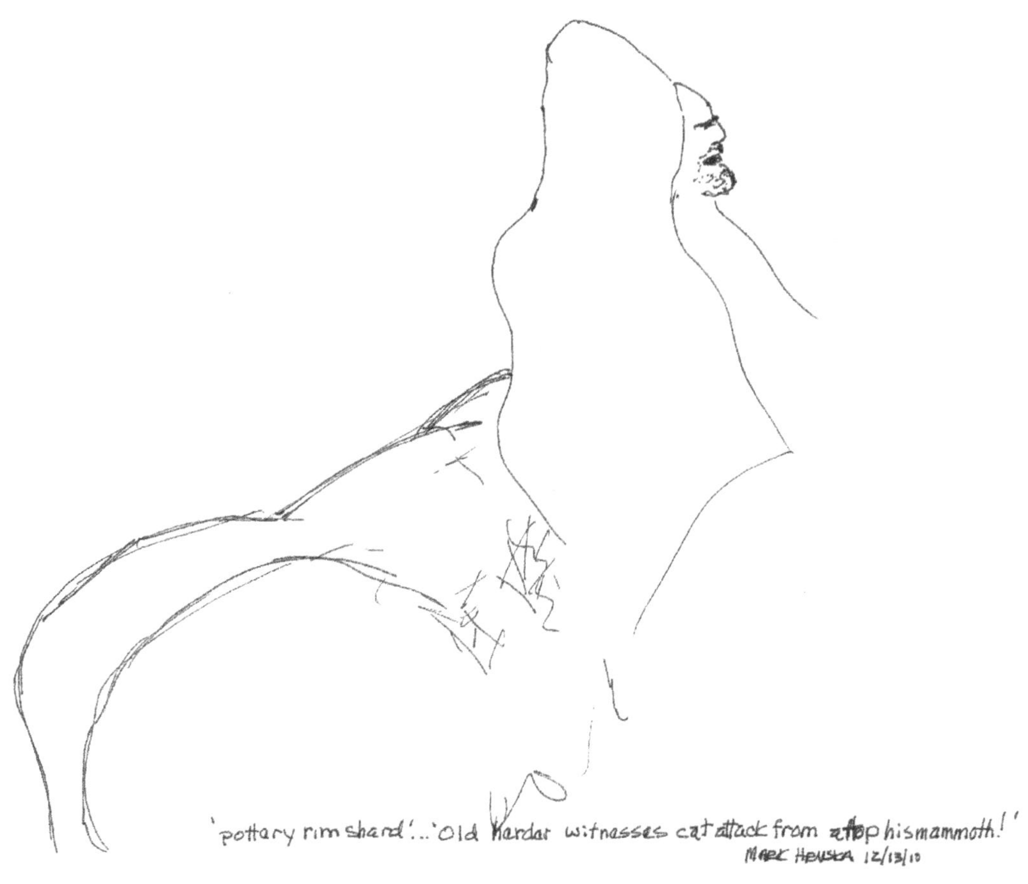

'pottery rim shard'... 'Old herder witnesses cat attack from atop his mammoth!'

15) This is undoubtedly grandpa riding the second back mammoth in the Mammoth People mammoth caravan of trekkers when they were trekking across the grasslands on their way to 'here'.

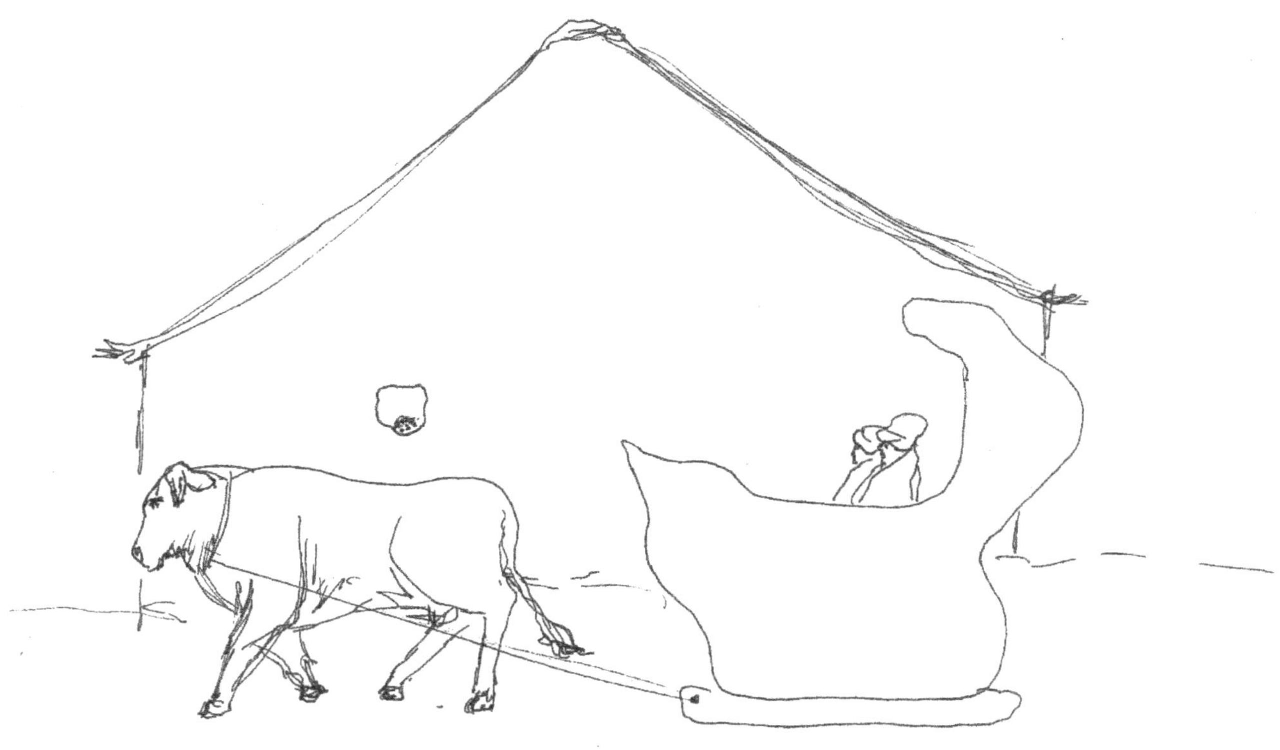

'pottery rim shard'... "Kids!"... 'We're home!"

16) I remember that the cool thing about this piece was seeing the small waist high young child peering out the cottages window.

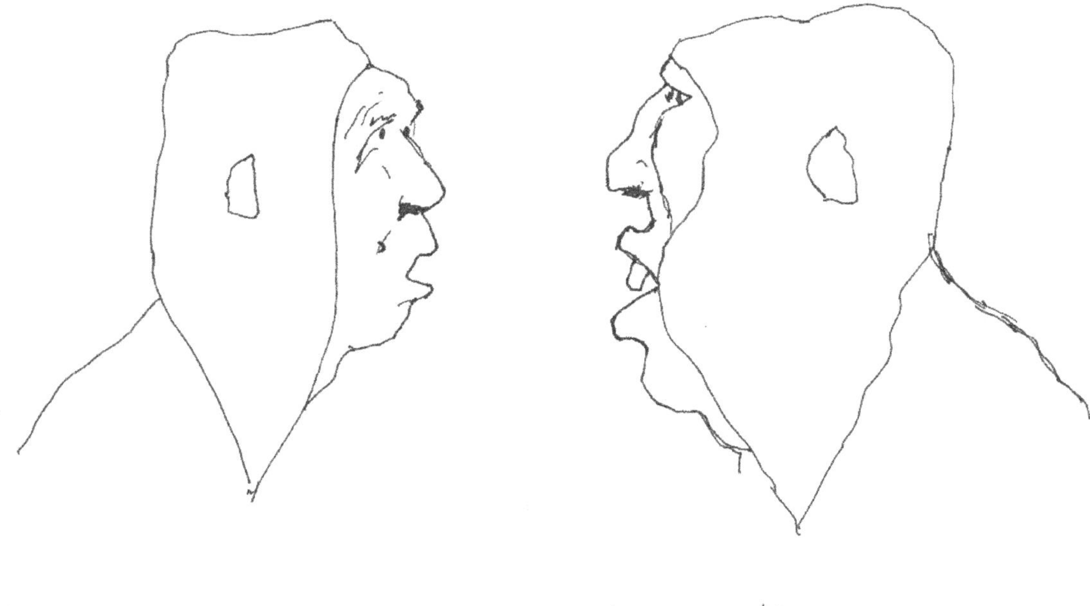

'pottery shard'... "...nobody ever believes me!"

17) What stood out in my 'mind's eye' when I saw this piece at the time of its interpretation is that the gossiping herdsman had holes in their hoods where there ears were. For all I know, the hunter herder abstract artist did it just to show that they were listening to each other. On the other hand, if you wanted to hear a twig snap when a predator was stalking you, perhaps you wouldn't want to cover your ears.

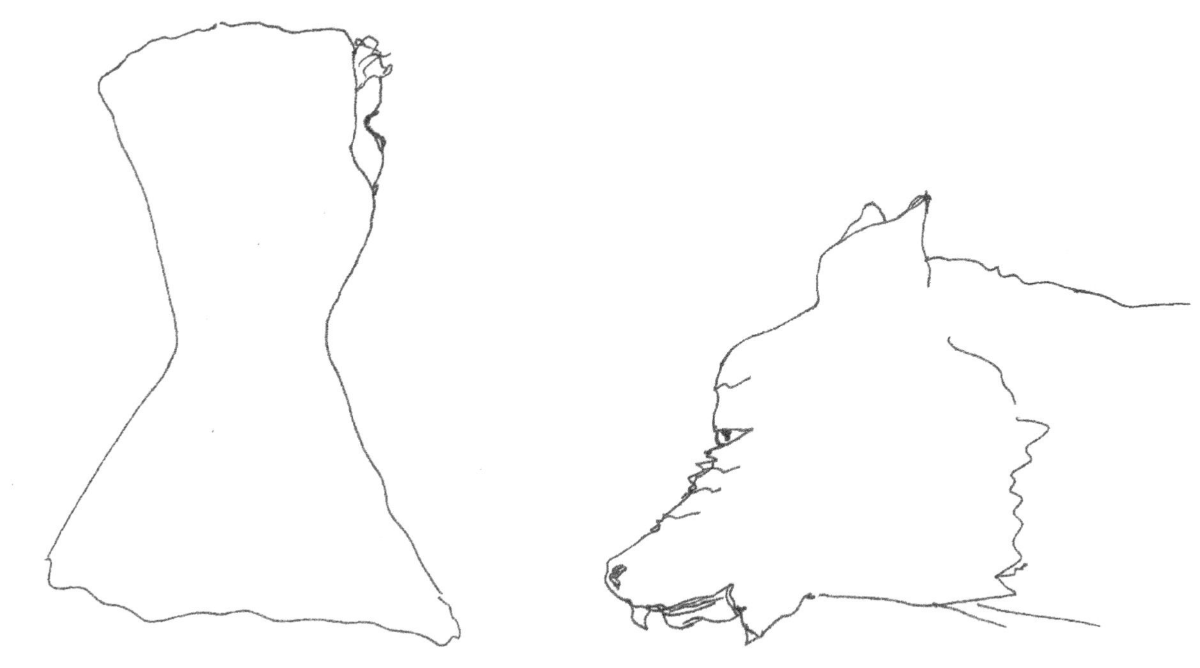

'pottery shard'... '...they want to silence
the horrific screams that were coming from those lips!'

18) This was a predator prey theme that clearly stood out in my 'mind's eye' simply because it reminded me of our own 'Little Red Riding Hood'. And now we know how long we've been thinking along those lines.

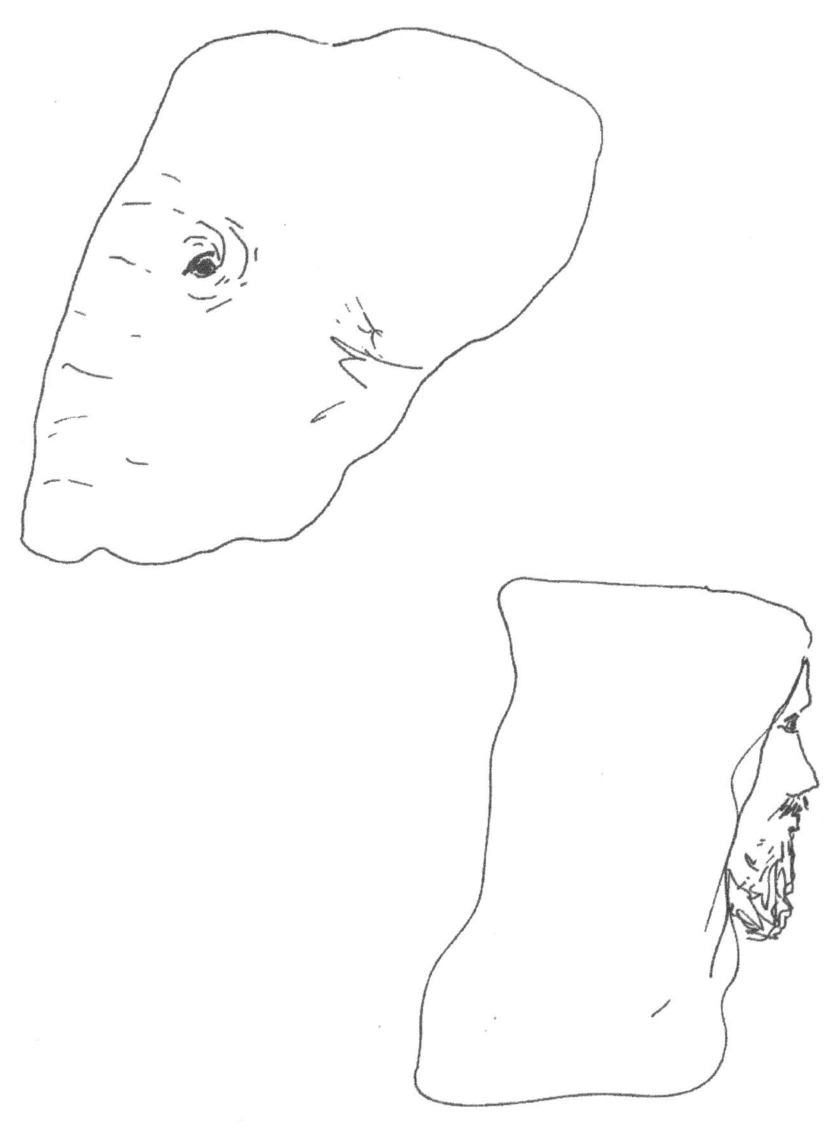

'What they each see!'

19) This piece is totally self-explanatory.

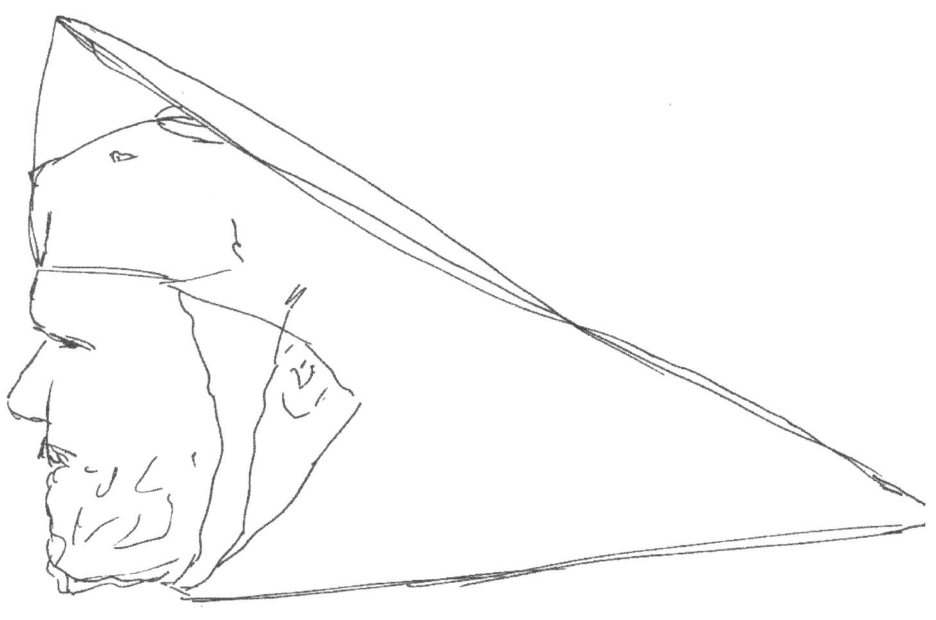

'flint backed knife'... '...the perfect image of the left side view of a
Patriot soldiers head and face!'

20) I later realized that this is simply how the lead hunter herders head gear looked. I later called it his vintage sailor style summertime hat that sloped to a point behind his shoulders and that was high in the front with a short visor on it. The left side view of a saber-toothed cat biting the top of his head from behind is how the Mammoth People perceived a stealthy hunter herder.

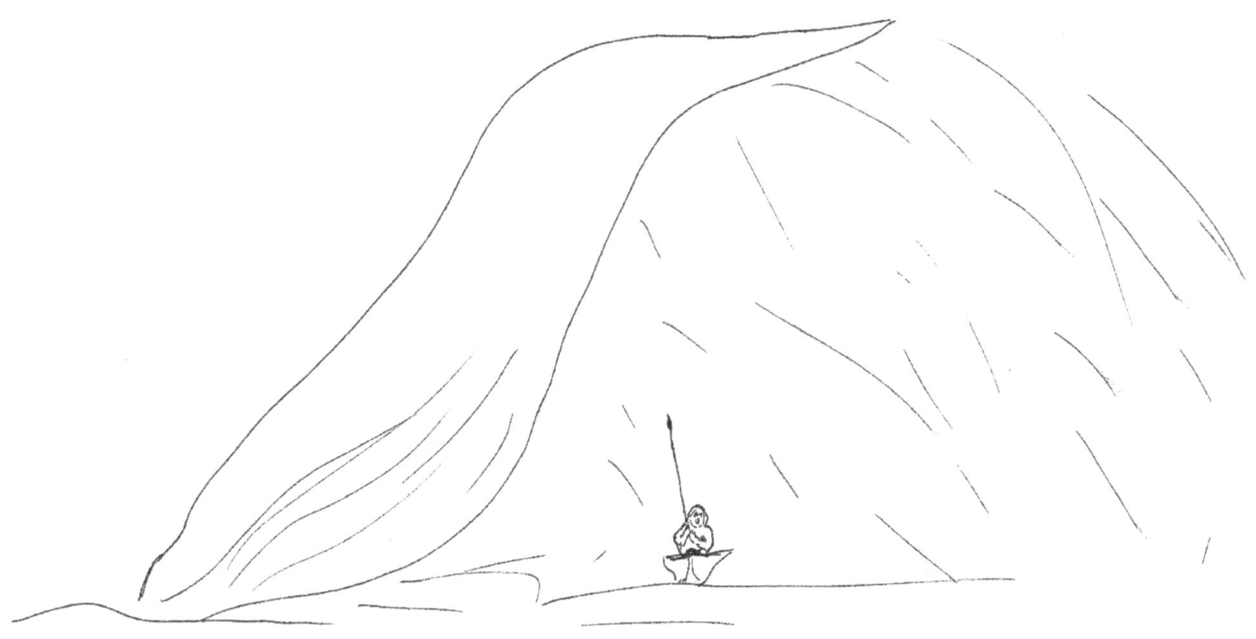

'prismatic knife'... 'Whale hunter... incredibly,
he really was an Ice Age humpback whale hunter!'

21) Imagine my euphoric surprise when I realized that I was seeing close-up imagery of a humpback whale on this piece along with the reflection imagery of the hunter herder with his harpoon type spear in his kayak.

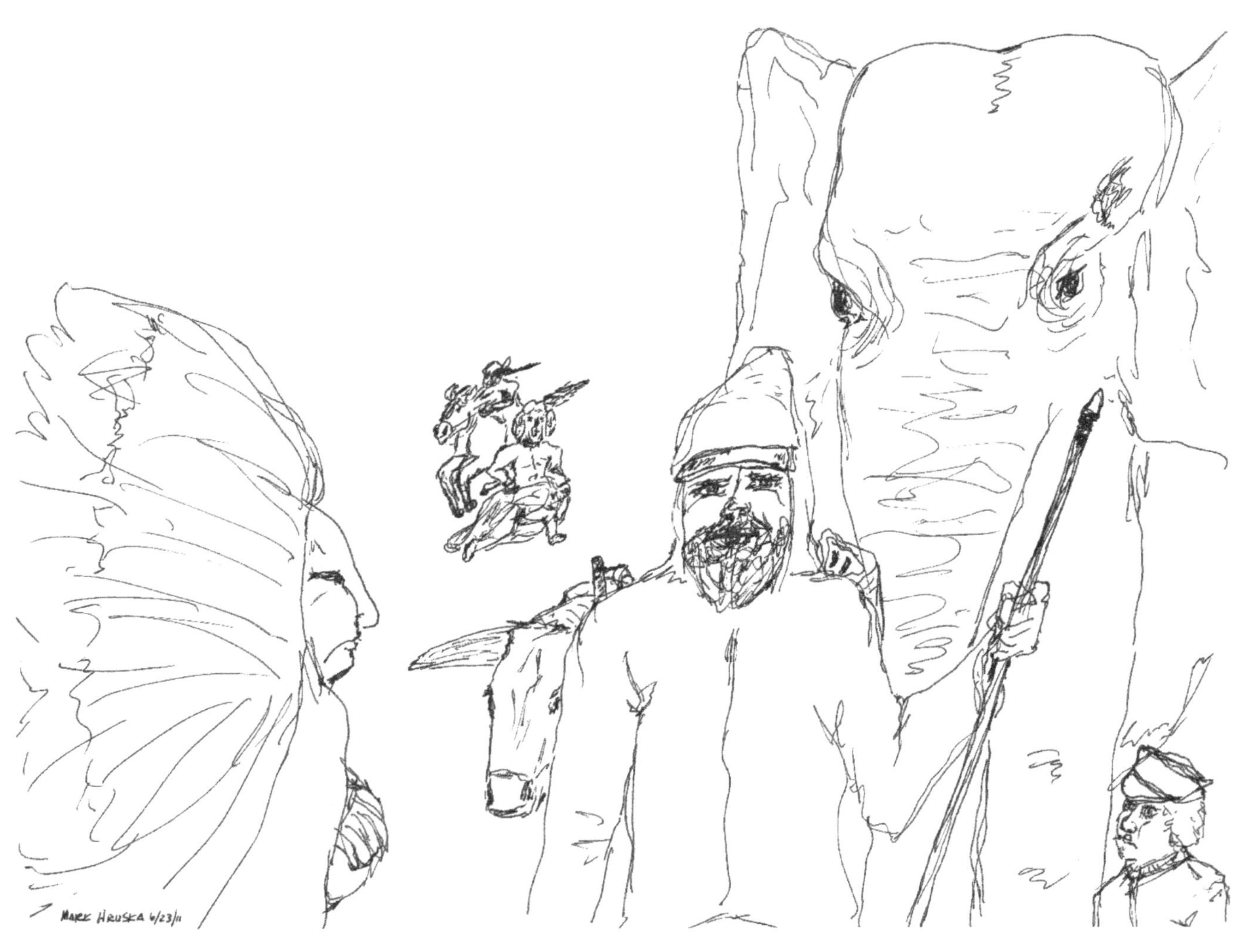

22) This line sketch was my very first attempt at bringing the known parts of the 'powwow' together up to that date in my research. It was remarkably accurate because nothing that you see in it changed with repeated interpretations only addendums of several more variances.

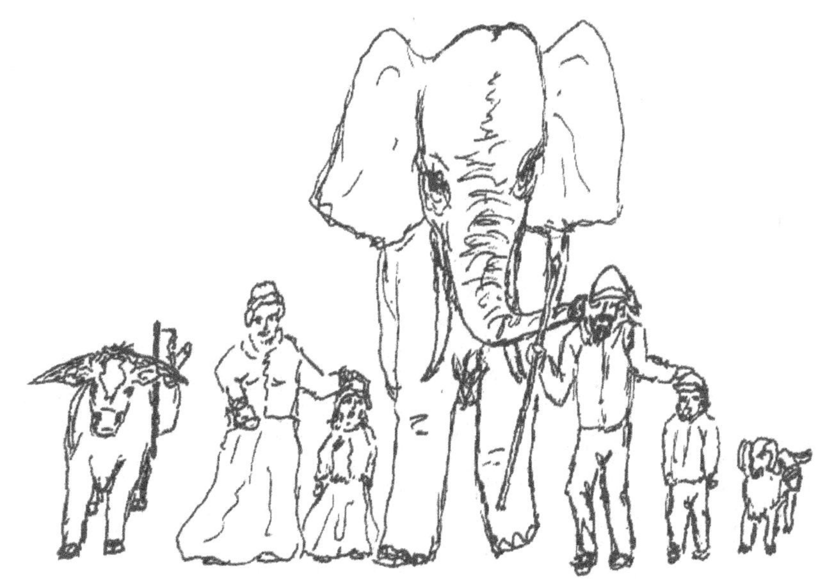

'Summertime' 'Mammoth People mammoth caravan' 'FRONT VIEW'

23) This is how the lead family of the Mammoth People mammoth caravan appeared as they trekked across the grasslands of our North American Continent. Sometimes grandma was sitting atop the lead mammoth but in this image she's most likely riding in the sled that the mammoth is pulling.

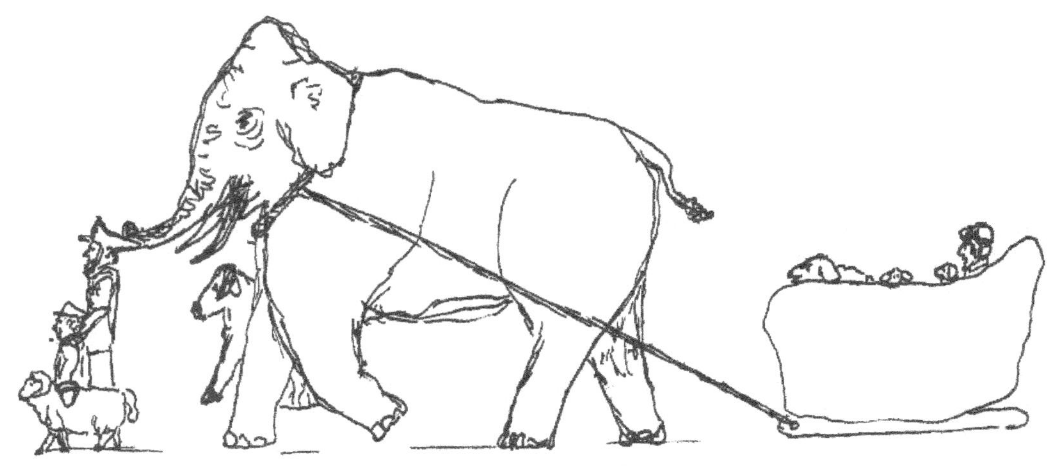

'SUMMERTIME' 'MAMMOTH PEOPLE mammoth caravan' 'Left' 'side view'

24) And here you see grandma sitting in the back seat of the sled with her pregnant ewe and all of the smallest lambs.

Let me give you an example of what the hunter herder microlithic abstract art is..........

I compare interpreting the Mammoth People hunter herder microlithic abstract art to reading 'Braille'. It's so foreign to our way of perception especially if you read normally with both of your eyes; nonetheless Braille gives its blind reader the perfect imagery that the writer wants them to see in their 'mind's eye'. So too, the hunter herder abstract artist creates a whole story, not from what your fingers touch across the pages of a 'book' or what your eyes read, but from what your fingers touch and what your eyes read around a tiny stone.....a 'microlith'! Instead of reading literal written words you're reading a figurative language that's comprised of figurative imagery that makes up individual scenes that when combined composes a theme.

.... "it just is what it is"....Mark Hruska

8/15/11

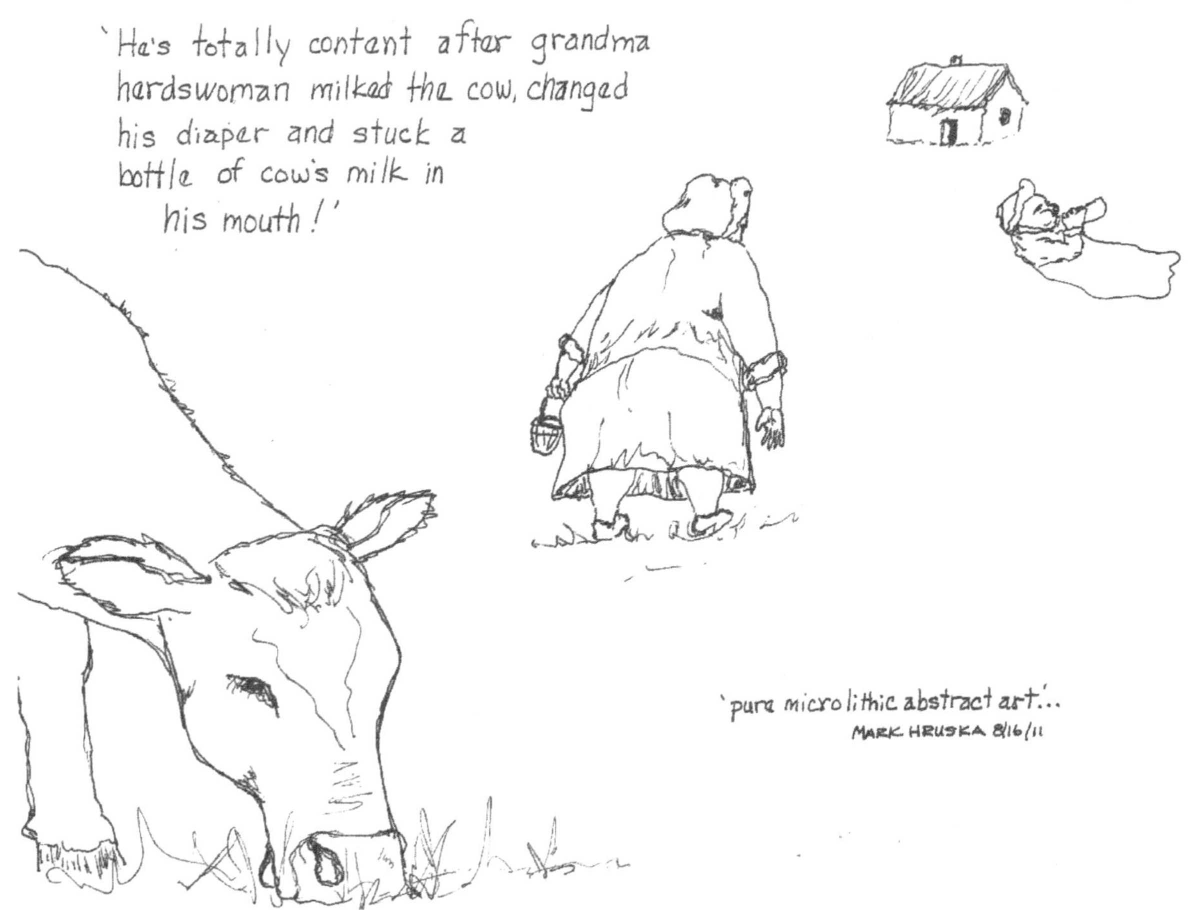

'He's totally content after grandma herdswoman milked the cow, changed his diaper and stuck a bottle of cow's milk in his mouth!'

25) This was no doubt one of the first pieces that showed me imagery of stout grandma walking away from the milk cow towards the cottage that's off in the distance with the infant in it.

"**IMAGES**.......are much more important than.......**words!**"

.... "it just is what it is"....Mark Hruska 8/21/11

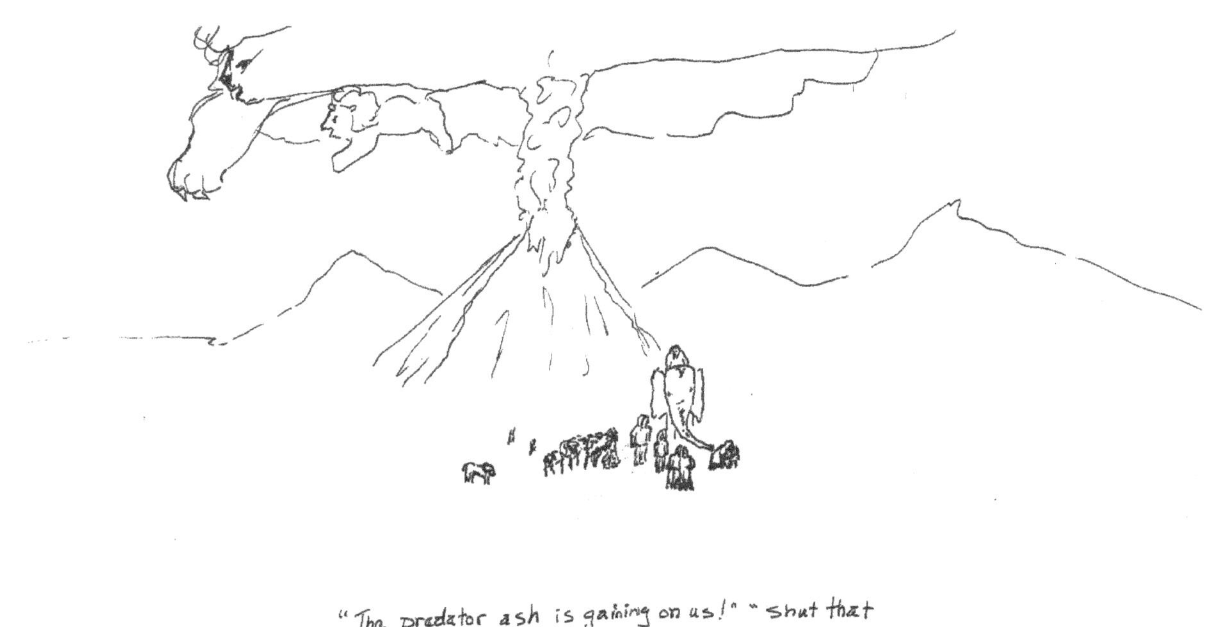

"The predator ash is gaining on us!" "Shut that kid up and move those sheep!"

26) This illustration shows how I was piecing together the 'volcanic mass exodus' epic folklore tale. It was most likely before I simply referred to grandma as 'crotchety' grandma instead of being more like their queen.

'RECORDED HISTORY'

There's no other form of recorded history that gives a clearer 'rock solid' picture of a culture than the Mammoth People hunter herder microlithic abstract art figurative language. Not even the Dead Sea Scrolls can give this intimate account of the daily lives of its authors and it's on a fragile rolled up piece of parchment that experts are trying to fill in the gaps of the missing pieces. There are no missing pieces when it comes to interpreting the Mammoth Peoples microlithic hunter herder abstract art figurative language, no special lights to bring out hidden letters, just a lit magnifier and the all-important genetics that our ancestors gave us......a 'mind's eye'!

.... "it just is what it is".....Mark Hruska 8/21/11

'FRUSTRATING'

"The most frustrating thing for me is that when I try to explain the Mammoth Peoples Stone age microlithic abstract art to someone, they want to see verification from an expert when no one else on the whole planet knows that it or they even existed!"

.... "it just is what it is"....Mark Hruska 8/21/11

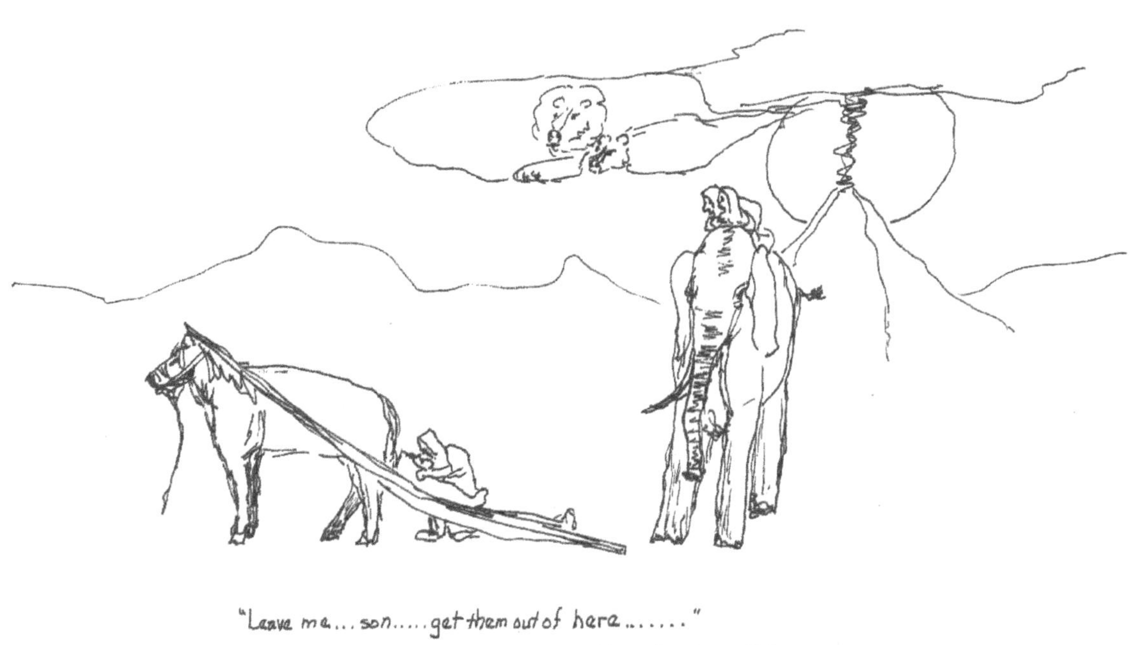

"Leave me...son...get them out of here...."

27) I'm gradually getting the 'volcanic mass exodus' repetitive theme, piece by piece. I'm also beginning to understand that it is the most common repetitive theme.

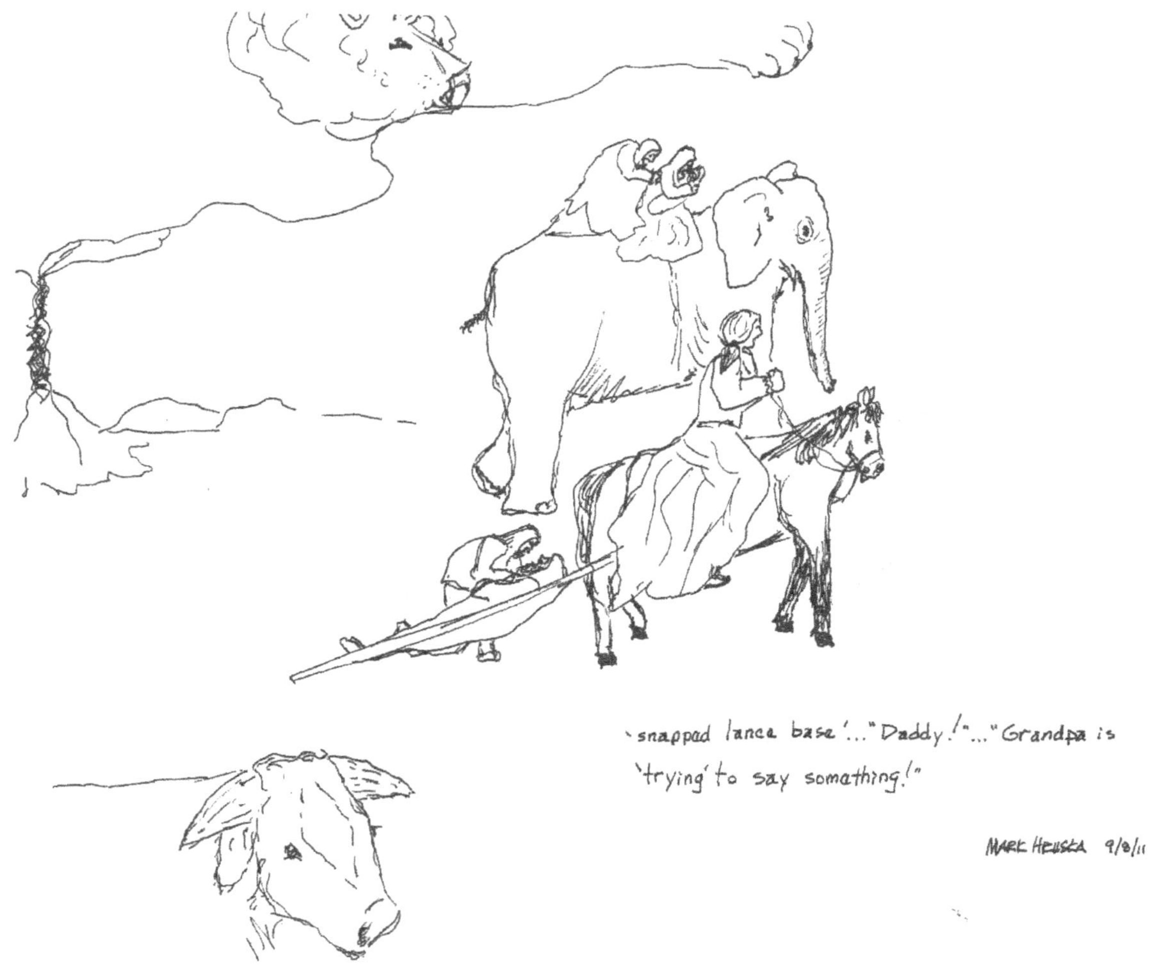

'snapped lance base'... "Daddy!"... "Grandpa is trying to say something!"

28) I'm building on the 'volcanic mass exodus' repetitive theme and am seeing a correlation between delirious grandpa who's always seen laying back at a forty five degree angle on his travois, and his fair young maiden or waist high young maiden granddaughter who is very concerned about his wellbeing.

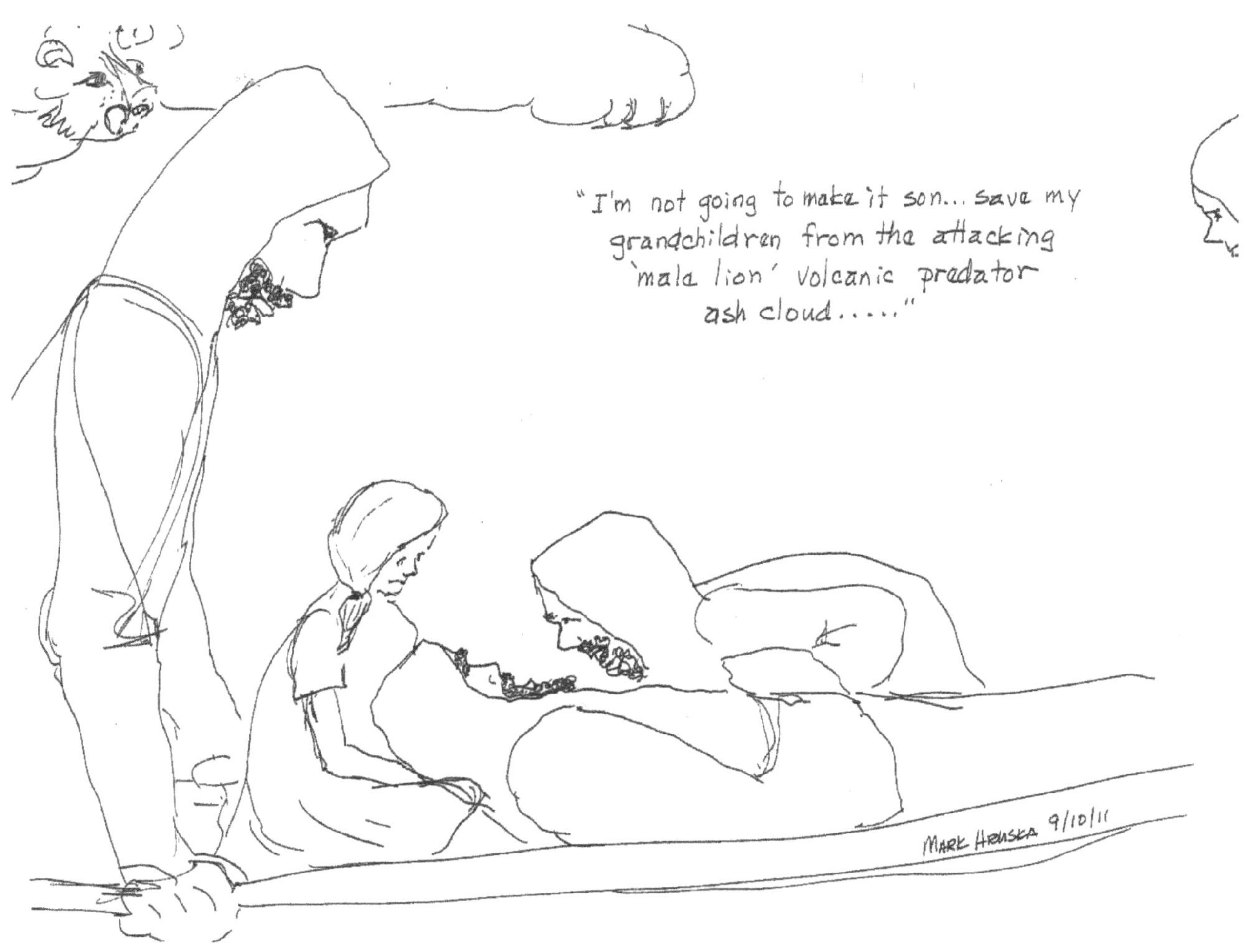

"I'm not going to make it son... save my grandchildren from the attacking 'male lion' volcanic predator ash cloud...."

29) Delirious grandpa and crotchety grandma are the ones that always seem to be seeing the roaring male lion up in the broiling ash cloud that's overtaking them. Its little wonder that delirious grandpa does because he's facing rearward towards it as they trek. And since the Mammoth People seemed to specialize in 'pareidolia' you can see how he could easily make out a male lions angry face in the broiling lightning filled ash cloud.

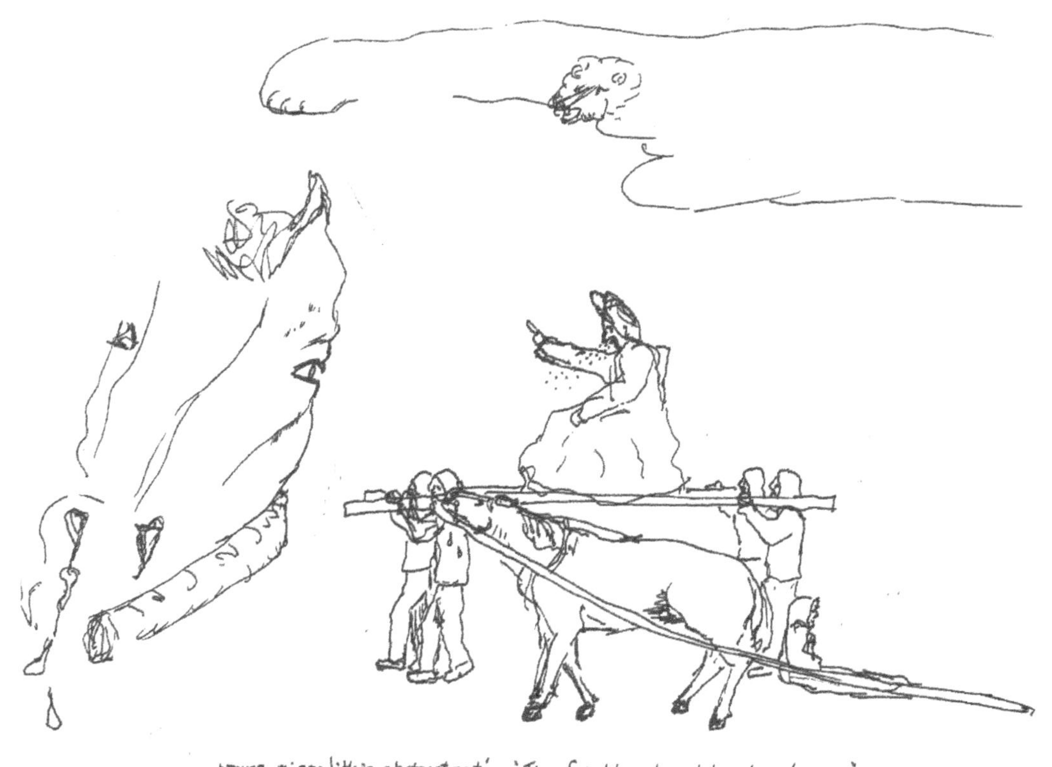

'pure microlithic abstract art'... 'The frightened and burdened pony's 'snorting snot' is how the porters portray their 'order barking' crotchety old queen!'

30) I'm still not referring to her as crotchety grandma, realizing that she is an important member of the 'lead' family. That still doesn't mean that she wasn't the fleeing Mammoth People's queen or matriarchal figurehead. This piece was instrumental in figuring out the microlithic abstract art because I realized that it was the teenage young lad front left porter who also felt like the beast of burden that had snot running from his nose, and that he saw close-up when he looked back to his left over his left shoulder.

"The Mammoth People are the ancestors to all of the Caucasian people on the entire planet!"

.... "it just is what it is"....Mark Hruska 8/26/11

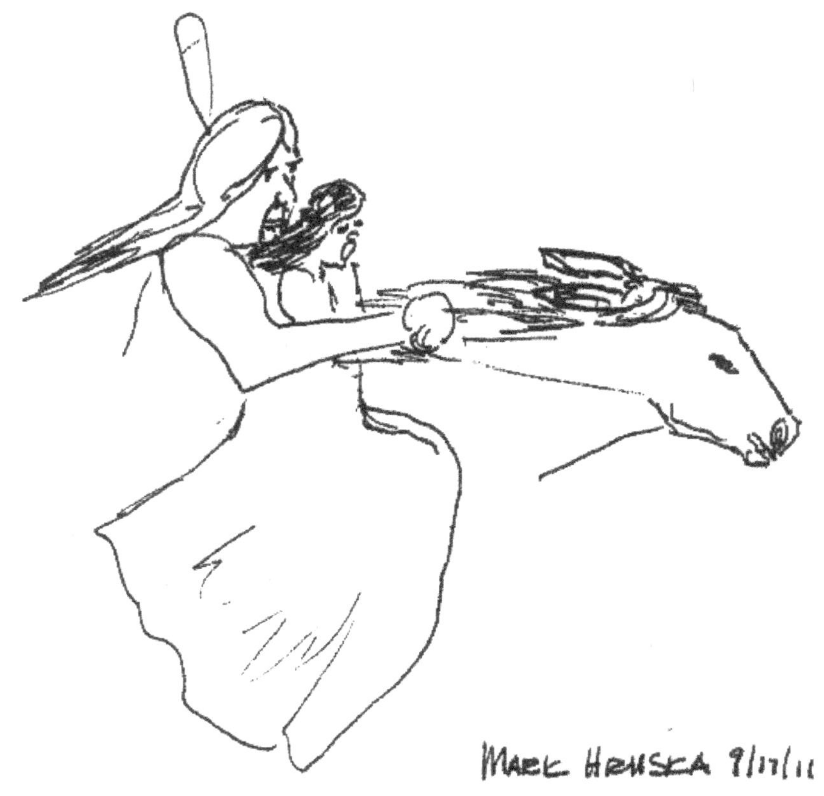

Line sketch dated 9/17/11

31) This one is obviously imagery that helped me put together the 'powwow' repetitive theme and was taking place when the whooping and hollering Palomino Pony People warrior braves raided the Mammoth People mammoth caravan of trekkers.

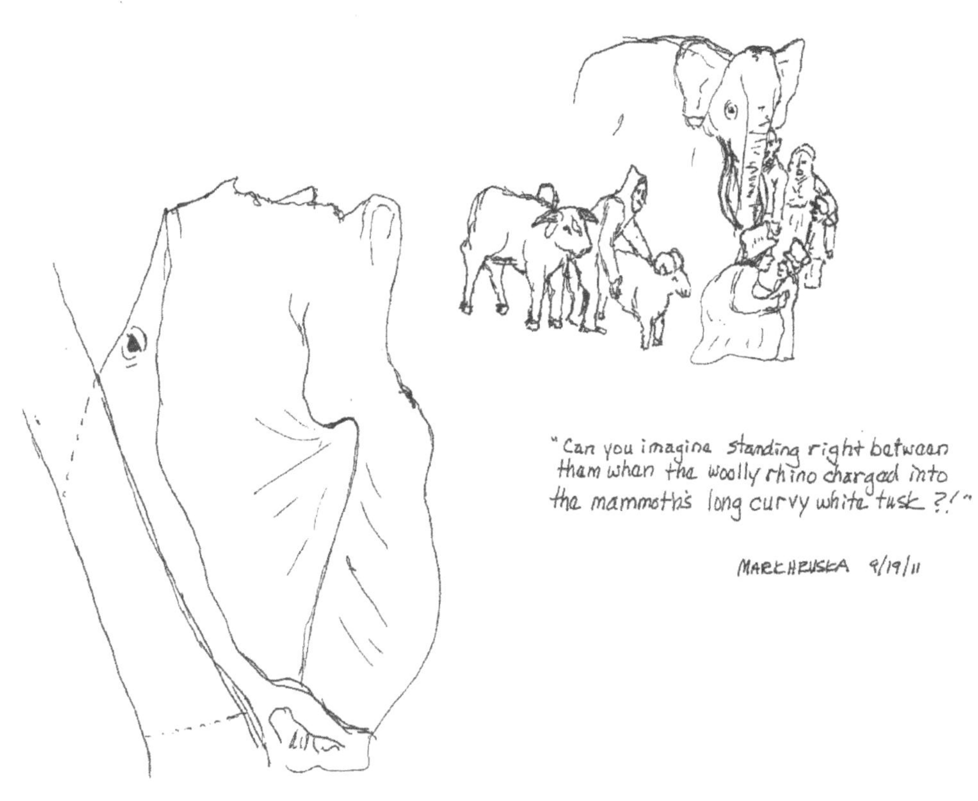

"Can you imagine standing right between them when
the woolly rhino charged into the mammoth's long curvy white tusk?!"

32) This was a rare glimpse of a rhino seen with the trekkers and may have been lost in the storytelling process early on.

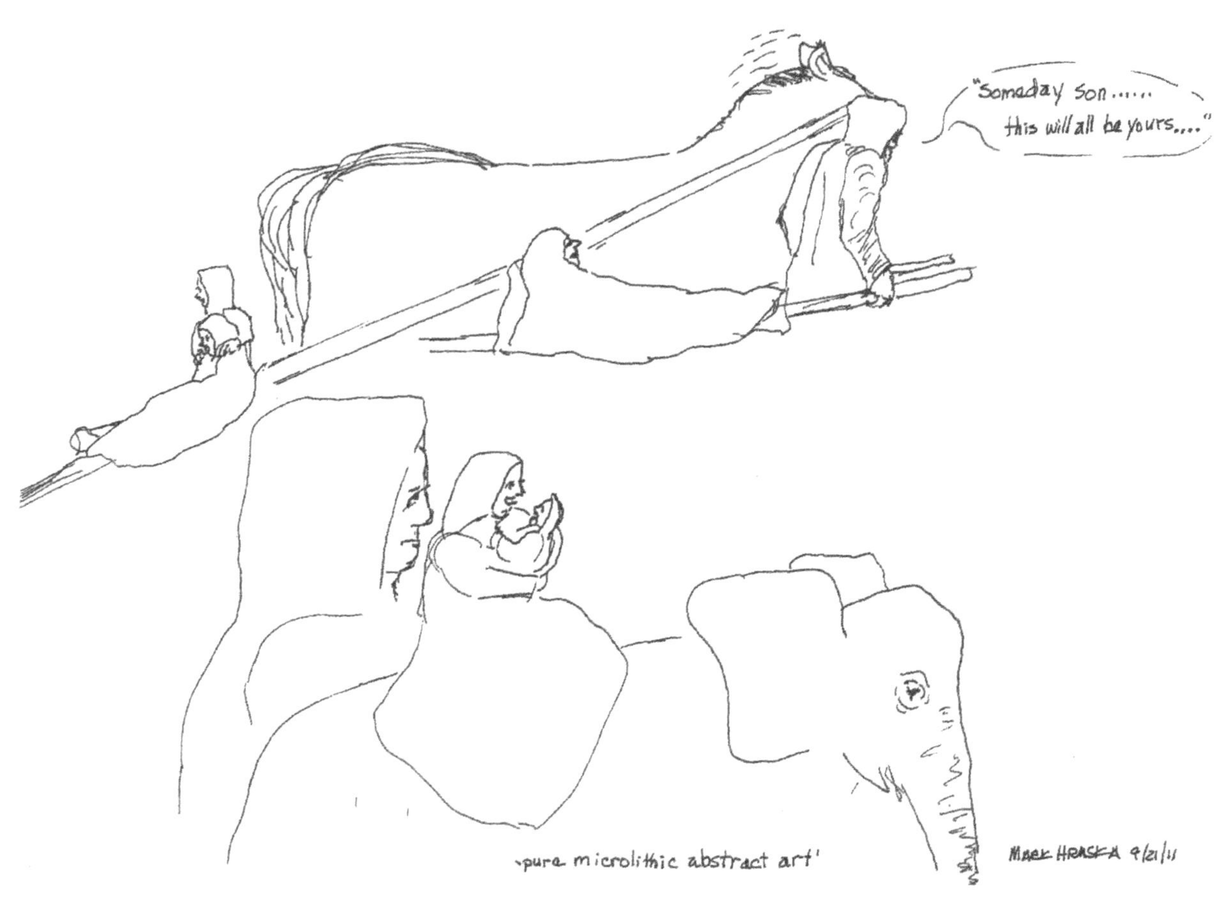

'pure microlithic abstract art'... "Someday son....this will all be yours..."

33) I still didn't grasp why or where they were trekking to when I interpreted this piece.

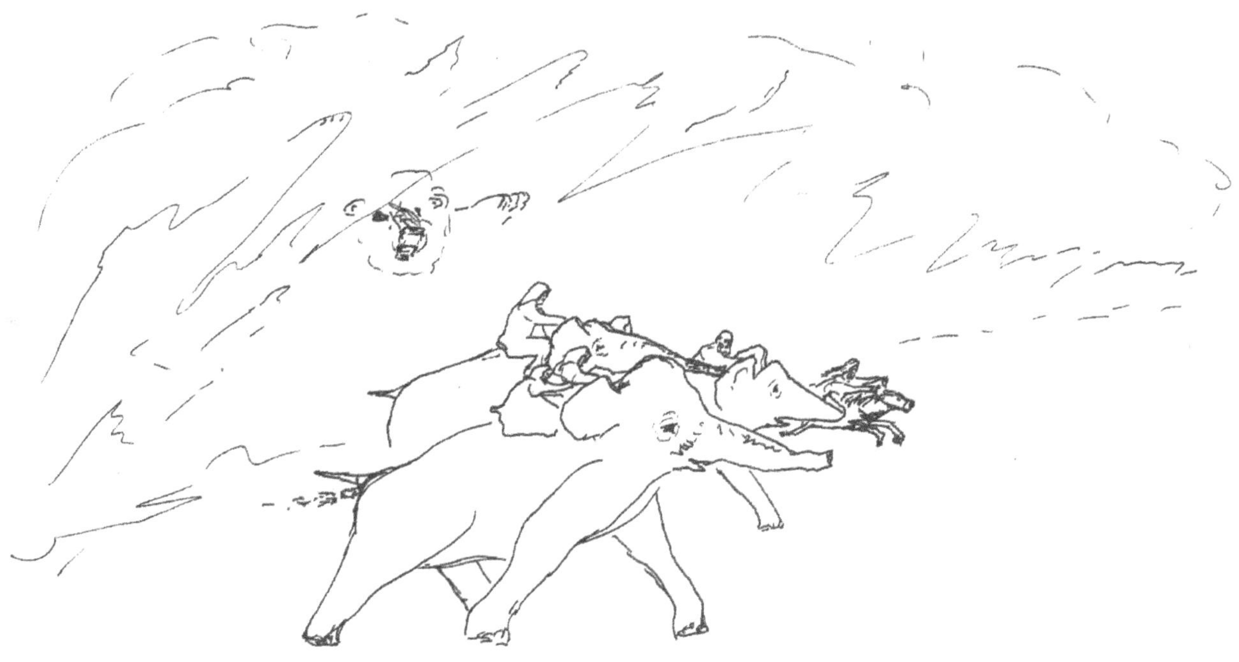

'Backed prismatic knife'... 'Clearly, the roaring and attacking predator male lion prairie grass fire scared the 's _ _ t' out of the fleeing mammoth!'

34) This heat treated flint prismatic knife left an indelible image in my 'mind's eye' all of this time later after I interpreted it. There is no doubt what I saw on this colorful 'rotational change-up' microlithic abstract artwork because I was as good as I was ever going to be at interpreting the art, I just didn't know exactly what I was seeing yet and was still learning piece by piece the entire folklore tales. One thing was clear though, and that is that the predator roaring male lion seemed to be an overwhelming attacking character in so many of their repetitive themes.

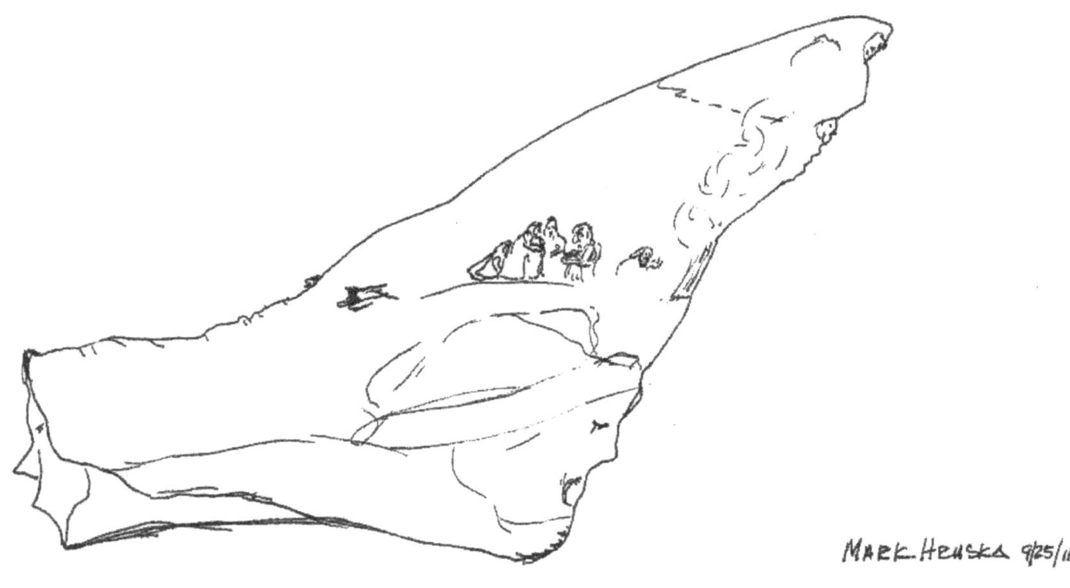

'pure microlithic abstract art'... "If you stay too late to gab, the dire wolves will have a feast!"

35) This repetitive theme no doubt was told to scare the living daylight out of the young maiden's and their mothers who couldn't resist the urge to overstay and gossip.

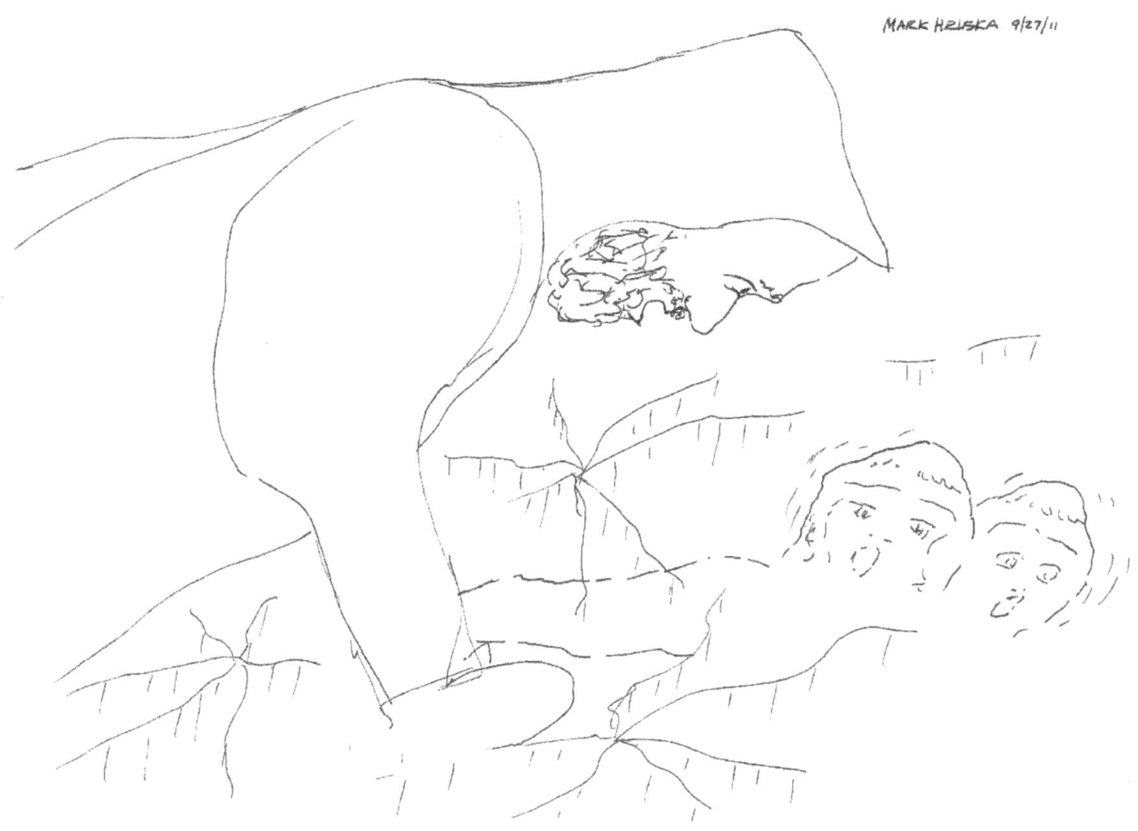

'pure microlithic abstract art'... 'Mom and dad peer helplessly thru the predator ice as
their beautiful vibrant and full of life young maiden daughter
sinks into the depths below....'

36) I love this line sketch that came out of me from the powerful imagery that the hunter herder microlithic abstract artist planted in my 'mind's eye'. It was one of the first attempts at portraying one of the variances of the 'predator ice' folklore tale when the Mammoth People mammoth caravan of trekkers were trekking across the vast expanse of sea ice on their way to 'here'.

43

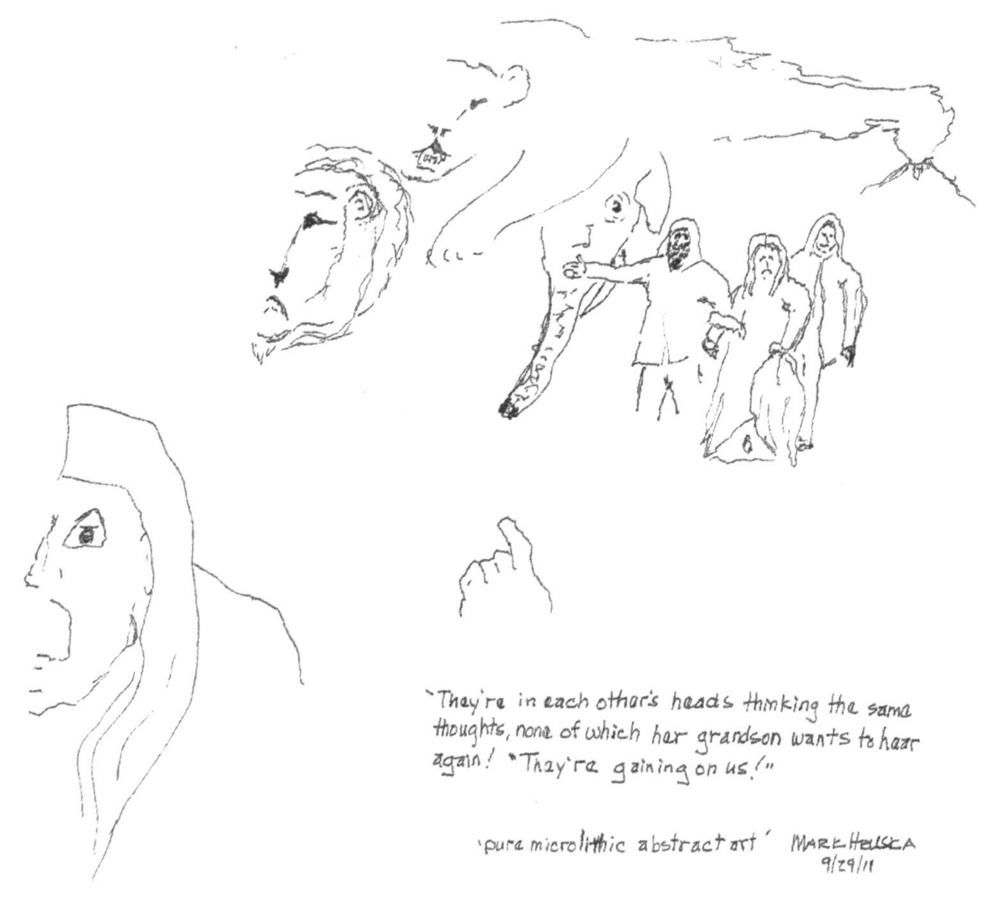

'They're in each other's heads thinking the same thoughts, none of which
her grandson wants to hear... "They're gaining on us!"

37) Her teenage grandson is her front left porter and she's often seen leaning down and forwards over her knees, yelling in his right ear. Of course she's yelling about the pair of lions that she sees up in the broiling ash cloud that's about to overtake them. I learned in subsequent pieces that she can figuratively lift her pointing index finger to touch the attacking male lion ash clouds top front fang in his roaring mouth.

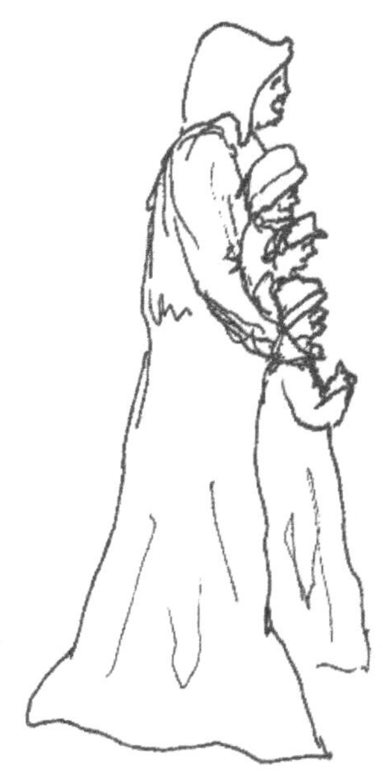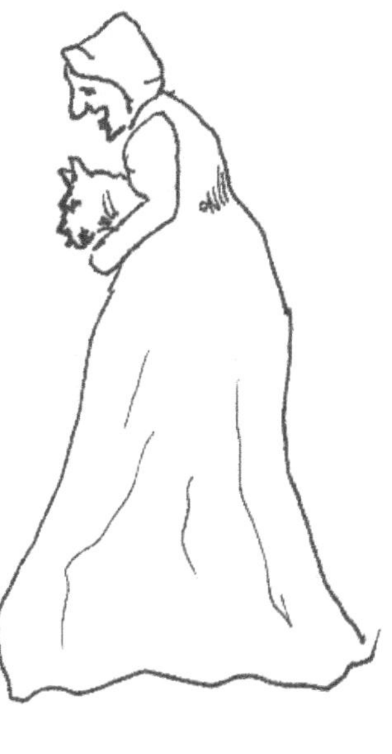

'pure microlithic abstract art'... 'It seems that the Scotties and Calico kitties
have been fighting like cats and dogs for thirteen millennia!'

38) This piece takes place at a springtime picnic gathering when proud mom herdswoman is showing off her growing children to the elderly neighbor lady and her Scotty. The waist high young maiden's kitty jumps from her arms to flee from the Scotty and he jumps from his owners arms to give chase.

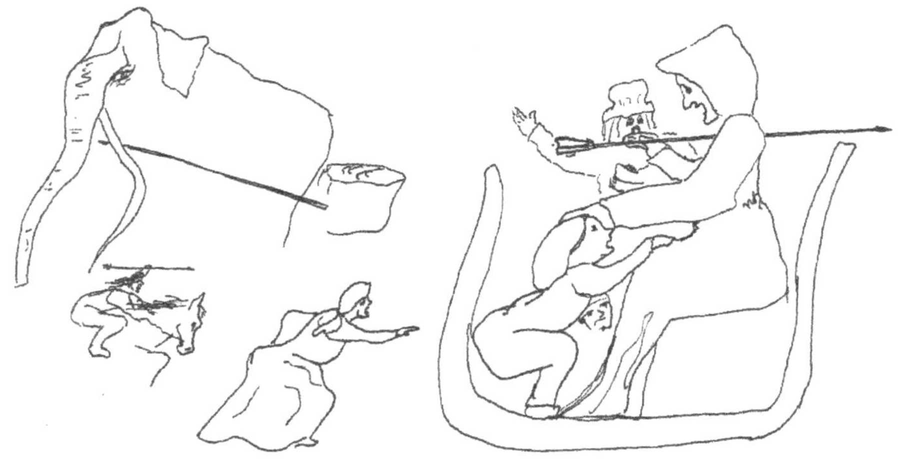

'stone knife'... 'The elderly shepherdess took a spear thru the chest to save her toddler grandson's lives while she was also trying to save her granddaughter!'

39) This scene was interpreted many times afterward which confirms the accuracy of the sketch, and it took place during the raid by the whooping and hollering Palomino Pony People warrior braves when grandma was riding in the sled that was pulled by the nervous lead mammoth. She was sheltering her toddler grandson's like a mother duck shelters her ducklings with her spread out wings when she took a spear through her chest.

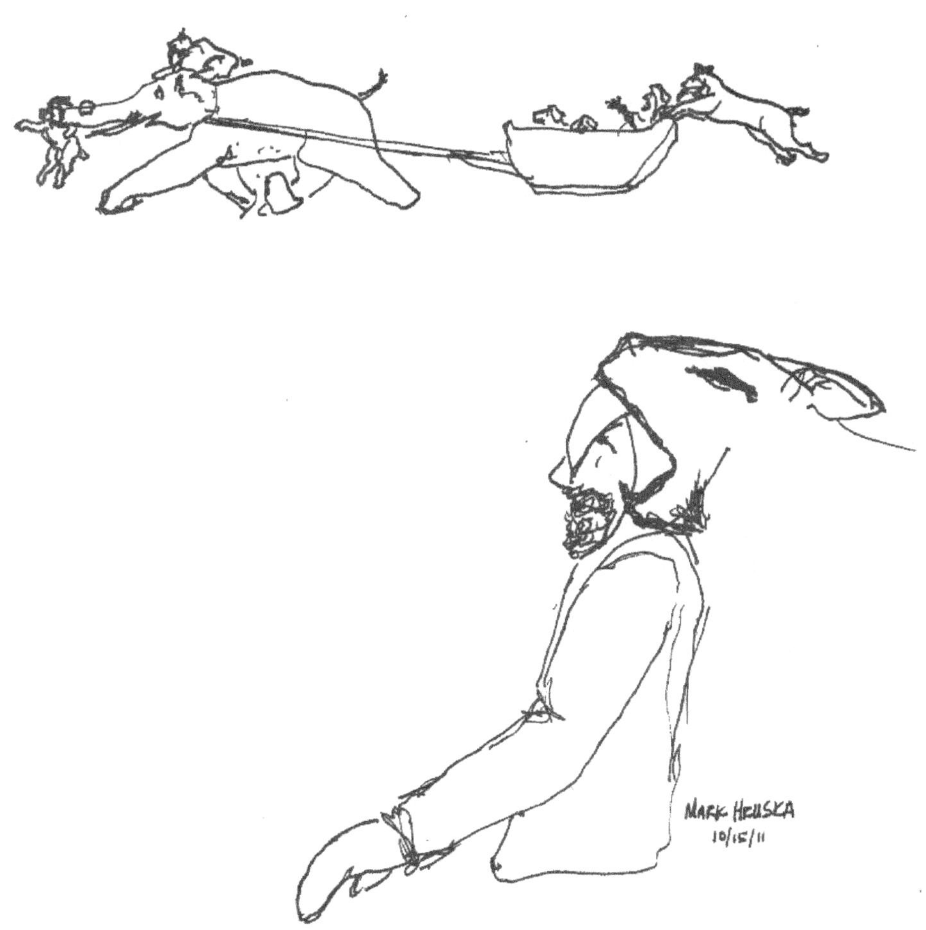

Line sketch 10/15/11.

40) This line sketch shows exactly how the marauding saber toothed cats worked together to bring down their fleeing prey. The object that you see between the running mammoth's legs is her sliced off left ear that's falling to the ground...and that will be chewed on by rats later...

"If you can't see the Mammoth People hunter herder microlithic abstract art it's probably because you think that you are smarter than they were. When you 'believe' that they had superior cognitive abilities to your own...only then will you most likely begin to see it and be humbled in a way that you never thought possible."

.... "it just is what it is"....Mark Hruska 10/17/11

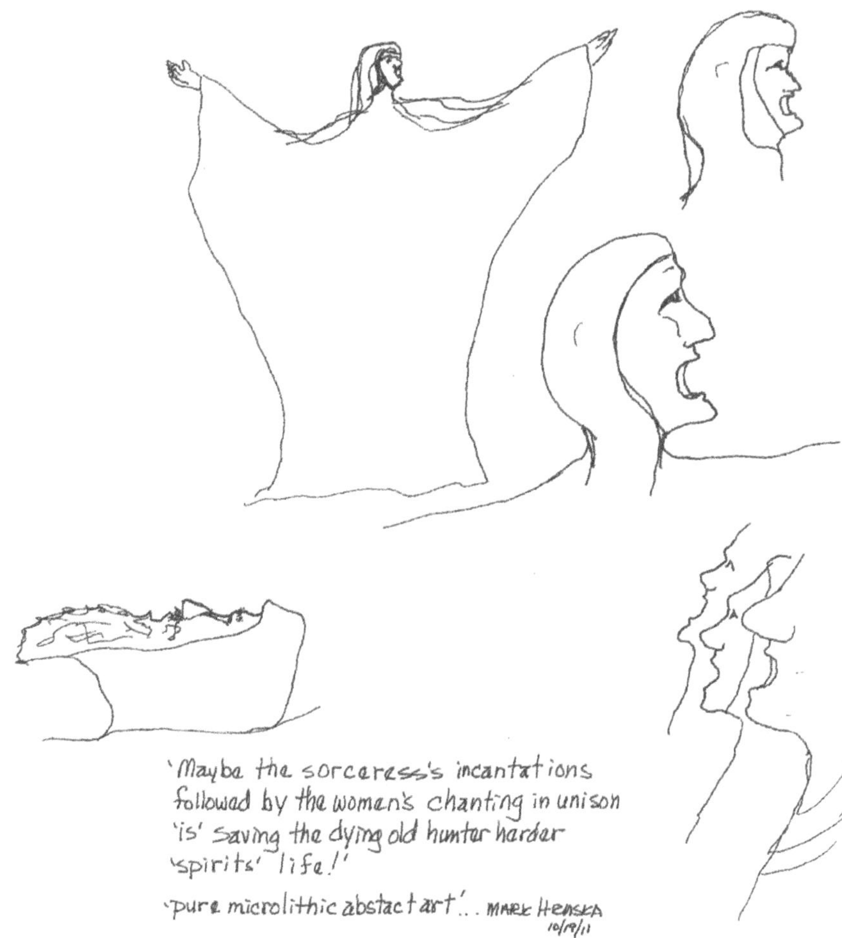

'pure microlithic abstract art'... 'Maybe the sorceress's incantations followed by the women's chanting in unison 'is' saving the dying old hunter herder 'spirits' life!'

41) After having interpreted several pieces with this repetitive theme on them, it was this one that showed the three chanting assistants as cognitive illusion silhouettes that were superimposed on each other that really brought it home to me in my 'mind's eye'.

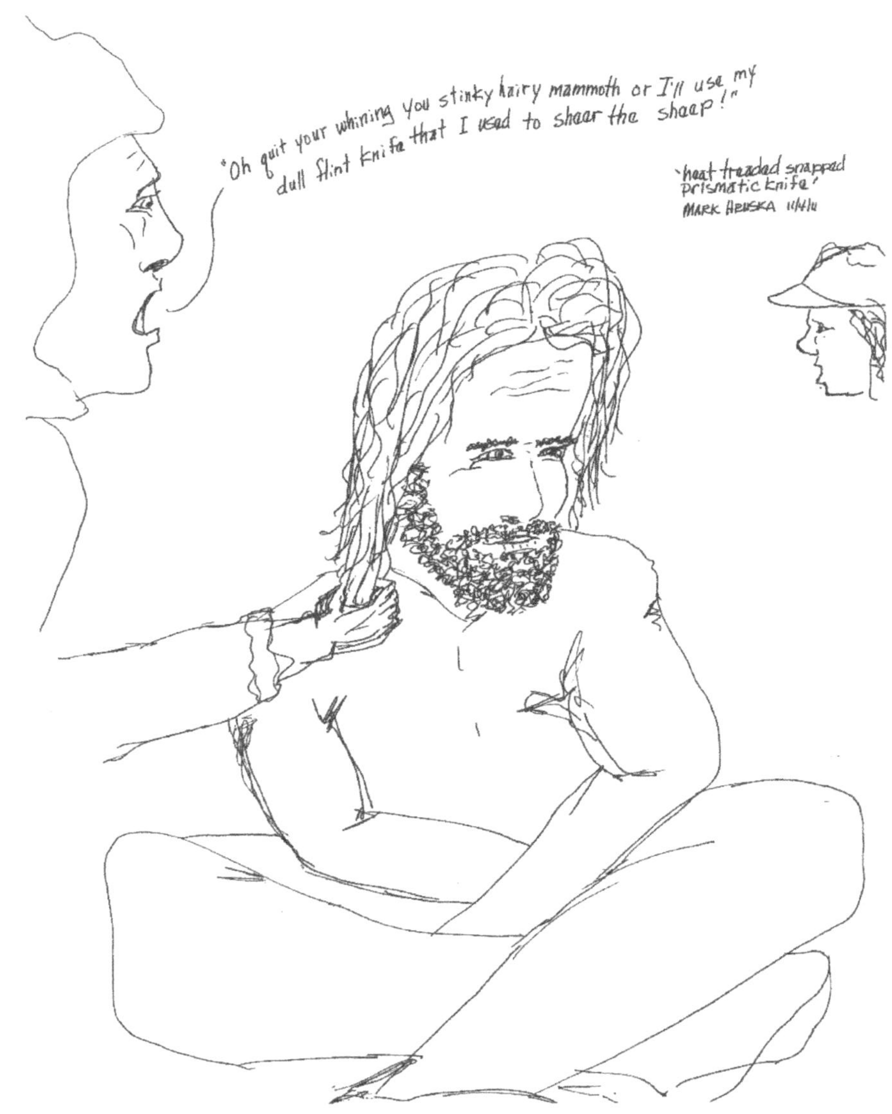

'heat treated snapped prismatic knife'... "Oh quit your whining you stinky hairy mammoth or I'll use my dull flint knife that I used to sheer the sheep!"

42) This is one of the few homestead yard scenes that I've been able to see and it was probably created by a hunter herder microlithic abstract artisan who was doodling instead of paying tribute to his ancestors.

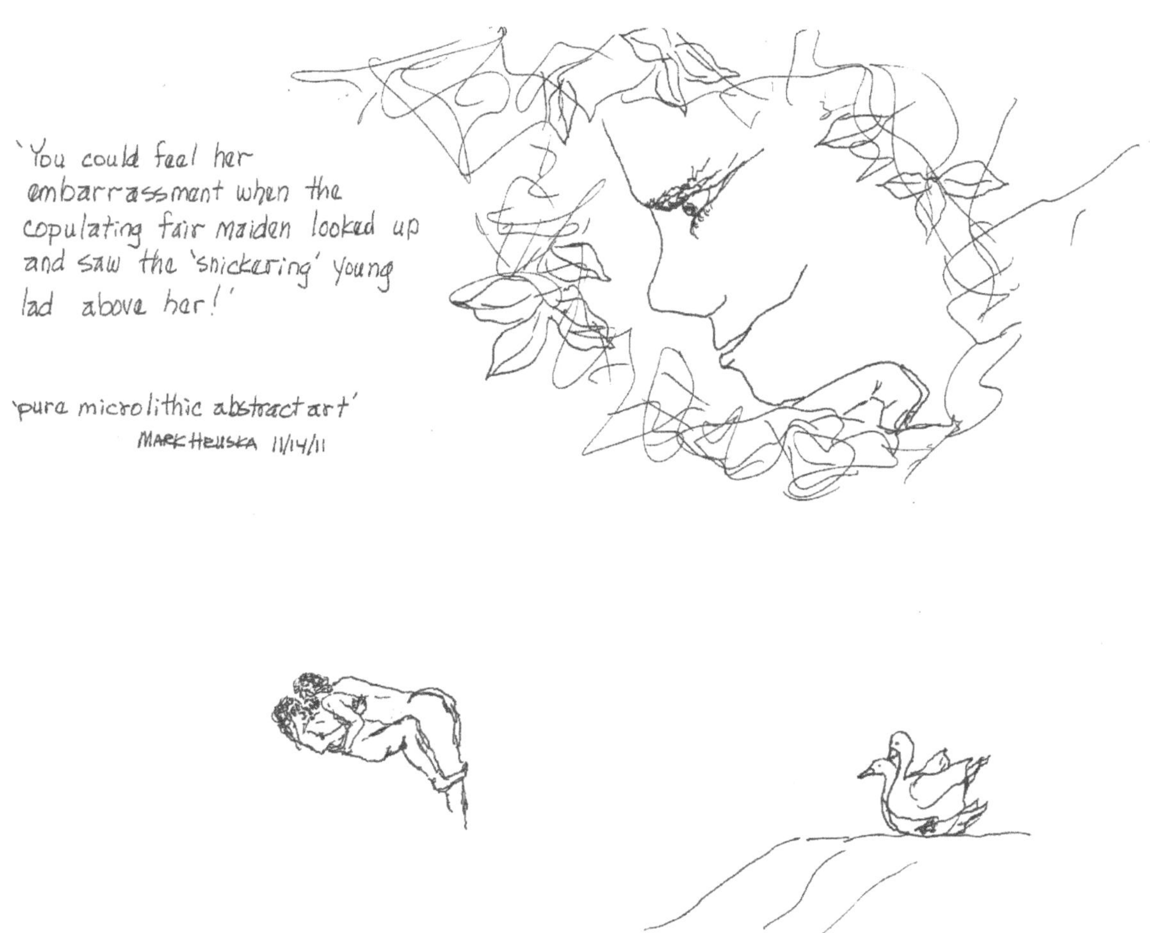

'pure microlithic abstract art'.... 'You could feel her embarrassment when the copulating fair maiden looked up and saw the 'snickering' young lad above her!'

43) Believe it or not, this pieces interpretation actually became a repetitive theme that I later realized was the folklore tale about the fair young maiden sneaking off with a handsome beau during the summertime picnic. They snuck off down to the brush covered river bank where the nesting and mating geese were. The snickering young lad is usually her ornery little brother who discovers the concealed couple when his bloodhound pup goes in the underbrush after a nesting hissing goose. He tells grandma and she spryly yanks the young lovers out with her shepherds crook. The point of the folklore tale is to warn fair young maidens of the immense embarrassment that this one had to live with.

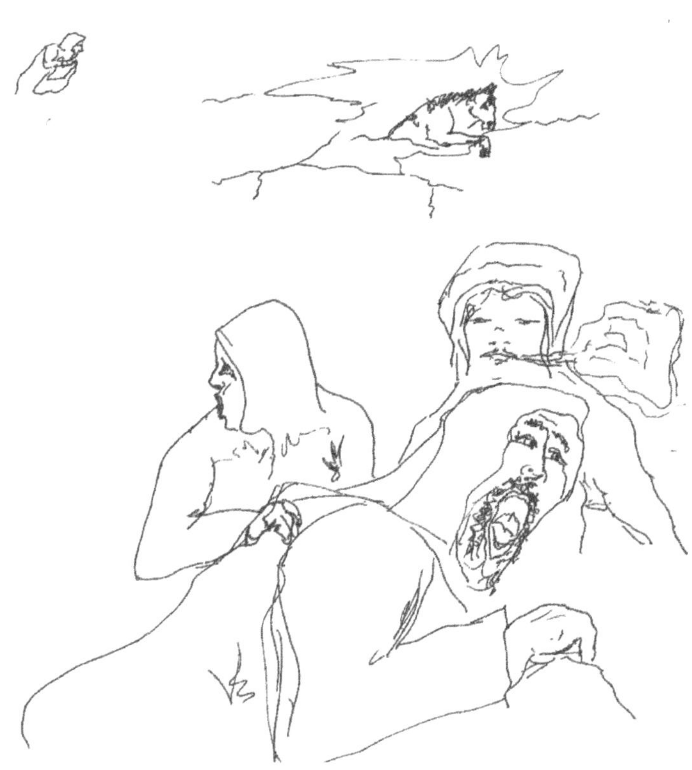

'backed flake knife'... 'Dad clearly saved her and mom is hollering
at grandpa to hurry up and to bring that blanket to warm her up!'

44) Sometimes the cooperating lead family saved the fair young maiden and her horse from the predator ice and sometimes they didn't, only to watch them both sink into the dark icy cold abyss.

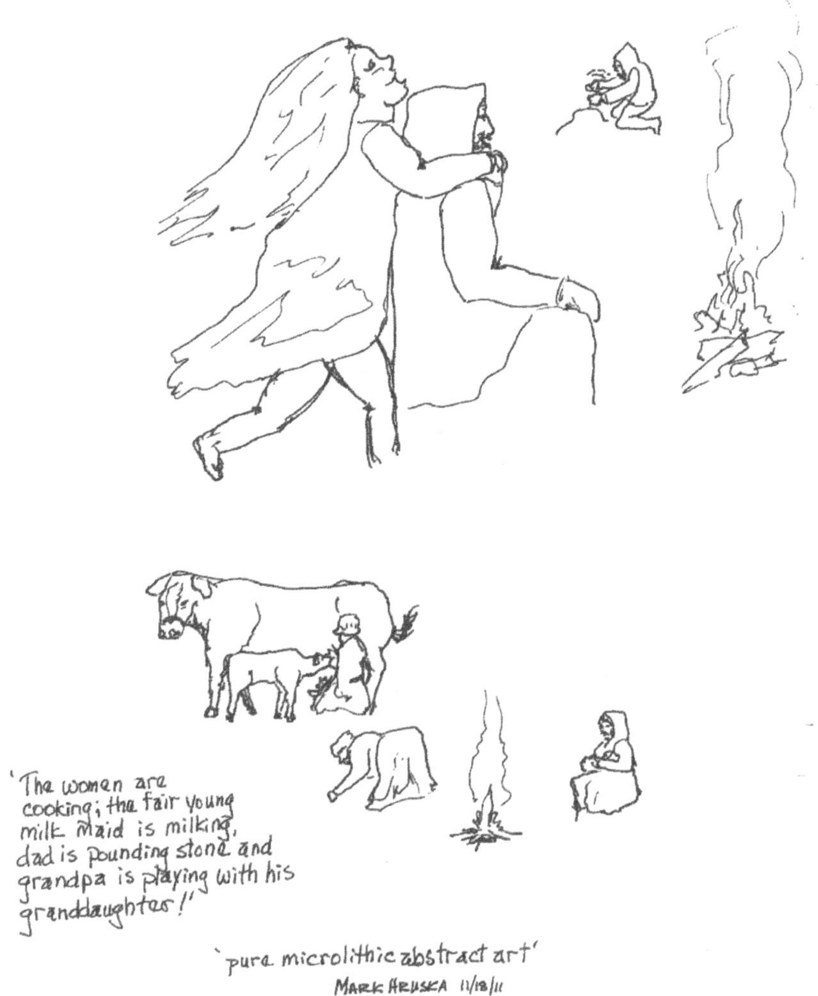

'pure microlithic abstract art'... 'The women are cooking; the fair young milk maiden is milking, dad is pounding stone and grandpa is playing with his granddaughter!'

45) This is obviously a Mammoth People camping scene after a long day of trekking to 'here'.

Interpreting the Mammoth People hunter herder
microlithic abstract art is like solving a miniature
'Rubik's cube'. You turn it every way possible in
order to see the optical and cognitive illusion close-
ups and the microlithic reflections that are on them
that flow into scenes that combine to create
repetitive themes.....that always have slight
variations. It's those combined variations that
eventually give you the entire picture of the
Mammoth People's lives!

.... "it just is what it is"....Mark Hruska

11/18/11

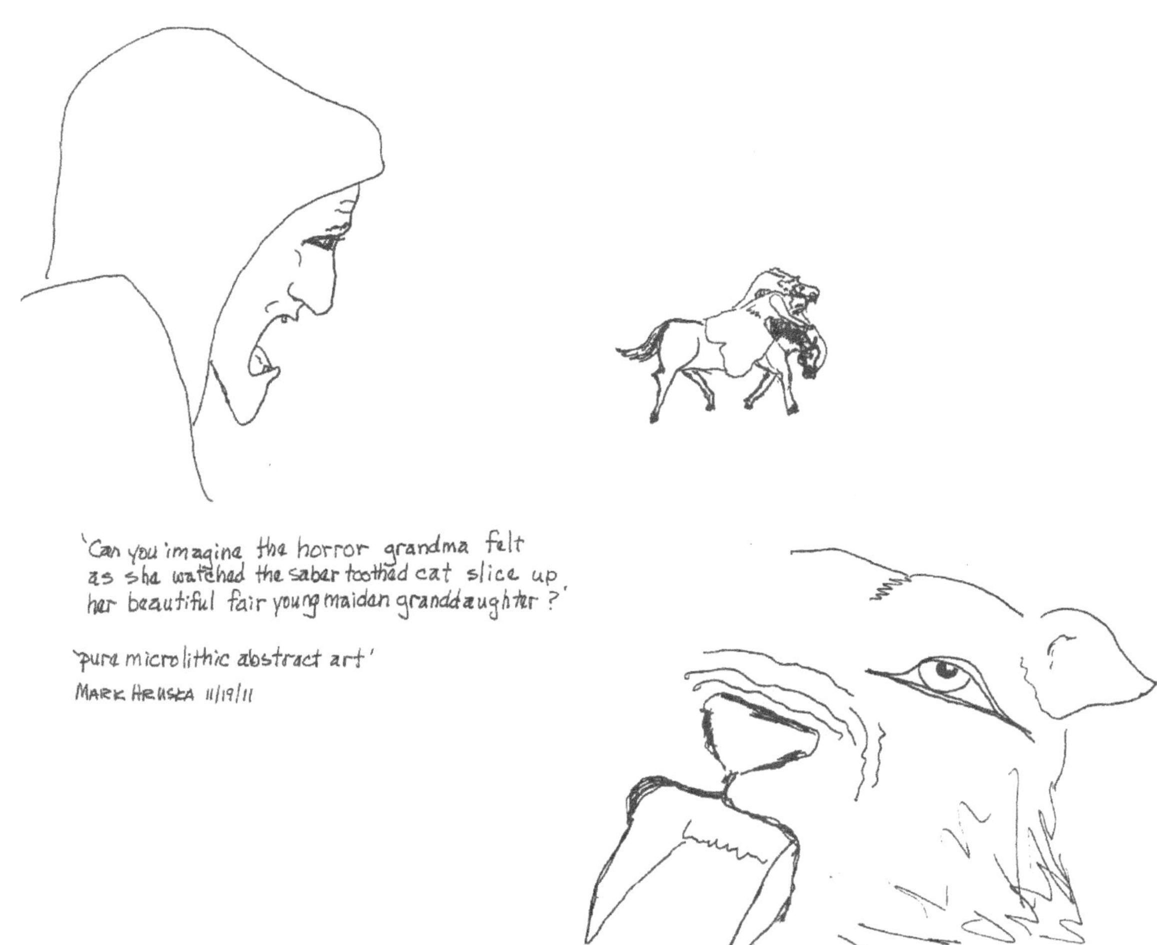

'pure microlithic abstract art'... 'Can you imagine the horror grandma felt as she watched the saber-toothed cat slice up her beautiful fair young maiden granddaughter?'

46) This scene turned out to be a fairly common one that is part of the epic folklore tale of when the Mammoth People mammoth caravan of trekkers trekked across the vast grasslands on their way to 'here'. If it wasn't the stalking saber-toothed cats that ambushed them it was the lurking lions.

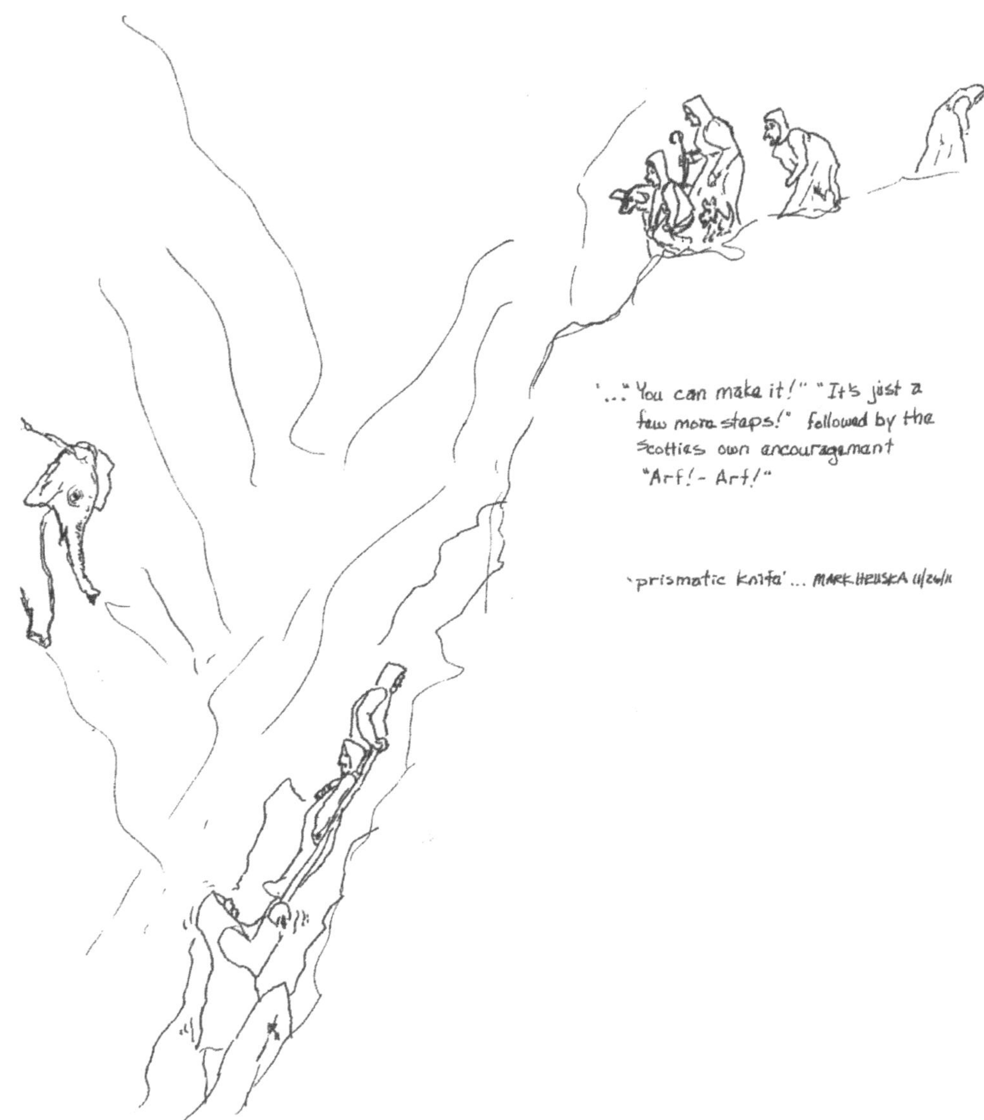

'prismatic knife'... '... "You can make it!" "It's just a few more steps!"
followed by the Scotties own encouragement "Arf!-Arf!"

47) This scene from the 'volcanic mass exodus' folklore tale demonstrates how extreme the volcanic mountainous terrain could be for the fleeing trekkers.

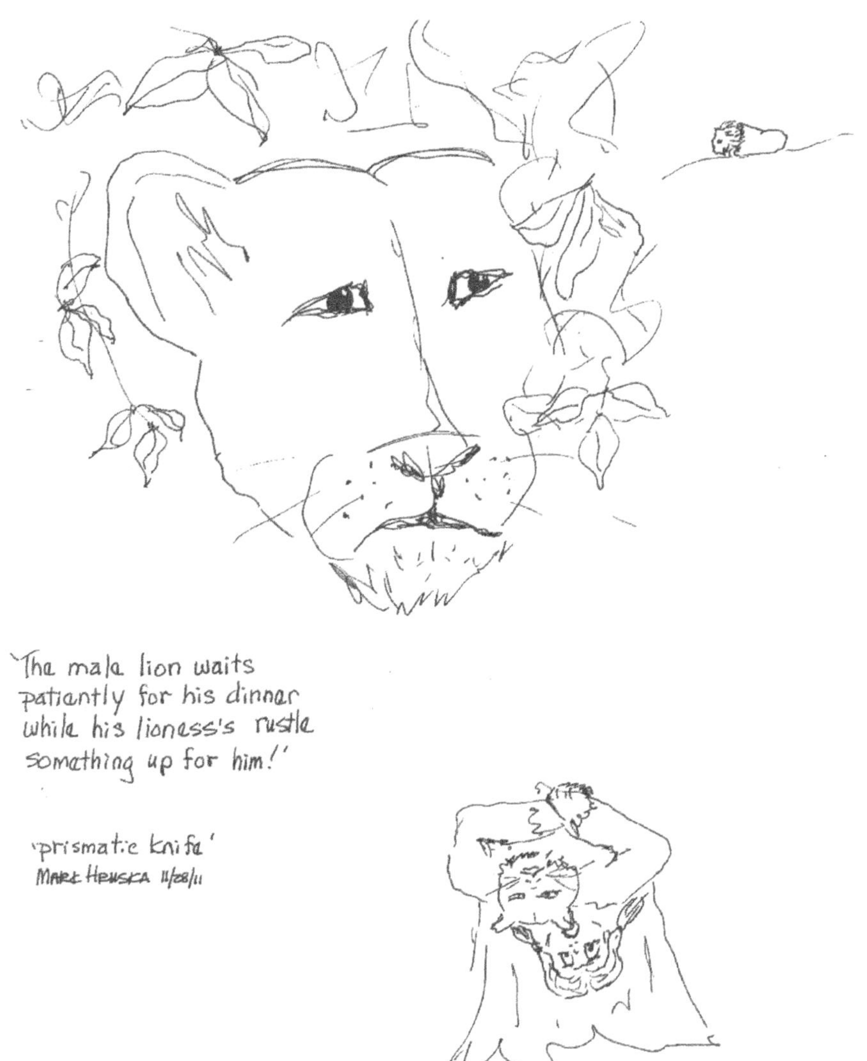

'prismatic knife'... 'The male lion waits patiently for his dinner while his lioness's rustle something up for him!'

48) This is another line sketch that pretty well sums up what is on the interpretation.

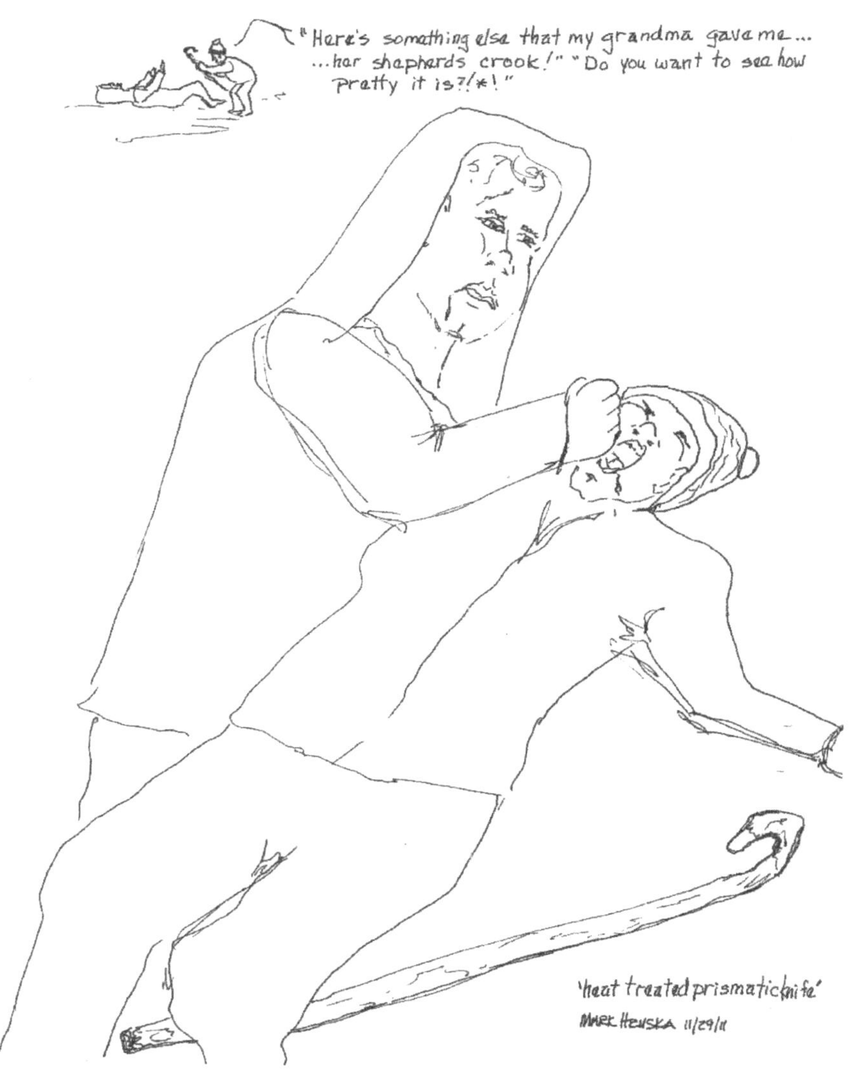

'heat treated prismatic knife'... "Here's something else that my grandma gave me.... her shepherds crook!" "Do you want to see how pretty it is?!"

49) This scene most likely took place on one of the Mammoth People school play grounds, and that was before I even knew that there were any...

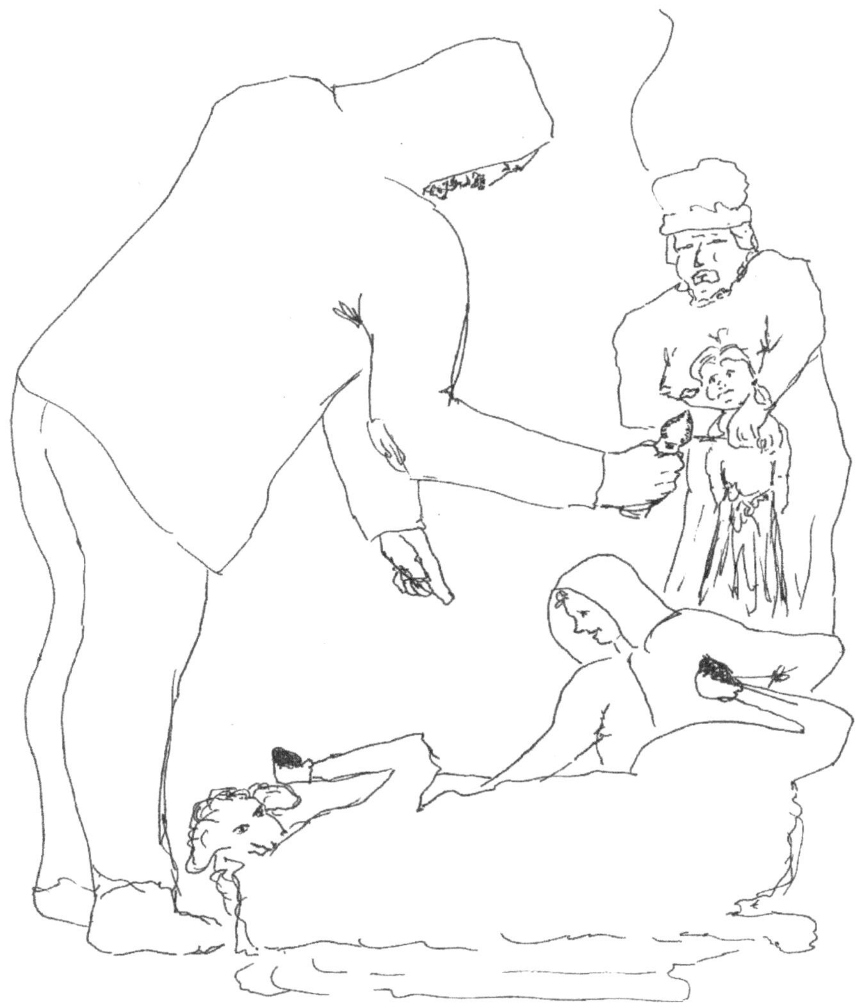

'pure microlithic abstract art'... MARK HRUSKA 11/30/11

'pure microlithic abstract art'... "Watch out for your fingers... dads in an all fiery hurry!"

50) Butchering was definitely a big part of all of the Mammoth People's lives.

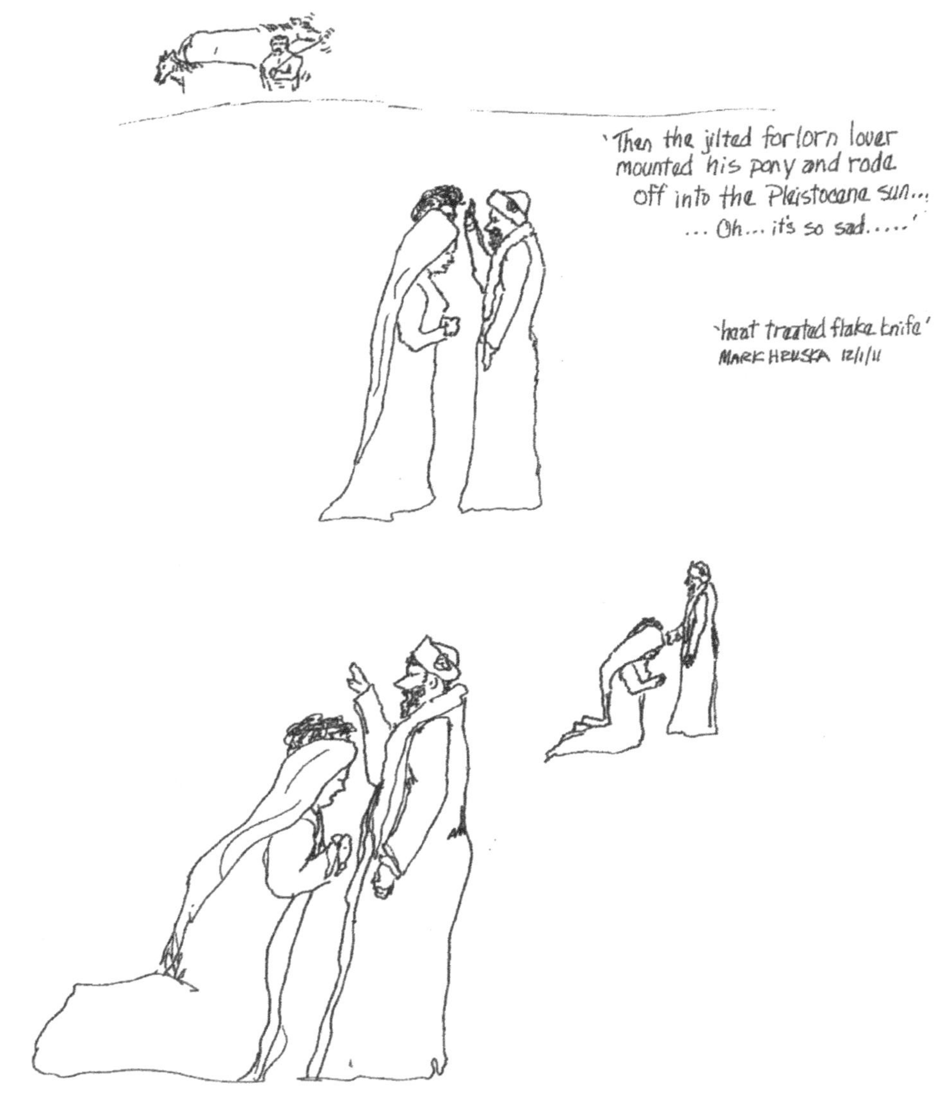

'heat treated flake knife'... 'Then the jilted forlorn lover mounted his pony and rode off into the Pleistocene sun... Oh... it's so sad...'

51) It's what happened after the boisterous pompous magistrate proclaimed them man and wife.

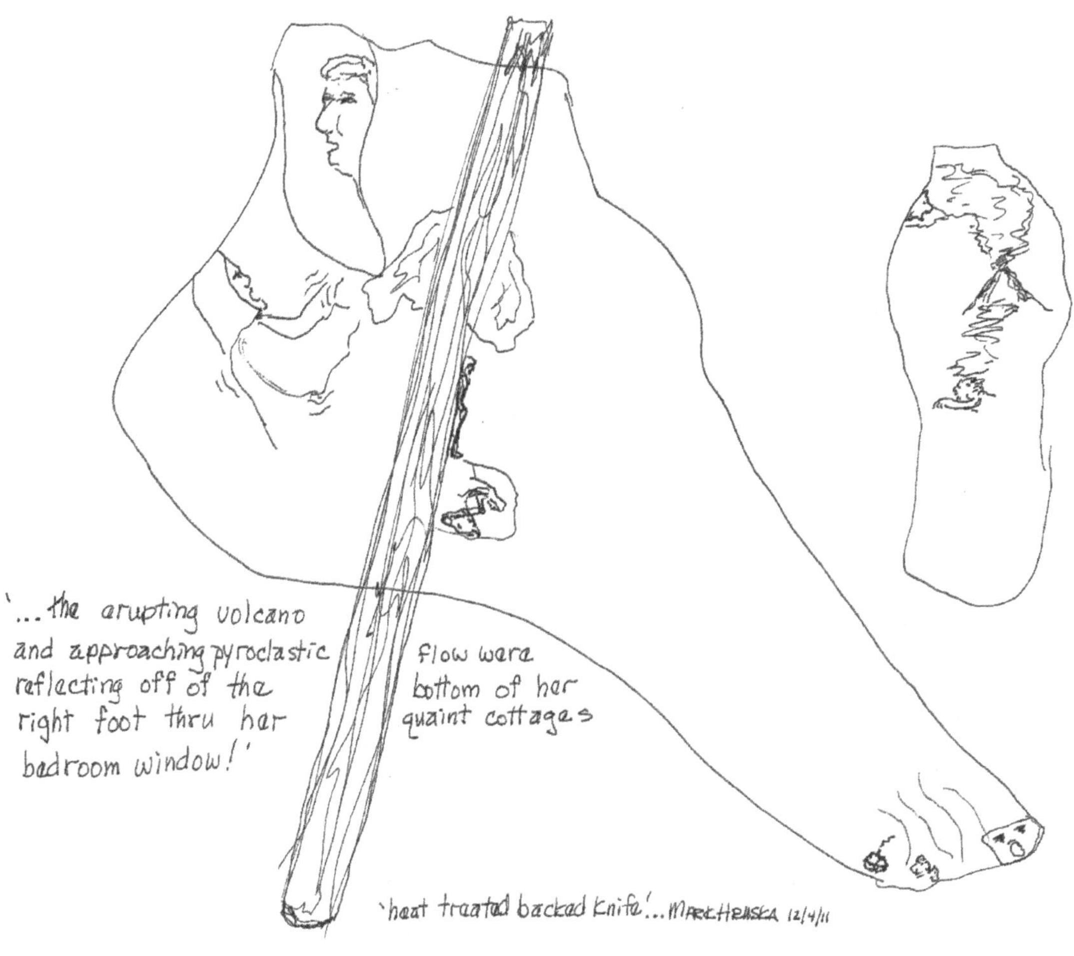

'heat treated backed knife'... '...the erupting volcano and approaching
pyroclastic flow were reflecting off of the bottom of her right
foot thru her quaint cottages bedroom window!'

52) Look closely to see all of the reflections that are reflecting off of her right foot as she lay on her bed in the bedroom of her cottage. Her fair young maiden granddaughter is riding her galloping horse to come and get her.

'A MEANS TO AN END'

Figuring out the Mammoth People hunter herders microlithic abstract art figurative language is in itself a means to an end 'dismissing' all other archaeological processes simply because no one alive today could replicate what the Mammoth People were creating using cognitive and dexterity skills that required vision that was three to five times more acute then ours is today. We can only imagine how much more acute their sense of hearing and smell were! The art alone is a testimonial to their incredible cognitive abilities. Collectively, the art from this one 'provenance' gives a complete picture of their entire lives along with the environment that they left behind when they left their erupting volcanic homeland and the new one that they 'settled' in that had entirely new predators! The art also proves that the Mammoth People were global travelers and could cover vast distances in one lifetime!   .... "it just is what it is"…..Mark Hruska 12/9/11

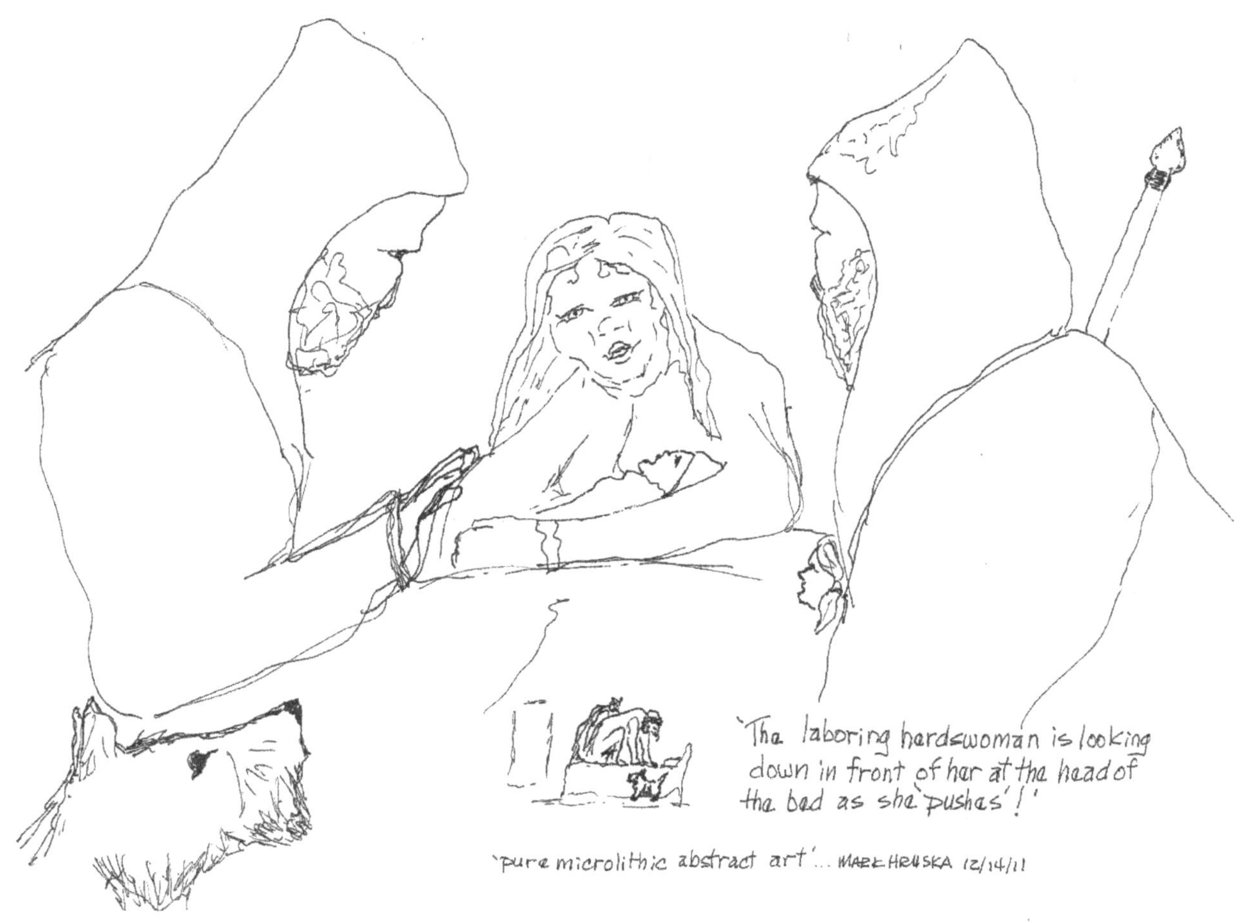

'pure microlithic abstract art'... 'The laboring herdswoman is looking down in front of her towards the head of the bed as she pushes!'

53) Birth was one of the most significant events for the Mammoth People. I've interpreted mammoth birth, cattle birth, horse birth and even sheep birth but the rarest birth folklore tale of all is that of human birth which makes it all the more precious. The most impressionable aspect that was left on my 'mind's eye' is that the birthing herdswoman always delivered her baby on all fours just like all of their domestic animals did. A midwife delivered the baby and she was usually grandma.

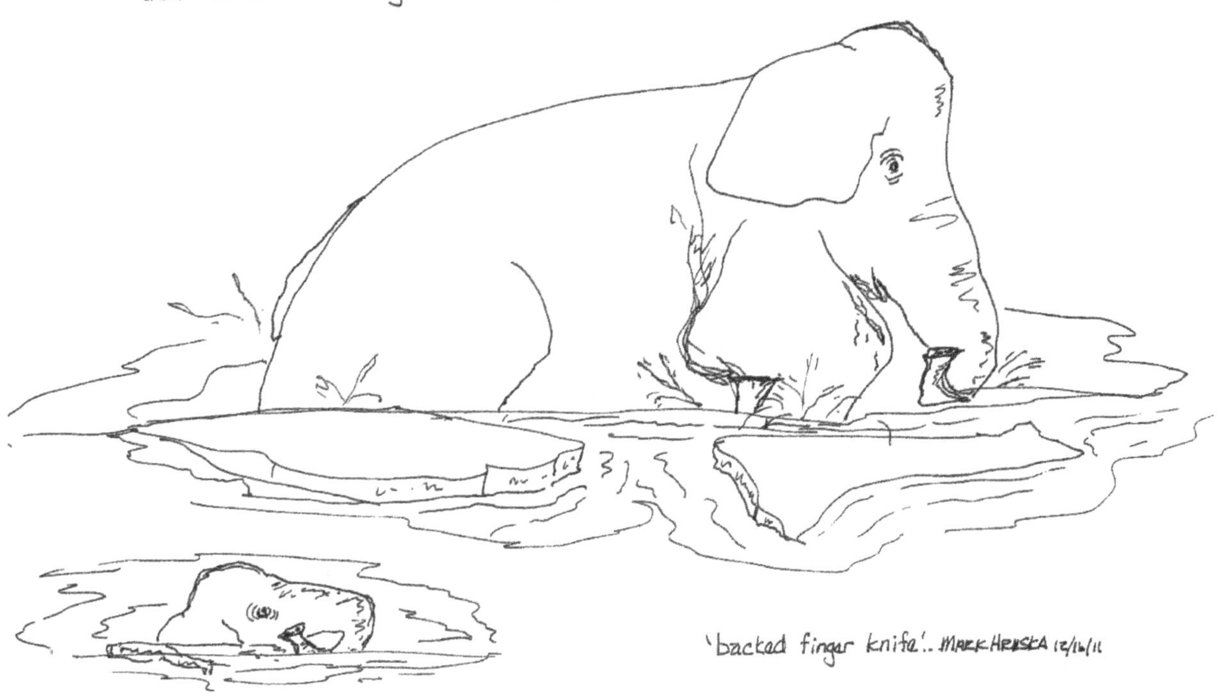

'backed finger knife'... 'The brown woolly mammoth battled the predator ice until her rear end finally sank with her head going down last like a sinking battle ship!'

54) This line sketch needs no further explanation.

'Drastically Changed Model'

As I try to get the discovery of the Mammoth People and their microlithic abstract art figurative language out to the general public I'm up against the same kind of skepticism that you would experience if you went up to a religious leader and tried to convince him that you found proof that there was no 'god' that his religion is based on. He would instantly discount you as some kind of psychotic 'kook' because he's so closed minded and brain washed about his beliefs. He wouldn't hear any of what you were telling him. Such is what I'm facing when I tell a local archaeologist of what I've discovered about the earliest people that lived in my State. 'It' seems so outlandishly foreign to what they've been taught all of their lives that they automatically dismiss it because 'it' would drastically change their comfortable model of who we always thought the first Americans were!

…… "it just is what it is"…..Mark Hruska

12/18/11

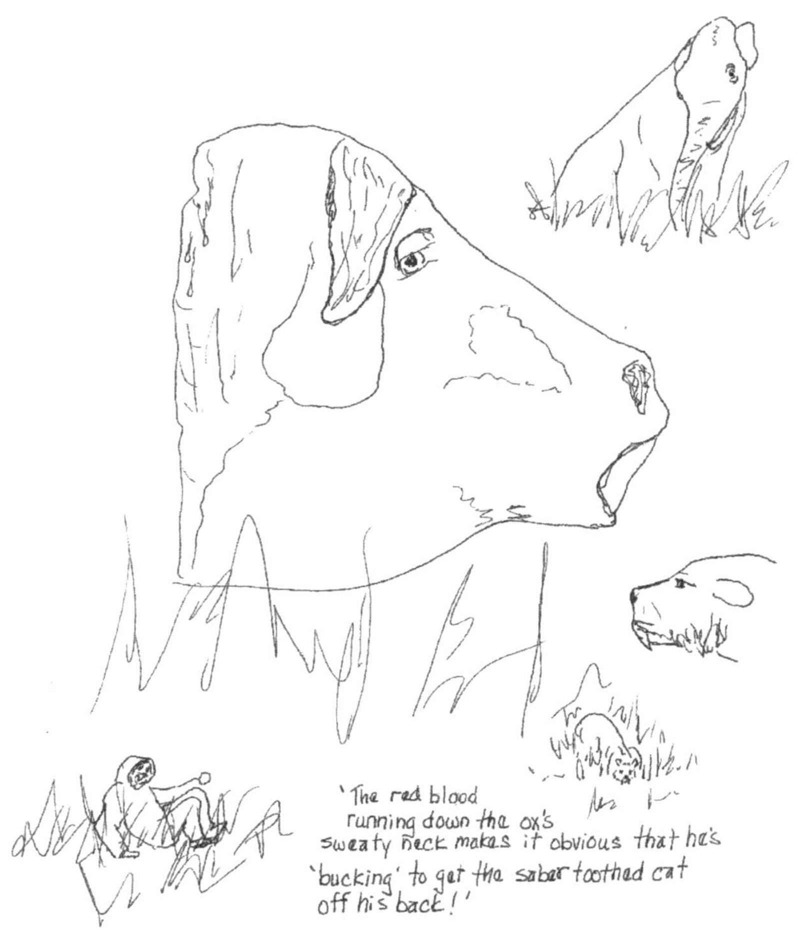

'backed knife'... 'The red blood running down the ox's sweaty neck makes it
obvious that he's 'bucking' to get the saber-toothed cat off his back!'

55) The scenes from this pieces interpretation are definitely from when the Mammoth People mammoth
caravan of trekkers was trekking across the vast grasslands. I interpreted it before I had pieced together
how the lurking cats jumped up on the domestic milk cow's back causing her to buck away with the infant
flopping on her left shoulder strapped to his carrier.

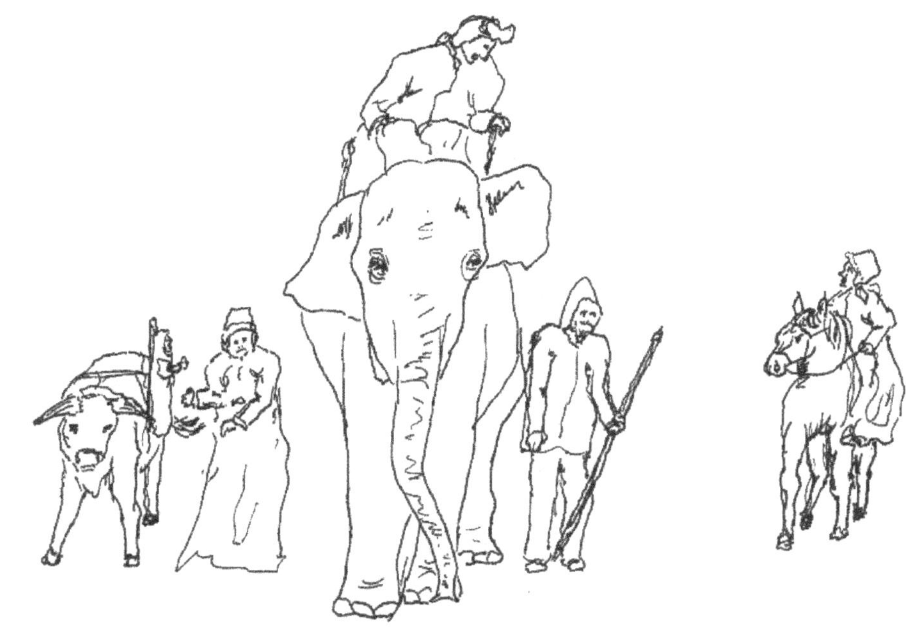

'Mammoth People mammoth caravan trekking to here!'

56) This is an updated view to that date of how I imagined them trekking from the combined scenes of the microlithic abstract artworks that had that repetitive theme or folklore tale on them.

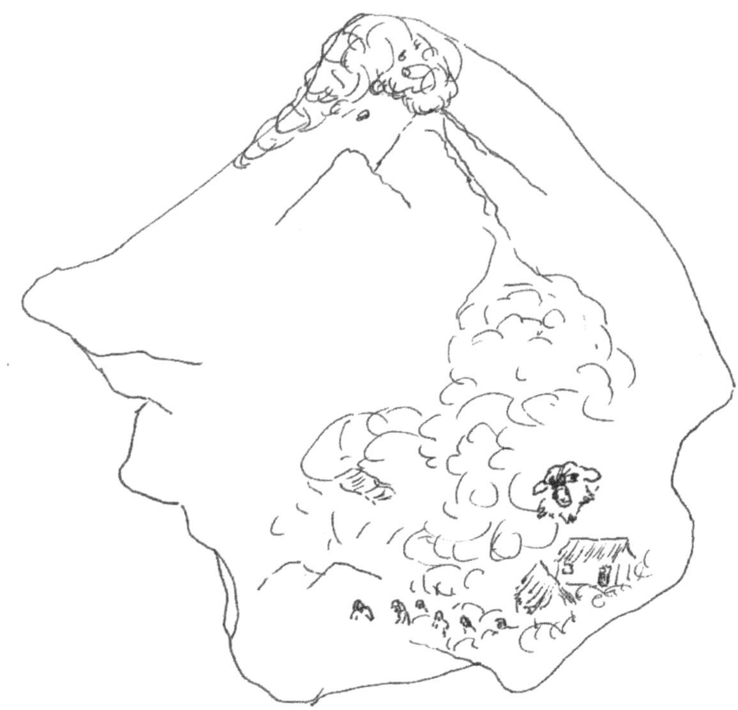

'flake knife'... 'The snarling male lion's head is above the fleeing
Mammoth People's heads as a pyroclastic flow that's pouncing on them!'

57) It's all reflecting off of the left side of a screaming fleeing herdswoman's cape hood that's over her bonnet.

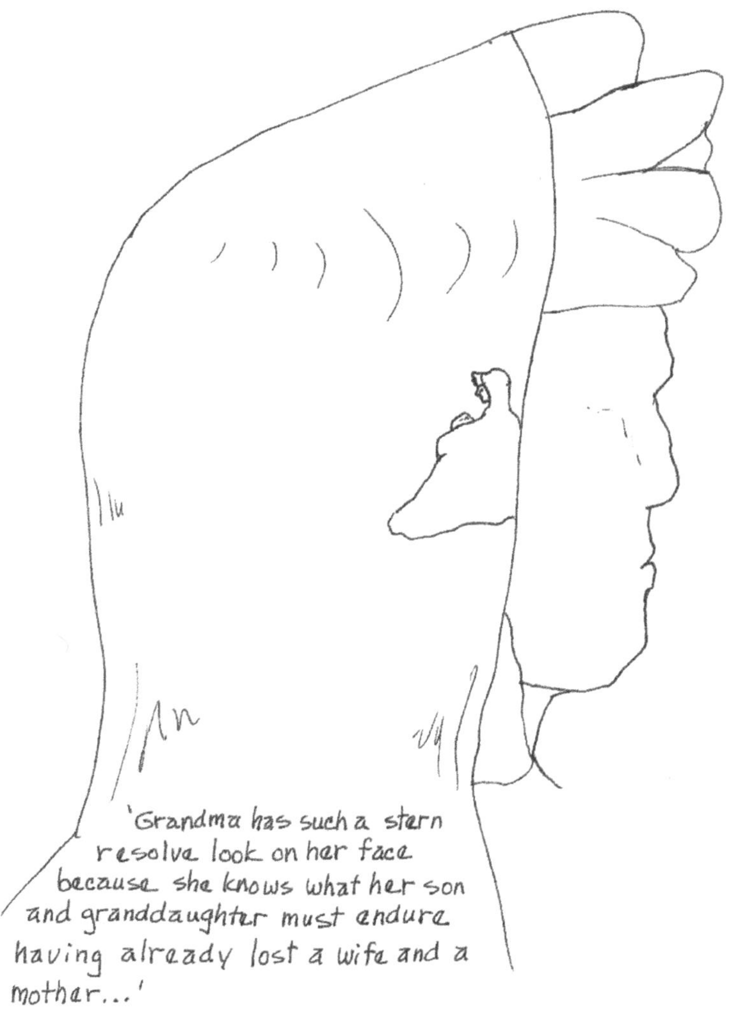

'prismatic knife midsection'... 'Grandma has such a stern resolve look on her face because she knows what her son and granddaughter must endure having already lost a wife and a mother...'

58) The Mammoth People's lives were full of tragedy.

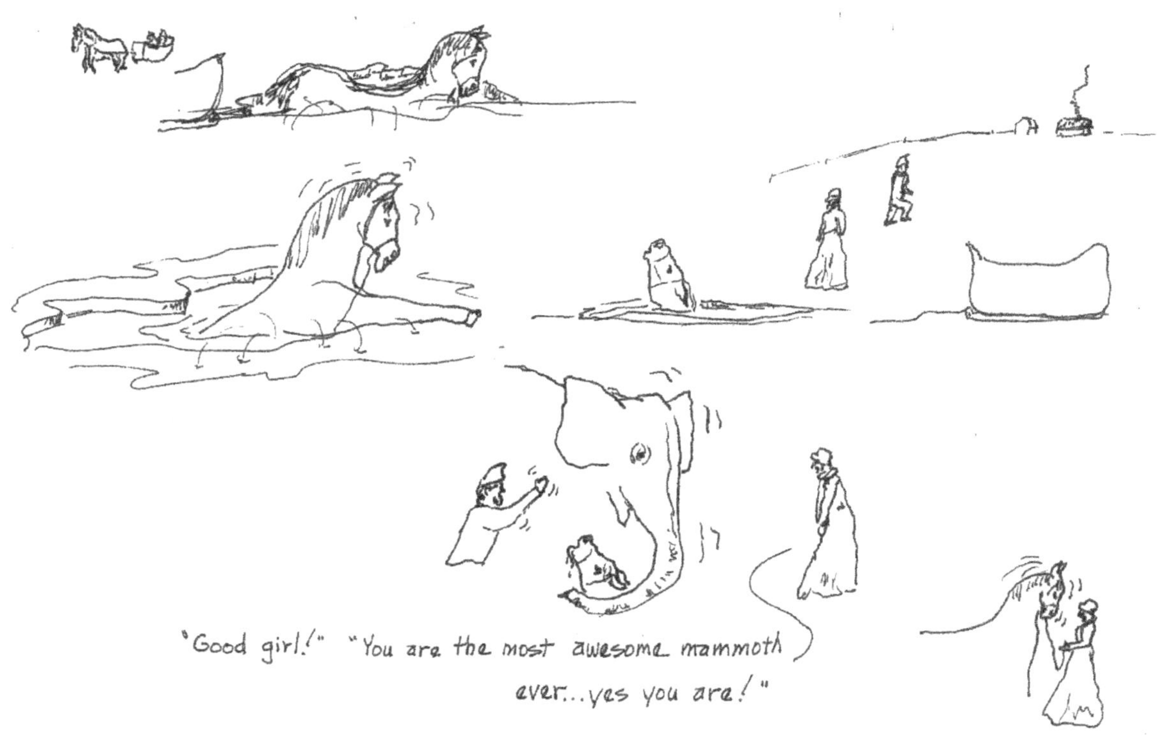

'rotational change-up'... "Good girl!" "You are the
most awesome mammoth ever...yes you are!"

59) I distinctly remember this piece because it didn't become a folklore tale from repetitiveness. It stood out as a lone story, one in which the young lad ran to the distant herd stead to commission its domestic mammoth to use her strong trunk to pull out a struggling horse that had fallen through the predator ice. She had been pulling the young couples sled at the time of the incident.

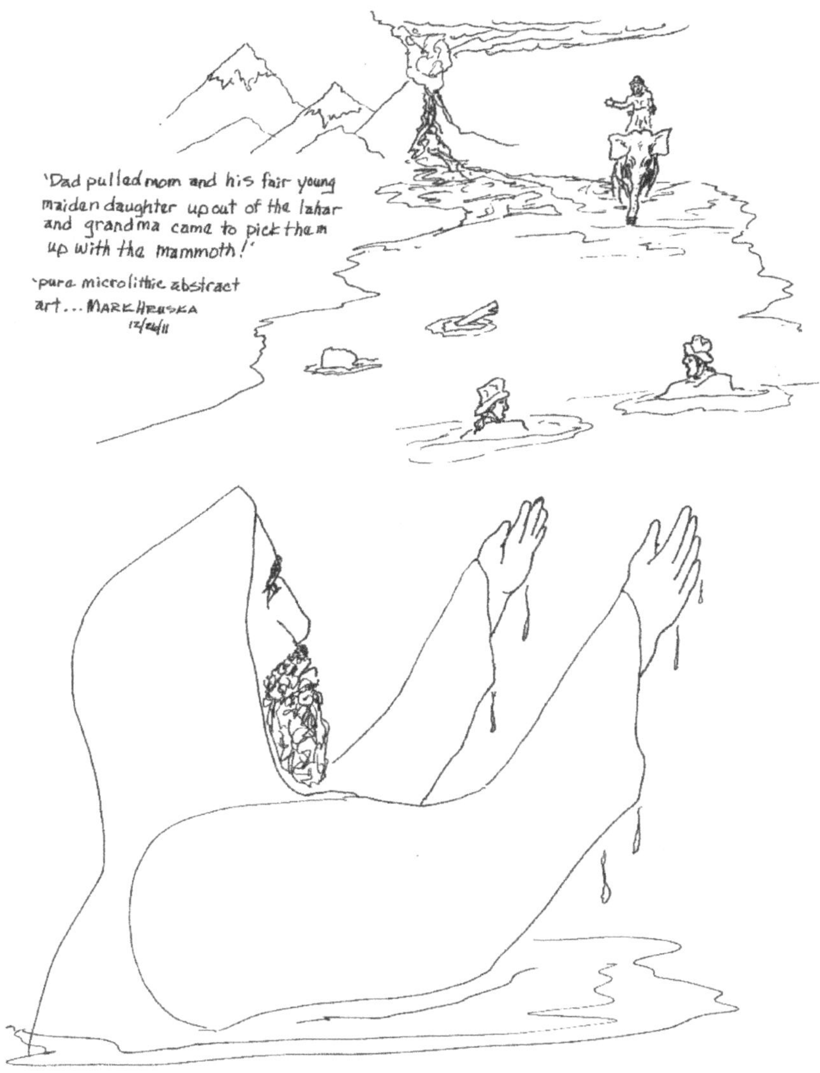

'pure microlithic abstract art'... 'Dad pulled mom and his fair young maiden daughter up out of the lahar and grandma came to pick them up with the mammoth!'

60) This is another self-explanatory line sketch that describes a piece with the 'lahar' repetitive theme.

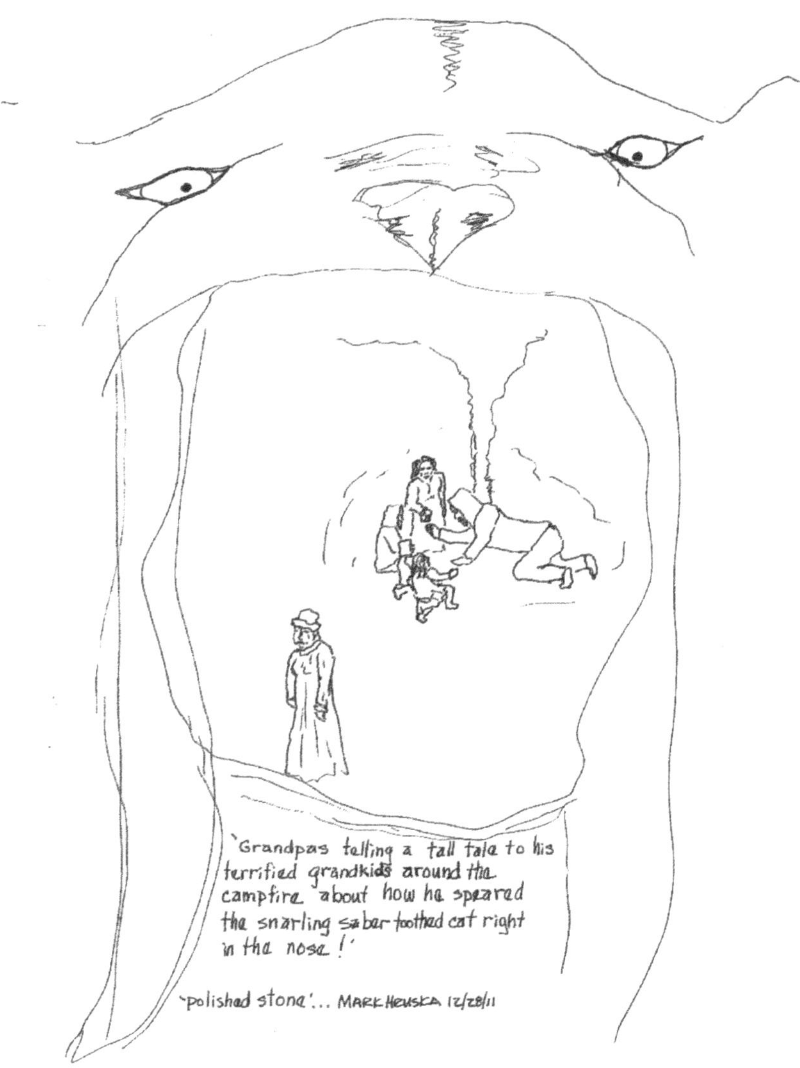

'polished stone'... 'Grandpa's telling a tall tale to his terrified grandkids around the campfire about how he speared the saber-toothed cat right in the nose!'

61) Storytelling was the primary form of entertainment but as you can see, grandma looks tired and disgusted as she slips away to bed. I clearly remember interpreting this amazing piece.

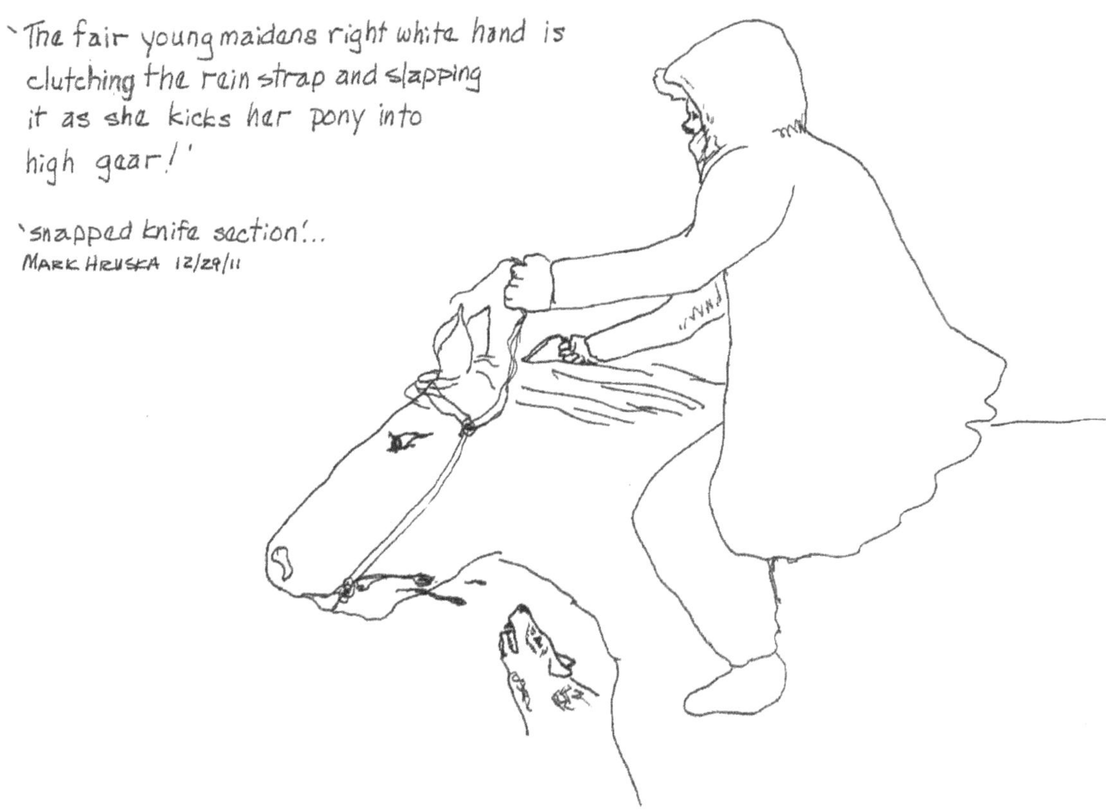

'snapped knife section'... 'The fair young maiden's right white hand is clutching the rein strap and slapping it as she kicks her pony into high gear!'

62) And it's because her life depends on it.

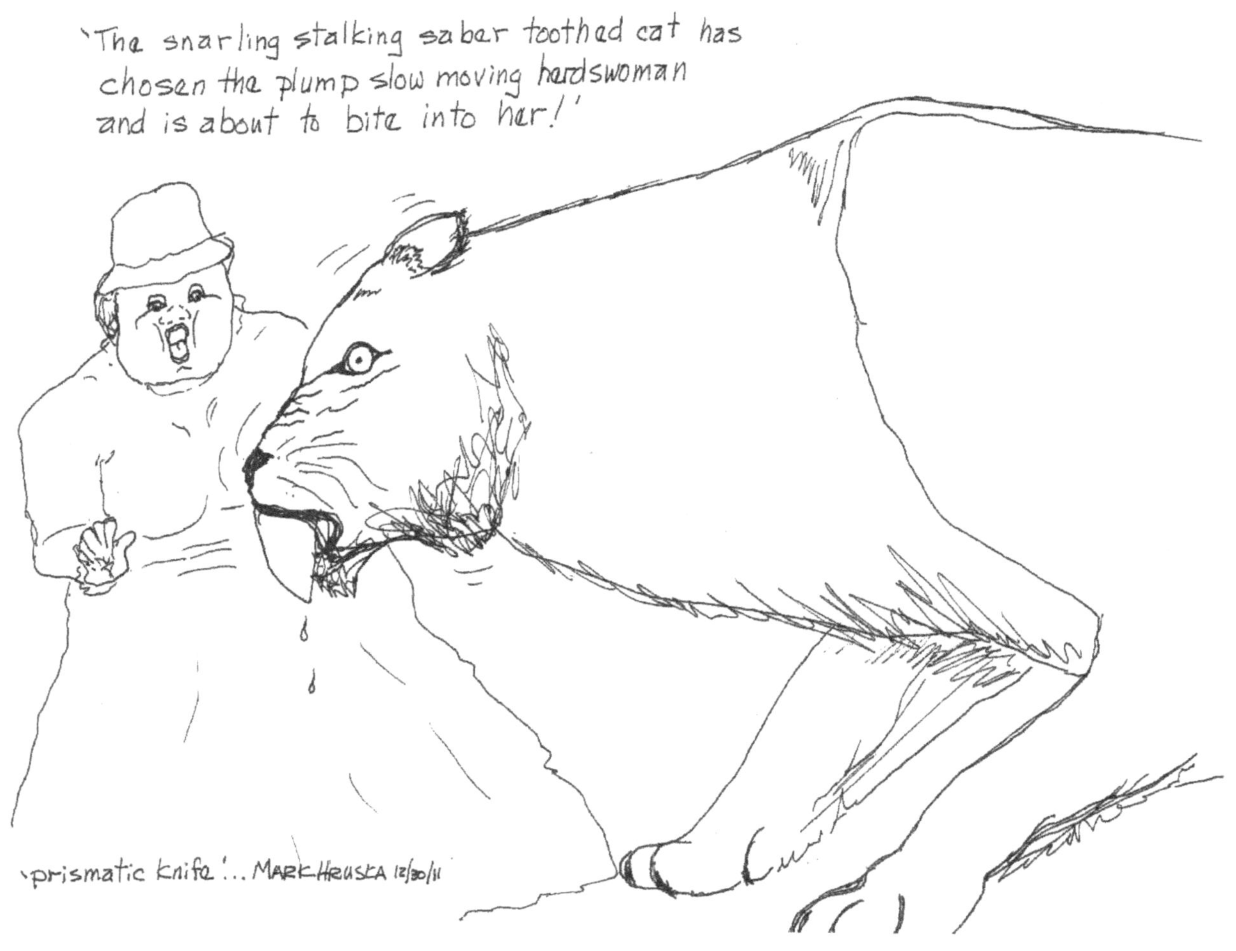

'prismatic knife'... 'The snarling saber-toothed cat has chosen the plump
slow moving herdswoman and is about to bite into her!'

63) This piece has the 'summertime picnic' folklore tale on it where either the saber-toothed cat, a pair of rogue male lions or a pair of dire wolves attack the picnic to have a little picnic of their own. The lesson to be learned by the Mammoth People children is to... not be plump.

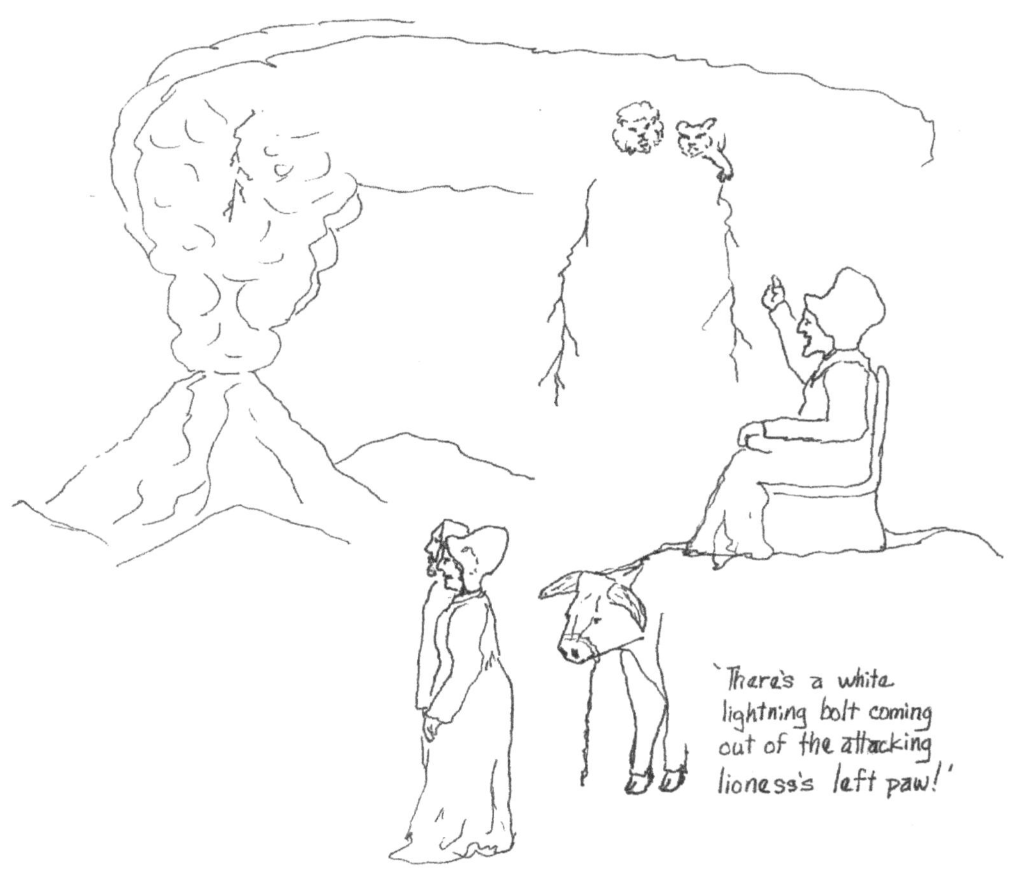

‘oval knife section’... ‘There’s a white lightning bolt
coming out of the lioness’s left paw!’

64) The ‘volcanic mass exodus’ repetitive theme is falling into place, but it has a long way to go even though I felt that I had it figured out at the time.

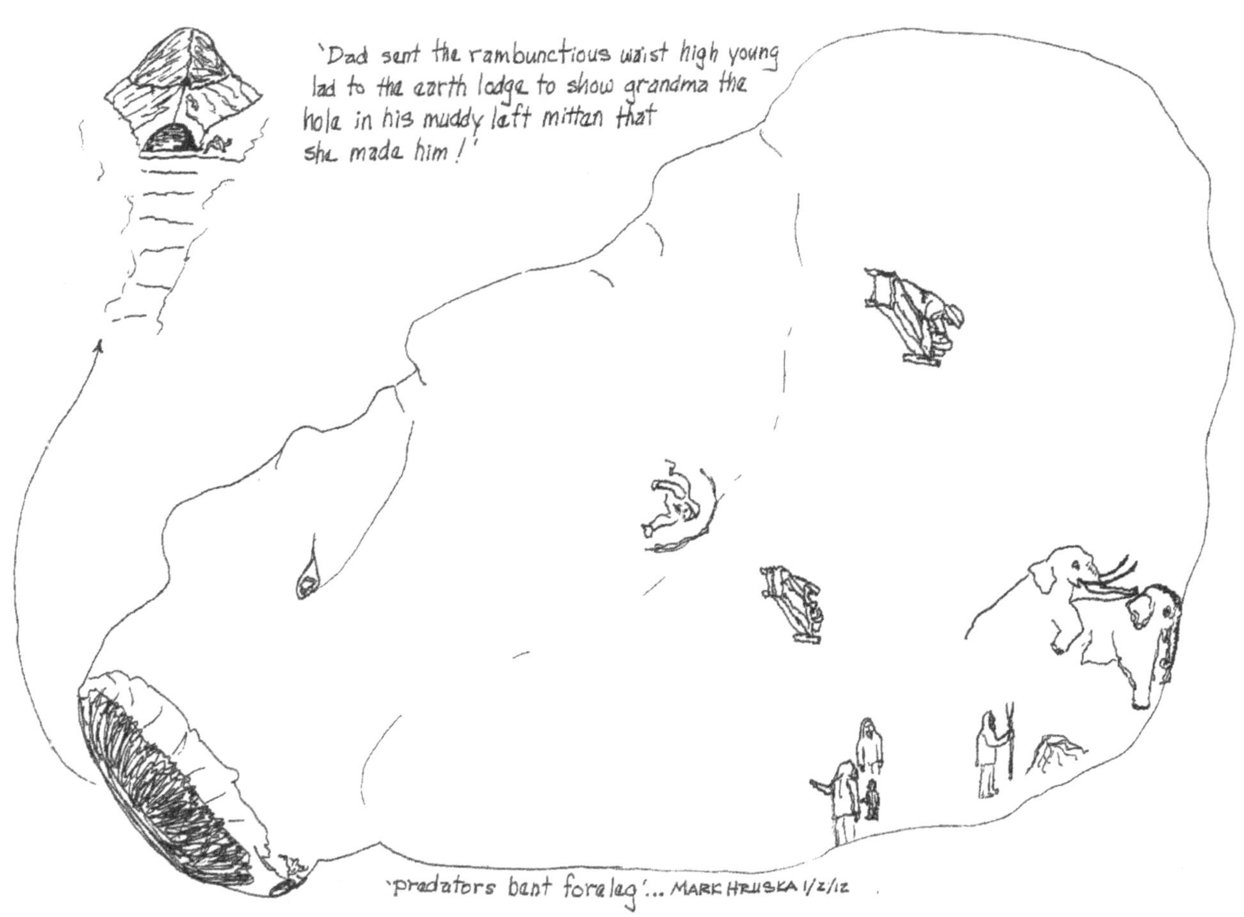

'predators bent foreleg'... 'Dad sent the rambunctious waist high young lad to the earth lodge to show grandma the hole in his muddy left mitten that she made for him!'

65) I distinctly remember interpreting this piece from the '2a' site and could actually picture how the lodge was at the top of the hill while the corral for the mammoth was down near the river. I also got the distinct impression that that site was older or one of the first sites that the Mammoth People settled at when they got 'here'.

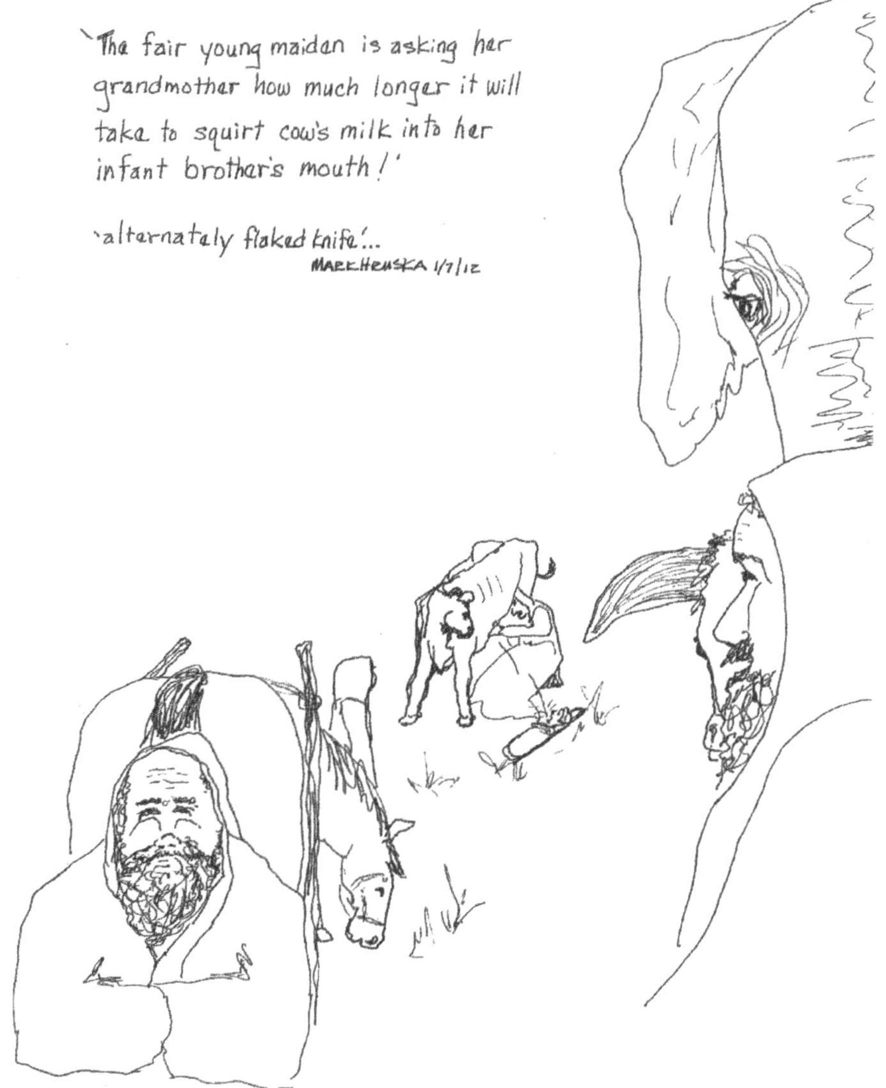

'alternately flaked knife'... 'The fair young maiden is asking her grandmother how much longer it will take to squirt cow's milk into her infant brother's mouth!'

66) The interpretation of this piece shows that I did not yet realize that it was frantic mom herdswoman and not grandma who was trying to appease the screaming infant before he raised tensions further during the 'powwow' and got them all killed.

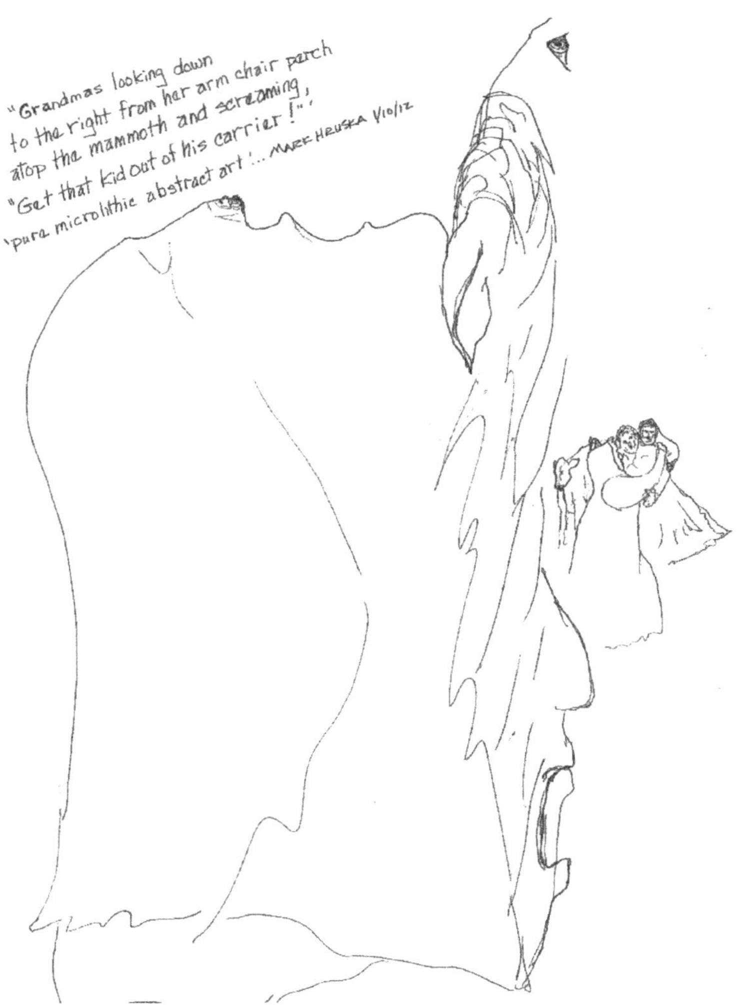

'pure microlithic abstract art'... 'Grandma's looking down to her right from her armchair perch atop the mammoth and screaming, "Get that kid out of his carrier!"'

67) This piece has the scenes of the 'powwow' on it when grandma's yelling at mom herdswoman to squirt cow's milk into the infants mouth while she also was looking out towards her screaming fair young maiden granddaughter who was being chased in towards her lead hunter herder dad in front of the nervous lead mammoth by the crazy whooping and hollering warrior brave on his galloping palomino horse. His and the top of his horses heads can be seen as opposing heads to 'yelling' grandma's head because they are sharing the backs of their heads and are in effect 'in' each other's heads thinking of each other.

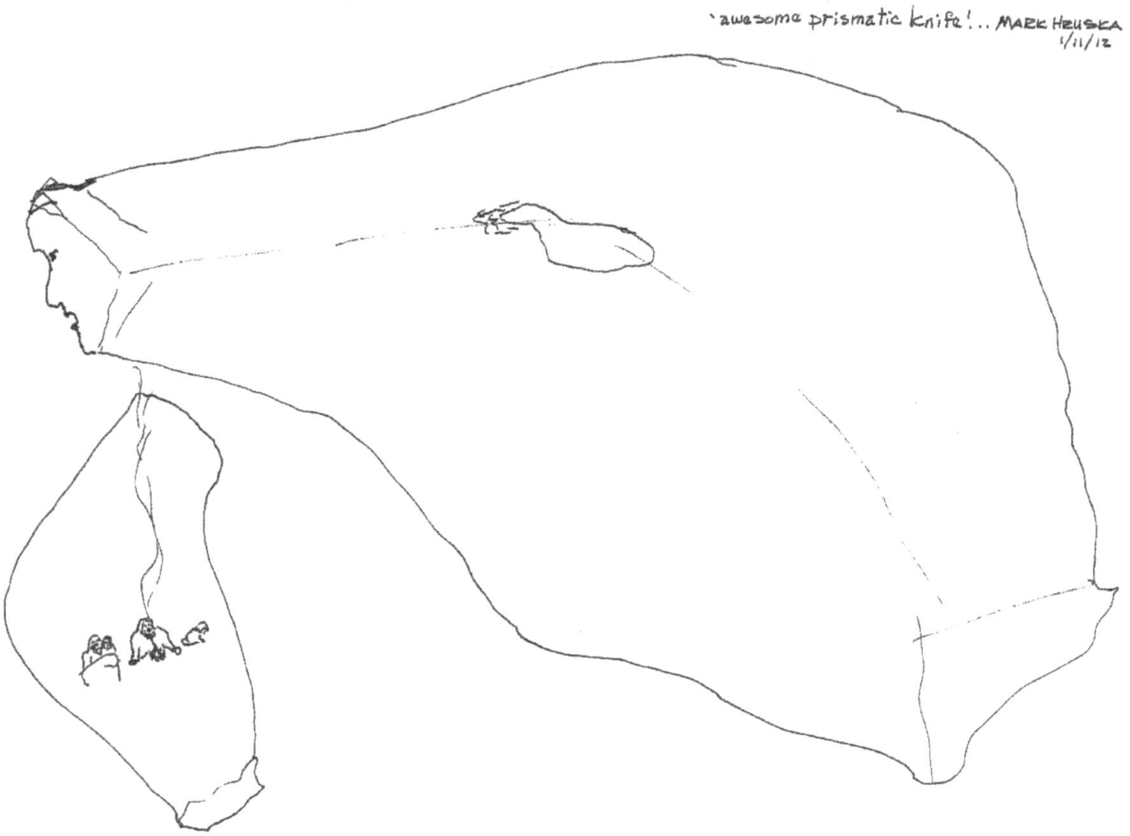

'awesome prismatic knife'... 'That's when the freezing waist high
young maiden yells, "Blow harder Daddy!" "Blow harder!"'

68) This pieces interpretation and its line sketch obviously show how important fire was to the Mammoth People.

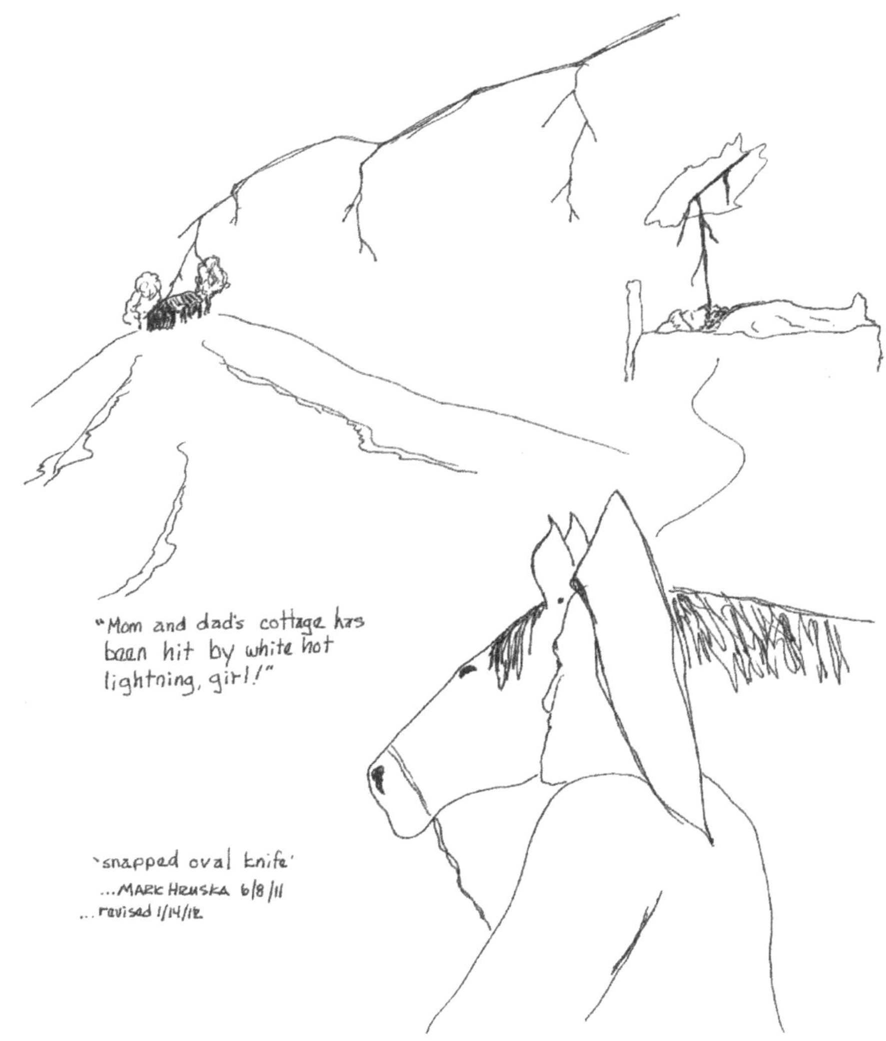

'snapped oval knife'... "Mom and dad's cottage has been hit by white hot lightning, girl!"

69) I remember this piece as a black flint knife that you had to just stare at until your eyes adjusted to the subtle differences in the black heat treated stone that actually was the combined optical and cognitive illusion close-up image of the left side view of the horses head during a nighttime rain storm. What you were seeing through the eyes of the microlithic abstract artisan's eyes was being seen during the flash of lightning that hit his parent's cottage that was on top of a hill.

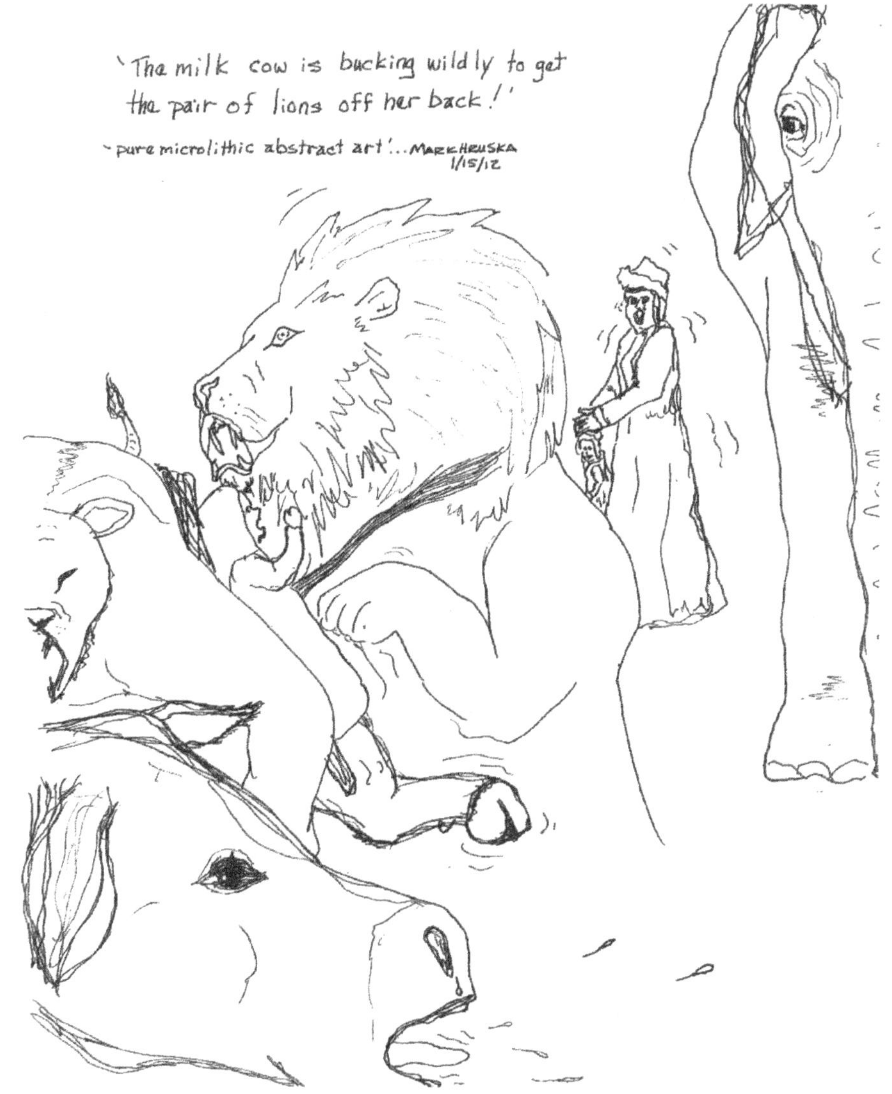

'pure microlithic abstract art'... 'The milk cow is
bucking wildly to get the pair of lions off her back!'

70) Mom and dad had no warning or chance to stop the domestic milk cow from bucking away from them with the pair of lions on her back.

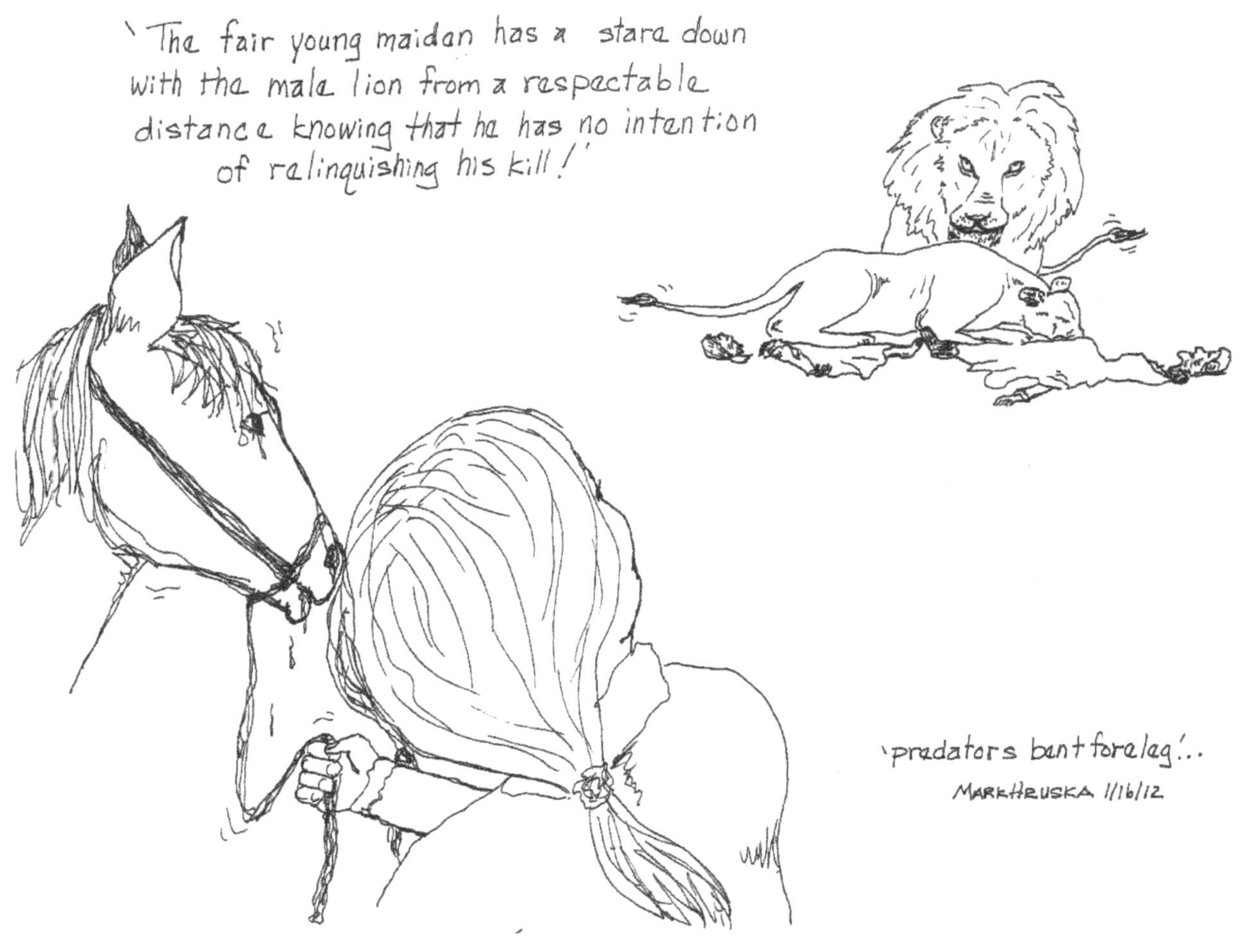

'predators bent foreleg'... 'The fair young maiden has a stare down with the male lion from a respectable distance knowing that he has no intention of relinquishing his kill!'

71) If I remember correctly, the fair young maiden went looking for her kind and loving grandma shepherdess who was babysitting her toddler little sister while out in the meadow watching over their domestic cattle and sheep. The singing of their traditional folk songs apparently sounded like wounded prey animals....

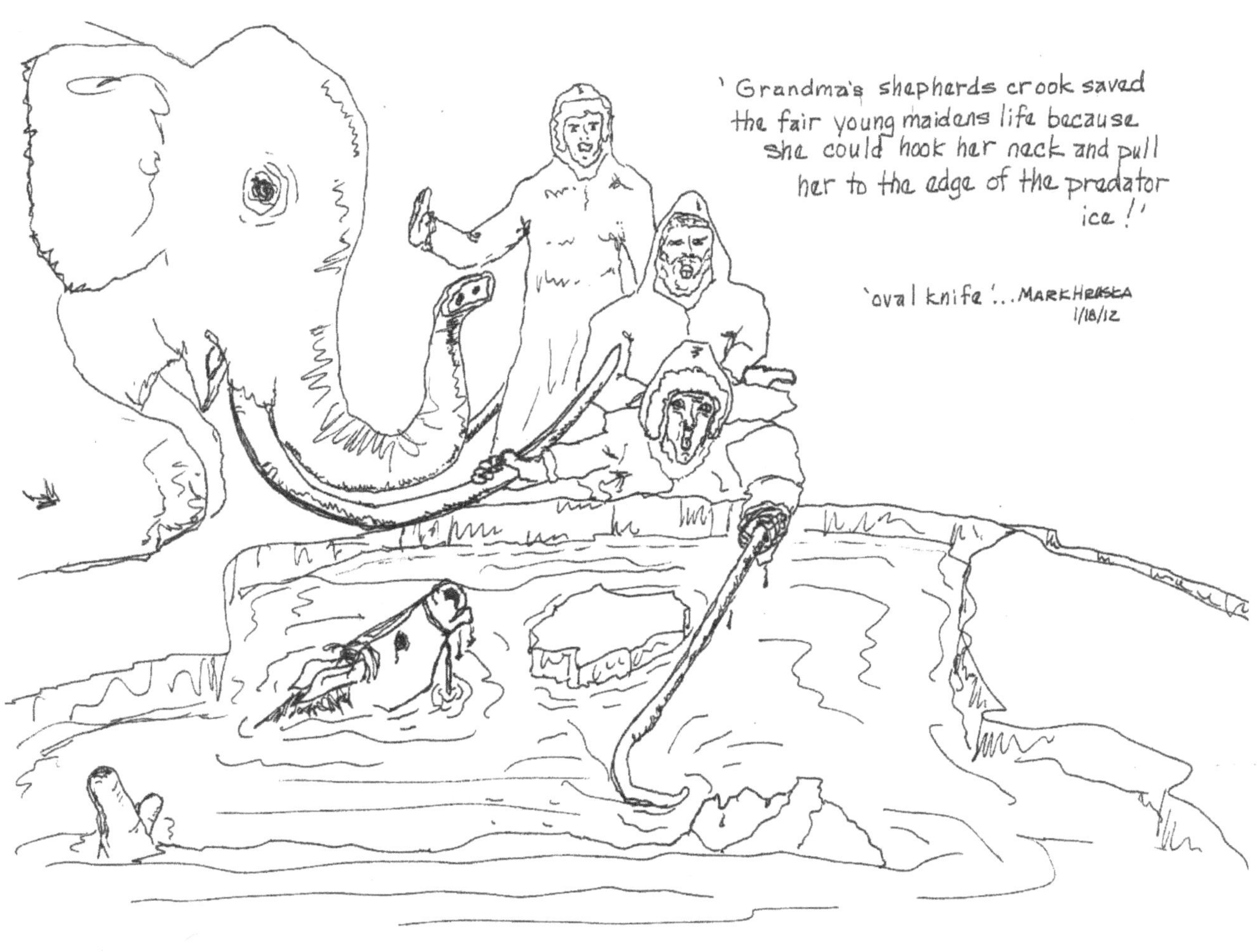

'oval knife'... 'Grandma's shepherds crook saved the fair young maiden's life because she could hook her neck and pull her to the edge of the predator ice!'

72) Sometimes the cooperation of the frantic lead family that included the kneeling nervous lead mammoth, successfully rescued the struggling fair young maiden and her thrashing horse, but most of the time one of the thrashing horse's flailing front feet's hooves kicked her in the head and sent her sinking into the dark icy cold abyss out of the reach of grandma's shepherds crook.

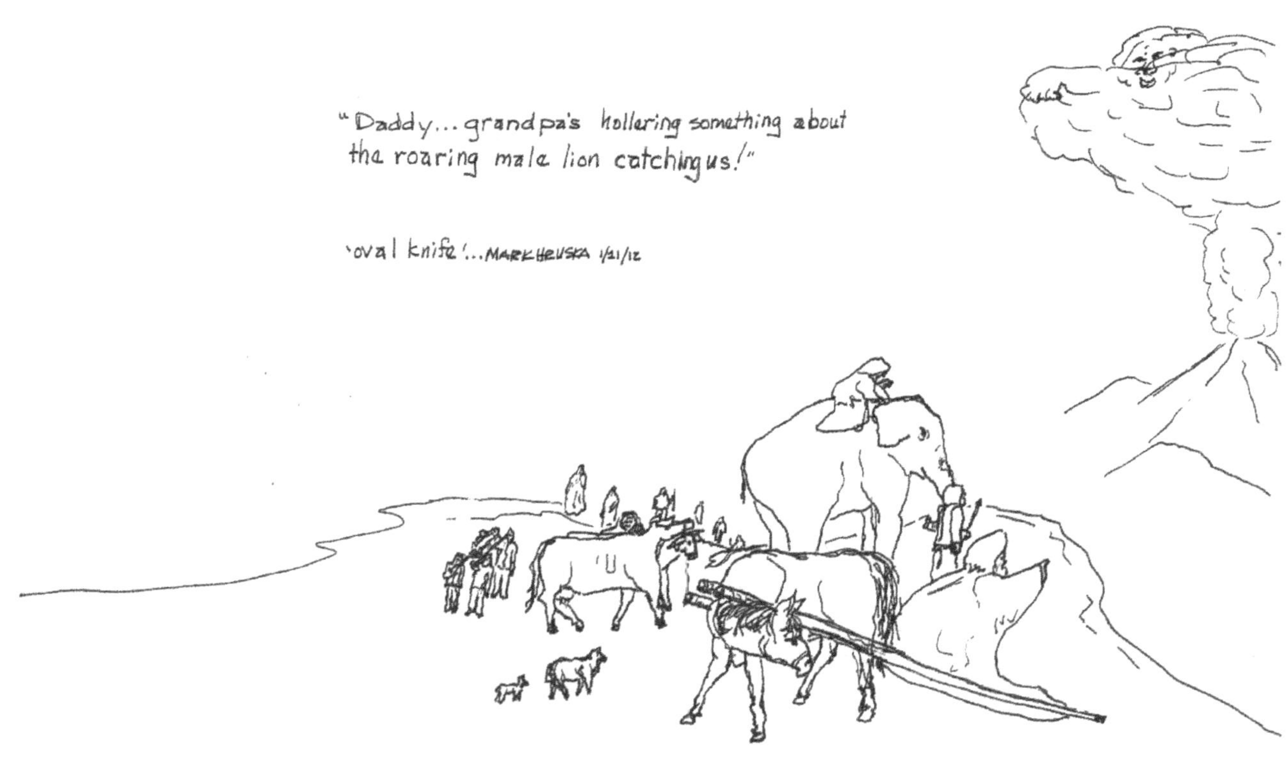

'oval knife'... "'Daddy.... grandpa's hollering
something about the roaring male lion catching us!'"

73) In this line sketch, I'm still piecing together all of the individual scenes that made up the entire epic folklore tale of the 'volcanic mass exodus'.

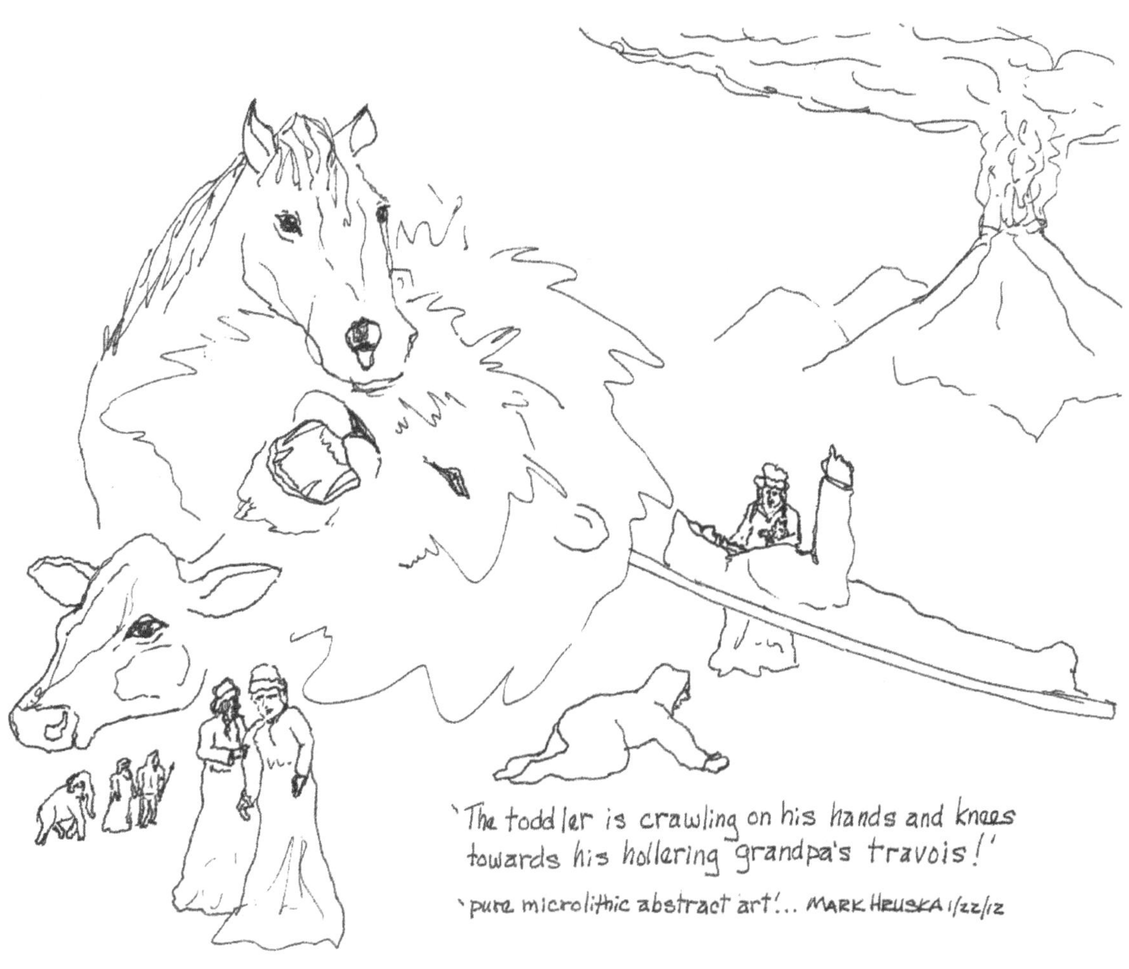

'pure microlithic abstract art'... 'The toddler is crawling on his
hands and knees towards his hollering grandpa's travois!'

74) As in the previous line sketch, I'm slowly and patiently piecing together the epic 'volcanic mass exodus' folklore tale by interpreting what will eventually turn out to be hundreds of artworks with its most popular repetitive theme.

'Why Do I Need To....?'

Why do I need to read or learn anything that
any archaeologist wrote or claims they know
about Paleo man that lived on this continent
when I can get all of the answers to the
questions that I have about our Paleo selves
from the Mammoth People hunter herder
microlithic abstract art that's on the debitage
that they left in the dirt near my home that I've
been picking up all of my life?

.... "it just is what it is"....Mark Hruska 1/23/12

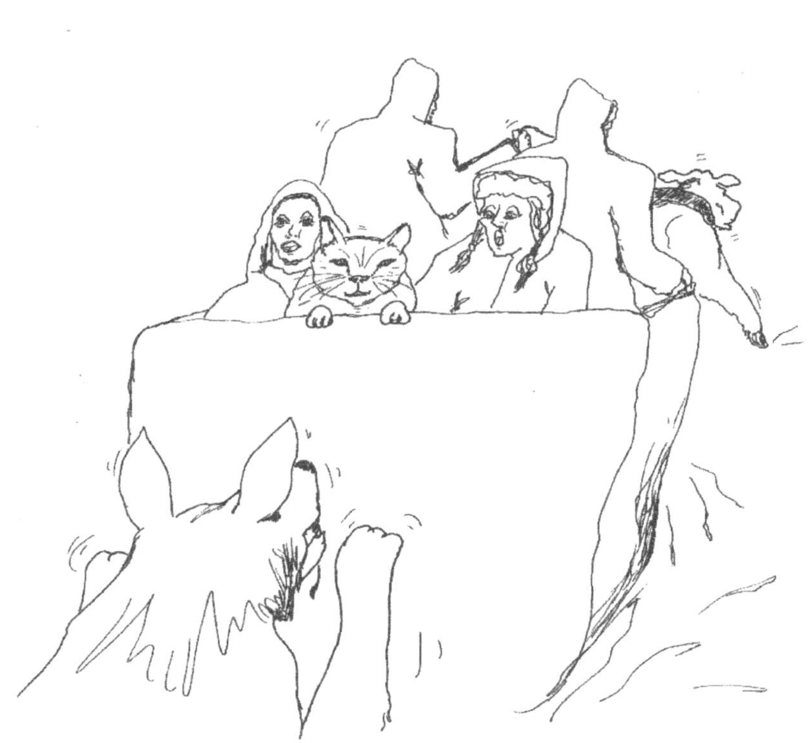

'heat treated flake knife'... '"Na, na, na, na...na!" "You can't catch me!"'

75) The horrified waist high young maiden's smug kitty is comfortably peering over the back wall of the sled face to face with the hungry dire wolf that's chasing them. I'd love to know how that story ended because on all of the succeeding interpretations that had that repetitive theme on them, it didn't bode well for the running ox that was hitched to the sled, nor for the occupants of the sled that he was pulling.

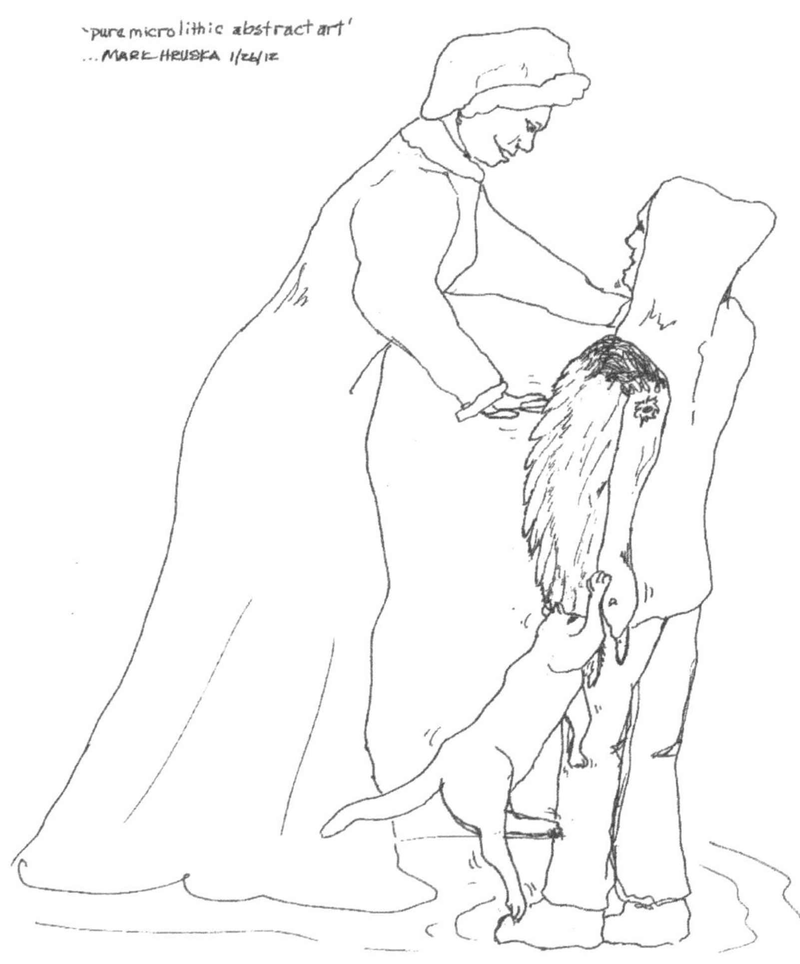

'pure microlithic abstract art'... 'The pair of oxen was driven home hard so that the young lad could show the rest of his family his first kill!'

76) This piece's line sketch makes it abundantly clear.

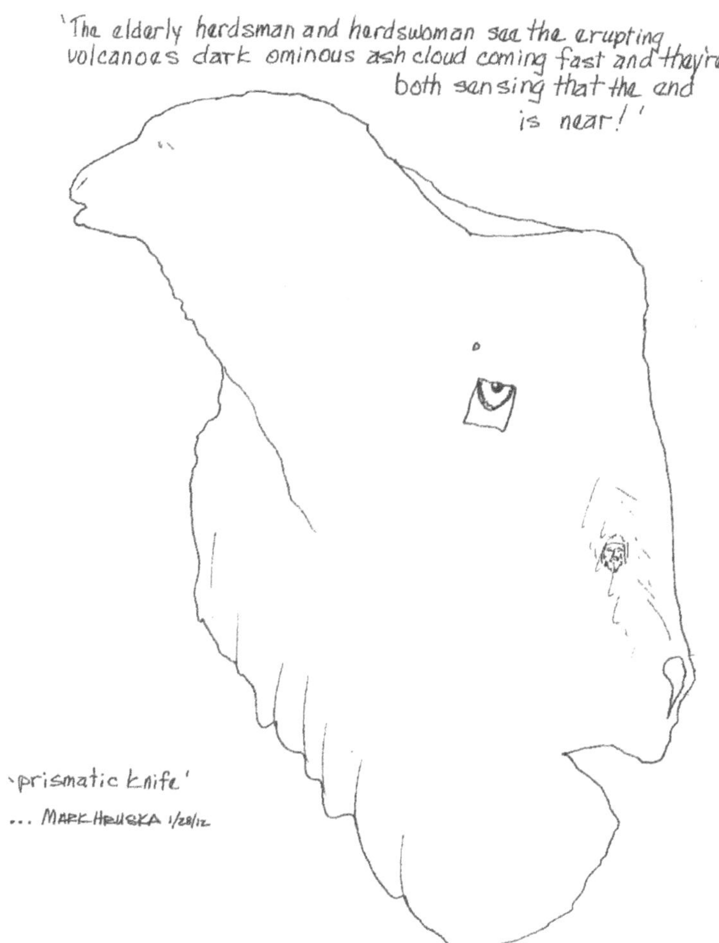

'prismatic knife'... 'The elderly herdsman and herdswoman see the erupting volcanoes dark ominous ash cloud coming fast and they're both sensing that the end is near!'

77) This piece has scenes from the 'volcanic mass exodus' on it. Delirious grandpa's bearded face is reflecting off of the right side of his rams face. The ram stays close to him as he lays on his travois because they were best buds when they watched over the sheep in the mountainous meadows of their beloved homeland. The flying submissive ewe spirits head and flying body are an opposing image to the rams head because delirious grandpa sees her as a reflection off of the ram's close-up head image which means that she's gliding in to possibly suck up their last exhaled breaths or their spirits giving this whole scene overtones of impending doom.

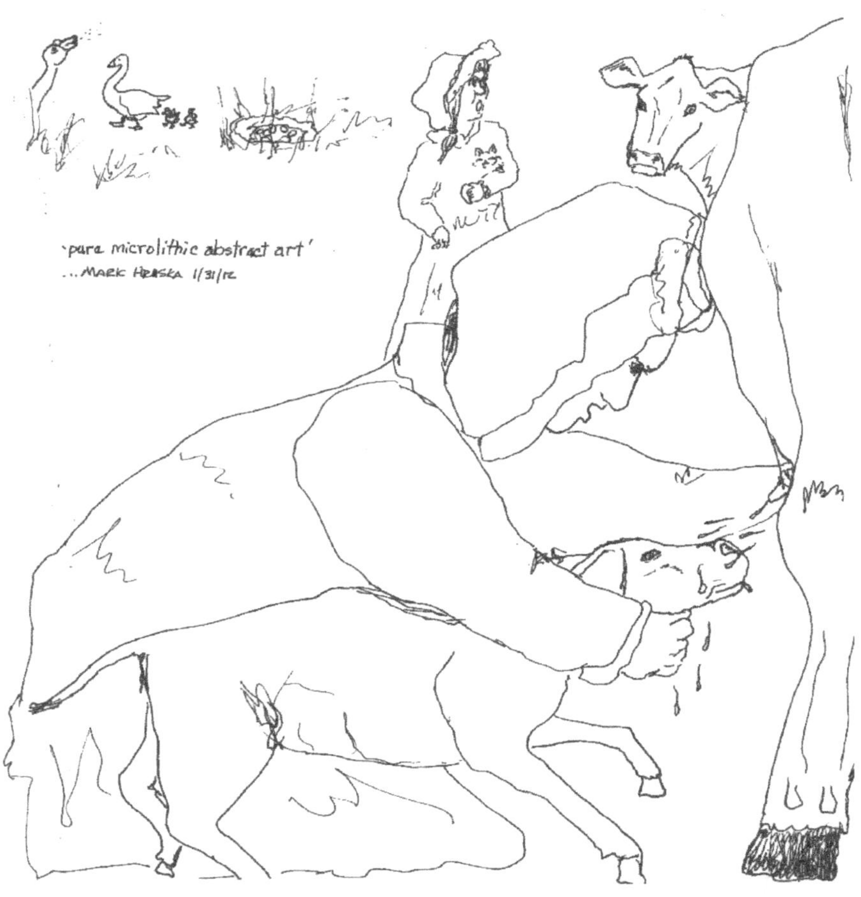

'pure microlithic abstract art'... '"Put the un-hatched goose eggs down sweetheart... or we'll both smell like rotten eggs!"'

78) This piece's interpretation takes place out in the springtime meadow near the herd stead yard while either mom or grandma was trying to get the newborn calf to nurse. It's the repetitive theme of springtime and rebirth which was so very important to the Mammoth People, especially after the long cold winter and its hungry predators.

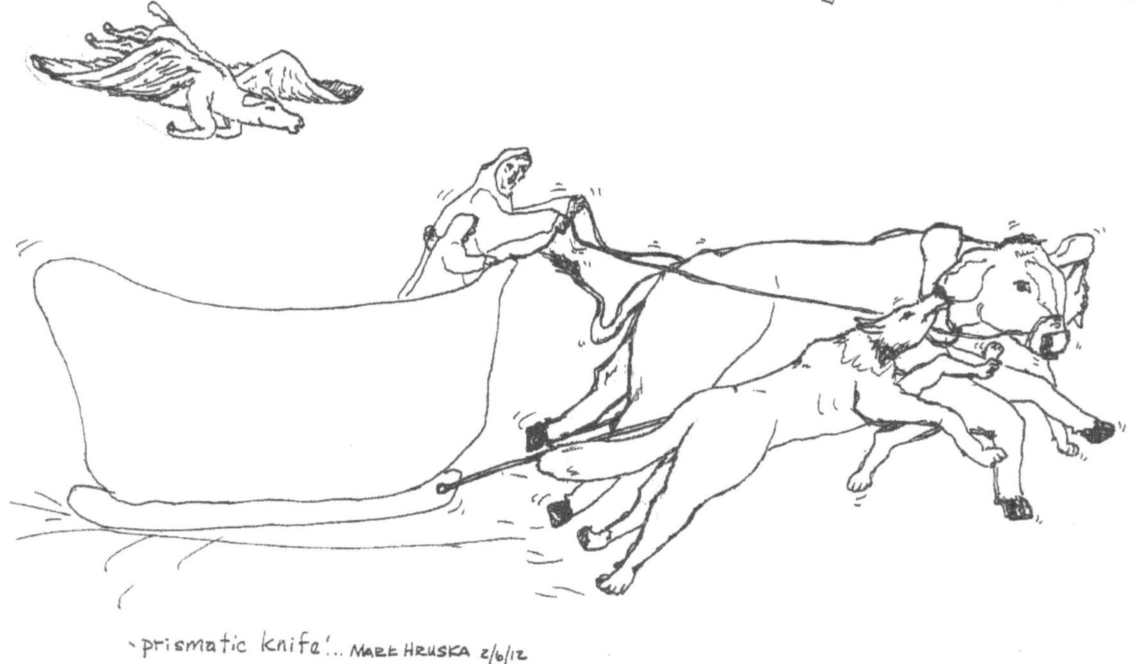

'prismatic knife'... '...when the dire wolves killed and ate his beloved wife and waist high young maiden daughter they ripped his heart right out of his chest too!'

79) This piece's interpretation has the folklore tale of when mom and her daughter or daughters attend the gossipy mother daughter gathering and overstay into the dusk hours when the hungry dire wolves come out looking for their supper. The alpha male leader and his she-wolf mate slow down the running ox or oxen by biting and then clinging onto their ears. These pieces will always have the flying submissive ewe spirit gliding down to suck up the dying Mammoth People's last exhaled breaths so that she can take their spirits into the heavens to be with their deceased loved ones.

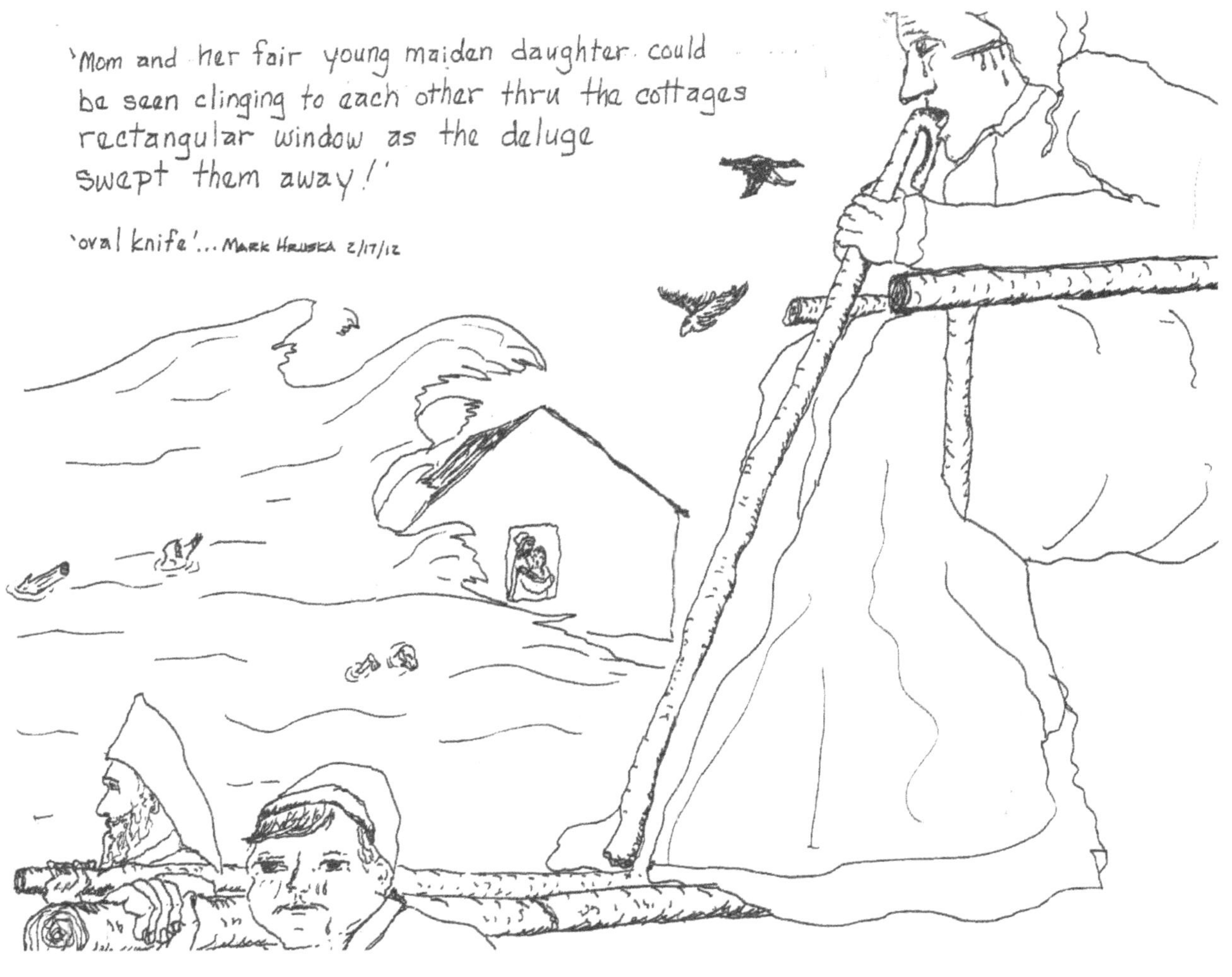

'oval knife'... 'Mom and her fair young maiden daughter could be seen clinging to each other thru the cottages rectangular window as the deluge swept them away!'

80) This piece shows how I was putting together what happened during the 'epic deluge'. You know that they're going to perish because the flying submissive ewe spirit can be seen gliding down from the heavens to suck up their last exhaled breaths or their spirits.

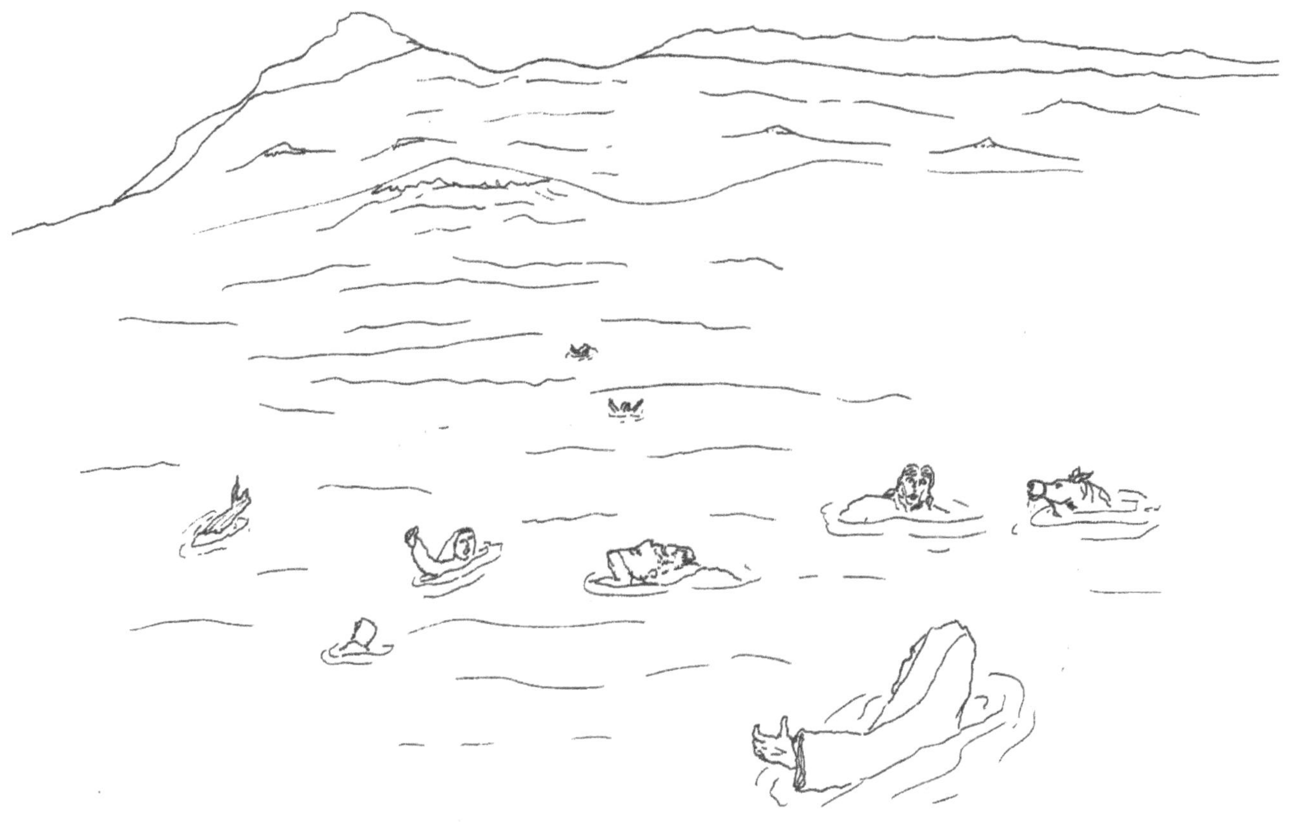

'pure microlithic abstract art'... 'The roaring male lion and his stalking
lioness mate breached the glacial ice damn wall and unleashed
an epic deluge on the trekking Mammoth People!'

81) Damn it! In my excitement to sketch what I had just seen through the eyes of the hunter herder microlithic abstract artist, I unintentionally misspelled dam, as in a glacial ice barrier.

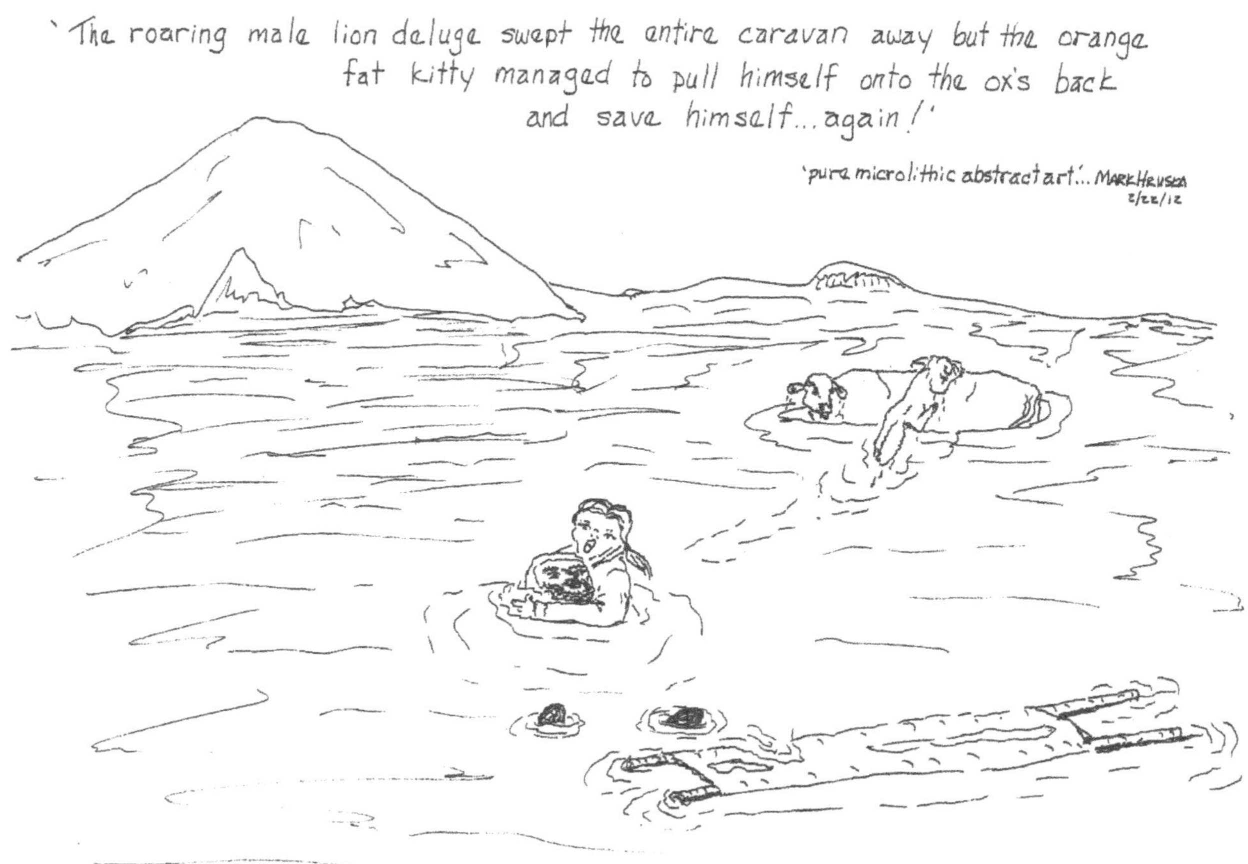

'pure microlithic abstract art'... 'The roaring male lion deluge swept the entire
caravan away but the orange fat kitty managed to pull himself
onto the ox's back and save himself....again!'

82) I sketched this interpretations line sketch before I realized that the ox was in fact the lead family's milk cow that carried the infant who was strapped to a backboard and slung over her left shoulder. Mind you, all of these folklore tales have overlapping imagery that ties all of them together but when you start telling the folklore tale of a particular piece, all of the scenes fall into place on the rotational change-up microlithic abstract artwork. This 'epic deluge' piece is showing what grandma sees from atop her swimming lead mammoth as they rescue the rest of the family.

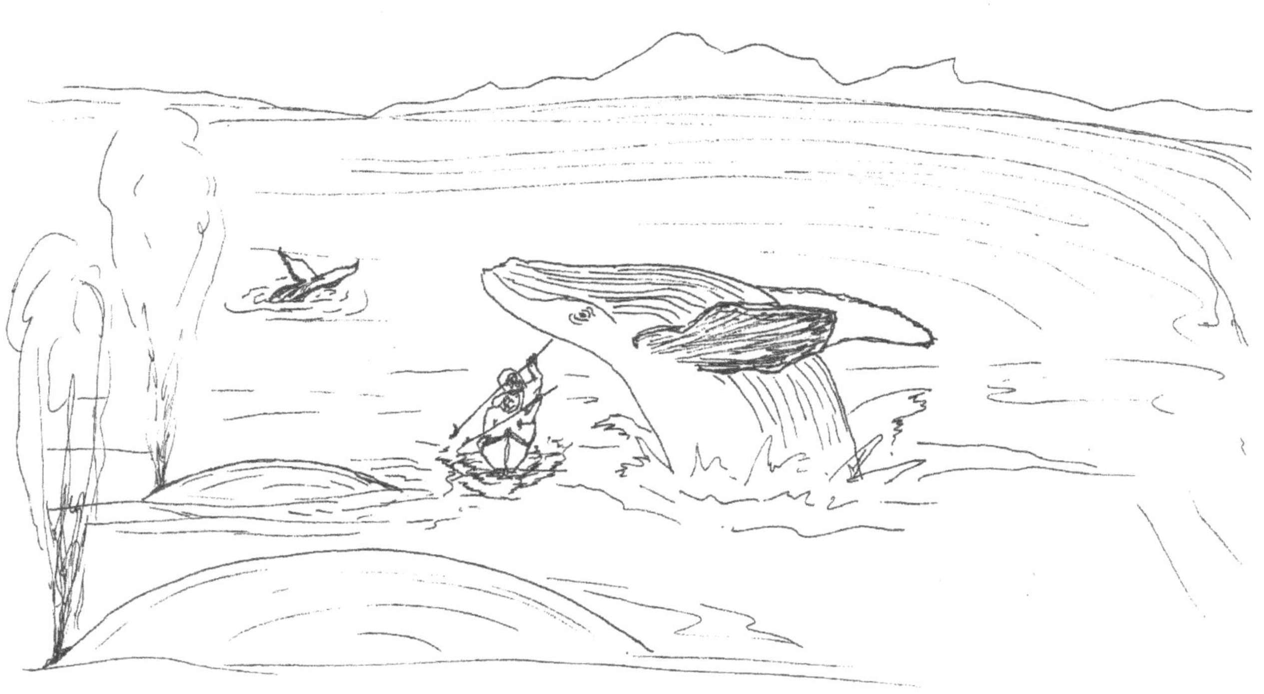

'bladelet knife'... 'Dad took his inexperienced young lad son
out in the kayak to hunt humpback whales but only one of them returned!'

83) The way that this folklore tale plays out is that since dad was teaching his inexperienced young lad son how to harpoon the easiest prey which is the calf, the mad breaching bull humpback whale smashes their kayak to pieces... along with dad. The inexperienced young lad lives and manages to make it back to shore to tell the tale. Consequently, an interpreter thirteen millennia later can also share it.

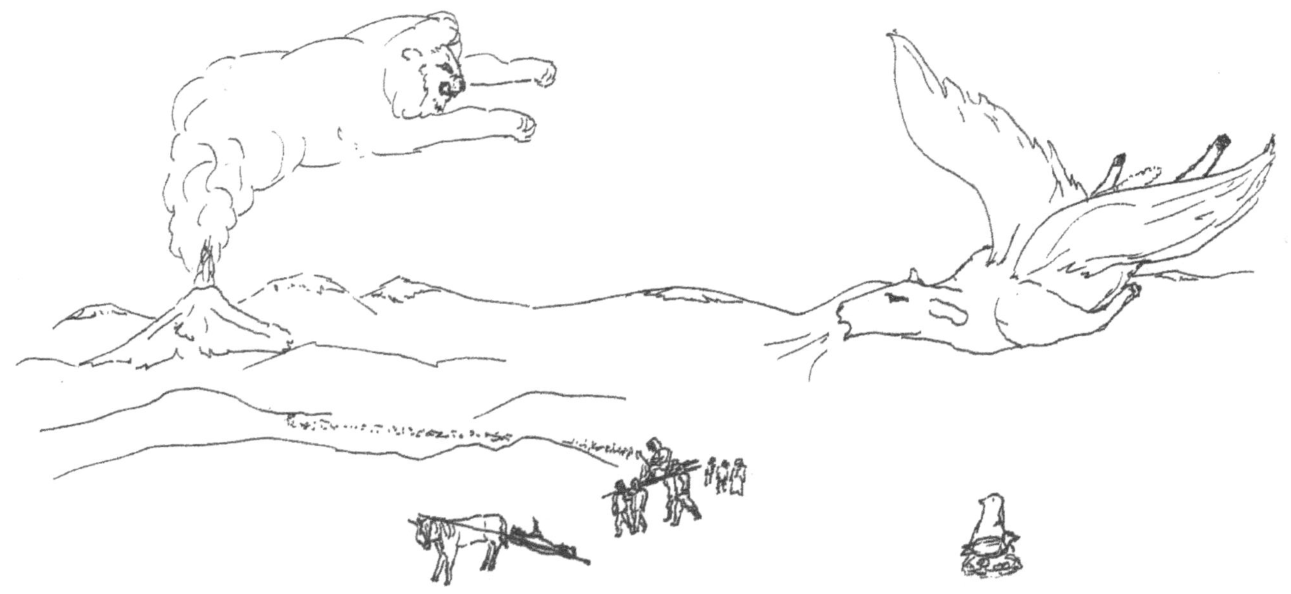

'heat treated flake knife'... 'The attacking roaring male lion ash cloud
is swiping at all of the weary trekkers including the alerted grouse family!'

84) Obviously, some of the weary trekkers are succumbing since the flying submissive ewe spirit is gliding down over them sucking up the dying ones last exhaled breaths so that she can take their spirits into the heavens to be with their deceased ancestors.

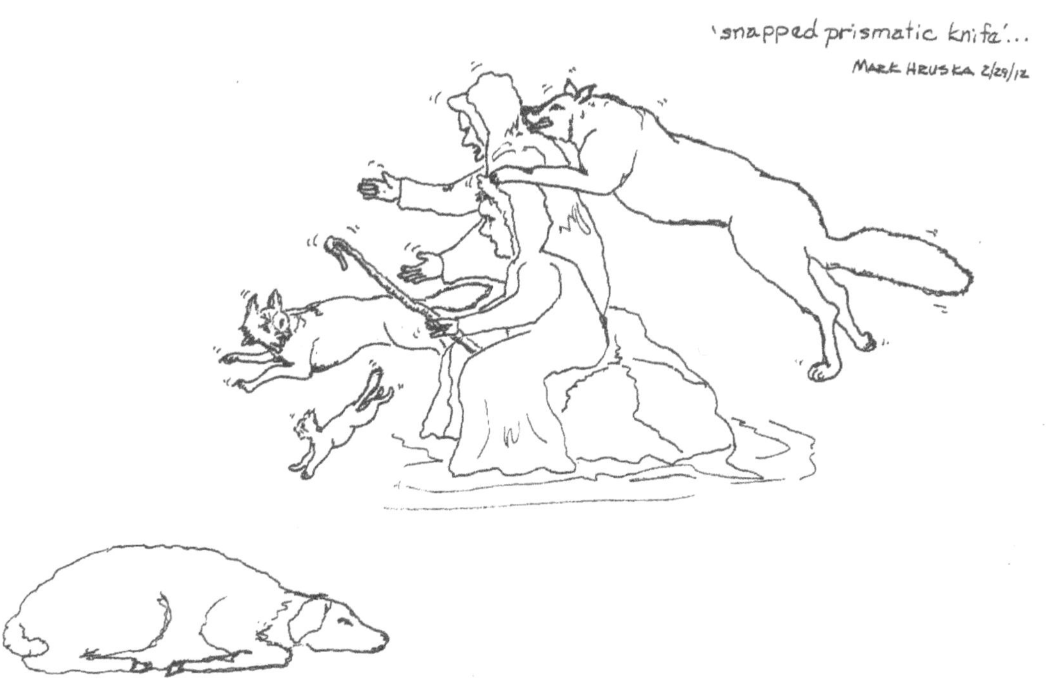

'snapped prismatic knife'... 'The alpha male dire wolfs front left paw is pushing the waist high young maidens head forward while he bites her grandmothers neck!'

85) As it happens in so many of these pieces' interpretations, it all takes place out in the meadow while kind loving grandma shepherdess was babysitting her granddaughter and also watching over their domestic cattle and sheep. Grandma is most likely teaching her granddaughter one of their folk songs and their combined screechy voices sound like a wounded prey animal. The message that's delivered loud and clear by dad or grandpa when they tell the folklore tale to the toddlers and waist high children is that you must be quiet and not cry out there so that you don't alert the large predators because they won't only eat you but they'll also eat your kind loving grandma as well. The dire wolves usually attack in pairs. The she dire wolf usually runs on past from the rear and knocks grandma off balance while the male dire wolf comes in behind her and goes for her exposed neck. The kitty always gets away...

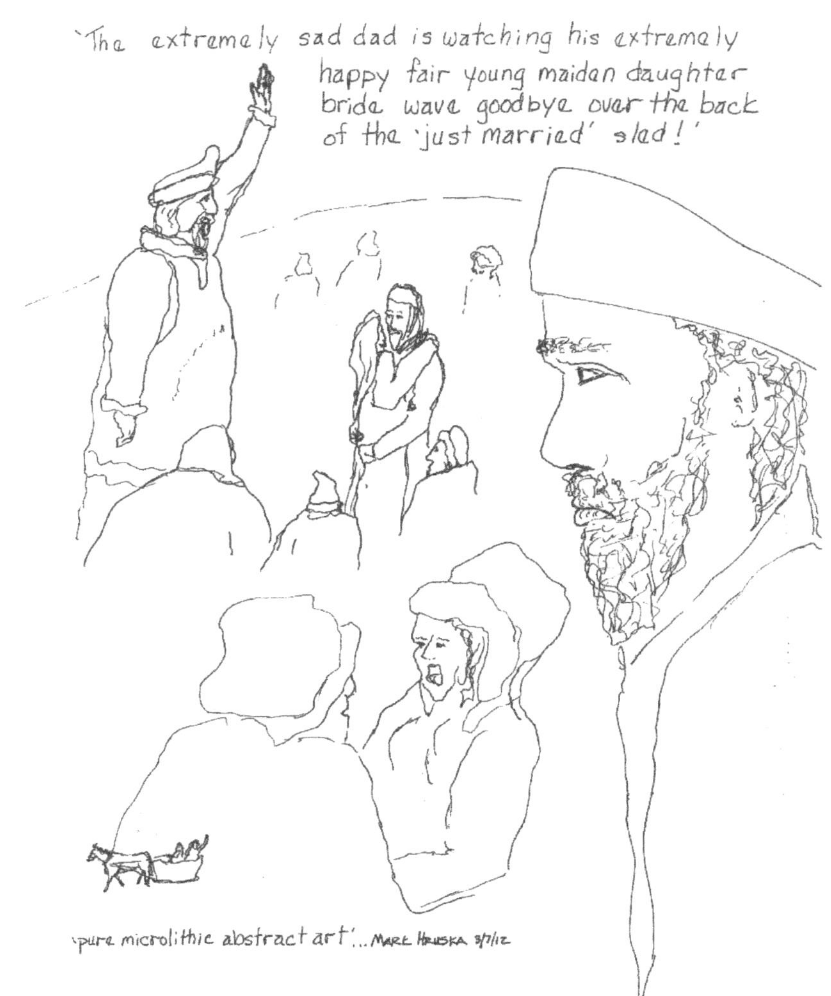

'pure microlithic abstract art'... 'The extremely sad dad is watching his extremely happy fair young maiden daughter bride wave goodbye over the back of the 'just married' sled!'

86) This is one of those interpretations that I hadn't quite gotten the complete folklore tale yet when I created this line sketch. For you see, I'm convinced that the sad dad is actually the upset forlorn lover who was jilted by the bride because she married one more handsome then he, and that he is not the sad dad. Never the less, I will never go back and change or correct an interpretation because it shows how I was gradually piecing together the complete folklore tales. It would be extremely difficult to get all of the scenes of one complete folklore tale on one artwork although some 'master' microlithic abstract artisans have come close.

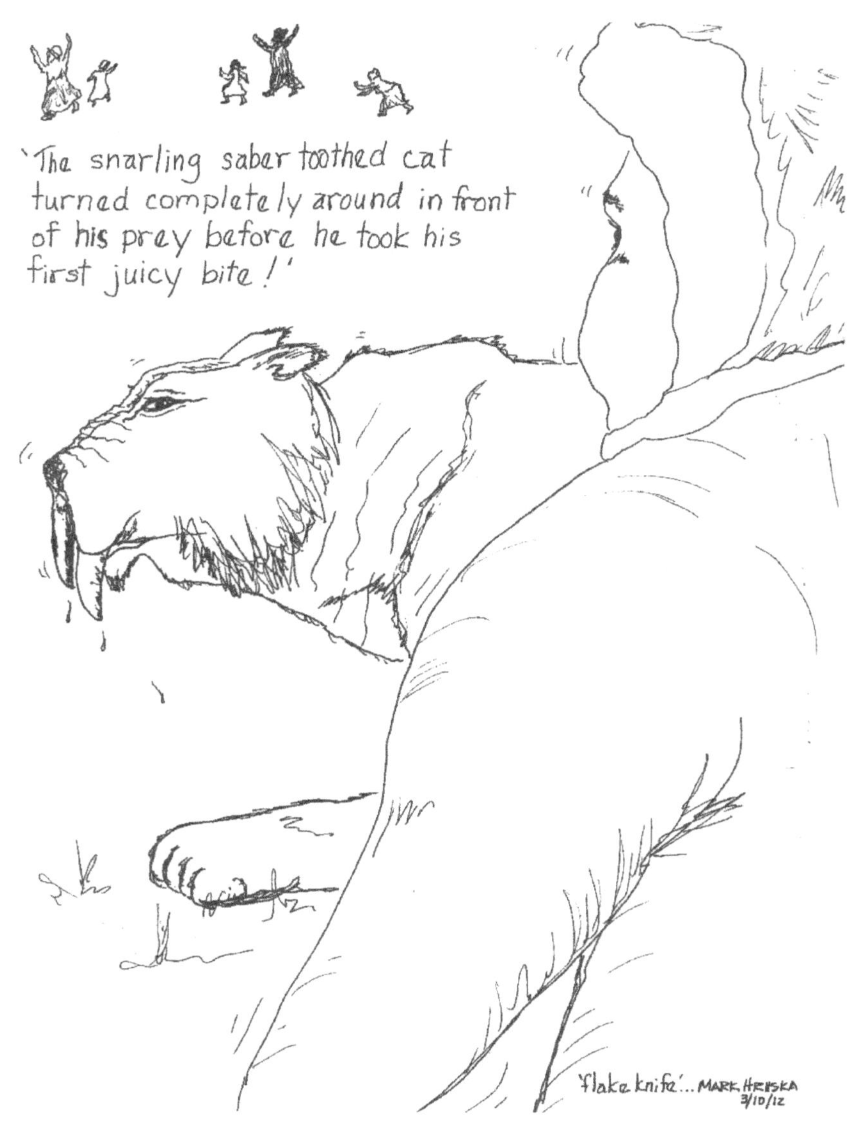

'flake knife'... 'The snarling saber-toothed cat turned completely around in front of his prey before he took his first juicy bite!'

87) The hungry saber-toothed cat decided to have his own picnic snack, cornering the plumpest fleeing Mammoth People picnicker!'

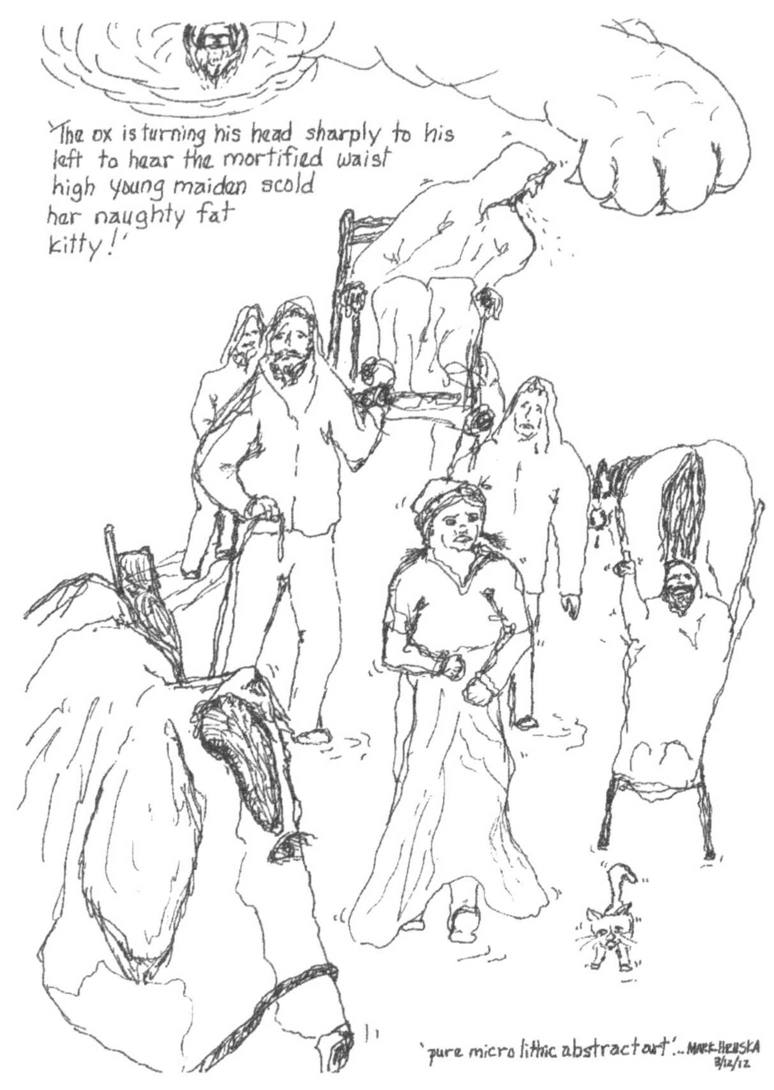

'pure microlithic abstract art'... 'The ox is turning his head sharply to
his left to hear the mortified waist high young maiden scold her naughty fat kitty!'

88) Once again, at this stage of my research I hadn't figured out yet that the ox was actually the domestic milk cow that had the infant who was strapped to a backboard, slung over her left shoulder. But I was slowly getting there, one interpretation at a time over a seven year time period.

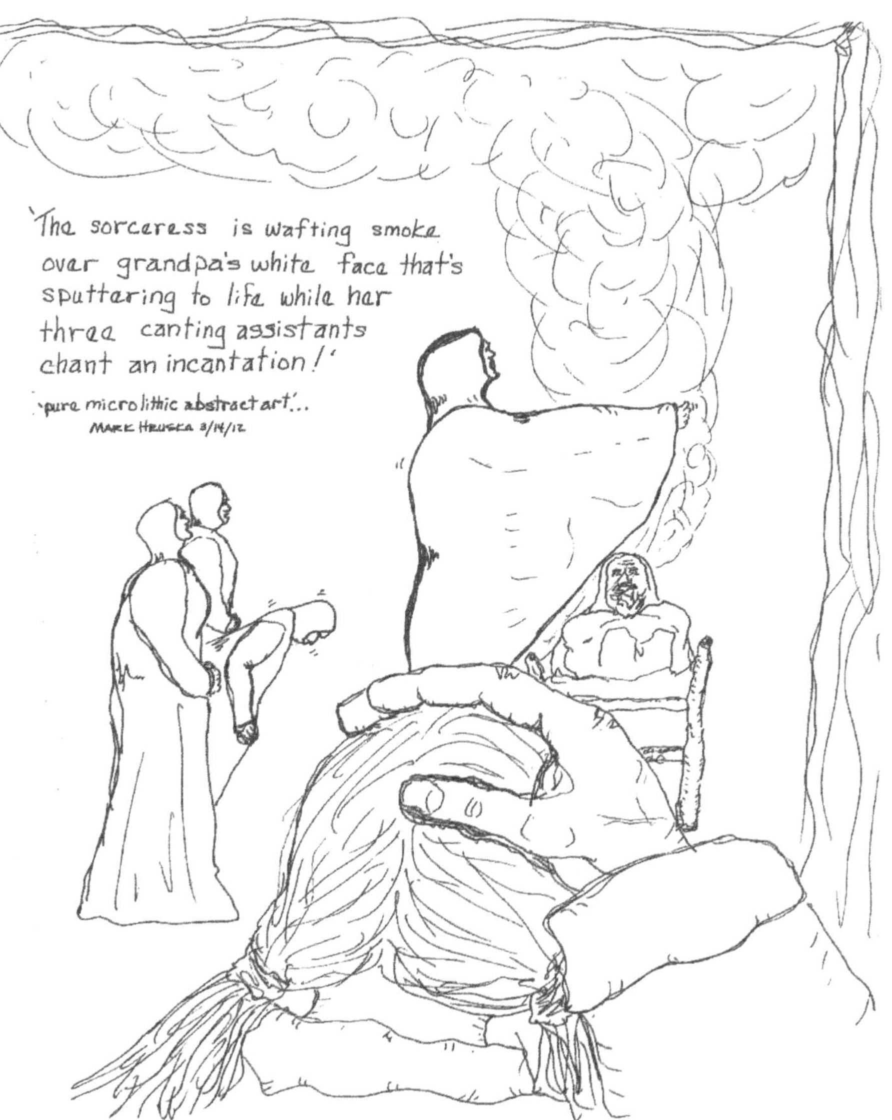

'pure microlithic abstract art'... 'The sorceress is wafting smoke over grandpa's white face that's sputtering to life while her three canting assistants chant an incantation!'

89) Concerned grandma is standing in the doorway of the cottage holding her granddaughter in front of her while the sorceress and her three chanting assistants perform the exorcism ceremony on unconscious grandpa.

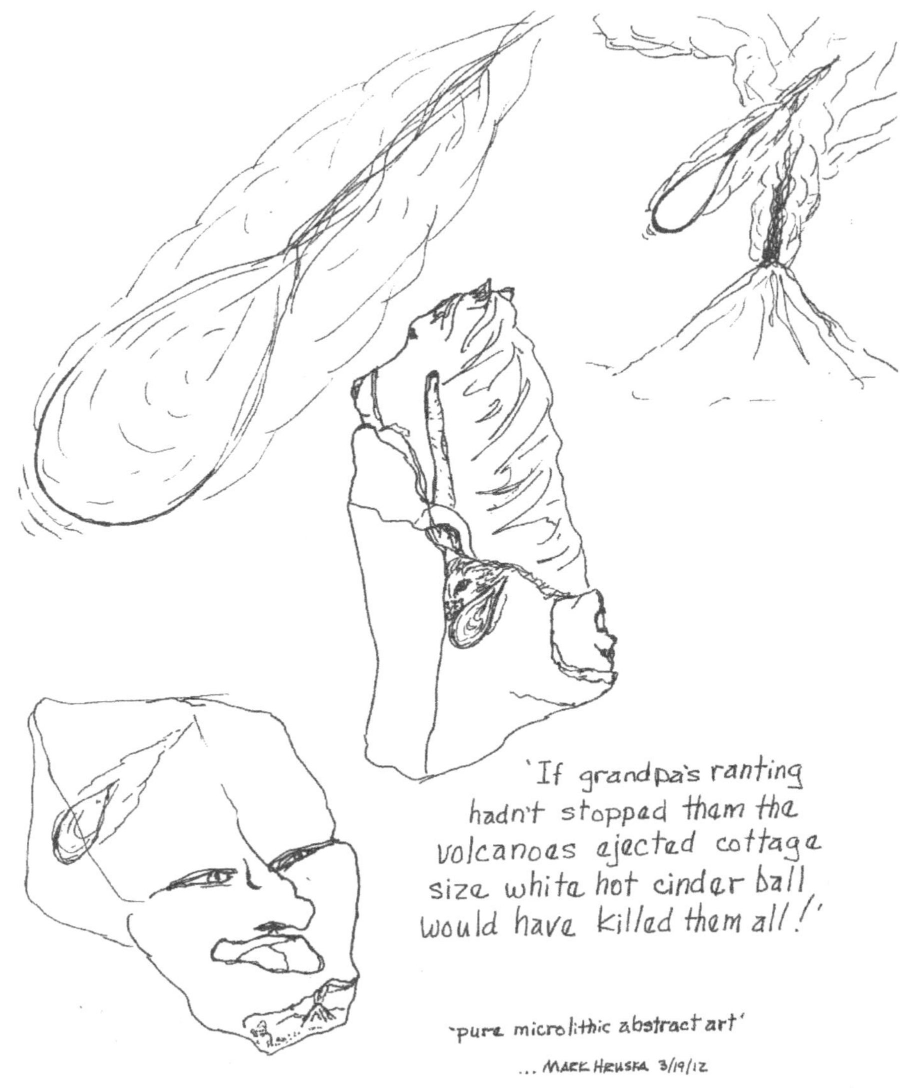

'pure microlithic abstract art'... 'If grandpa's ranting hadn't stopped them the volcanoes ejected cottage size white hot cinder ball would have killed them all!'

90) It's fairly evident that I tried to sketch what I was actually seeing on the rotational change-up microlithic abstract artwork.

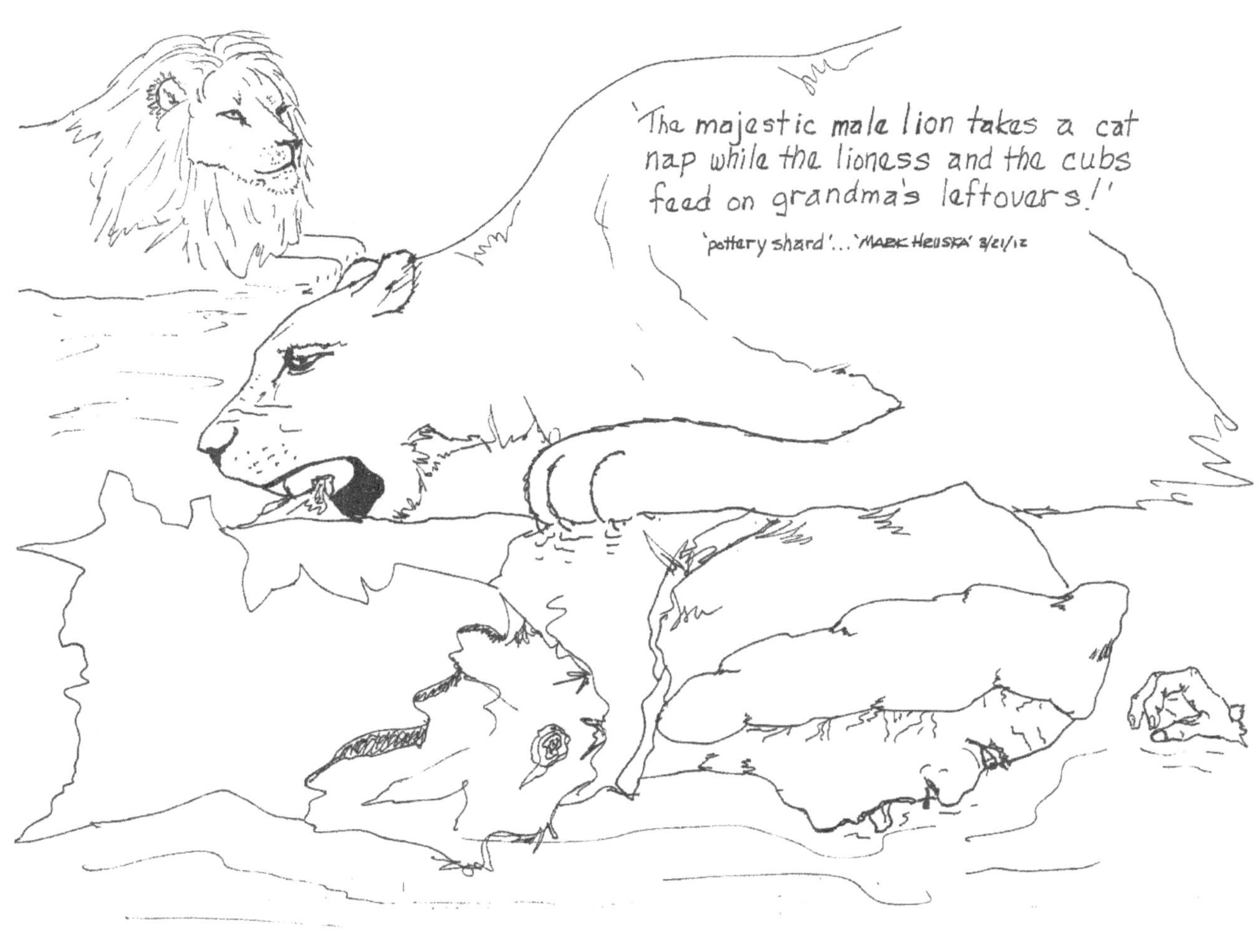

'pottery shard'... 'The majestic male lion takes a
catnap while the lioness and the cubs feed on grandma's leftovers!'

91) I don't know how much more graphic this line sketch could be to get the point across. Is that the end of her right arms humerus sticking out of her right shoulder?

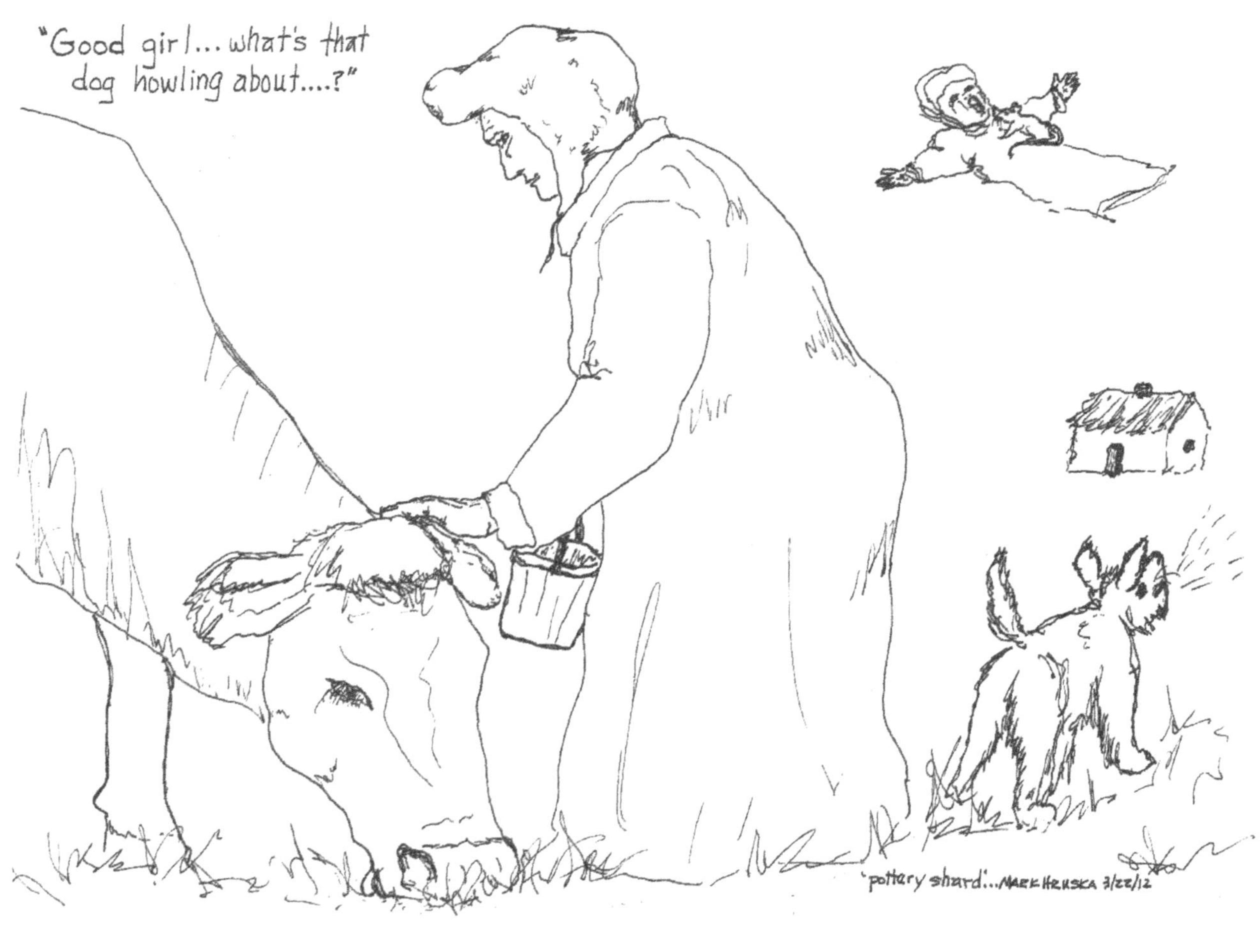

'pottery shard'... "Good girl... what's that dog howling about....?"

92) The pesky house rat took advantage of the time that grandma spent away from the cottage when she had to get fresh warm cow's milk for her crying infant grandchild.

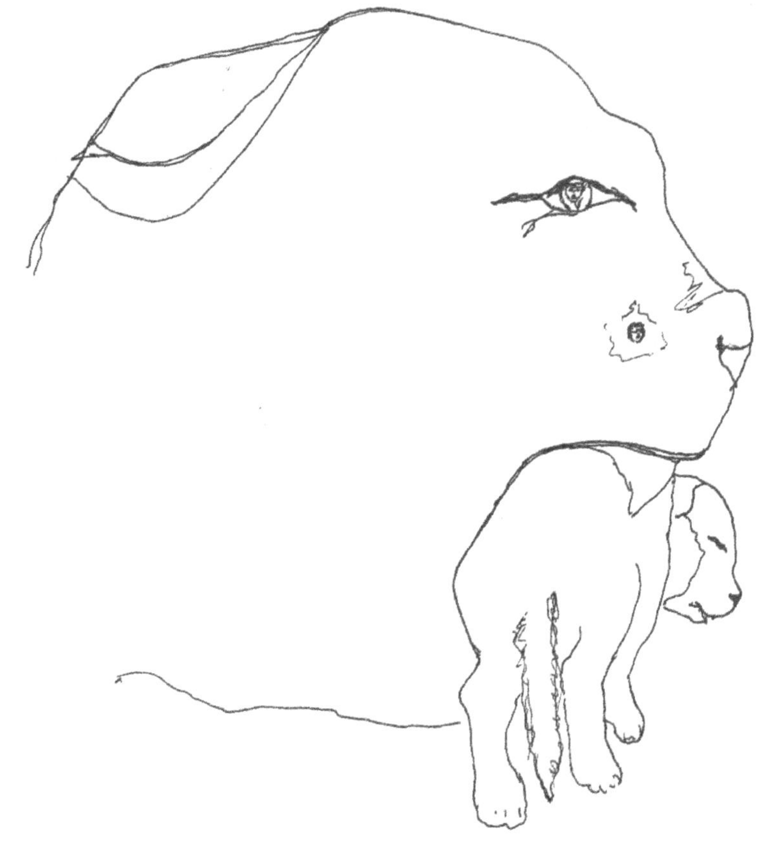

'hammer stone'... 'The cute little kitties won't stay
hidden from the persistent waist high young maiden for long!'

93) If I remember correctly, this interpretations artwork was a fairly simple piece that was easy to see
because it's on a large hammer stone.

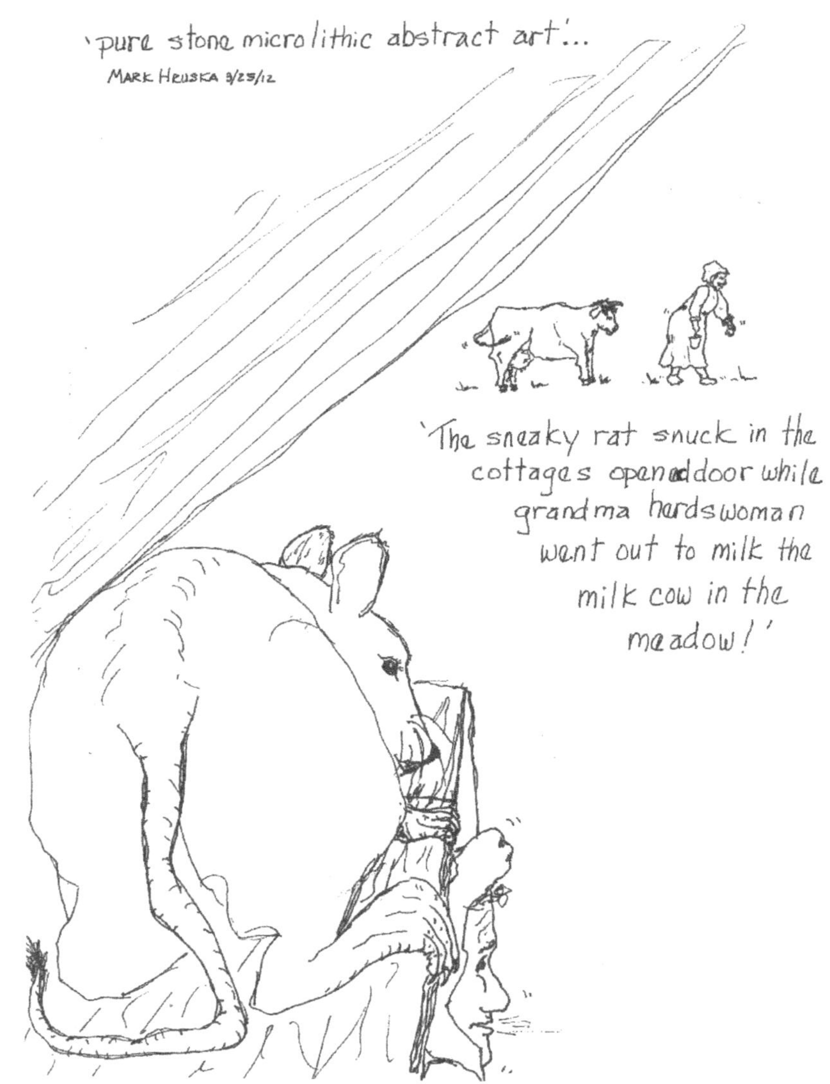

'pure stone microlithic abstract art'... 'The sneaky rat snuck in the cottages opened door while grandma herdswoman went out to milk the milk cow in the meadow!'

94) This interpretations artwork is also a fairly large stone which makes it easier to see the combined optical and cognitive illusion close-up images.

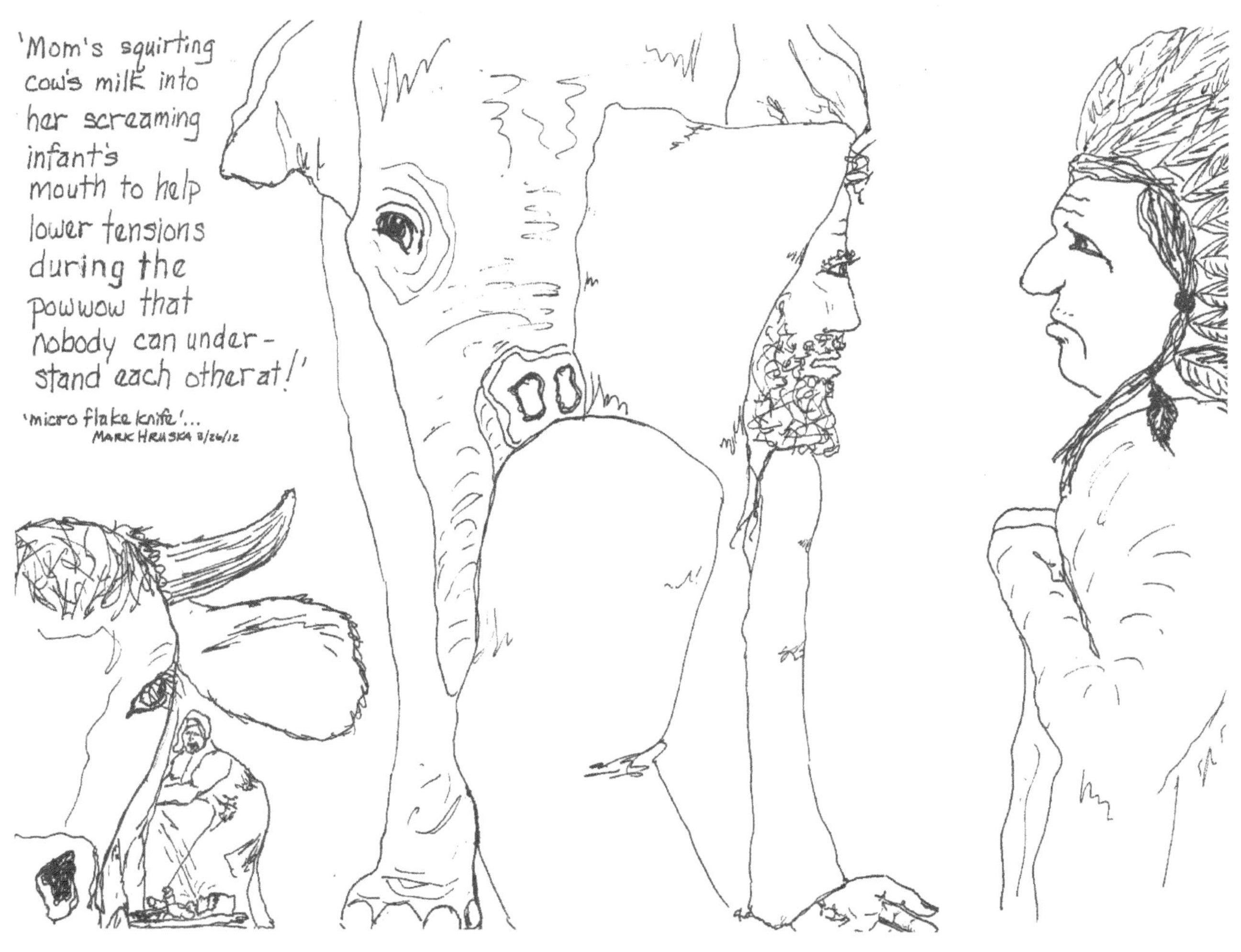

'micro flake knife'... 'Mom's squirting cow's milk into her screaming infant's mouth to help lower tensions during the powwow that nobody can understand each other at!'

95) There's so much going on during the 'powwow' that even the nervous lead mammoth needs reassurance as she continually sniffs over the lead hunter herders shoulders towards his bearded face.

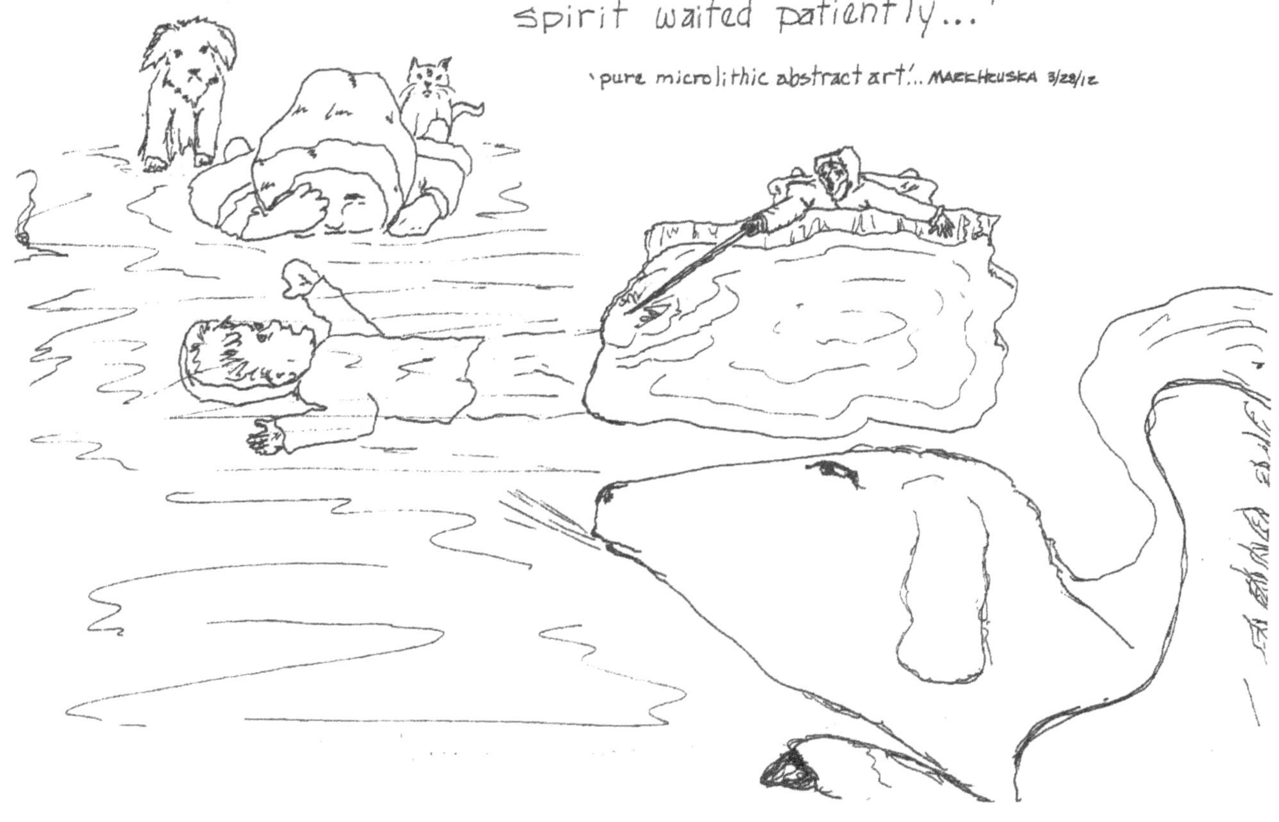

'pure microlithic abstract art'... 'The sharp predator ice slowly separated
the inseparable Pleistocene twins while the submissive ewe spirit waited patiently!'

96) The kitty and the Scottie seem to be able to see that the submissive ewe spirit is sucking up the drowning twins last exhaled breath or spirit so that she can take him up into the heavens to be with the Mammoth People's deceased loved ones.... while grandma tries frantically to recover his out of reach body.

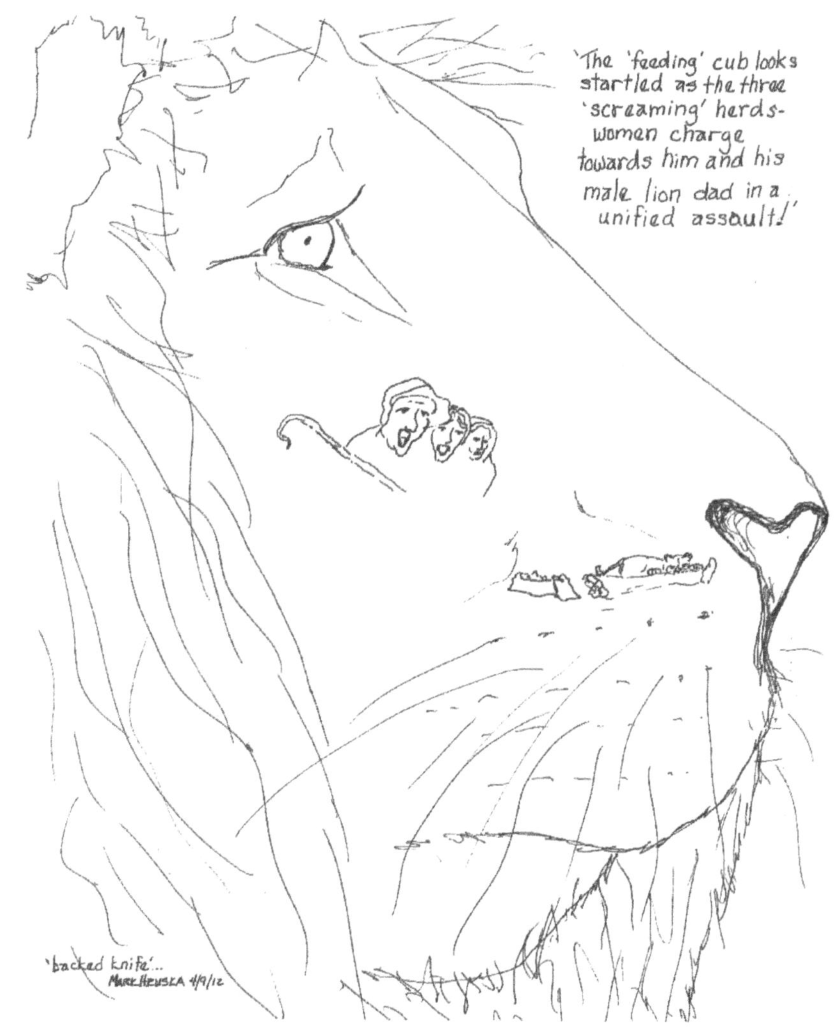

'backed knife'... 'The 'feeding' cub looks startled as the three
screaming herdswomen charge towards him and his male lion dad in a unified assault!

97) It's fairly obvious from the reflections off of the right side of the lounging majestic male lion's face that they were trying desperately to recover what they could of the 'nosey' teenage young lad who had been sticking his big nose where it didn't belong. That's because he was trying to get as close as he could to see the lions mating and didn't realize that another lioness was above him in the tree that he was hiding under.

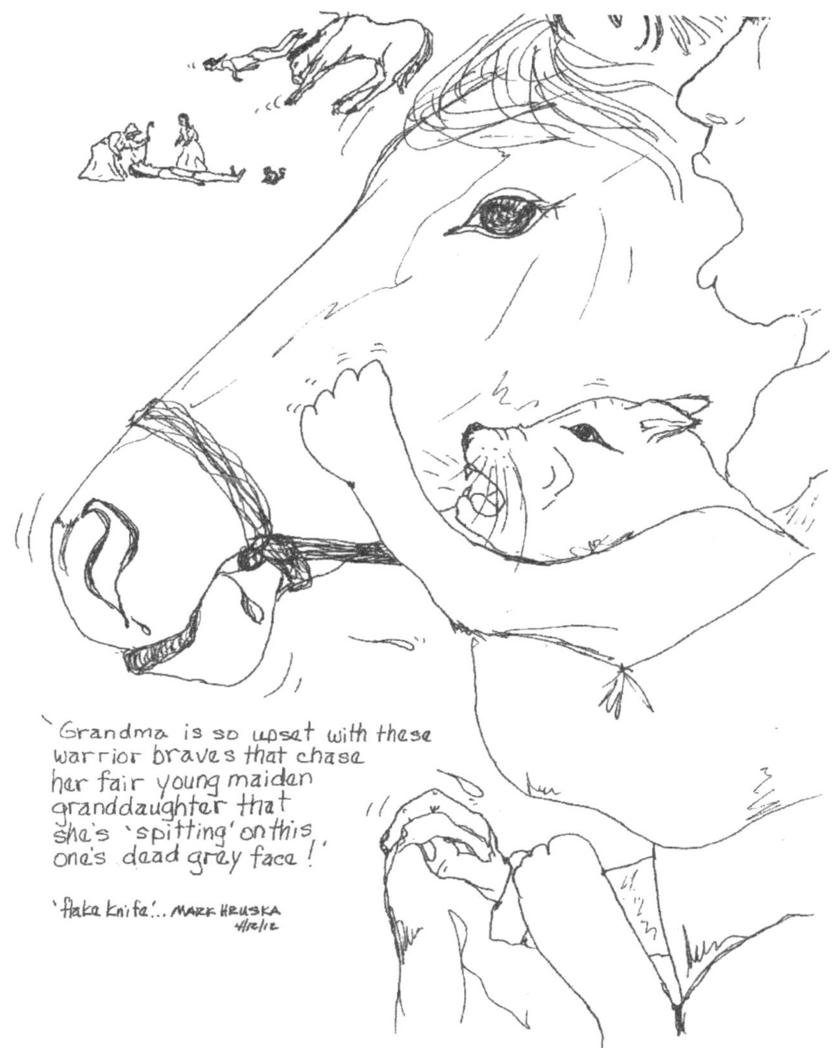

'flake knife'... 'Grandma is so upset with these warrior braves that chase her fair young maiden granddaughter that she's spitting on this one's dead grey face!'

98) At this point in time I've almost figured out this variation of the 'powwow'. All that's missing yet is the discovery of pissed off cursing grandpa who hobbles up to the scene of the incident and urinates on the supine dead warrior braves war painted white face (even though it looked grey in this pieces interpretation).

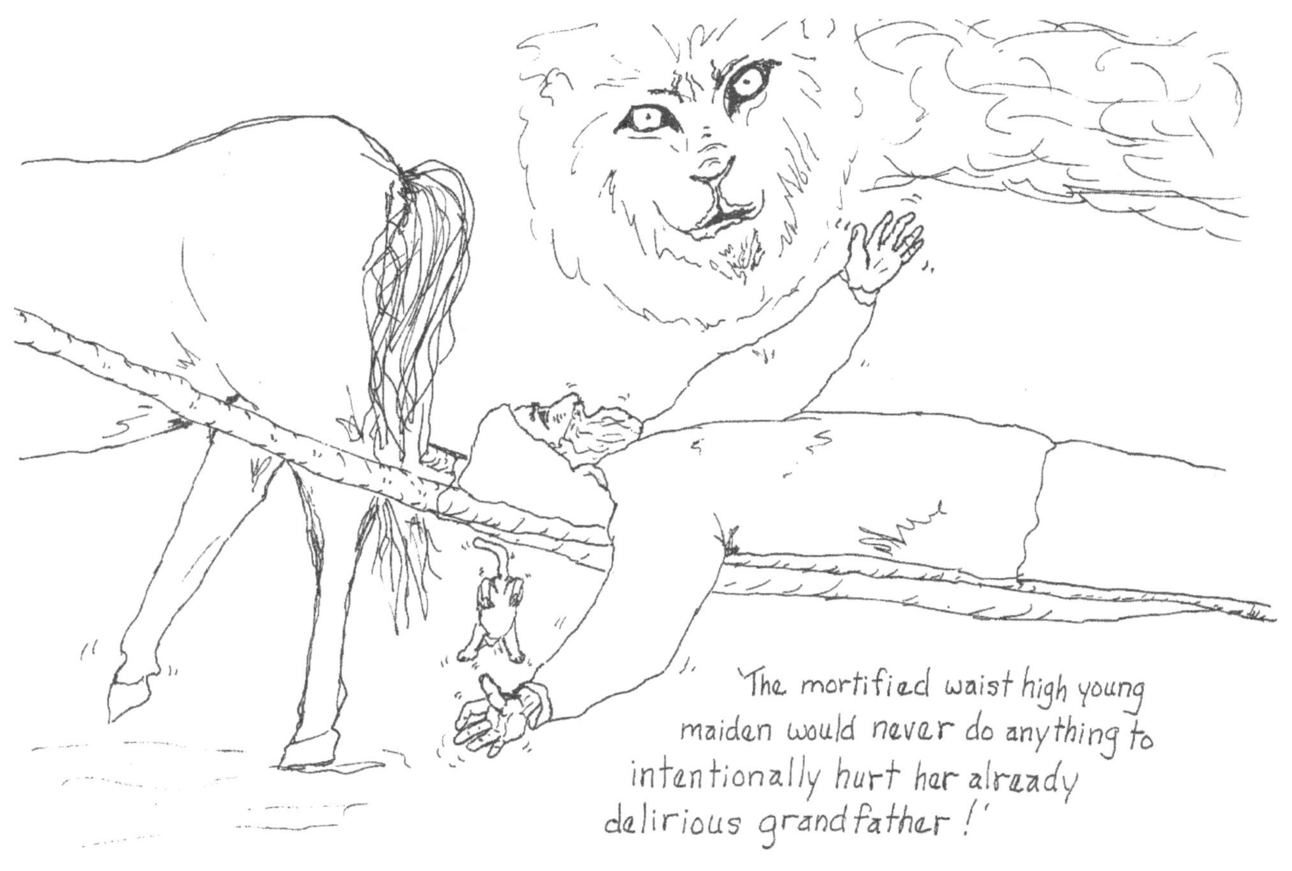

'pure microlithic abstract art'... 'The mortified waist high young maiden
would never do anything to intentionally hurt her already delirious grandfather!'

99) The waist high young maiden's frightened kitty has just scratched grandpa's face making him more delirious than he already was because he thought that he was seeing the roaring male lion volcanic ash cloud that close up.

Do you remember the 'Indiana Jones' movie where Indiana (what his dad called him) has to step out and down onto an invisible narrow stone beam in a 'leap of faith' in order to get across a cavernous abyss in his search for the Holy Grail? The invisible stone beam was an optical illusion and Indiana had to rely on 'blind faith' that it was indeed real before he took that first step. Then, having done his research ahead of time, he throws the sand that he had in his jacket pocket out over the narrow stone beam to highlight it so that he could see exactly where it was. Such is the Mammoth People hunter herder microlithic abstract artist's figurative language. Once you know that it 'is' indeed there....only then will you 'see' it!

.... "it just is what it is"...Mark Hruska 4/18/12

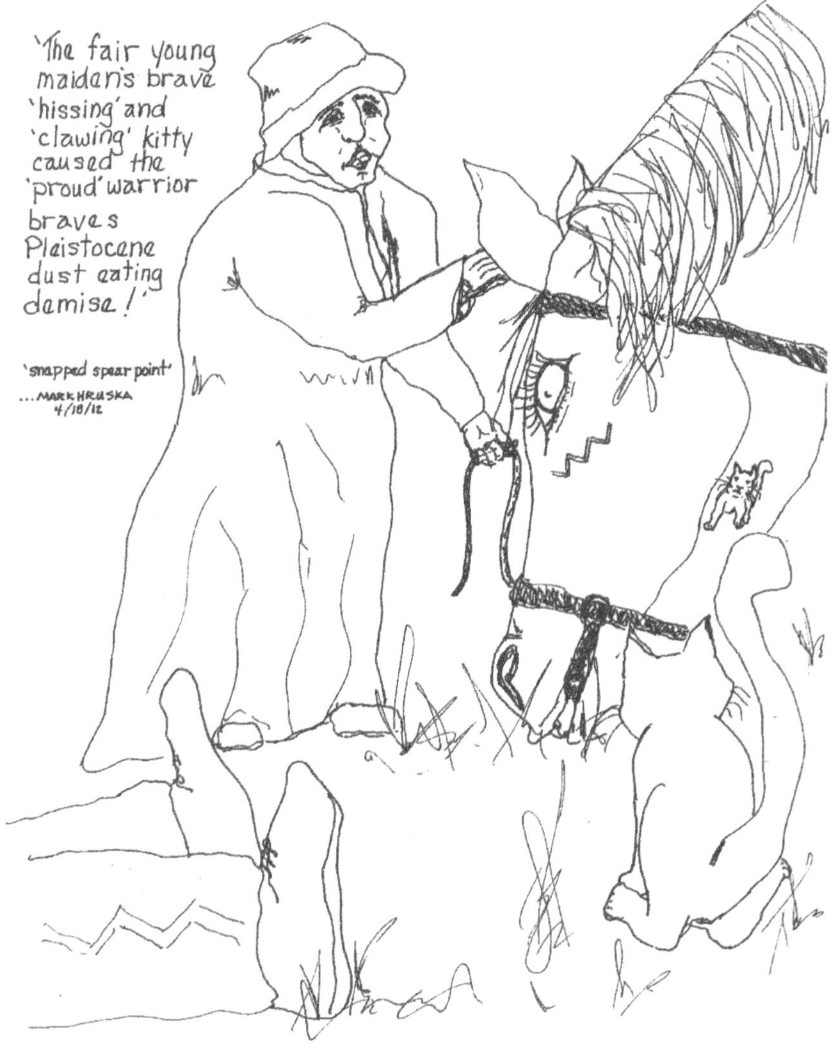

'snapped spear point'... 'The fair young maiden's brave 'hissing' and 'clawing' kitty caused the 'proud' warrior braves Pleistocene dust eating demise!'

100) As he sits on his haunches and keeps his eyes on the fine animals wide opened left eye so that he doesn't try anything else, the brave golden kitty reflects off of the underside of the golden horses chin while he nervously grazes on prairie grass.

"How is it that humans can look at crocodiles and 'except' the fact that they haven't changed much over the last ninety five 'million' years in light of fossil records and yet...believe that humans have changed immensely in only thirteen 'thousand' years?!"

.... "it just is what it is"....Mark Hruska 4/19/12

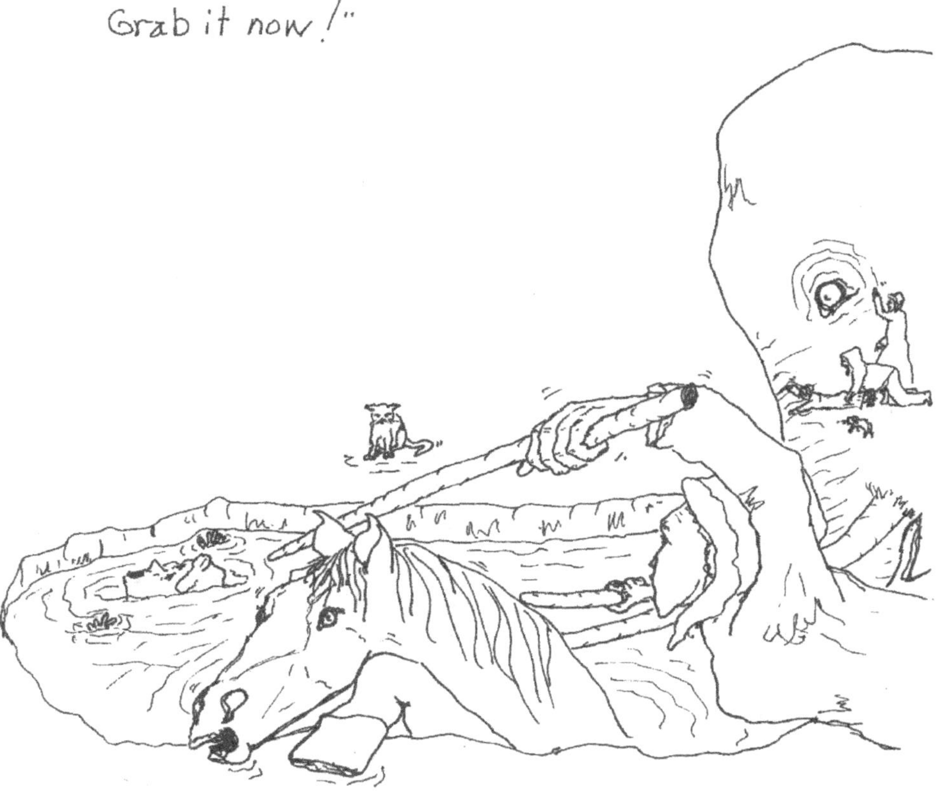

'pure microlithic abstract art'...'Amongst all of the commotion, grandma's yelling back at her struggling granddaughter...."Grab the end of my crook sweetheart....grab it now!"'

101) The Mammoth People lead family is cooperating to rescue the struggling fair young maiden and is reflecting off of the left side of the kneeling nervous lead mammoth's head!

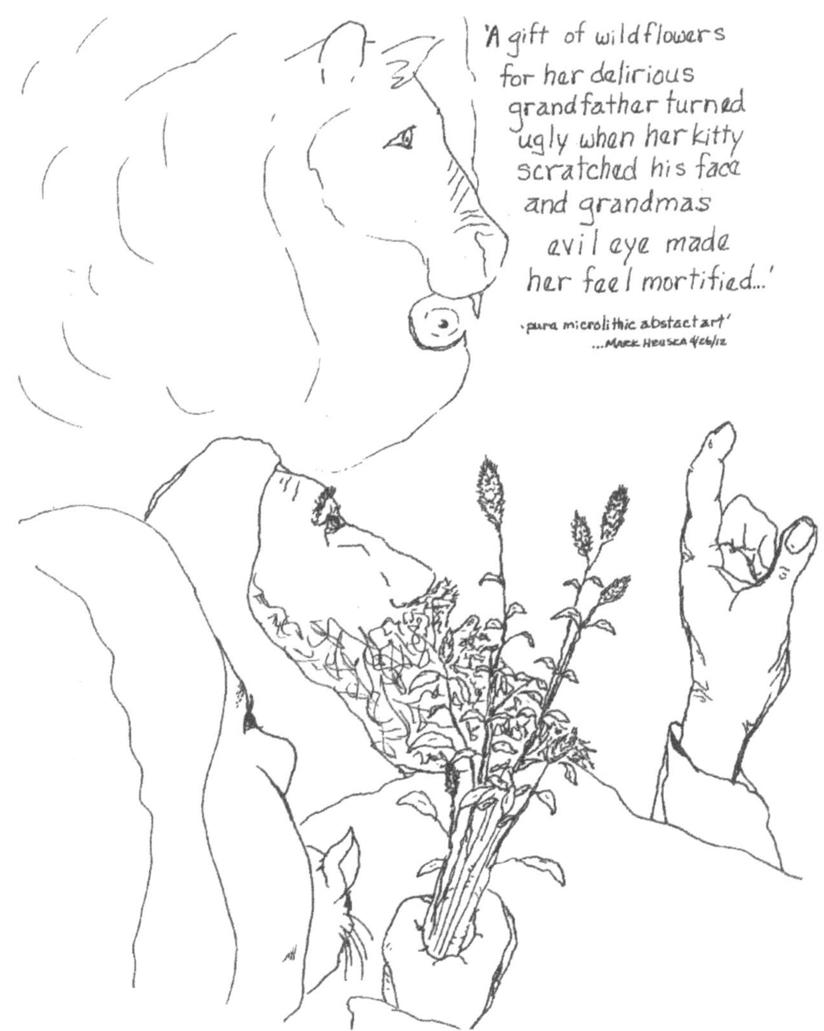

'pure microlithic abstract art'... 'A gift of wildflowers for her delirious grandfather turned ugly when her kitty scratched his face and grandma's evil eye made her feel mortified!'

102) Delirious grandpa is pointing skyward towards the roaring male lion that both he and his crotchety wife both see up in the broiling ash cloud that seems to be about to pounce on them. The poor sweet innocent waist high young maiden and her kitty seem to be the victims caught up in the horrible life changing Pleistocene event.

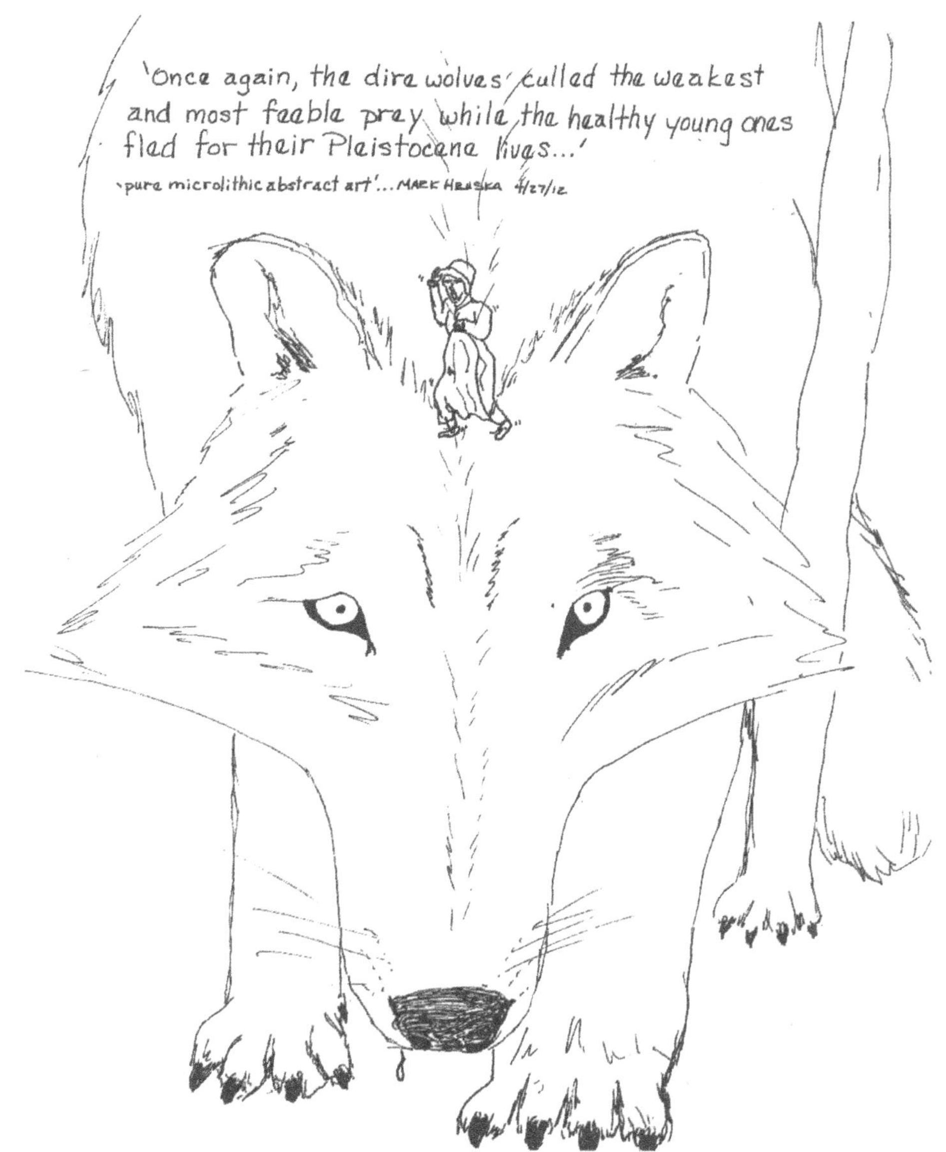

'pure microlithic abstract art'... 'Once again, the dire wolves culled the weakest and most feeble prey while the healthy young ones fled for their Pleistocene lives!'

103) It's usually a pack or a pair of dire wolves that attack the summertime picnic event.

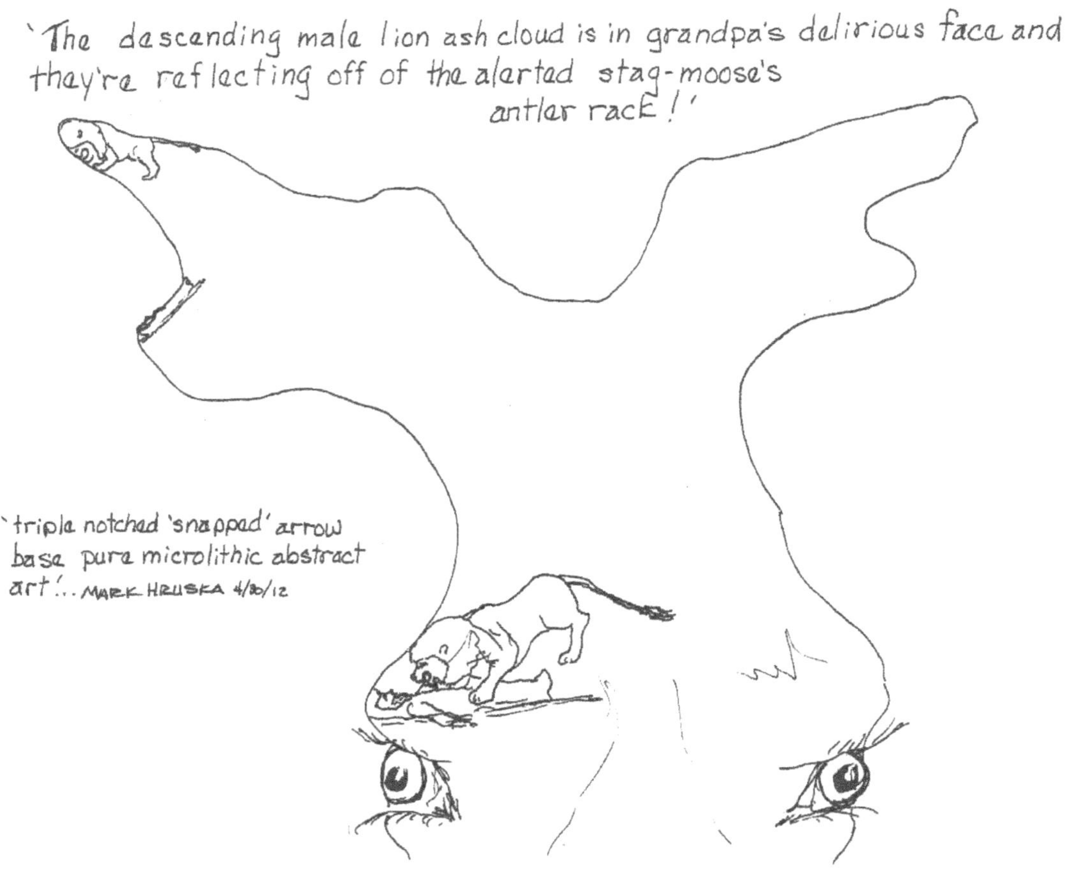

'triple notched 'snapped' arrow base, pure microlithic abstract art'...
'The descending male lion ash cloud is in grandpa's delirious face and
they're reflecting off of the alerted stag-moose's antler rack!'

104) Imagine in your 'mind's eye' that the stag-moose's antler rack 'is' the base of the triple notched arrow that has the pointy end of it 'snapped' off. Then you'll understand how it was used as a combined optical and cognitive illusion close-up image of his rack with those microlithic cognitive illusion reflection images reflecting off of it. In this scene the tip of his right antler is the anvil of the broiling ash cloud that appears to be pouncing on delirious grandpa as he lays back at a forty five degree angle on his travois.

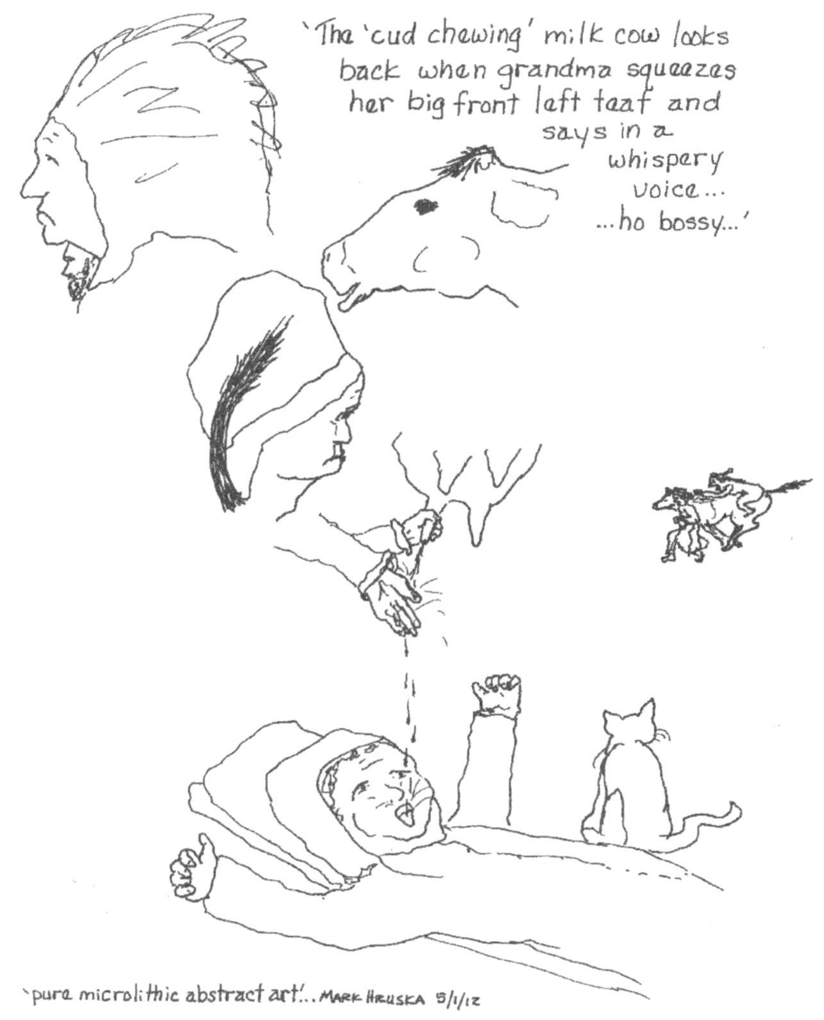

'pure microlithic abstract art'... 'The 'cud chewing' milk cow looks back when grandma squeezes her big front left teat and says in a whispery voice...ho bossy....'

105) This is clearly a scene from the 'powwow' folklore tale when irate grandma spryly dismounted her nervous lead mammoth and removed her screaming infant grandson's carrier from the milk cow's left shoulder and plopped it on the ground so that she could squirt warm fresh cow's milk into his screaming mouth to appease him before the gruff chief and his taunting warrior brave lost their patience.

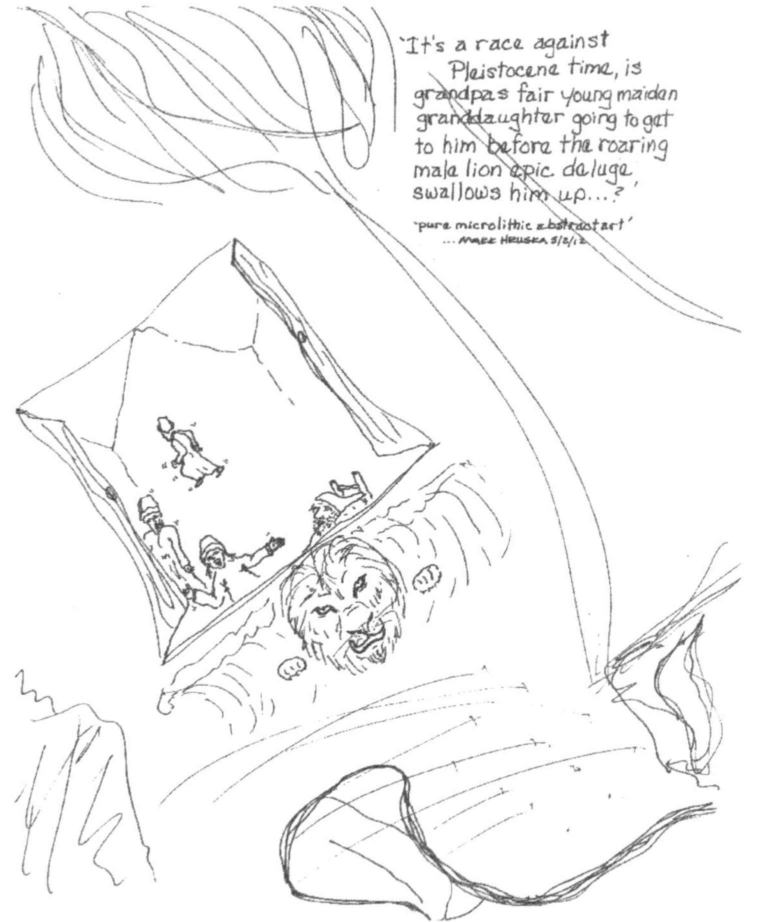

'pure microlithic abstract art'... 'It's a race against Pleistocene time, is grandpa's fair
young maiden granddaughter going to get to him before the roaring
male lion epic deluge swallows him up?'

106) It's this sort of artwork and its interpretation of its folklore tale that lead me to believe that the displaced Mammoth People were reestablished on the coast of present day Washington State living in cottages before the epic deluge swept them away. The reasoning for that is because you were viewing this scene through the window of the cottage that the rapidly approaching roaring male lion epic deluge wave was about to overtake. He is reflecting off of it and is the one that was seeing this scene the way that I sketched it. And in case you're wondering, the large imagery to your lower right is the epic roaring waves own flared nostrils that he sees with his squinting eyes extremely close up at the end of his roaring wrinkled up muzzle. This should give you a good feel for how the microlithic abstract art figurative language works.

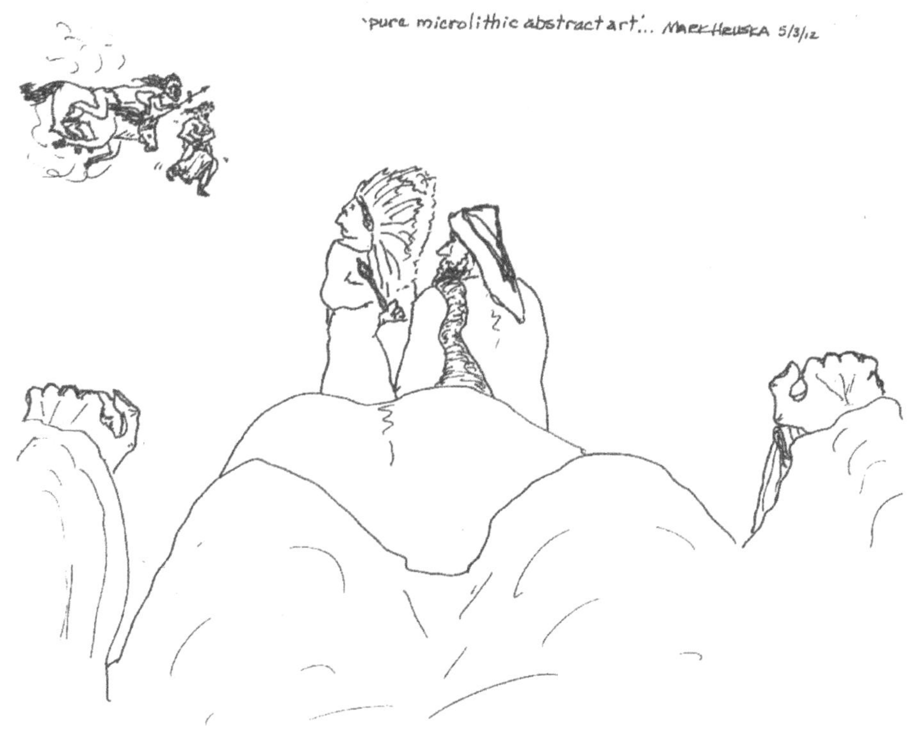

'pure microlithic abstract art'... 'Looking down over the forehead of her mammoth
at the powwow below, grandma speaks in her crotchety old voice...
"Use your spear to convince him...son..."'

107) The imagery and description on this line sketch pretty much gives you the bird's eye view from irate grandma's perspective while everything around her was in turmoil during this scene from the 'powwow'.

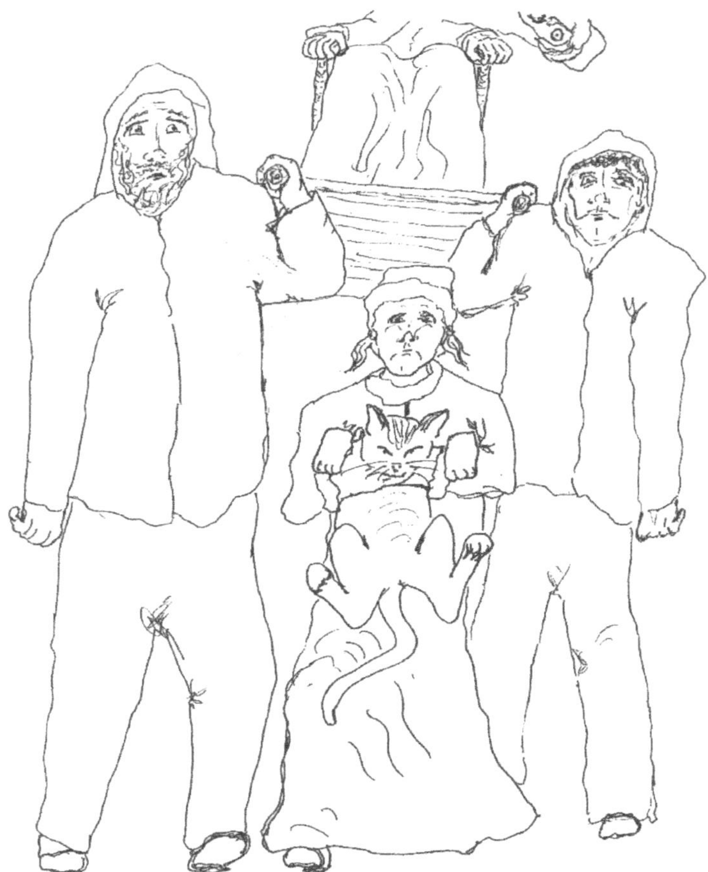

'pure microlithic abstract art'... 'Her frightened kitty's rear left paw
scratched grandpa's delirious white face while grandma's
white eyeballs glared at her mortified granddaughter...'

108) The upset waist high young maiden is 'madly marching' towards the other miserable weary trekkers who have to go around her held up, dysfunctional lead family.

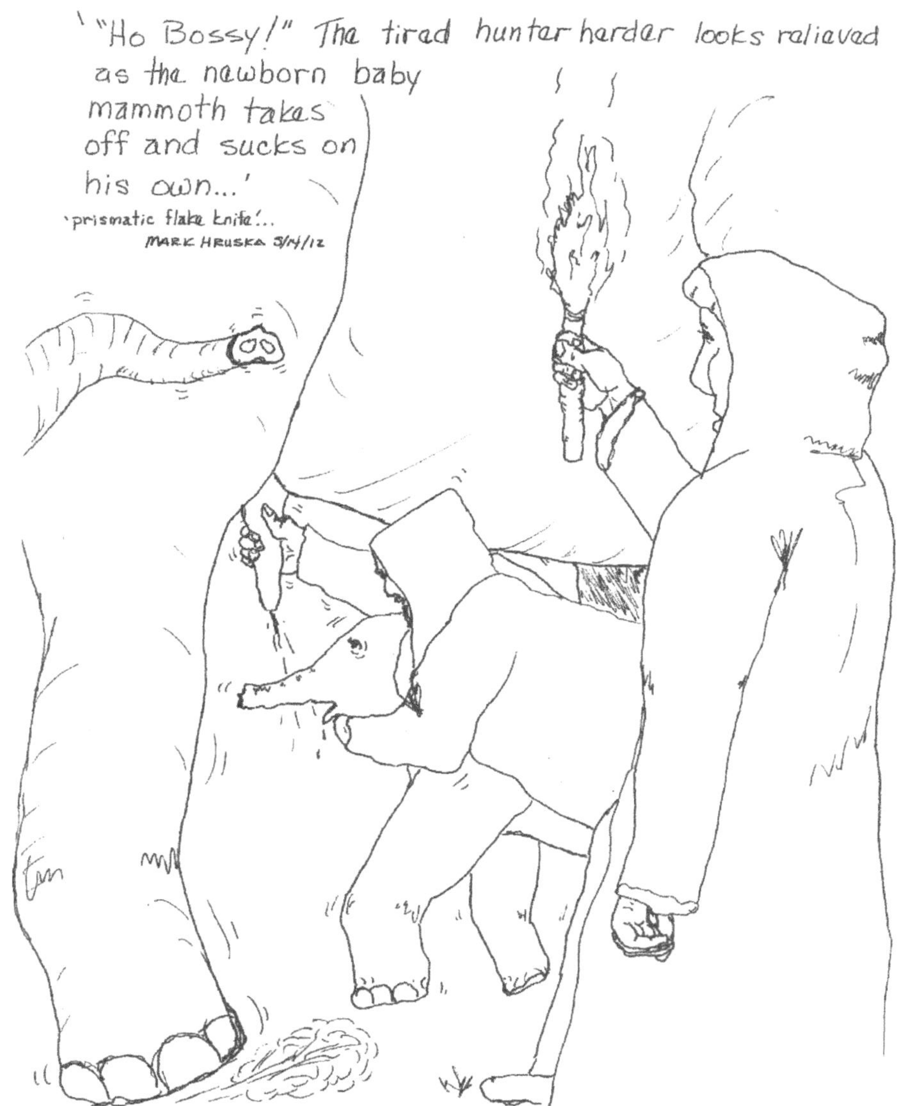

'prismatic flake knife'... '"Ho Bossy!" The tired hunter herder looks relieved as the newborn baby mammoth takes off and sucks on his own...'

109) Sheep, cattle and human birth could all be difficult but the mammoth birth was especially difficult for dad who then had to get the clumsy newborn to nurse.

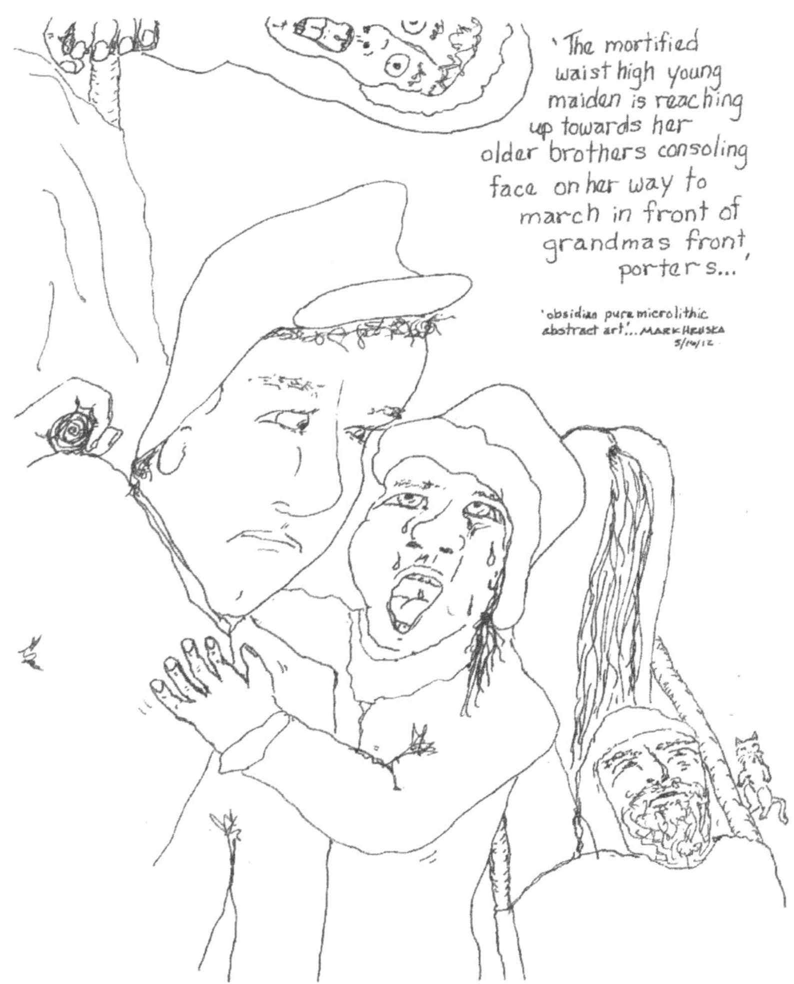

'obsidian pure microlithic abstract art'... 'The mortified waist high young maiden is reaching up towards her older brothers consoling face on her way to march in front of her grandma's front porters...'

110) The complete story of the Mammoth People's most popular folklore tale of the 'volcanic mass exodus' is slowly coming together in my 'mind's eye'.... through repetition. Once I knew that I was viewing that folklore tale, I could predict what I would see next on the rotational change-up microlithic abstract artwork. Occasionally, something that hasn't been seen before would present itself which is why you just keep interpreting until you never see anything new.

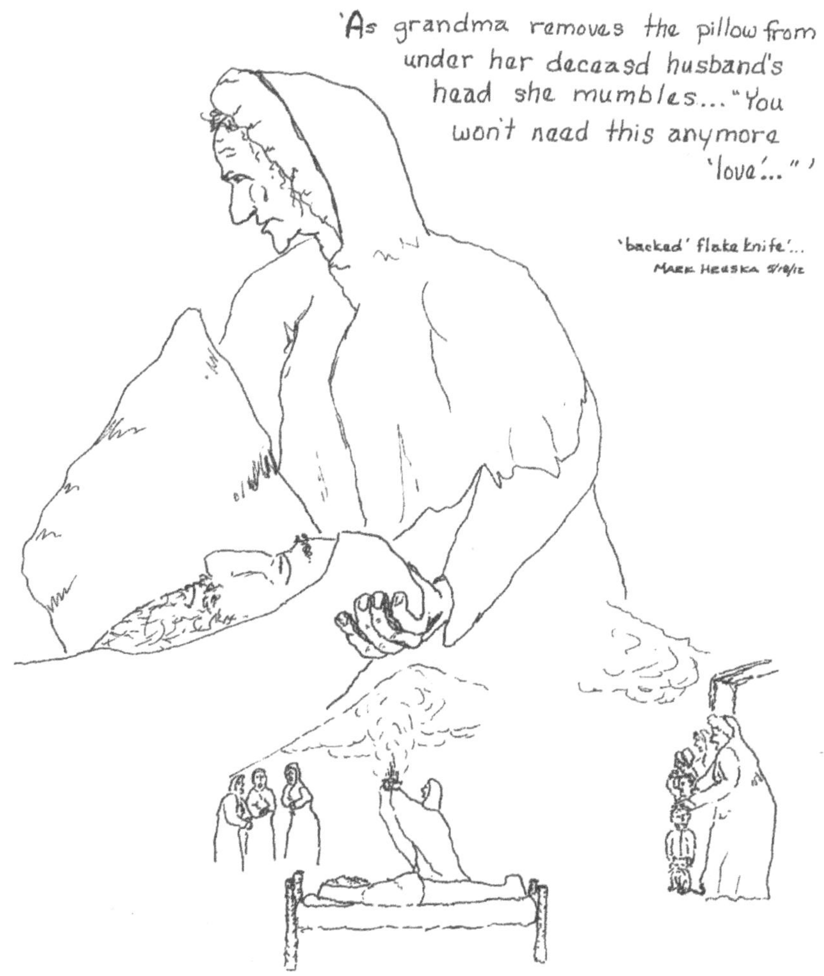

'backed flake knife'... 'As grandma removes the pillow from under her deceased husband's head she mumbles... "You won't need this anymore 'love'..."'

111) What I hadn't figured out yet in this 'sorceress' folklore tale is that grandpa isn't dead, just in a deep slumber that he's rudely awaken from by the suffocating smoke that the sorceress is wafting over his face from the fireplace while she loudly recites incantations followed by the chants of her three bowing assistants. This all takes place in the quaint cottage with the enthralled family watching intently from the doorway and the rats coughing and choking from the thick smoke that's accumulating up in the ceiling rafters that they're clinging to.

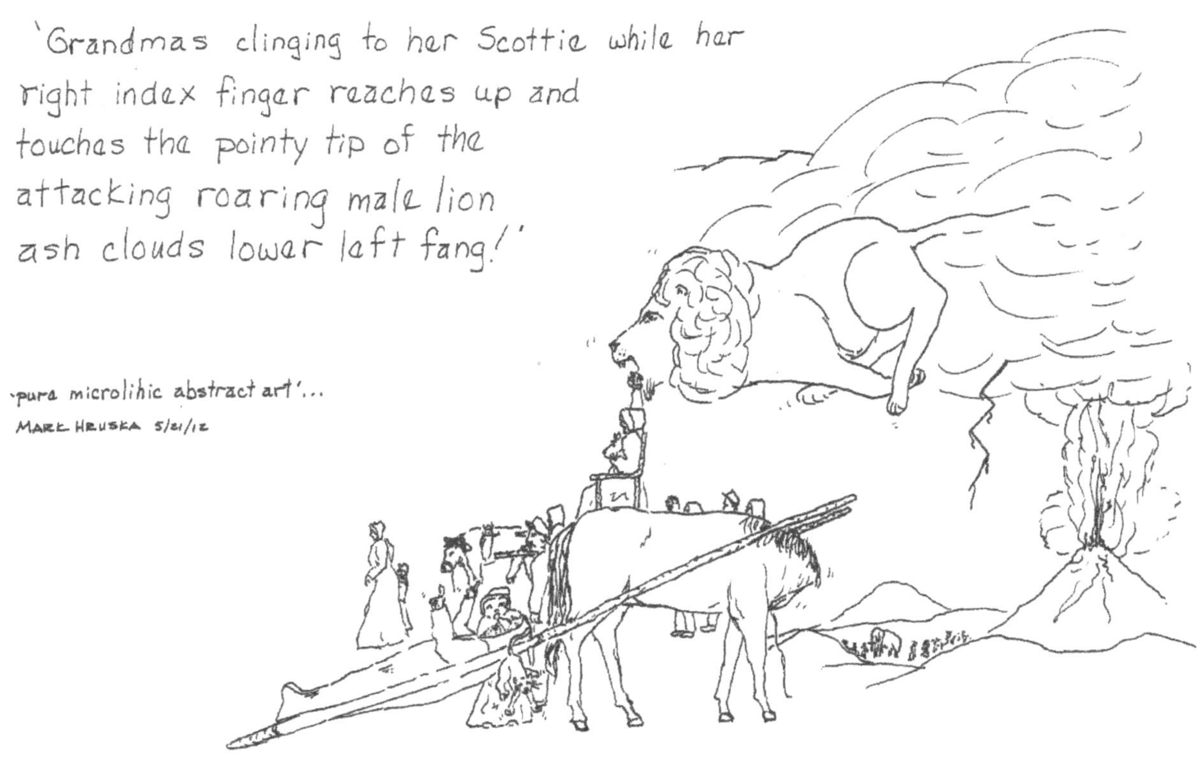

'pure microlithic abstract art'... 'Grandmas clinging
to her Scottie while her right index finger reaches up and touches
the pointy tip of the attacking roaring male lion ash clouds lower left fang!'

112) This is the way that the hunter herder microlithic abstract artist demonstrates to his children as he tells the folklore tale, of just how close crotchety grandma was to the broiling ash cloud that was descending on them and that appeared to be pouncing on them with crotchety grandma being the closest or first in line to the predators bite.

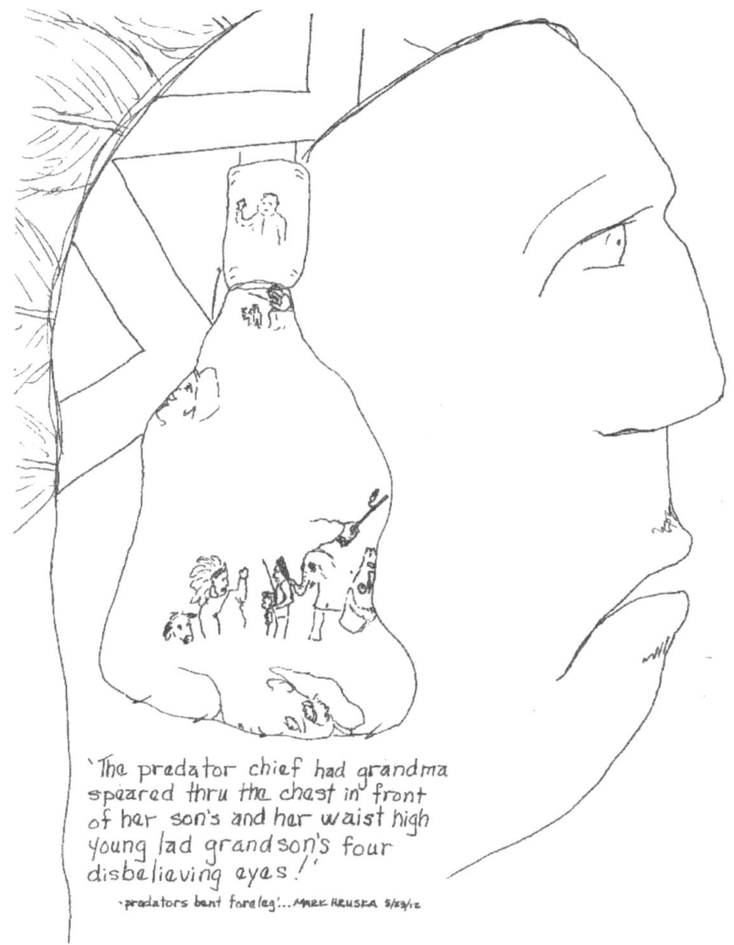

'predators bent foreleg'... 'The predator chief had grandma speared thru the chest in front of her son's and her waist high young lad grandson's four disbelieving eyes!'

113) The reflections on this line sketch pretty much tell what's going on in this scene of the 'powwow'. Some of them are reflecting off of the sea lion pup pelt flipper that's dangling from the right side of the gruff chief's headdress's headband. And if you look closely, it's what the waist high young lad is so mesmerized with because he's looking directly at it while he points at it. Below the front view of his reflection is the reflection of the left side view of irate grandma with a spear through her chest atop the nervous lead mammoth. This variation is not very common though, usually she's speared through the chest while riding in the sled that's being pulled by the nervous lead mammoth. I guess it was the storyteller's preference and over time who knows what the original story was....

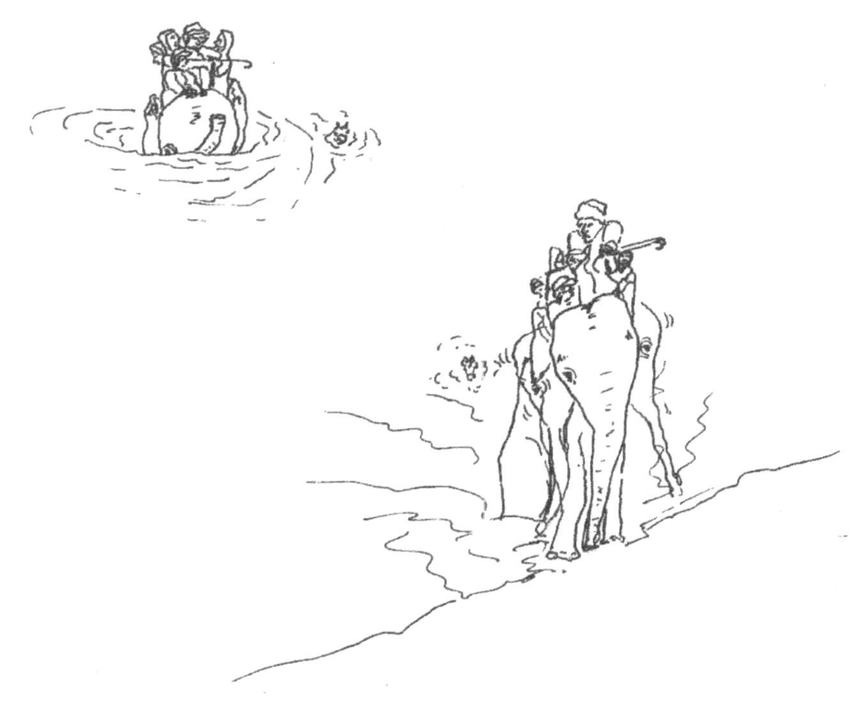

'pure microlithic abstract art'... 'After the mammoth rescued the trekkers from the epic deluge she pulls herself up on dryland and looks both ways!'

114) This is obviously an attempt to show 'motion' or a proto-cinema scene. By doing so the hunter herder microlithic abstract artist created the sense of being totally displaced and not knowing where to go next.

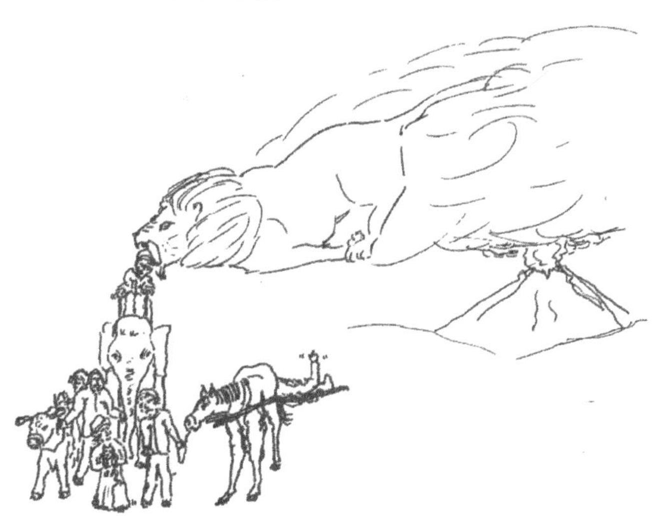

'pure microlithic abstract art'... 'After the mortified waist high young maiden's frightened kitty scratched grandpas delirious face, grandma made her march in front of the tan mammoth so that she could keep a glaring eyeball on her!'

115) The tan colored mammoth may have been how she looked during a flash of lightning but if you look closely at this line sketch, you'll see how accurately I'm getting the positions of the characters in this the Mammoth People's most popular folklore tale. If you substitute the mammoth with the stretcher that grandma's special armchair is normally attached to, dad and his teenage young lad son would still be in the positions that you see them in this sketch with dad being the front right porter and his son being the front left one. This particular piece had to have taken place early in their exodus though because crotchety grandma is still sitting on her special armchair atop the lead mammoth. When they were trekking over the steep mountainous terrain her special armchair was attached to a stretcher and being carried on her four porters shoulders or hanging from their arms which ever kept her the most level.

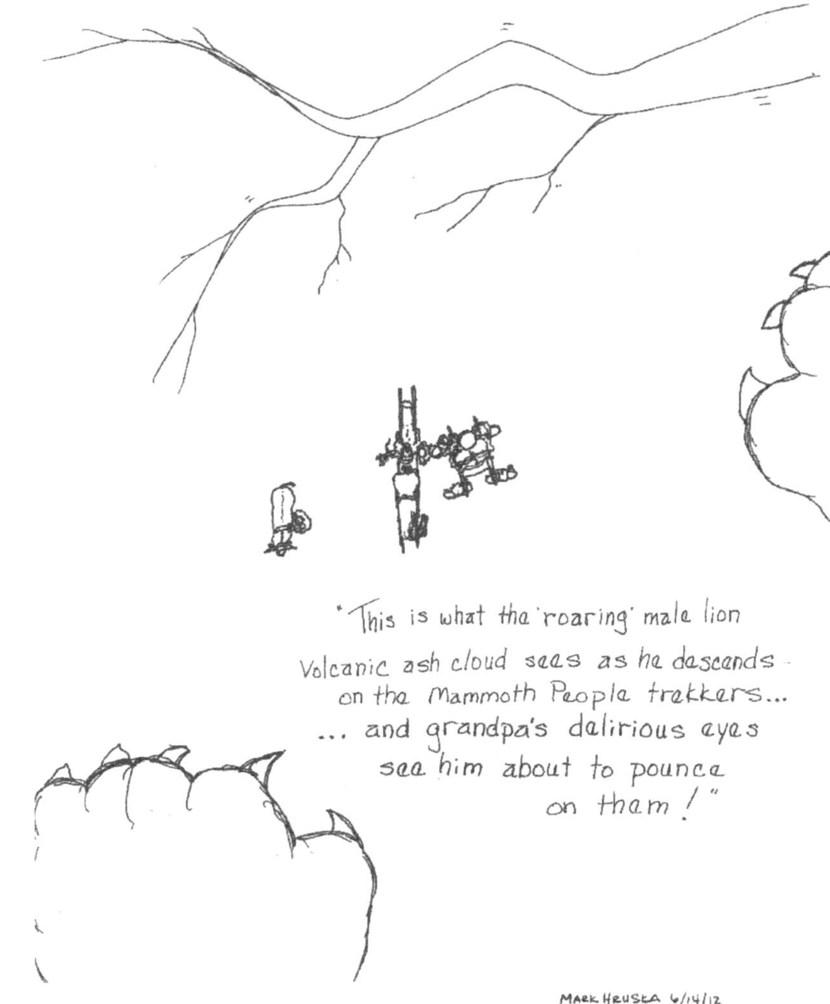

'6/14/12'.... 'This is what the 'roaring' male lion
volcanic ash cloud sees as he descends on the Mammoth People
trekkers.....and grandpa's delirious eyes see him about to pounce on them!'

116) Zoom in and peer intently and you'll even be able to see the beast of burden horse turning his head sharply to his left under the left travois pole to look back towards the mortified waist high young maiden who's kitty has just scratched delirious grandpa's face and is jumping down on the other side of the travois where he'll go and sit on his haunches and lick off his paws and swipe them down over his face to clean himself.

'Responsibility'

It's the responsibility of the individual that
makes an unprecedented discovery, one that has
no words to describe it, to bring it to fruition in
a clear concise manner...because no one else
will be capable of doing so in a single
lifetime......

.... "it just is what it is"....Mark Hruska 12/21/12

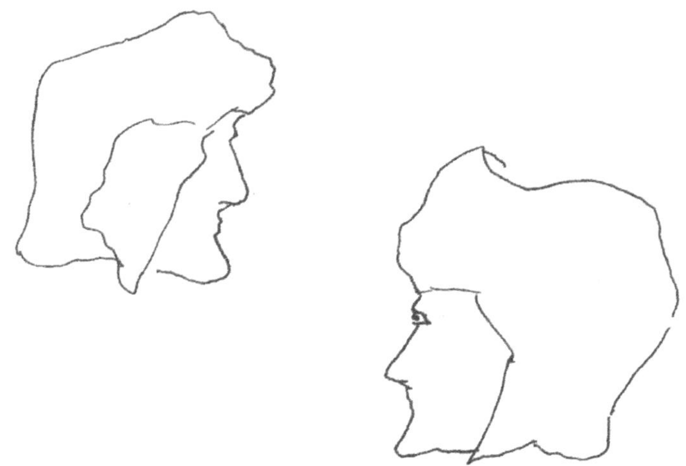

'heat treated stone microlithic abstract art'... 'That left side close-up view of grandma's bonnet covered head and crotchety face with her 'glaring' left eyeball 'Rocks'!'

117) This piece obviously has a very good image of the left side of crotchety grandma's bonnet covered head and crotchety face.

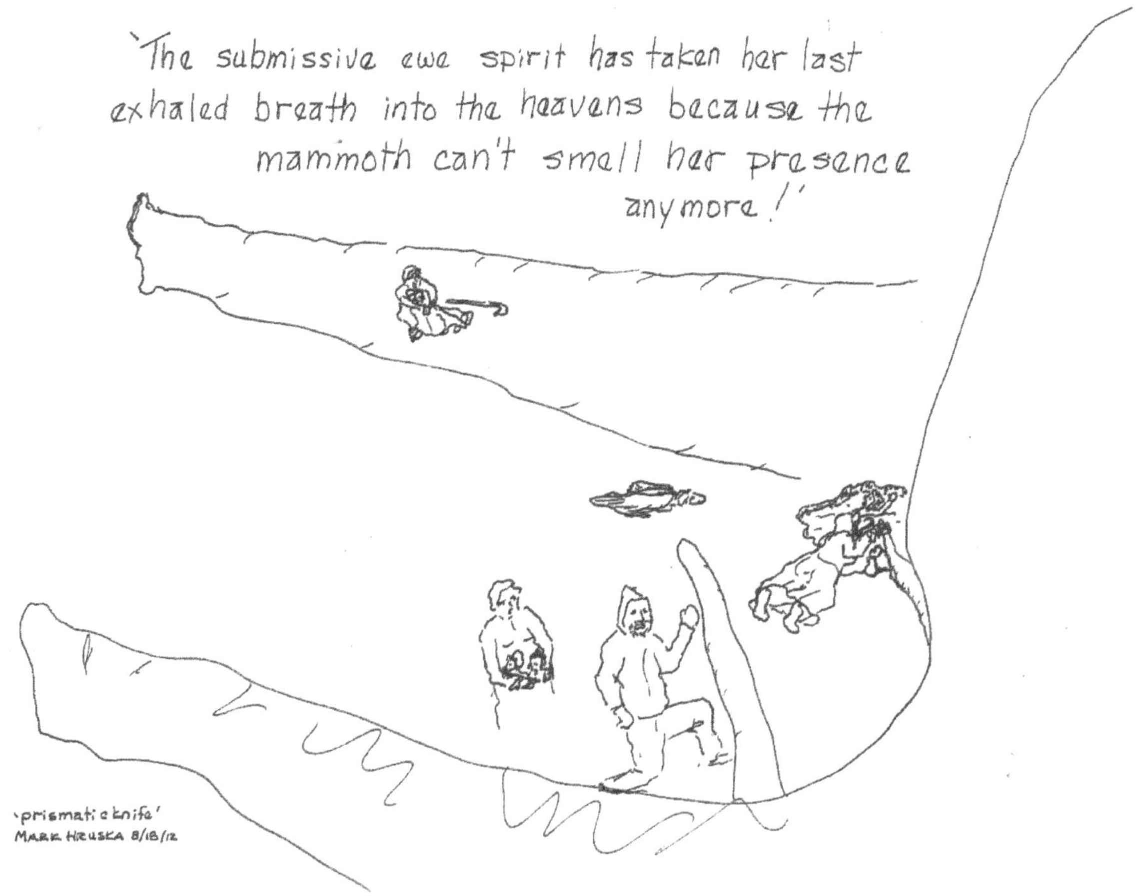

'prismatic knife'... 'The submissive ewe spirit has taken her last exhaled breath into the heavens because the mammoth can't smell her presence anymore!'

118) After the cooperating lead family's mammoth helped pull the struggling fair young maiden out of the icy cold sea water and then pulled out her struggling horse by his neck, her long wrinkly trunk sniffed at the expired fair young maiden over wailing grandma's shoulders and knew that she wasn't there anymore...

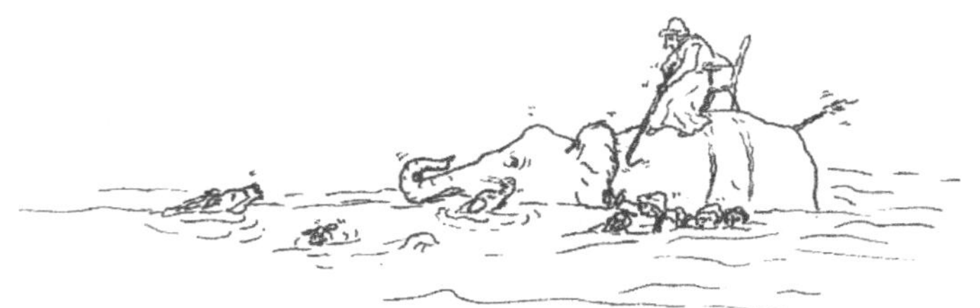

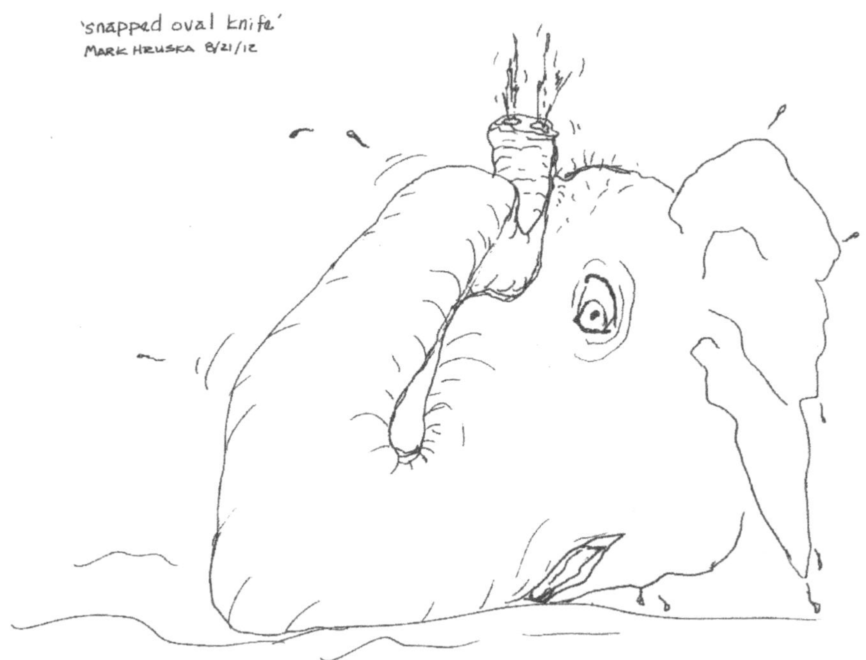

'snapped oval knife'... 'All of the surviving trekkers including the baby mammoth are swimming towards grandma and the mother mammoth that she's sitting atop!'

119) What's so cool about this line sketch is that if you zoom in and peer intently at the swimming baby mammoth in the further away image, you'll see that the left side of his head is close to the left side of his swimming mothers head. His swimming mother's left eye sees her struggling baby with his snorting little trunk raised high the way that you see him in the close-up image of him. This 'epic deluge' folklore tale usually ends well with grandma and the swimming mammoth rescuing all of the lead family with even the baby mammoth draped across her back.

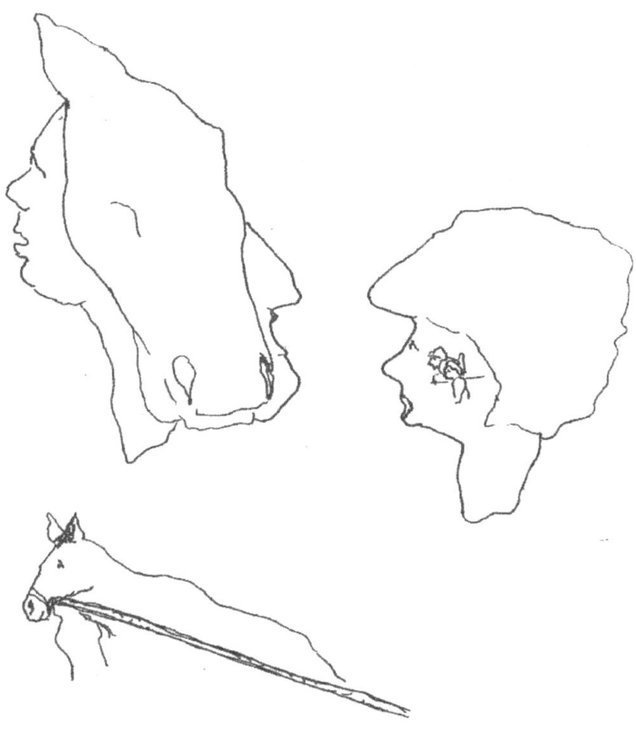

'heat treated stone'... MARK HRUSKA 8/26/12

'heat treated stone'... 'The horse is turning his head from right to left to try
to get it either over or under the travois poles to see what's going on behind him!'

120) This line sketch and its description relate how the beast of burden horse tries relentlessly to get his head over or under the travois poles to look behind him and see what all of the commotion is about. When he does get his head over or under the left travois pole, his left eye usually locks with the teenage young lad front left porters eyes. Seeing the horse's snotty nose the teenager realizes that he's a beast of burden too, no different than the poor horse.

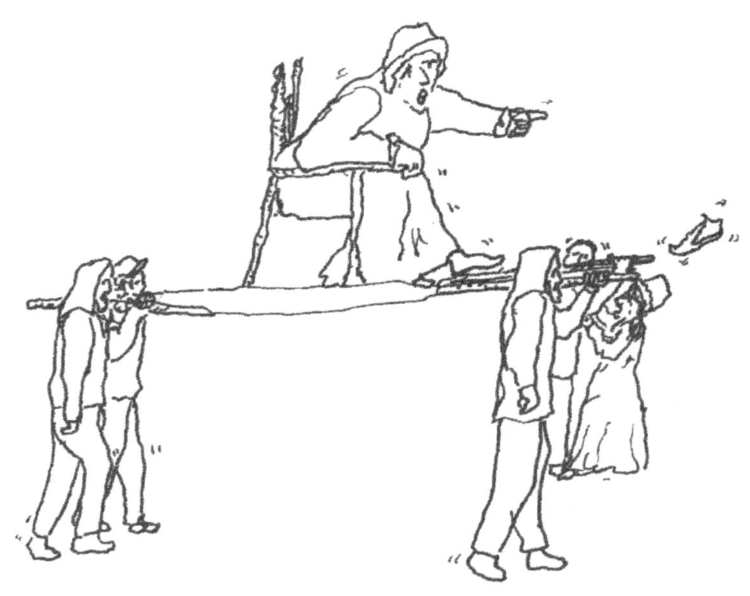

'pure microlithic abstract art'... '...now you know that
grandma's crotchety face is reflecting off of her 'kicked off' left shoe!'

121) The shoe is being kicked off towards the mortified waist high young maiden's naughty kitty but it always barely misses the poor teenage young lad's face which ends up extremely close to crotchety grandma's old bare foot.

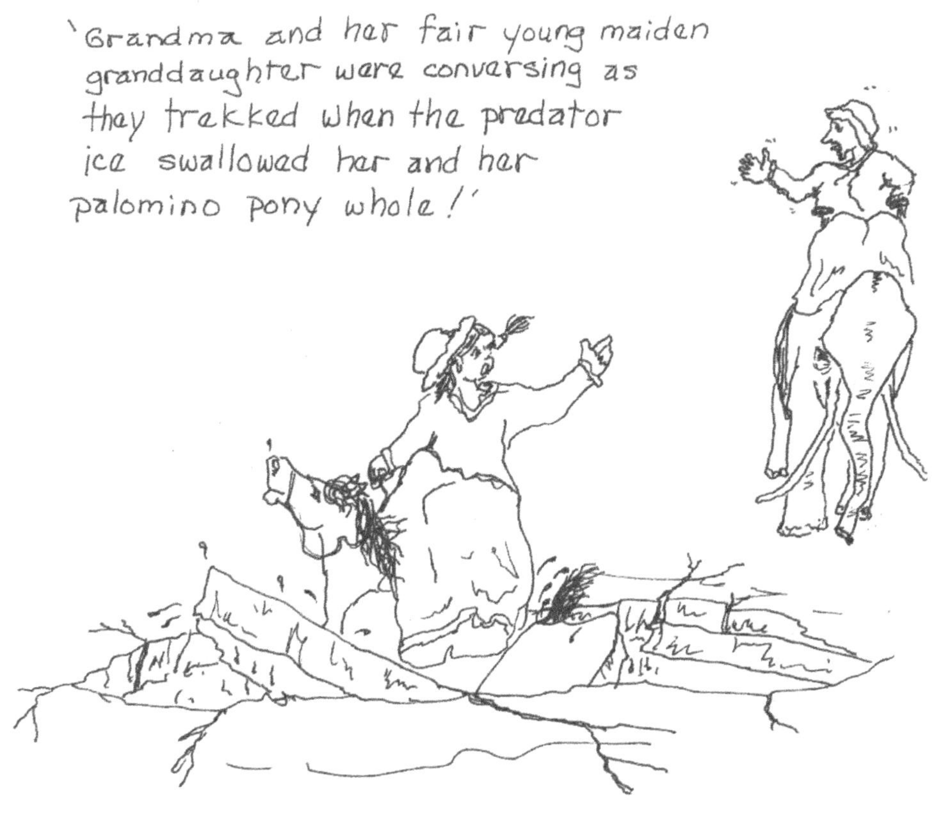

'heat treated flake knife'... MARK HRUSKA 9/6/12

'heat treated flake knife'... 'Grandma and her
fair young maiden granddaughter were conversing as they
trekked when the predator ice swallowed her and her palomino pony whole!'

122) This is of course what happened prior to the lead family that included the lead mammoth, frantically cooperating to rescue them.

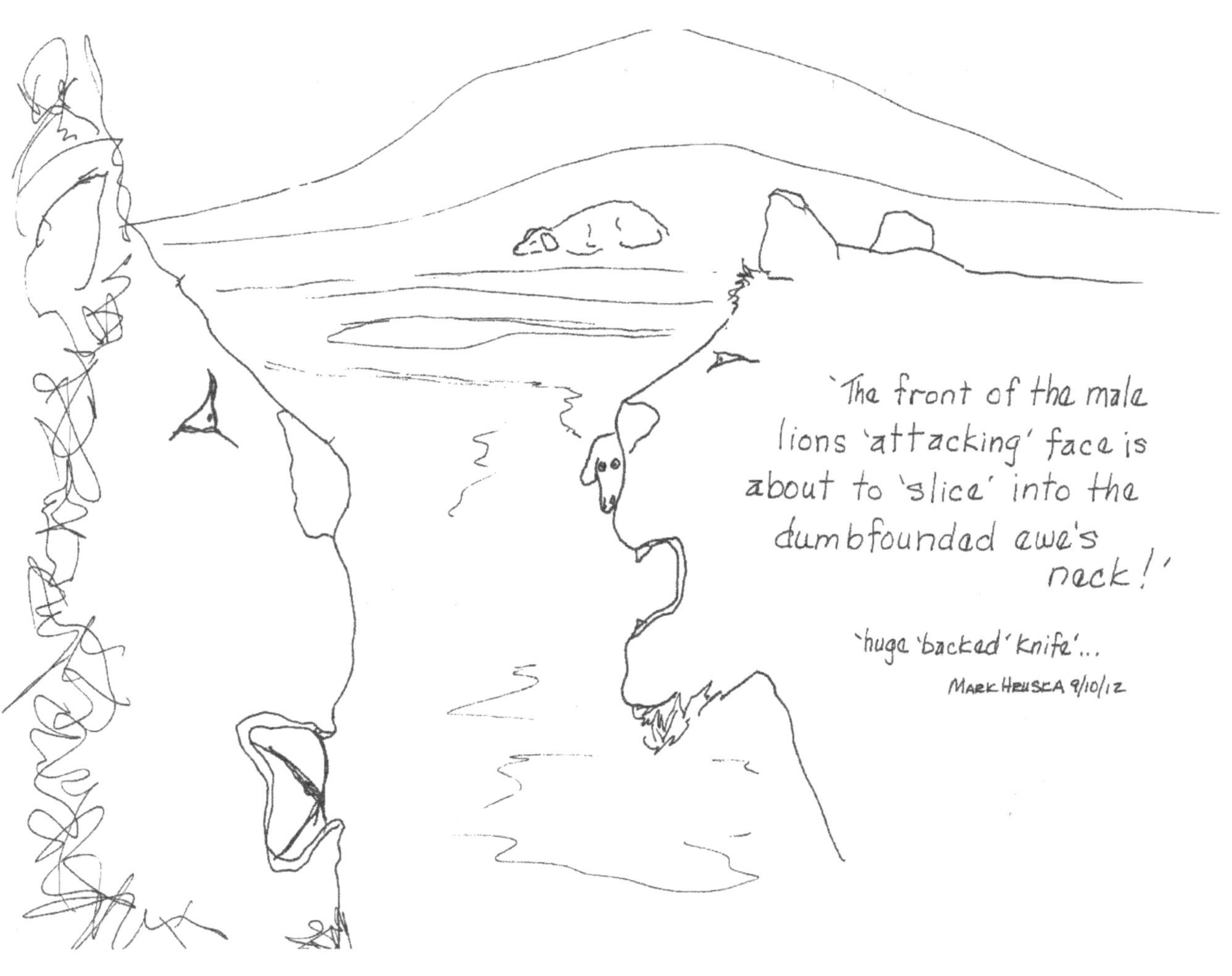

'huge backed knife'... 'The front of the male lions
'attacking' face is about to 'slice' into the dumbfounded ewe's neck!'

123) I'm pretty sure that the one that he bit into the nape of the neck of is the one that has the 'deer in the headlight' expression on its face and that's poking out from the other side of the lioness's snout, that's superimposed over the rest of the dumbfounded ewe's fleecy body.

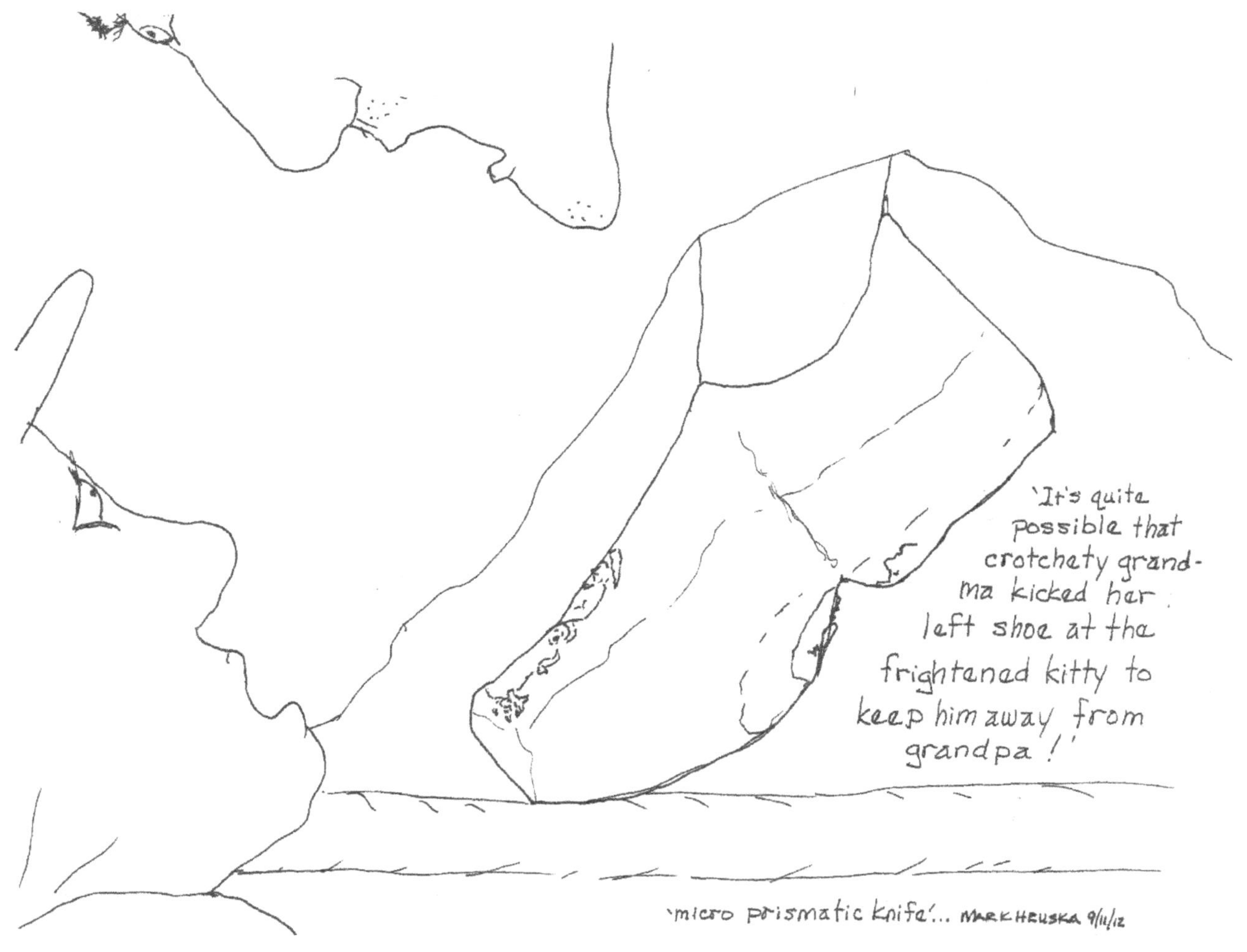

'micro prismatic knife'... 'It's quite possible that crotchety grandma kicked her shoe at the frightened kitty to keep him away from grandpa!'

124) After several pieces that focused on crotchety grandma kicking her shoe off towards the kitty, you eventually understand why she was doing it.

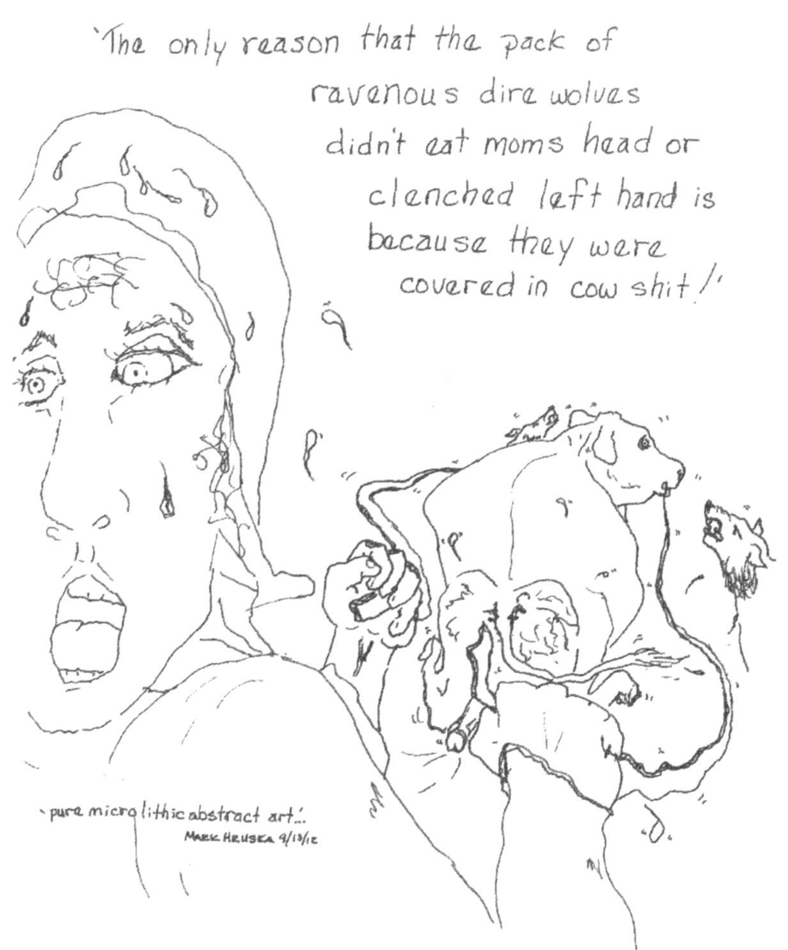

'pure microlithic abstract art'... 'The only reason that the pack of ravenous dire wolves didn't eat mom's head or clenched left hand is because they were covered in cow shit!'

125) No, I don't like using Ice Age profanity, but I made a commitment to the hunter herder microlithic abstract artist when I discovered their Ice Age microlithic abstract art figurative language to be as true as possible to them above all else. This is one of my favorite pieces and I just couldn't imagine not calling it the way that I saw it especially when I grew up milking cows by hand and having my hands in what we always simply called.... cow shit! Besides, it just wouldn't have had the same impact if I would have called it cow dung, cow excrement, etc. You can imagine the impact the folklore tale would have had on the young maidens when grandpa or dad told it in order to make them and their mother get home at a reasonable time after the gossipy mother daughter gatherings... before the howling dire wolves came out.

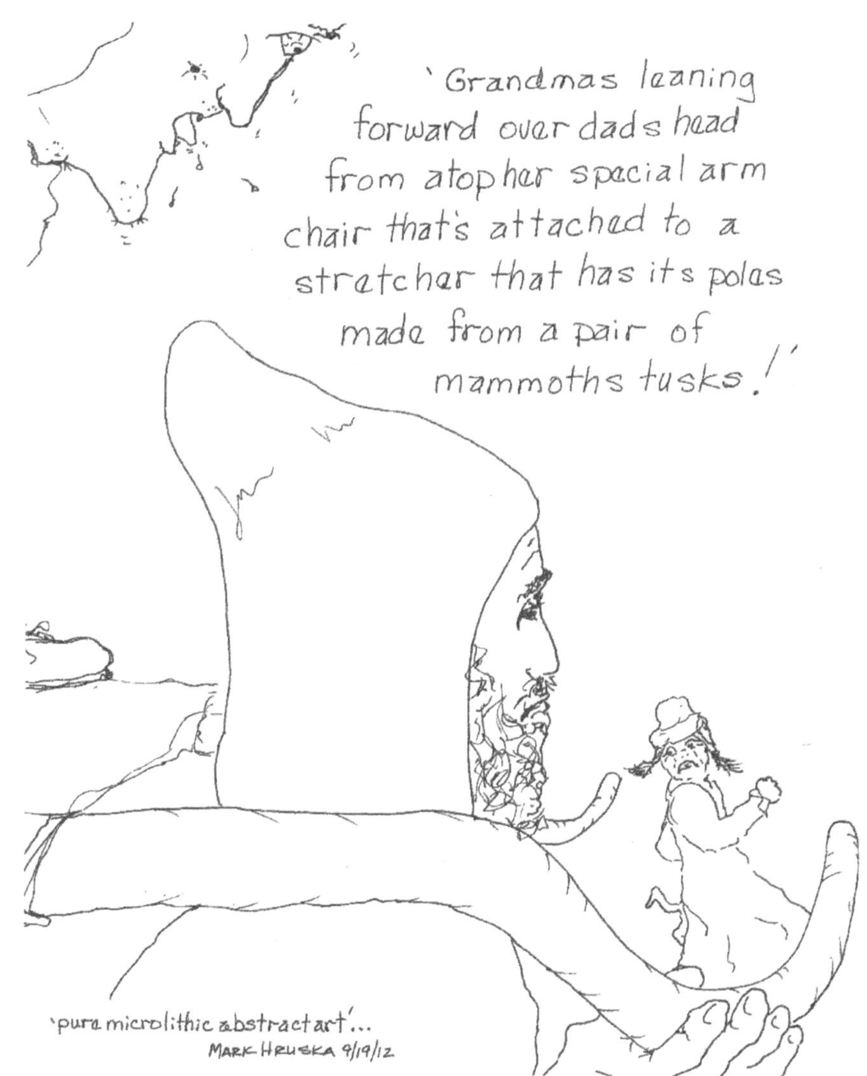

'pure microlithic abstract art'...'Grandma's leaning forward over dads head from atop her special armchair that's attached to a stretcher that has its poles made from mammoth tusks!'

126) I very rarely saw the poles of the stretcher that crotchety grandma's special armchair was attached to be made from mammoth's tusks on the subsequent interpretations of the 'volcanic mass exodus'. But since I did see it on this microlithic abstract artwork I'm sure it motivated me to sketch it.

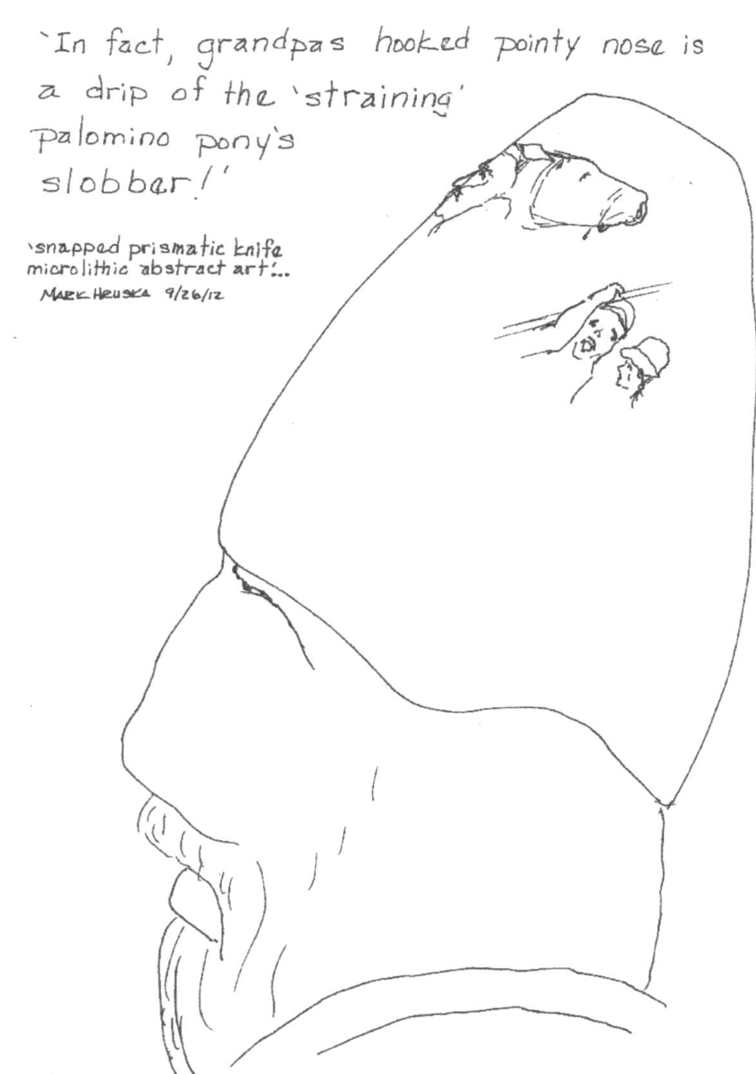

'snapped prismatic knife microlithic abstract art'... 'In fact, grandpa's hooked
pointy nose is a drip of the 'straining' palomino pony's slobber!'

127) This artwork has the 'volcanic mass exodus' folklore tale on it and when you look at the line sketch to see the close-up image of the rear left side view of the stern lead hunter herder's head.... all of those reflections are reflecting off of him. His teenage young lad front left porter son is turning towards him to his left to complain to him for not doing anything about crotchety grandma to get her to quit yelling at his little sister. Back behind him is the reflections of the 'opposing heads' of delirious grandpa and the other 'beast of burden' or the horse that has slobber dripping from his snorting snout.

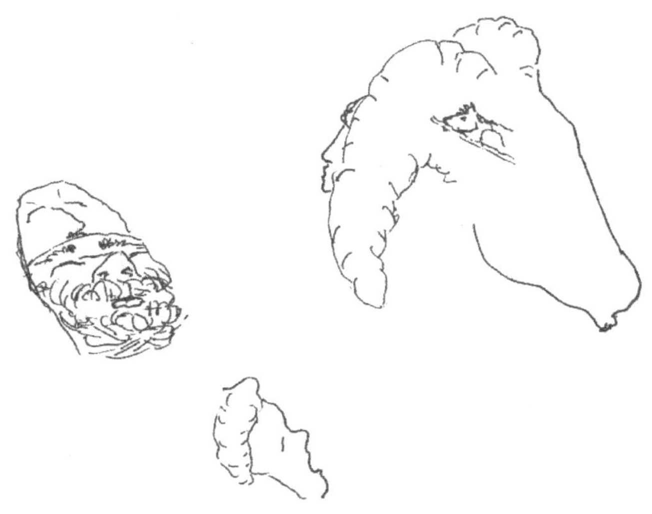

'pure microlithic abstract art'... 'Both of the mortified
waist high young maiden's grandparents are extremely irritated!'

128) Look closely and you'll see who's looking at whom. Crotchety grandma's face is reflecting off of the top half of delirious grandpa's face as he peers up towards her from his travois. When she looks down to the left of his travois which is right below the left arm of her special armchair she sees the mortified and now sobbing waist high young maiden the way you see her, and she's looking towards her compassionate big brother who is an opposing head to the black faced ram that's on the right side of delirious grandpa's travois near his feet which makes the two of them face to face because he's crotchety grandma's front left porter who's turning to his left towards the ram. As the ram looks towards the beast of burden teenage young lad front left porter, the other beast of burden (the horse that's pulling delirious grandpa's travois) is reflecting off of the right side of his face as he struggles to get his head either over or under the left travois pole. Now do you see how the microlithic abstract art figurative language works?

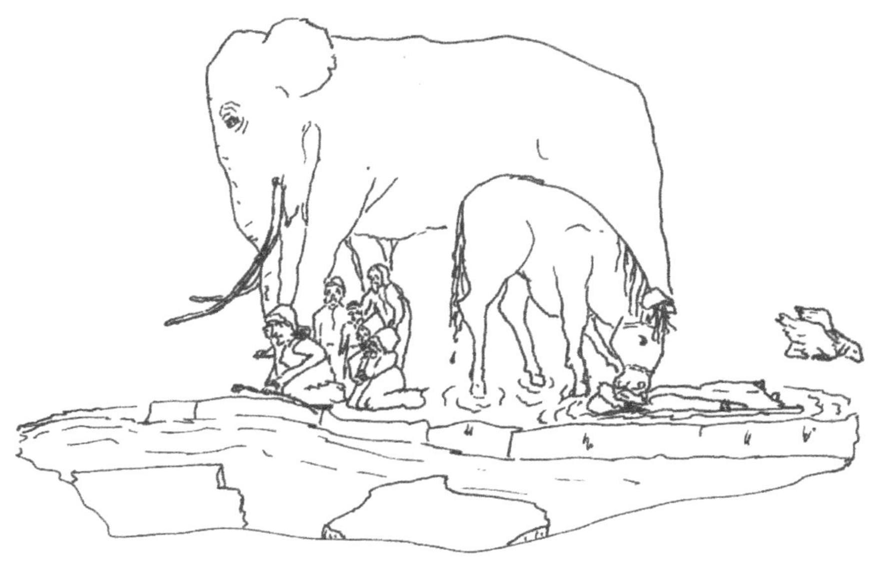

'pure microlithic abstract art'... 'The family of Mammoth People trekkers are all grieving inconsolably along with the mammoth and the fair young maiden's pony!'

129) After the mammoth pulled the fair young maiden's struggling horse out of the hole in the predator ice he too is sniffing her and saying his goodbyes... It appears that the submissive ewe spirit is patiently waiting for that last exhaled breath that is the fair young maiden's spirit so that she can take it up into the heavens to be with her deceased ancestors.

144

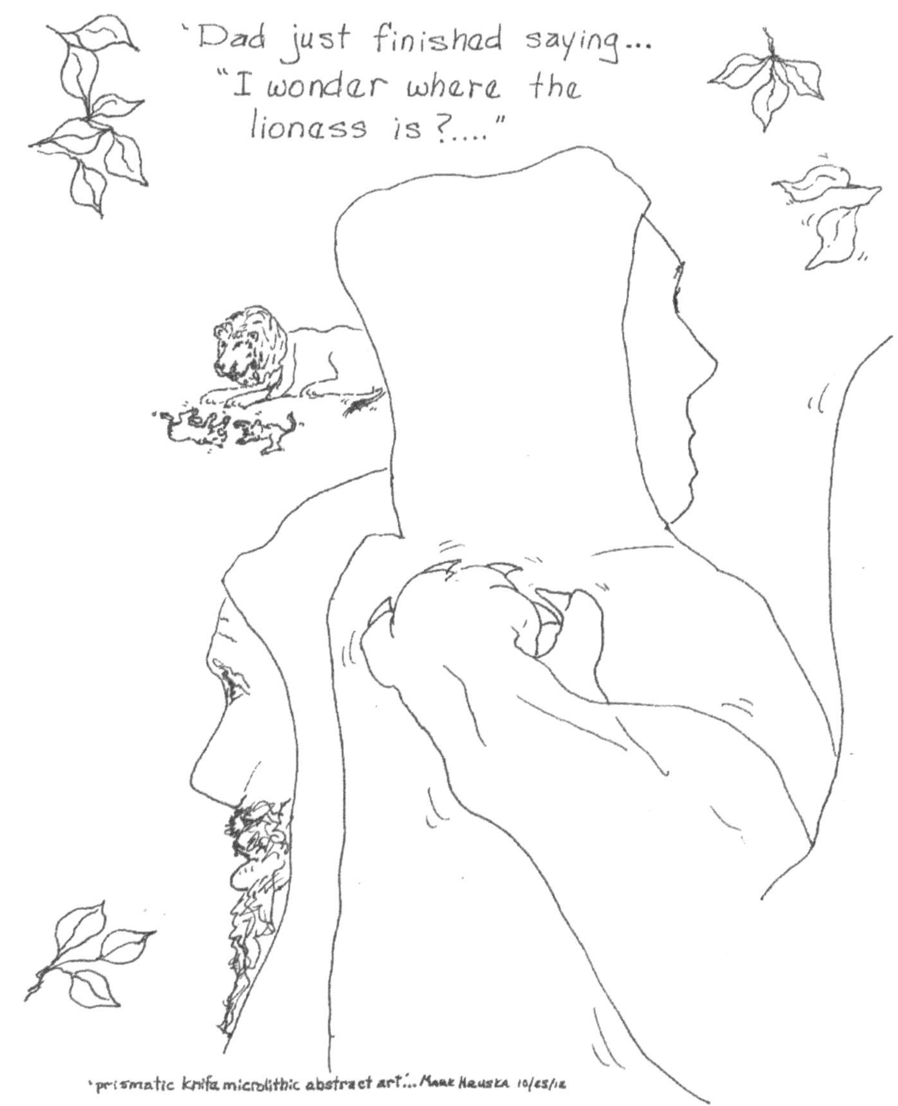

'prismatic knife microlithic abstract art'...
'Dad just finished saying... "I wonder where the lioness is?..."'

130) This interpretation's line sketch and description pretty much say everything you need to know. Obviously, this folklore tale was told to the inexperienced teenagers so that they never let their guards down and would always be totally aware of their surroundings.

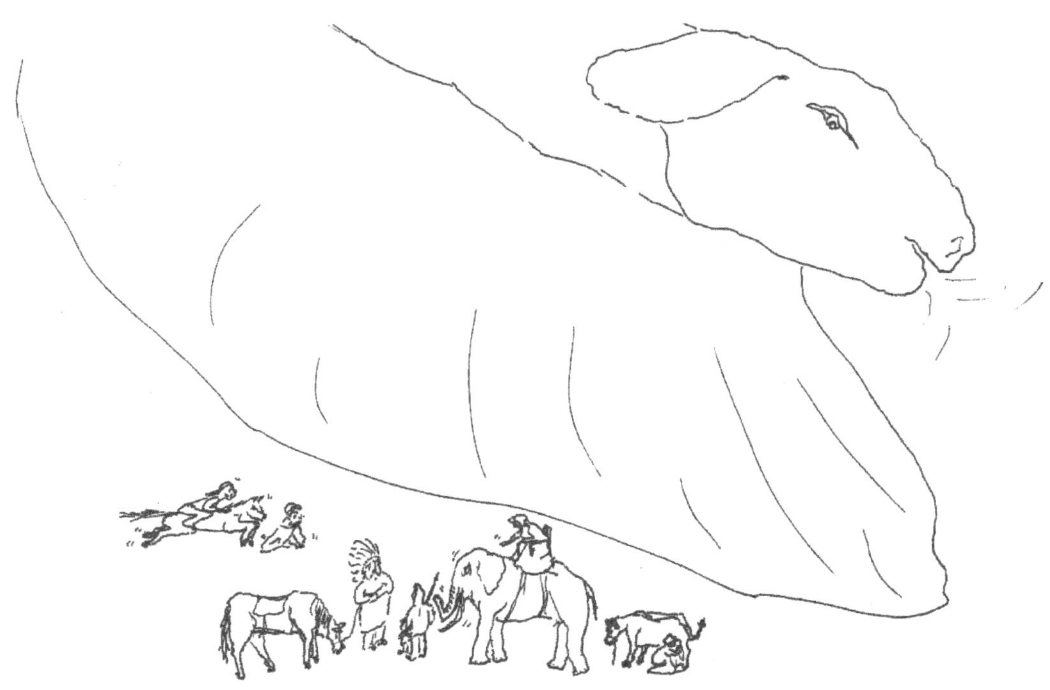

'backed knife microlithic abstract art'... 'The submissive ewe spirit is 'gliding'
in for a landing to collect the Mammoth Peoples exhaled last breaths!'

131) This is one 'powwow' interpretation that didn't end well for the trekkers, although it is a rare one. It may have been because of that bawling infant...

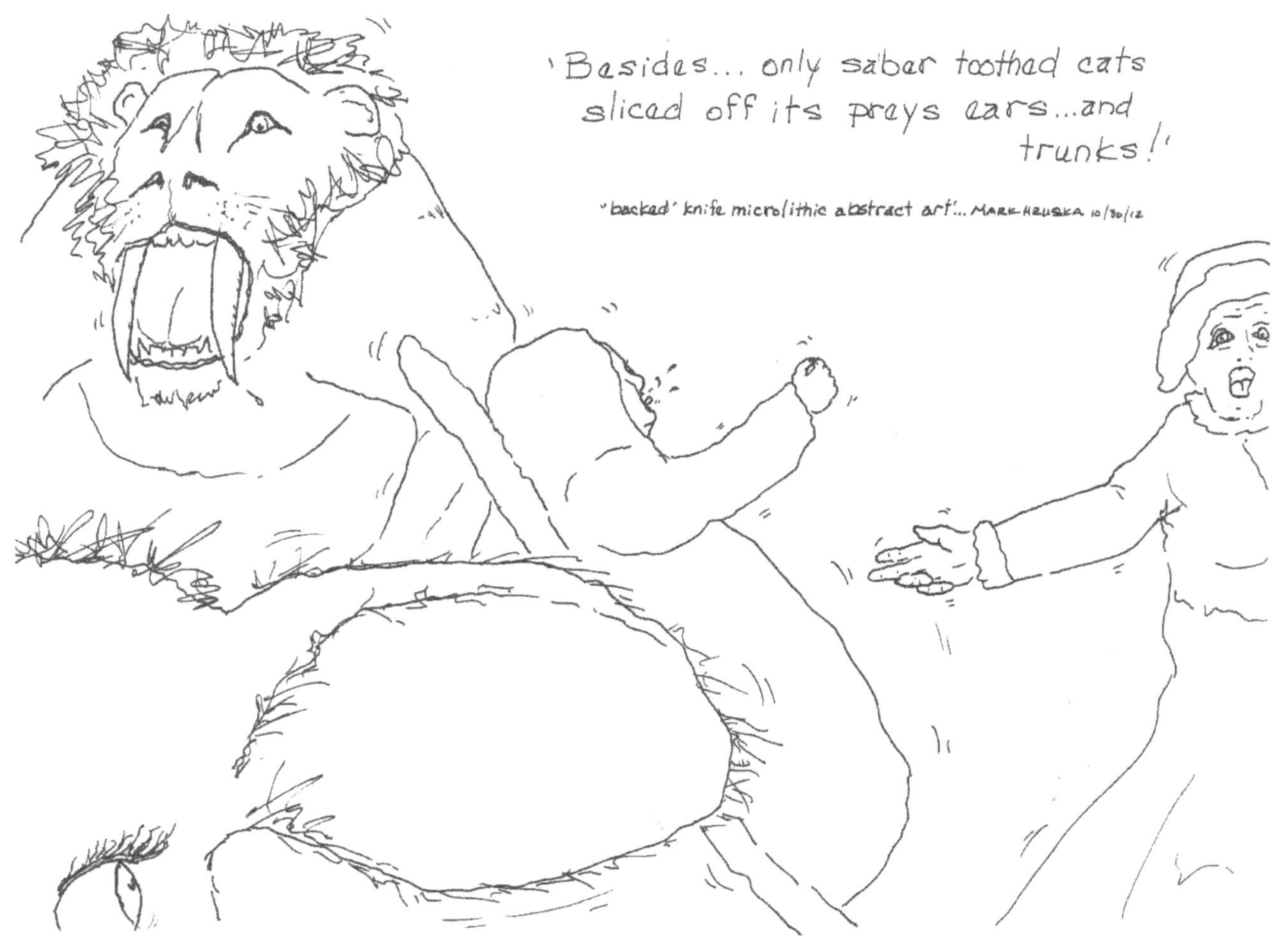

'backed knife microlithic abstract art'... 'Besides...only
saber-toothed cats sliced off its preys ears...and trunks!'

132) This is a scene from when the Mammoth People mammoth caravan of trekkers was trekking across the vast expanse of grasslands that had big cats lurking in it. The big cat that's jumping up on the back end of the bucking milk cow looks like a male lion but the male saber toothed cat had somewhat of a mane too. Think of a Bengal tiger without its stripes but with a tan hide that has pock marks or splotches. Either way, whichever big cat decided to ambush the lead family, mom and dad were totally helpless as their infant flopped around on the left shoulder of the milk cow as she wildly bucked away from them.

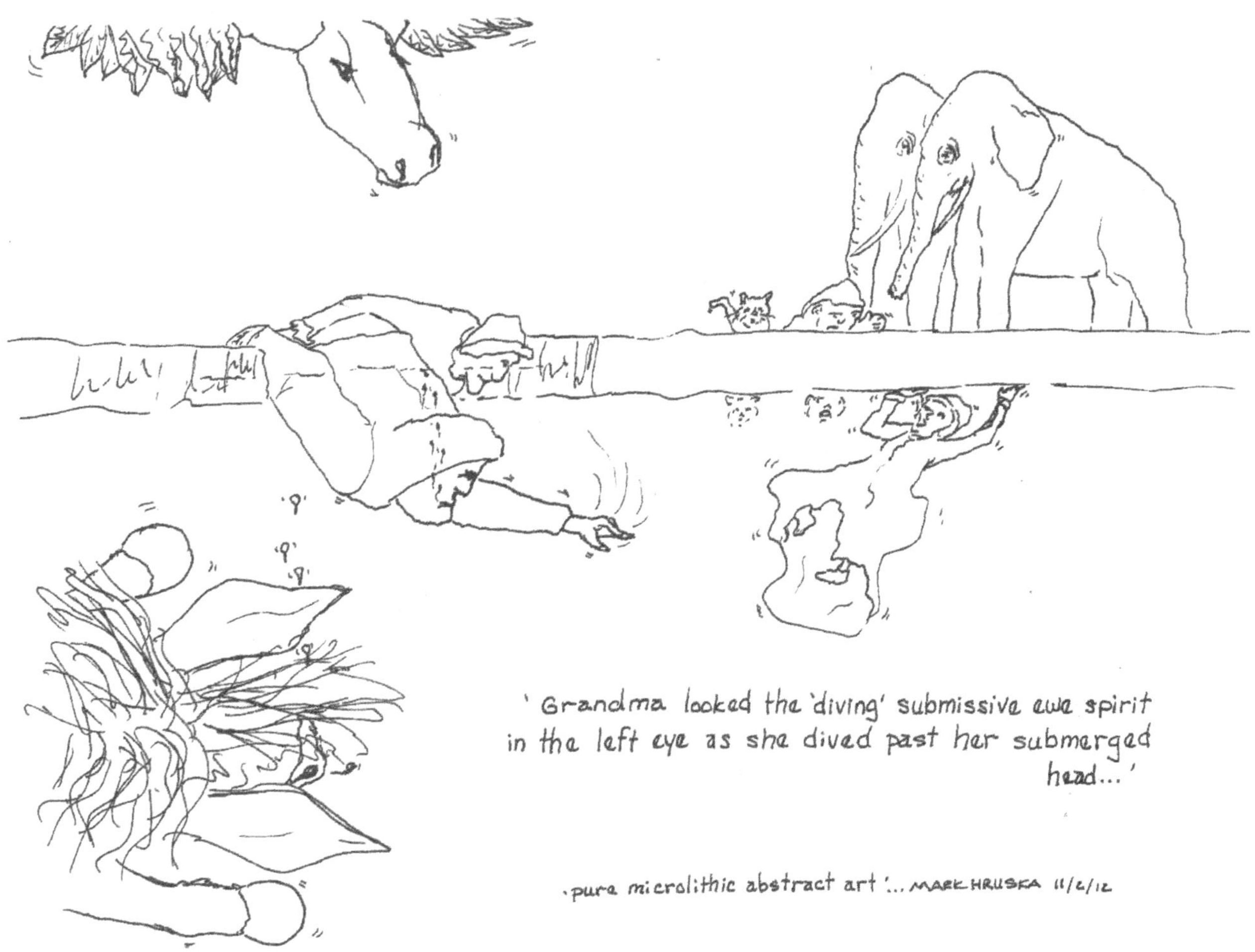

'pure microlithic abstract art'... 'Grandma looked the 'diving'
submissive ewe spirit in the left eye as she dived past her submerged head...'

133) The supine fair young maiden could see her worried sibling and her kitty through the thick ice as she clawed for the hole that she and her sinking horse had fallen through. The appearance of the flying submissive ewe spirit can only mean one thing and that is that this was going to end with grandma and dad watching their vibrant fair young maiden sink into the dark icy cold abyss...along with her horse that unintentionally forced her under the predator ice out of dad or grandma's reach.

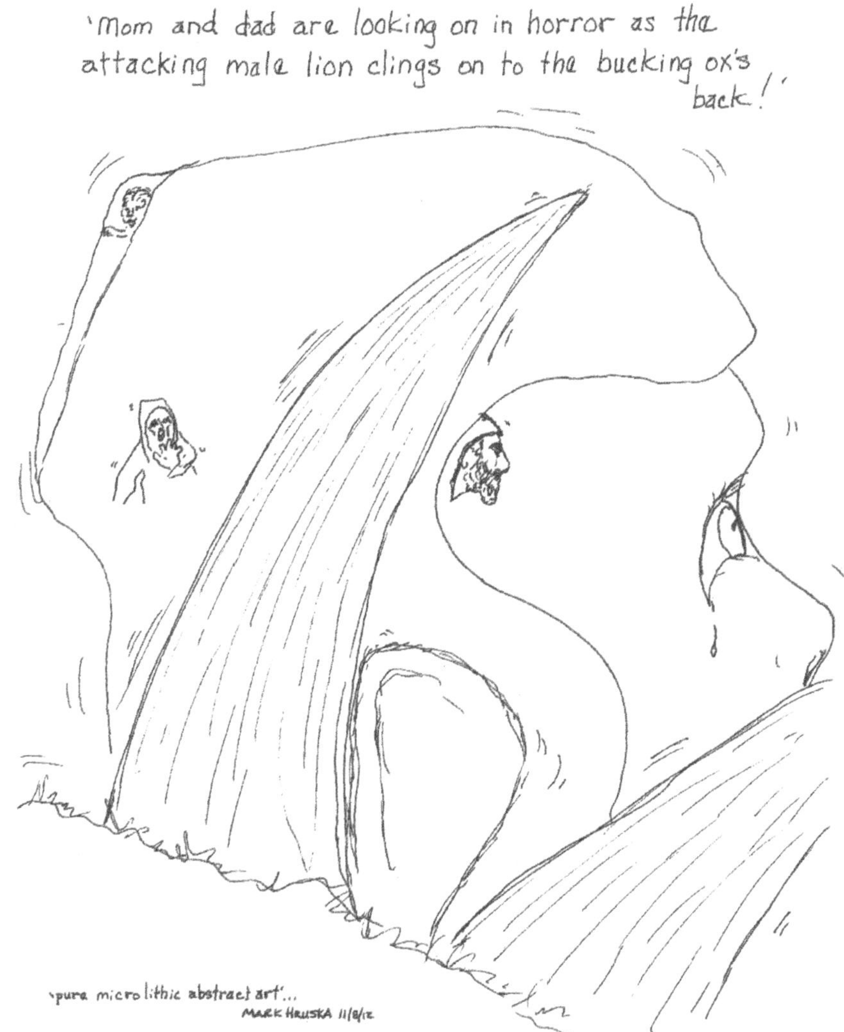

'pure microlithic abstract art'... 'Mom and dad are looking on in
horror as the attacking male lion clings on to the bucking ox's back!'

134) This artwork was interpreted before I figured out that the bucking ox was in fact the bucking domestic milk cow. Her left horn is seen twice, superimposed on the left side of the crying infant's baby bunting hood covered head as a way to show motion. The proto-cinema scene clearly shows the positions of the main characters of the scene as they reflect off of the flopping infants head.

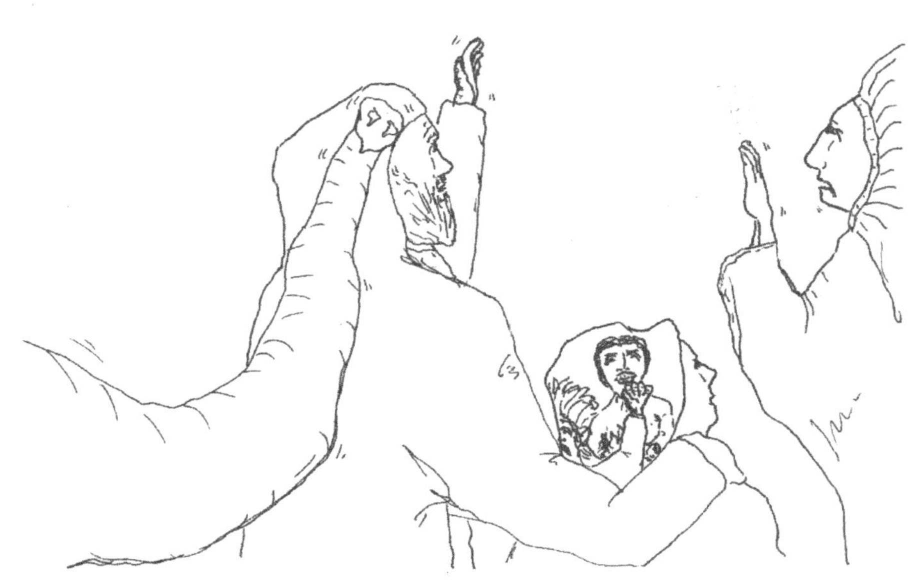

'flake knife'... 'The 'jeering' warrior brave is sitting atop
his pony behind the chief's raised purple arm with the amber
setting Pleistocene sun setting on the horizon to the right of him!'

135) The taunting warrior braves head and jeering face is reflecting off of the right side of the mesmerized waist high young lad's hood covered head in this line sketch of the interpretation. the gruff chief's raised hand seems to be making that "Howw!" sign language expression to the lead hunter herder or 'dad' and it's superimposed over the taunting warrior brave who is (as I later referred to him) 'sitting on his high horse' behind the gruff chief.

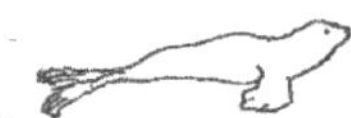

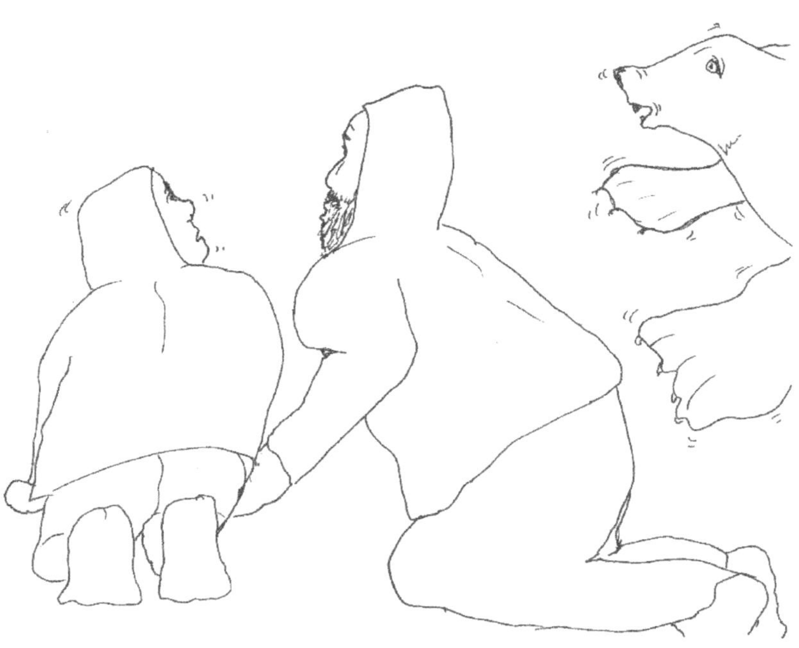

'stone prismatic knife'... 'The angry charging mother sea lion has the
'predators bent foreleg featuring the prey that it's stalking'...
it's her right flipper... and she's gaining on them!'

136) This artworks interpretation shows that the 'predators bent foreleg featuring the prey that its stalking' art form doesn't always have to represent the swiping front foreleg or paw of a saber-toothed cat, lion, bear or dire wolf. It can be the flipper of an angry mother sea lion, a human's arm and gloved hand or even the waist high young maiden's kitty's paw that's swiping at her face because he wants her to pick him up and carry him. All of these swiping appendages will have the prey that they're swiping at reflecting off of the underside of the swiping paw. The 'bent' part of the art form describes the wrist but sometimes the piece just has the predator's front paw as the art form.

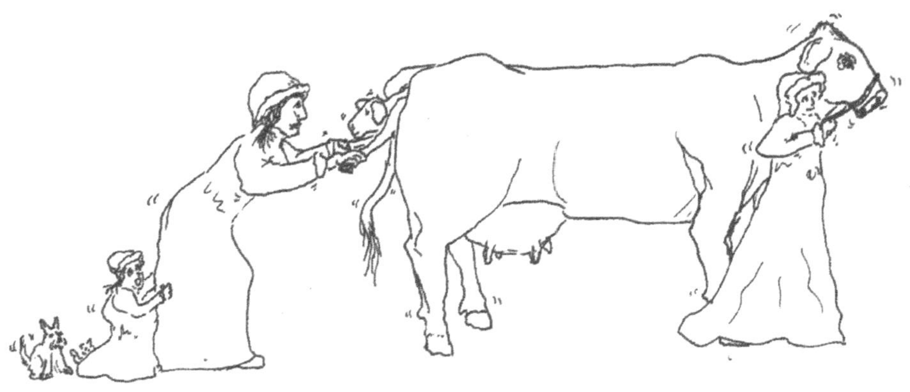

'pure microlithic abstract art'... 'I'm sure that mom's doing her
best to answer all of the waist high young maidens perplexing questions!'

137) This artworks interpretation and line sketch is self-explanatory. In subsequent interpretations of sheep, cattle, mammoth or human birth I refer to the waist high young maiden with all the perplexing birth questions as the 'inquisitive' waist high young maiden. And since all birth was paramount to the Mammoth People, mom or grandma or whoever was working diligently to assist the birthing mother, always answered the inquisitive waist high young maiden's relentless questions.

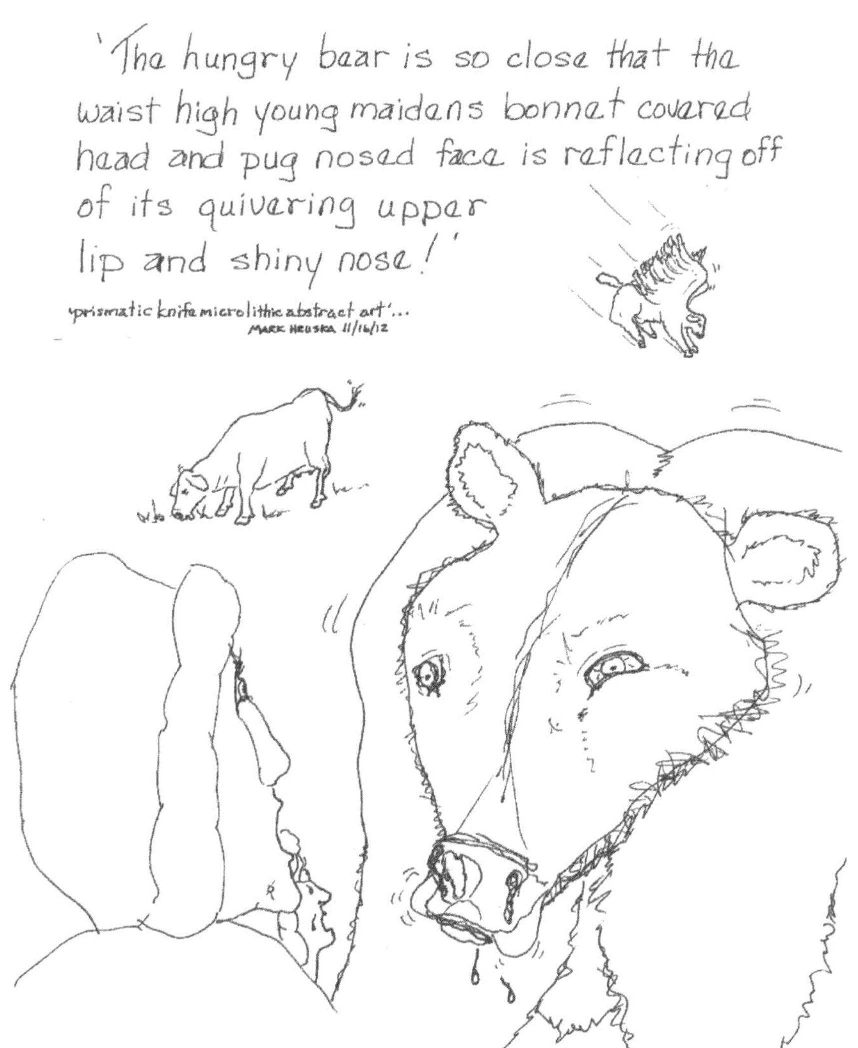

'prismatic knife microlithic abstract art'...
'The hungry bear is so close that the waist high young maiden's bonnet covered
head and pug nosed face is reflecting off of its quivering upper lip and shiny nose!'

138) Obviously the hungry bear is going to eat the frightened waist high young maiden and her horrified
grandma because the flying submissive ewe spirit is gliding in to suck up their last exhaled breath's which
is their spirits that she will take up into the heavens to be with their deceased ancestors.

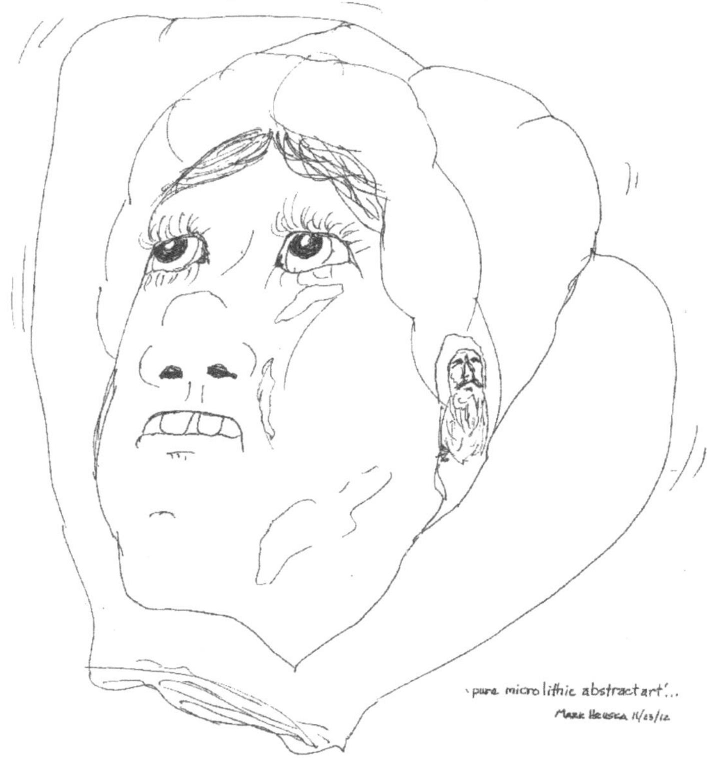

'pure microlithic abstract art'... '...you'll see that the waist high young
maiden's face is reflecting off of the back of the kitty's 'swiping' left paw!'

139) This scene is from the folklore tale of the 'volcanic mass exodus'. In it the upset sobbing waist high young maiden is going over to the other side of delirious grandpa's travois to retrieve her naughty kitty that had just scratched his face. The kitty is sitting on his haunches nonchalantly grooming himself. To verify that, you'll see delirious grandpa's bearded face reflecting off of the frilled edge of the waist high young maiden's bonnet that's over her left ear. We are actually seeing the reflection of the front 'right' side view of her bawling face which means that delirious grandpa is over to the right of her sitting up on his travois while the kitty swipes his left paw down over his left ear and his face after having licked it thereby reflecting his upset waist high young maiden's face in the process while she bends over to pick him up. It also means that delirious grandpa's reflection is a 'double' reflection. Now, do you see how the hunter herder microlithic abstract art...works?

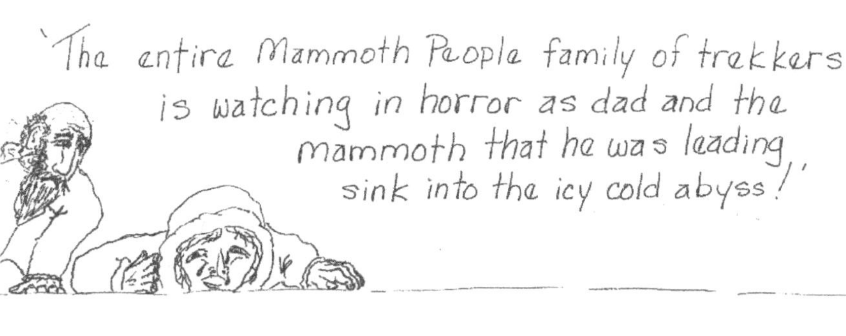

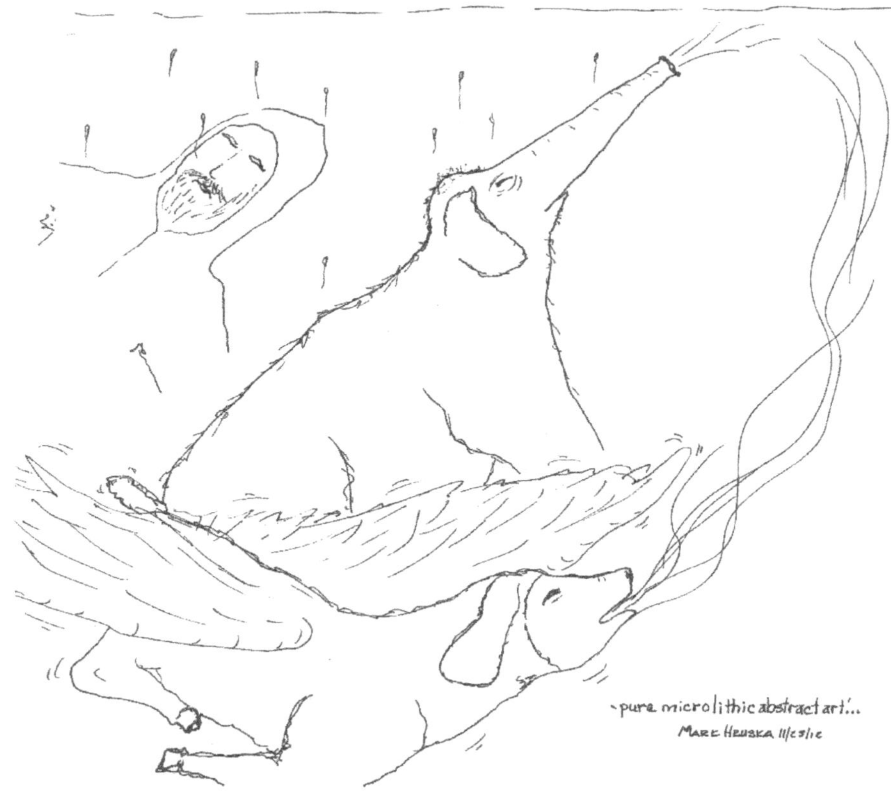

'pure microlithic abstract art'...
'The entire Mammoth People family of trekkers is watching
in horror as dad and the mammoth that he was leading sink into the icy cold abyss!'

140) If a picture is worth a thousand words then this line sketch says plenty.

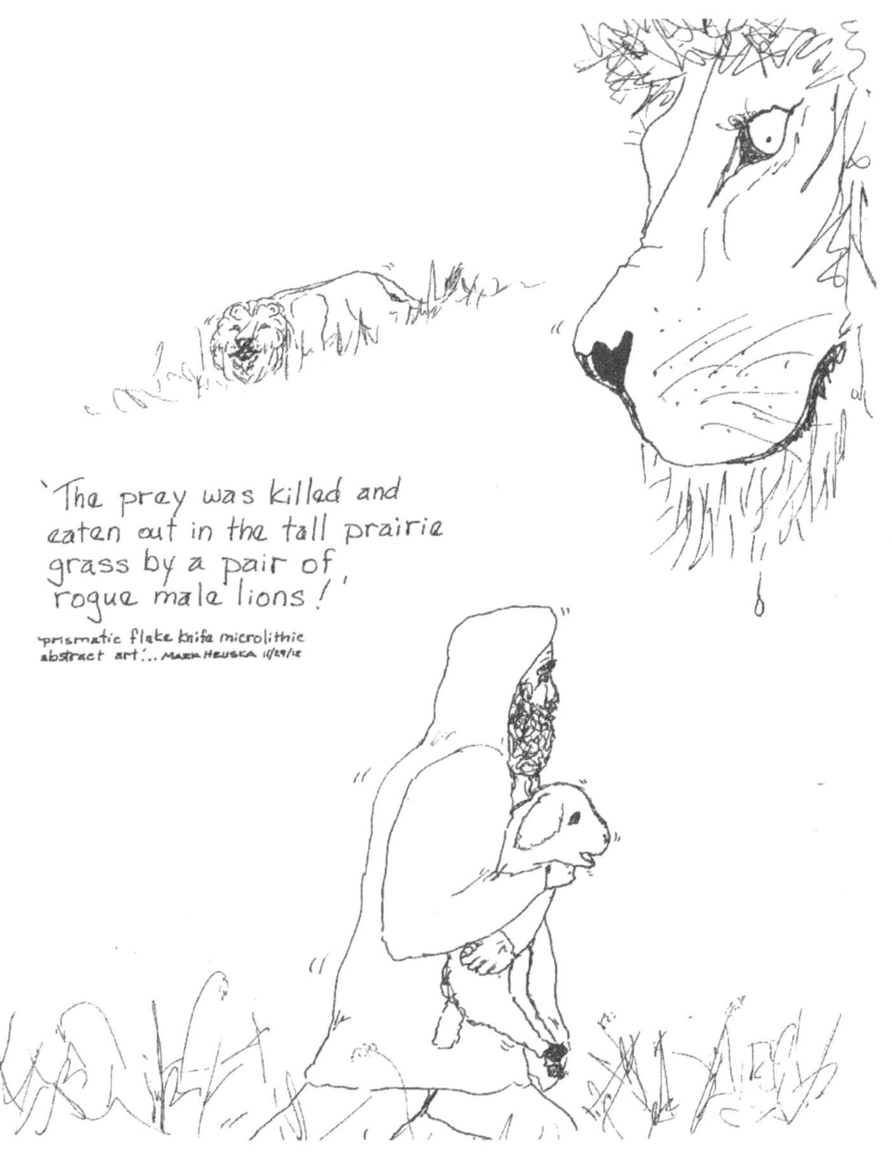

'prismatic flake knife'... 'The prey was killed and
eaten out in the tall prairie grass by a pair of rogue male lions!'

141) This pieces interpretations line sketch is another one of those that needs no explanation.

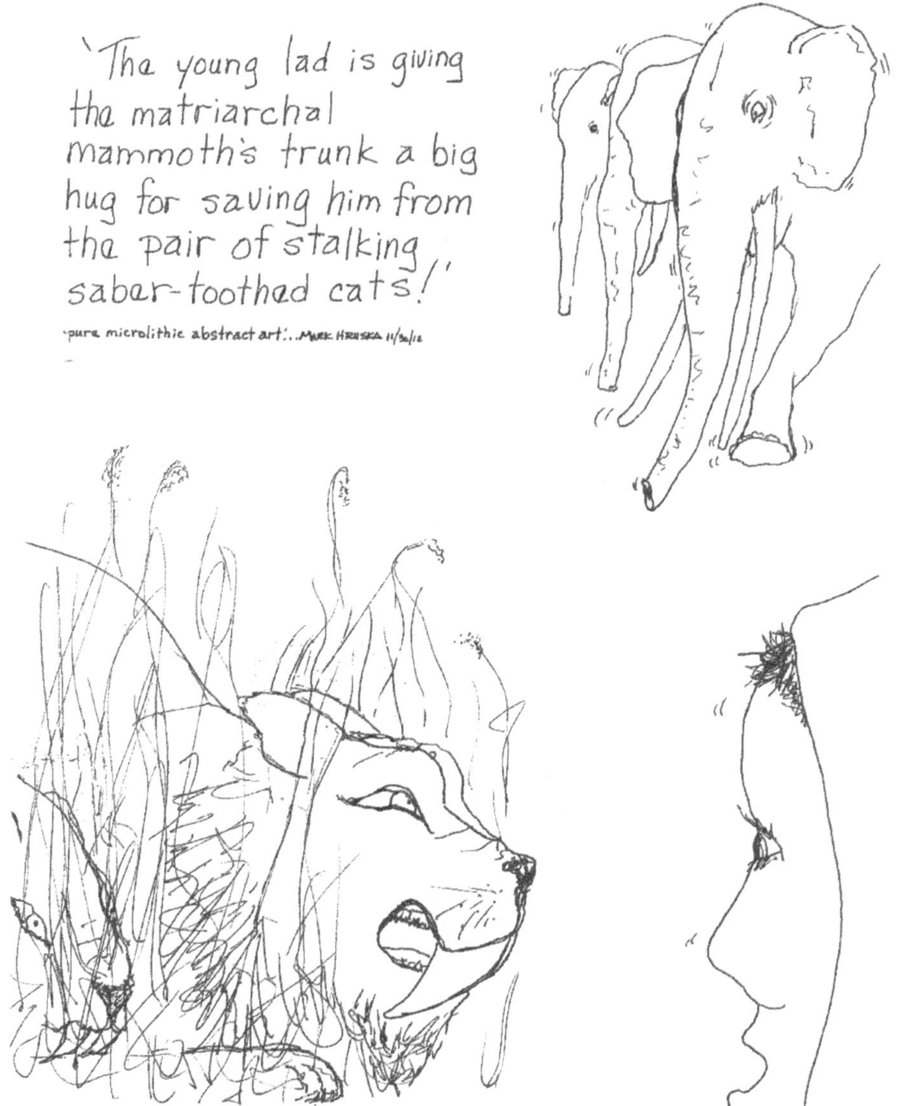

'pure microlithic abstract art'... 'The young lad is
giving the matriarchal mammoth's trunk a big hug for saving his life!'

142) I was clearly getting better at capturing one two dimensional scene from the multiple three dimensional rotational change-up microlithic abstract art images that combined to create it.

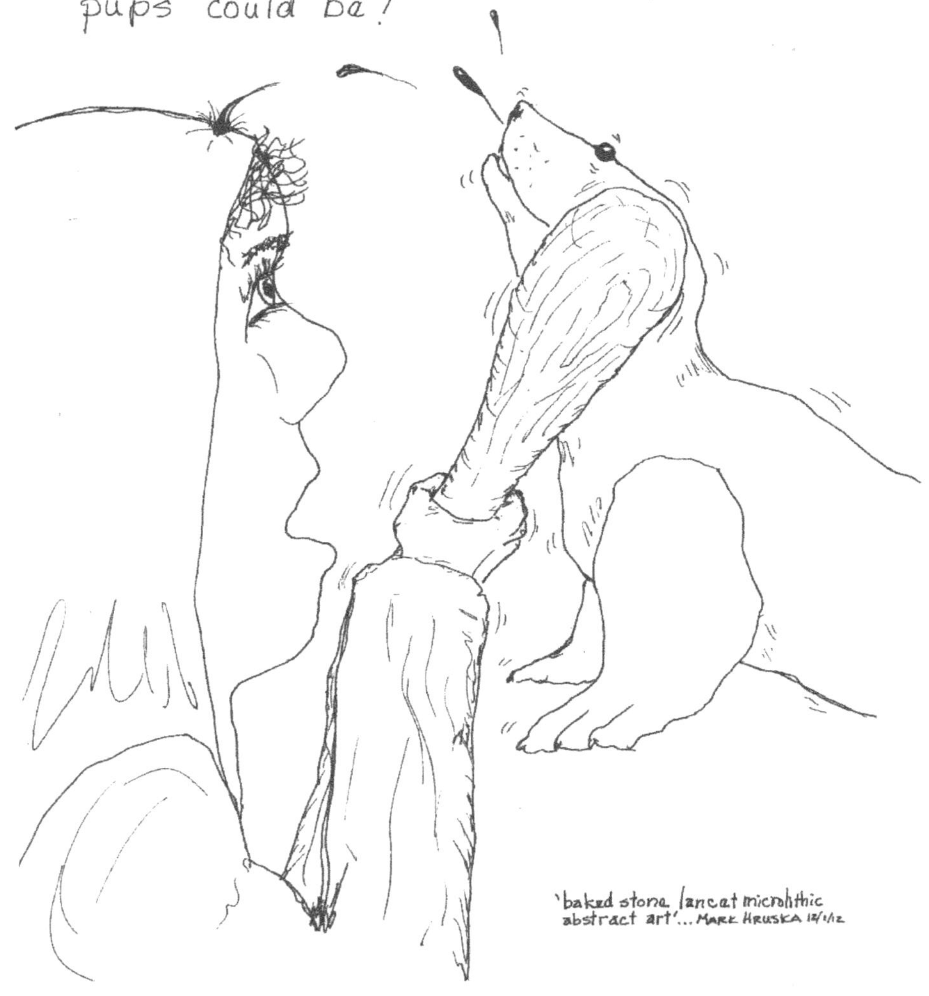

'baked stone lancet microlithic abstract art'... 'The inexperienced young lad had no idea how 'messy' bludgeoning baby sea lion pups could be!'

143) This is another line sketch that represents the artwork itself as well as it possibly could.

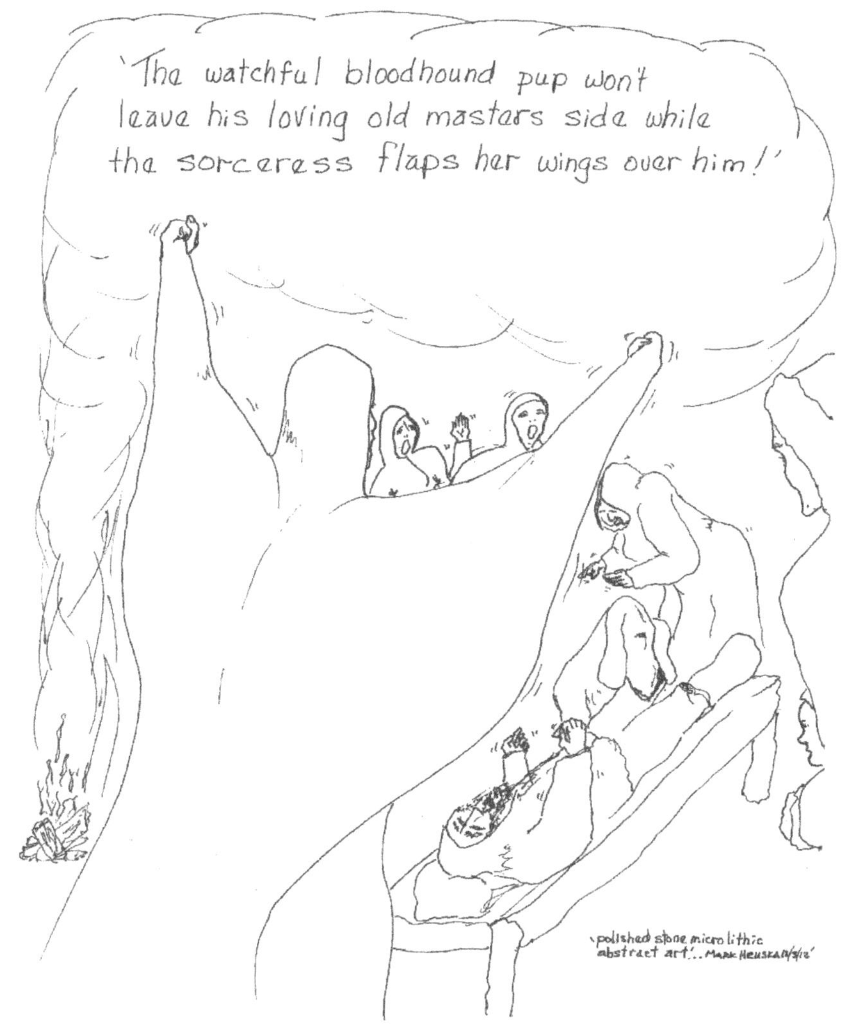

'polished stone microlithic abstract art'... 'The watchful bloodhound pup
won't leave his loving old masters side while the sorceress flaps her wings over him!'

144) Up to this point in time, I still hadn't figured out a key part of this folklore tale which was that there is a pair of coughing and choking rats that are above grandpa's cot on the ceiling rafters near the sorceress's head. They're coughing and choking because all of the smoke that the sorceress is wafting over unconscious grandpa's face is collecting up in between the wooden ceiling rafters of the cottages gabled thatched roof.

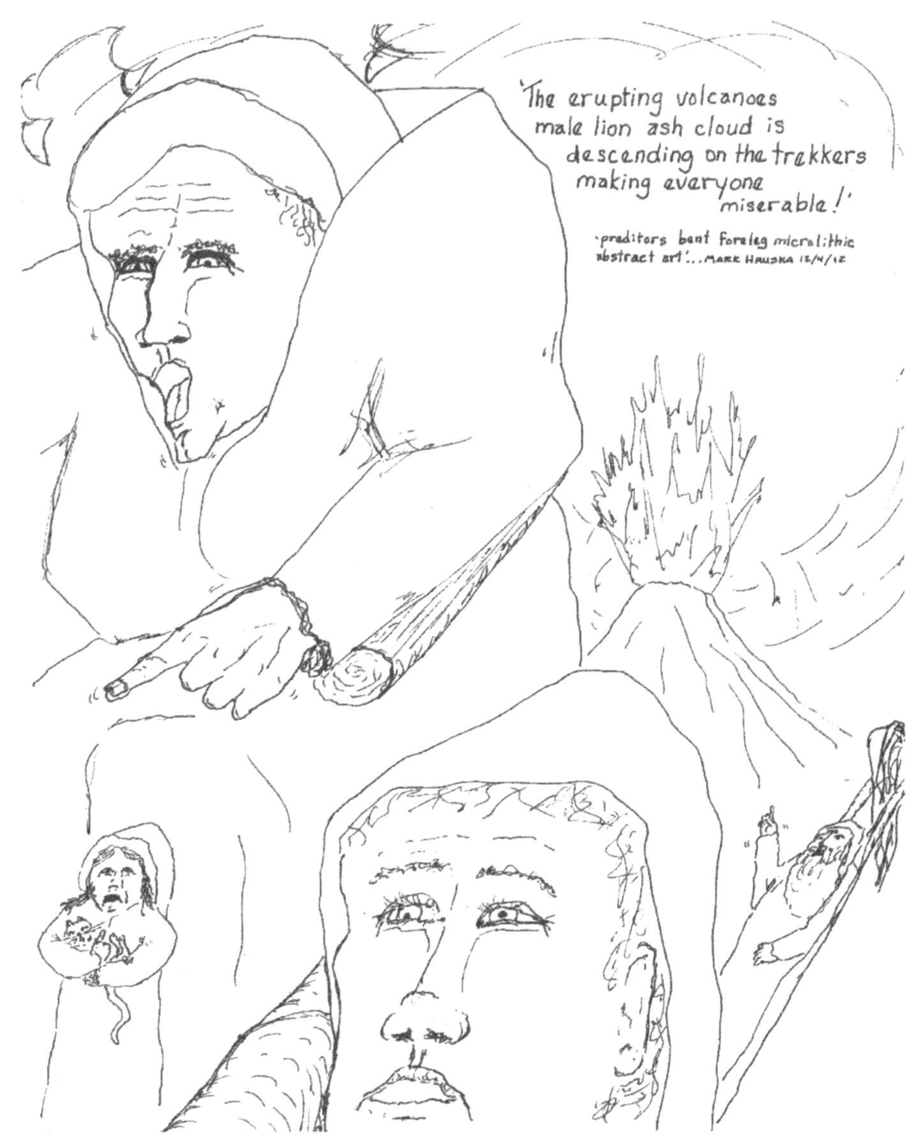

'predators bent foreleg microlithic abstract art'... 'The erupting volcanoes male lion ash cloud is descending on the trekkers making everyone miserable!'

145) And as you can see, his extended forelegs' paws claws are closest to the top of crotchety grandma's head.

160

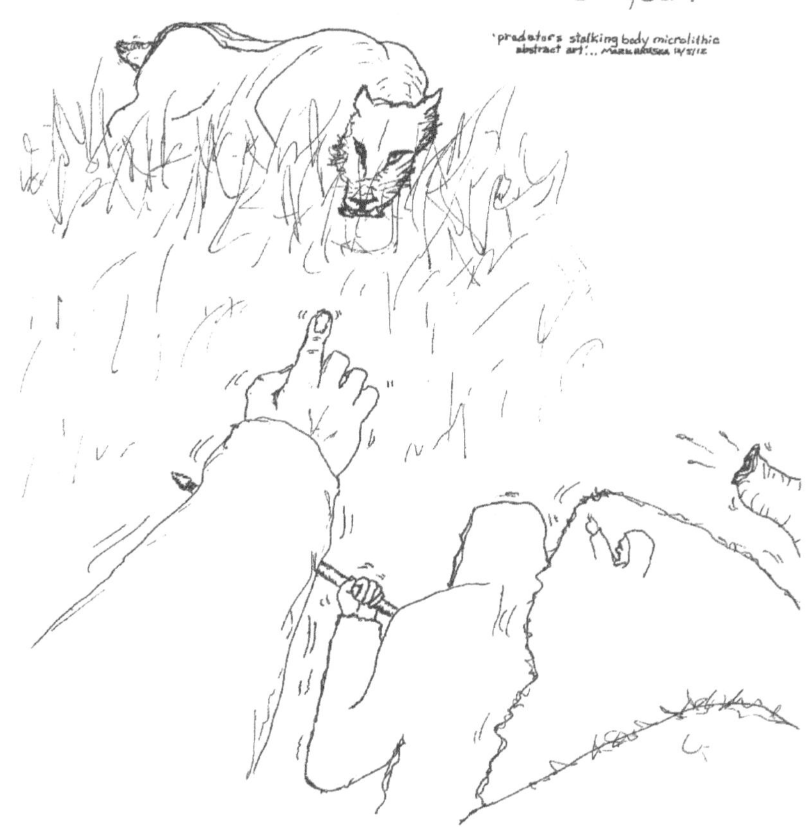

'predators stalking body microlithic abstract art'... '"It's the biggest stalking saber-toothed cat that you've ever seen and it's less than an ox length in front of you!"'

146) Notice how irate 'pointing' grandma's reflection is reflecting off of the back top part of the nervous lead mammoth's outwardly flapping left ear. This is the way that the hunter herder microlithic abstract artist can show how she looks from her exact position on her special armchair without actually having to show a close-up image of her yelling down at her lead hunter herder son who's out in front of the flapping ear. In fact, the whole Mammoth People 'backed' knife scraper eating utensil artwork may be just the close-up statuesque image of the nervous lead mammoth's flapping left ear that everything behind and in front of is reflecting off of, and the backed edge is the invisible outline of the 'stub' end of the ear.

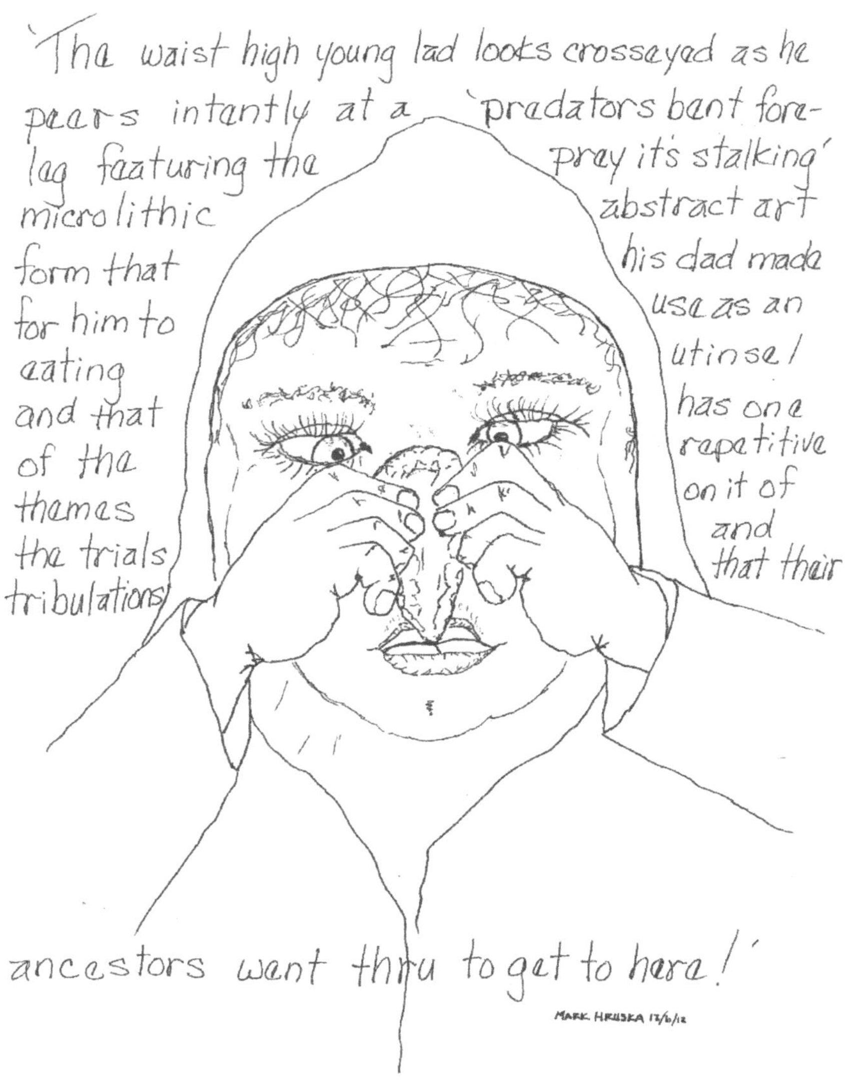

12/6/12… 'The waist high young lad looks cross-eyed as he peers intently at the 'predators bent foreleg featuring the prey its stalking' microlithic abstract art form that his dad made for him to use as an eating utensil and that has one of the repetitive themes on it of the trials and tribulations that their ancestors went thru to get to here!'

147) The only thing that I would add to this statement after several more years of research after having written it… is that they were all 'epic' trials and tribulations and that those repetitive themes were the basis for the popular folklore tales being told the Mammoth People children.

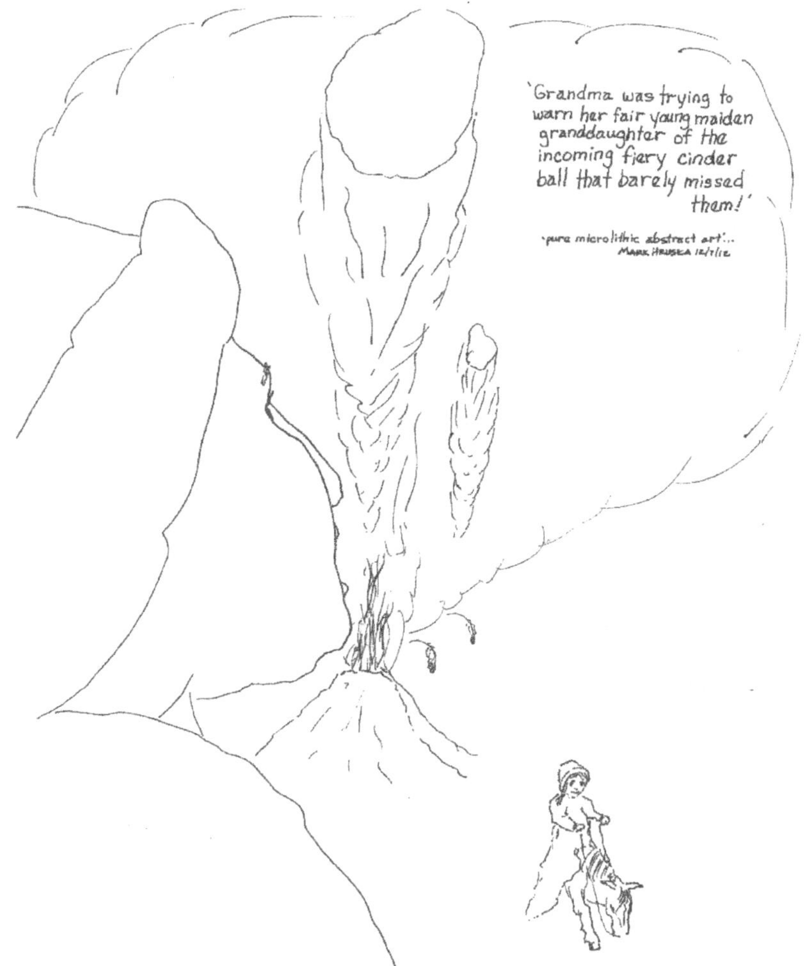

'pure microlithic abstract art'... 'Grandma was trying to warn her fair young maiden granddaughter of the incoming fiery cinder ball that barely missed them!'

148) The screaming white hot cinder balls were seen by grandma as the roaring male lion ash cloud's lioness mate that he sent 'screaming' towards the fleeing trekkers. Sometimes the screaming lioness cinder ball, albeit much smaller than the ones seen in the illustration, landed on the back of crotchety grandma's neck or on the back of one of her gnarled old hands and scorched a hole in them which is what made her so crotchety in the first place. When she looked down at the fiery white hot cinder ball on the back of her gnarled old hand that was gripping the end of her special armchair in agonizing pain, she saw the lioness cinder ball sitting on her scorching haunches with her back turned towards crotchety grandma while she looked smugly back at her over her left shoulder as if to say "Mine... all mine...'"

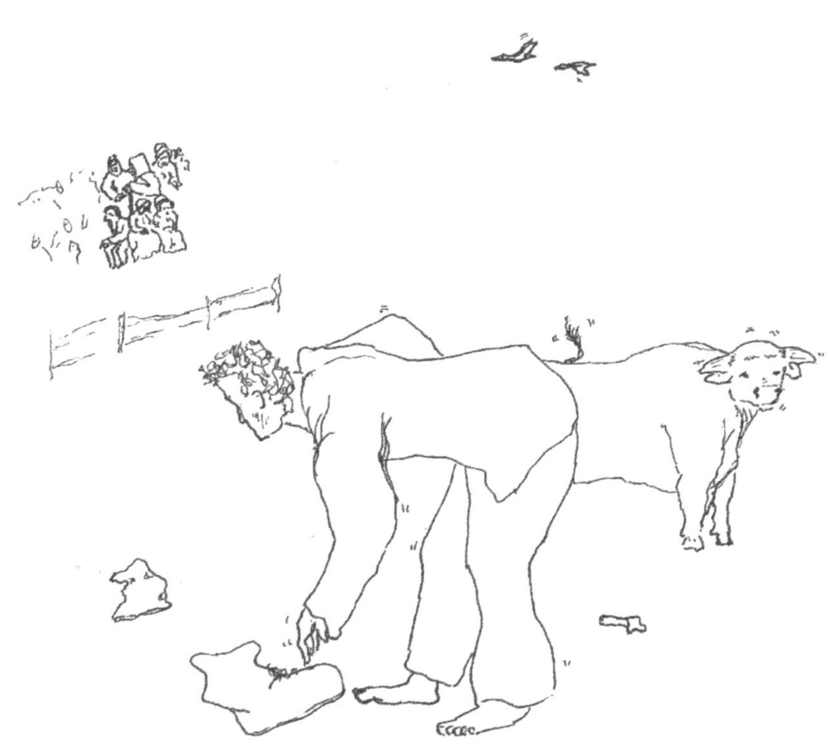

''boot' microlithic abstract art'... 'Grandpa's cursing at the poor performance after the bucking bull jerked his grandson cleanly out of his sea lion pup pelt boots!'

149) This piece shows the flying ducks for two reasons. One is that it places the bull riding rodeo event in the spring or more likely in the fall during waterfowl migrations. The second reason was to show exactly how high the bucked off teenager flew when he was jerked cleanly out of his fancy boots.

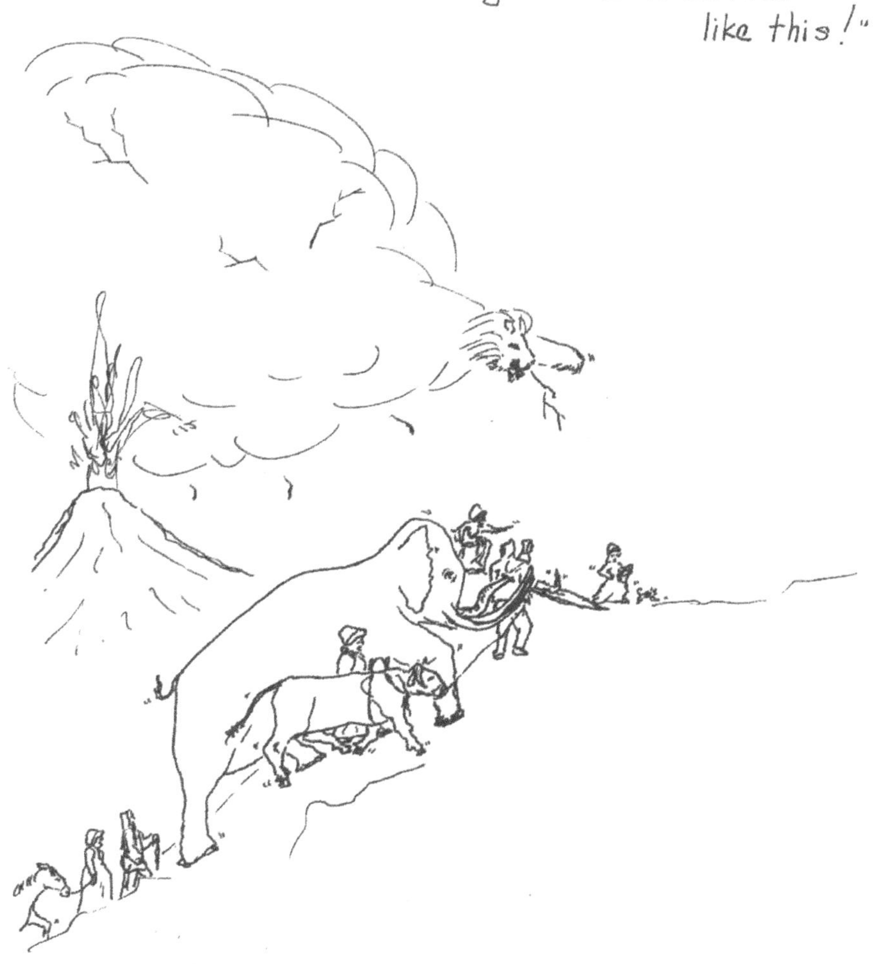

'pure microlithic abstract art'... Mark Hruska 12/9/12

'pure microlithic abstract art'... 'Mom doesn't realize that they're just getting started on their epic journey... "Honey...we can't go much further like this!"'

150) This microlithic abstract art works illustration is totally self-explanatory.

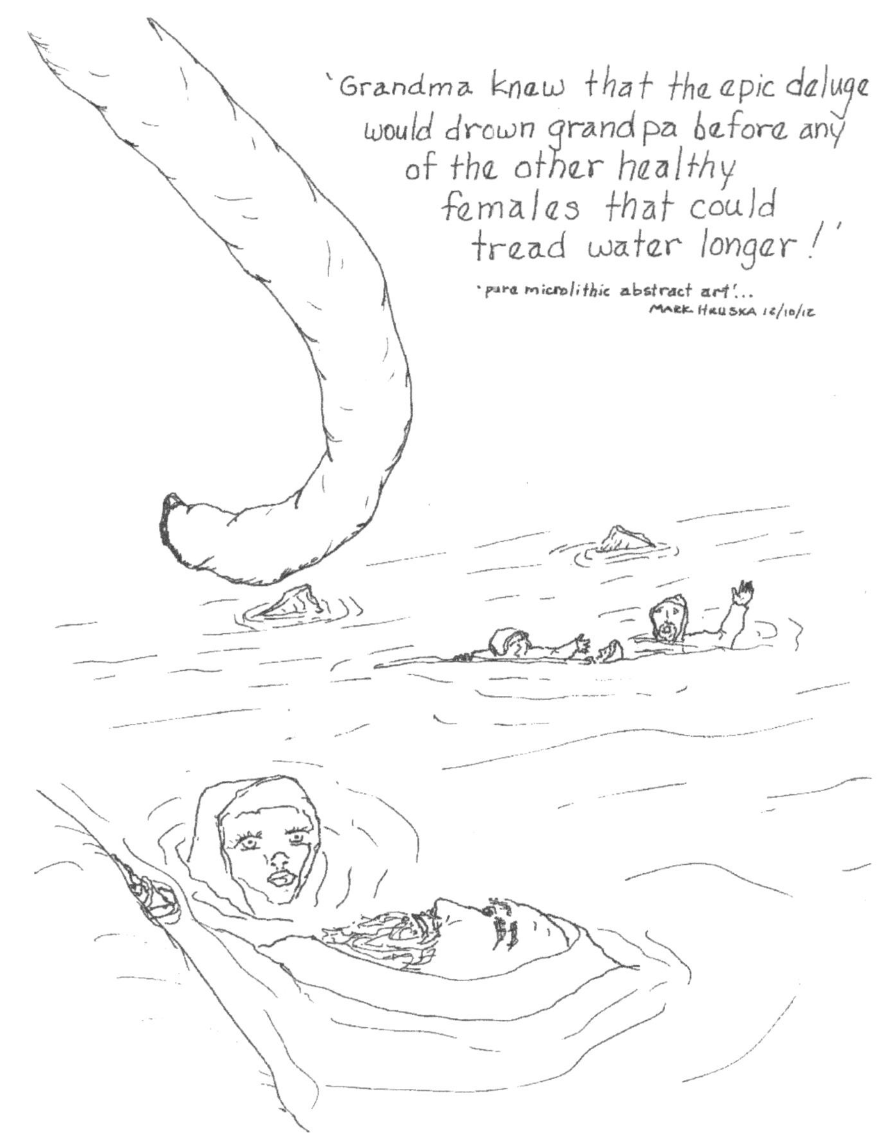

'pure microlithic abstract art'... 'Grandma knew that the epic deluge would drown grandpa before any of the other healthy females that could tread water longer!'

151) She's rescuing them with her shepherds crook and the help of her vivacious fair young maiden granddaughter, from her special armchair atop the swimming lead mammoth... and they're starting with grandpa.

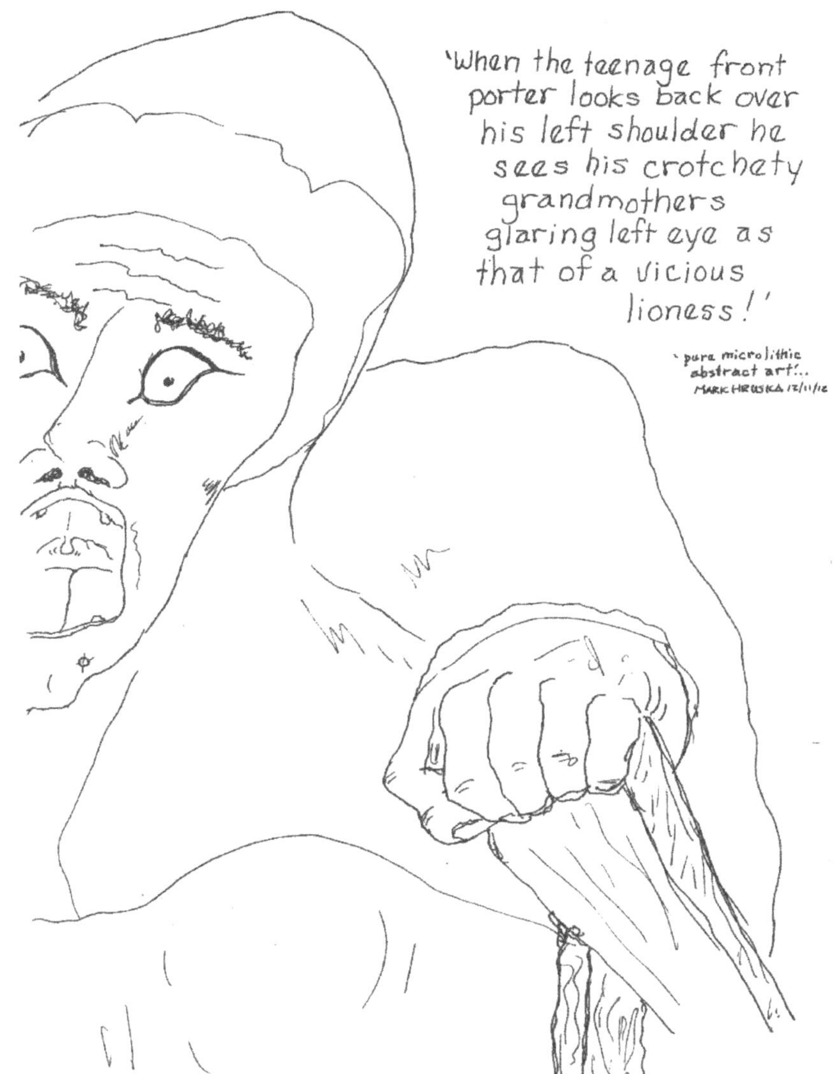

'pure microlithic abstract art'... 'When the teenage front porter looks back over his left shoulder he sees his crotchety grandmothers glaring left eye as that of a vicious lioness!'

152) Her left eye most likely looks like that of the lioness cinder ball that's sitting on her haunches scorching a hole on the back of one of crotchety grandma's old gnarled hands that are gripping the ends of her special armchair. The scorching lioness cinder ball would be looking smugly back at crotchety grandma over her left shoulder as she holds down her fresh prey.

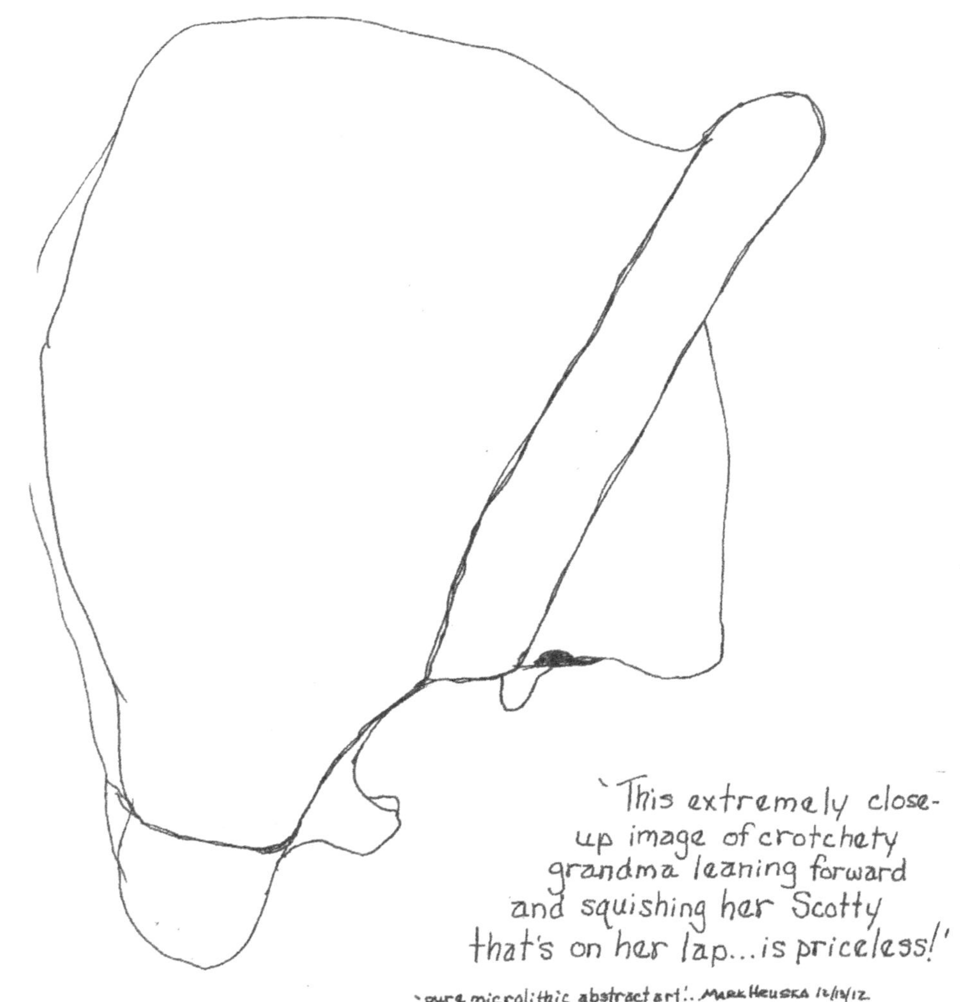

'pure microlithic abstract art'... 'This extremely close-up image of crotchety grandma leaning forward and squishing her Scotty that's on her lap...is priceless!'

153) On this pieces' illustration I was obviously trying to sketch the right side view of crotchety grandma's head as you saw it at that one distinctive angle on the microlithic abstract artwork. She's always wearing her cape hood over her bonnet and it's the frilled front edge of her bonnet that's encompassing the top and the right side of her yelling old face. If you could see that top tooth from the front of her it would appear to be a snaggletooth.

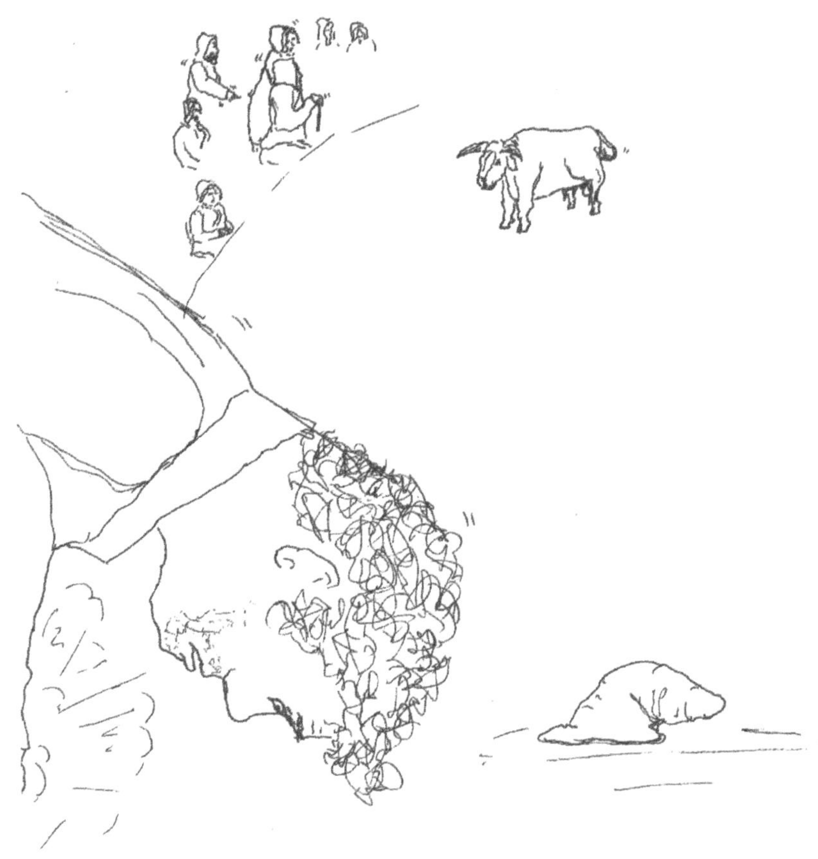

'prismatic flake knife' 'microlithic abstract art'...
'Grandma and grandpa are so disappointed in their
grandson's bull riding performance that they're getting up to go home!'

154) You'll also notice that the attractive fair young maiden who was sitting down to your lower left of them is the one that the teenage bull rider was trying too hard to impress, ignoring all the skills that his grandpa had coached him to apply.

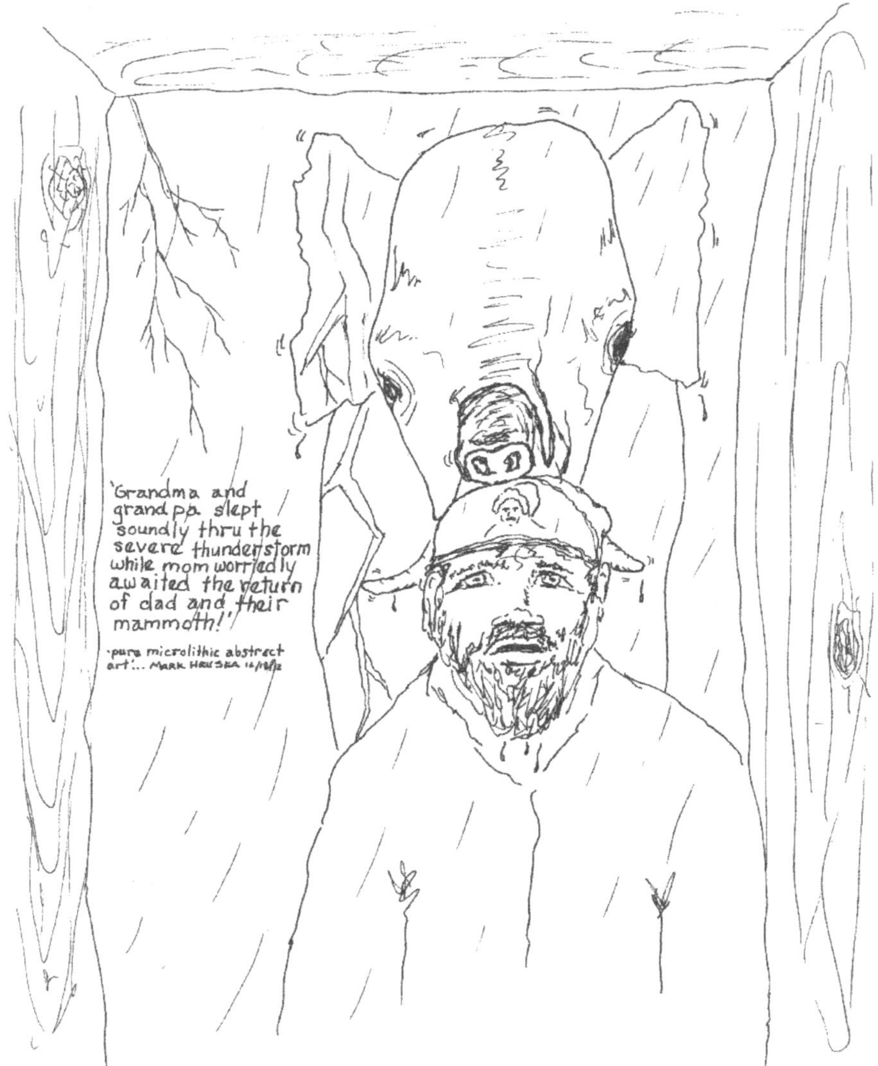

'pure microlithic abstract art'... 'Grandma and grandpa slept soundly thru the severe thunderstorm while mom worriedly awaited the return of dad and their mammoth!'

155) If you look closely, you'll see how I knew that mom looked worried when she opened the front door of their cottage to see that dad and their mammoth had made it back safely from checking on the folks while lightning snapped all around them. We also know that mammoth detest lightning. She appears to want to get into the cozy cottage with mom after that last close snap that's reflecting off of her right ear and on down the front right side of her front right leg. Do you suppose that dad walked all the way home just so he wouldn't be sitting on the highest object around as he rode atop the frightened mammoth?

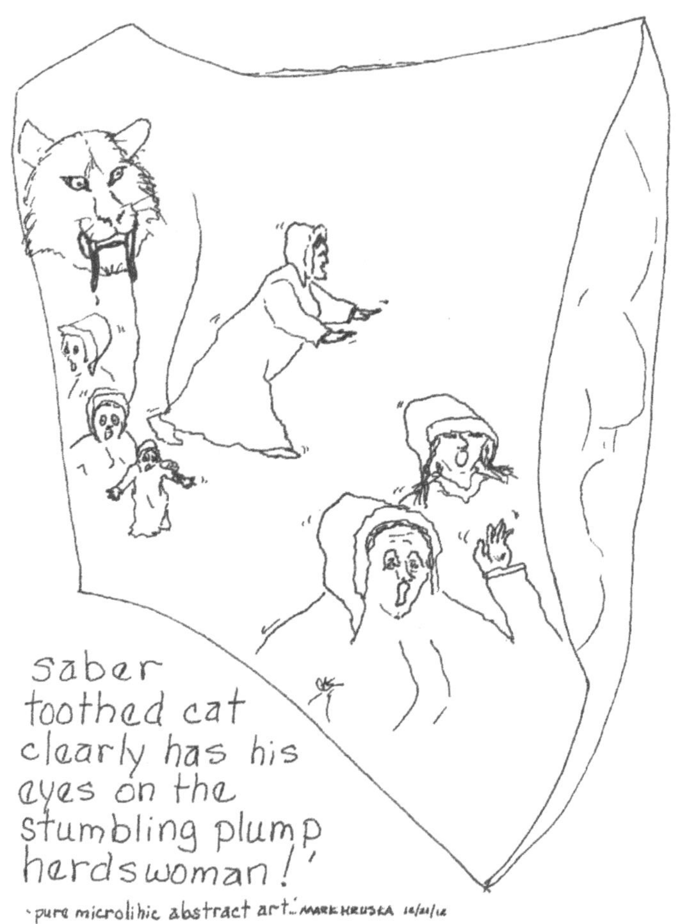

'pure microlithic abstract art'...'The youngsters
bonnet is slipping down over her eyes as she flees but the
saber toothed cat clearly has his eyes on the stumbling plump herdswoman!'

172

156) I just love this illustration that goes along with the pieces interpretation. The piece itself was most likely a flake knife eating utensil. You are to imagine in your 'mind's eye' that this summertime picnic scene is reflecting off of the right side of the fleeing herdswoman's cape hood that's over her bonnet and that's encompassing the right side of her horrified face. The whole artwork 'is' the combined optical and cognitive illusion close-up image of the right side view of her head. The concave curving edge that's to your lower left 'is' the invisible outline of the top of her right shoulder. Once you see this scene in your 'mind's eye' it's as if you are seeing this fleeing herdswoman's head this close up through the eyes of the saber-toothed cat...as if you could zoom into that further away image of her that's nearest the predator by simply taking a step back and viewing the whole piece. Notice too, how the top of her bonnet or cape hood that's covering her bonnet, is also the top of the stalking saber-toothed cats back and stalking left shoulder. The upper left corner of the piece is his right one. His combined optical and cognitive illusion image is an opposing image to his prey victims head because they are sharing the backs of their heads but instead of being face to face, he's looking towards her while she flees. Either way they're 'in' each other's heads thinking of each other in a predator prey way.

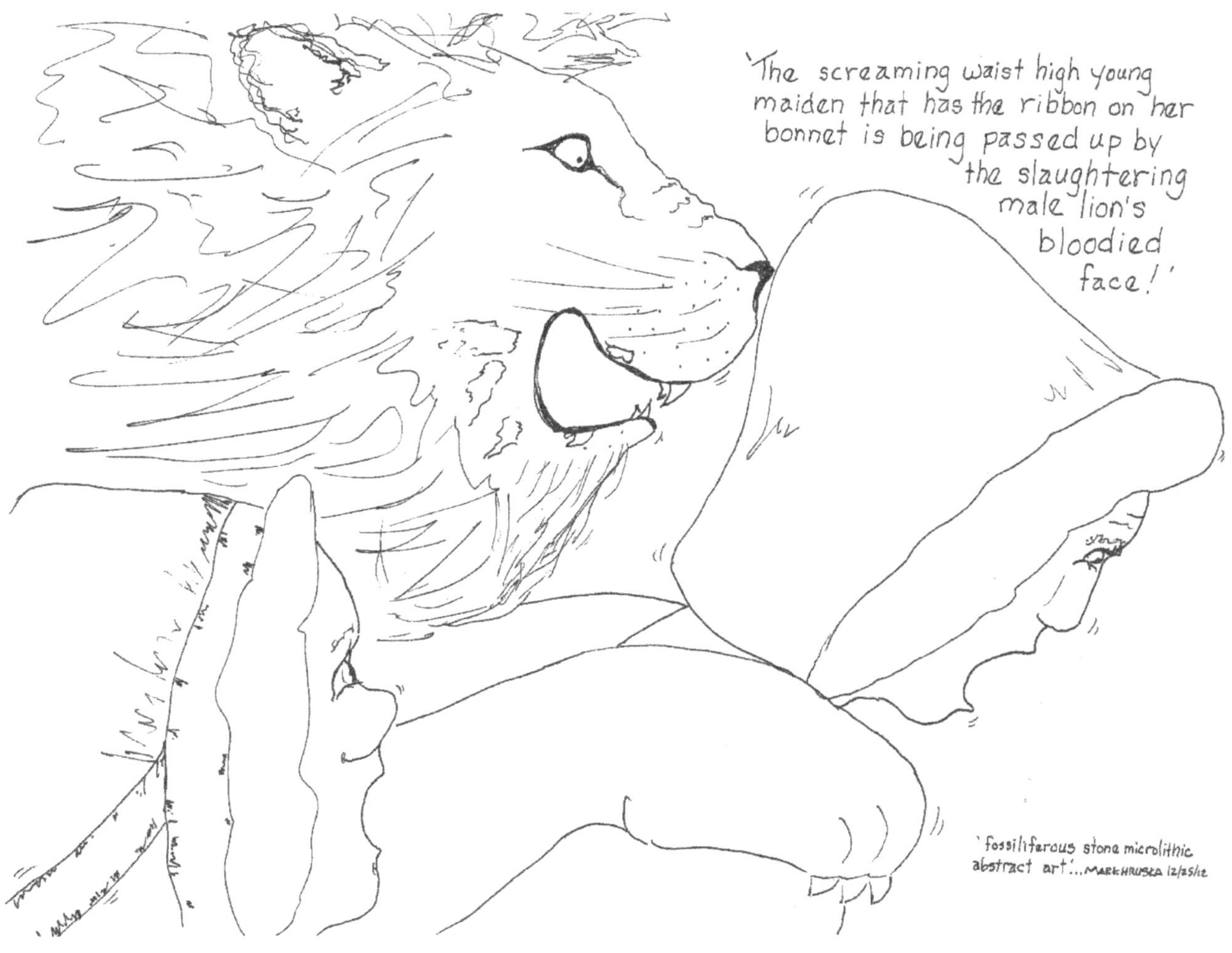

'fossiliferous stone microlithic abstract art'... 'The screaming waist high young maiden that has the ribbon on her bonnet is being past up by the slaughtering male lions bloodied face!'

157) This illustration is of the Mammoth People's summertime picnic that most likely had a pair of rogue male lions picnicking too.

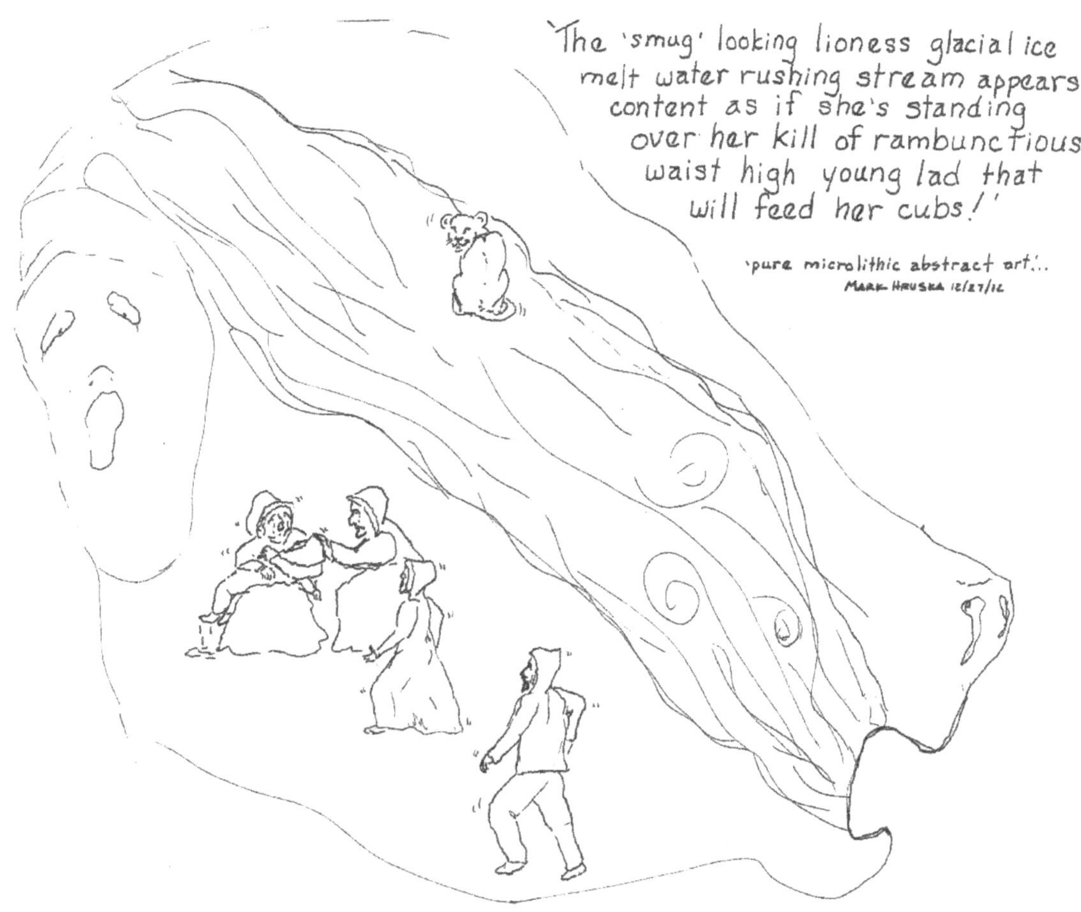

'pure microlithic abstract art'... 'The 'smug' looking lioness
glacial ice melt water rushing stream appears content as if she's standing
over her kill of rambunctious waist high young lad that will feed her cubs!'

158) It's how wailing grandma sees the roaring glacial ice meltwater stream when she and the rest of the lead family recover the waist high young lads limp body on a sandbar further downstream. He got away from grandma while she was busily helping prepare the evening meal and rambunctiously went down to the bank of the stream. The dizzying fast flowing water caused him to lose his balance and he fell in as prey to the predator glacial ice meltwater lioness stream.

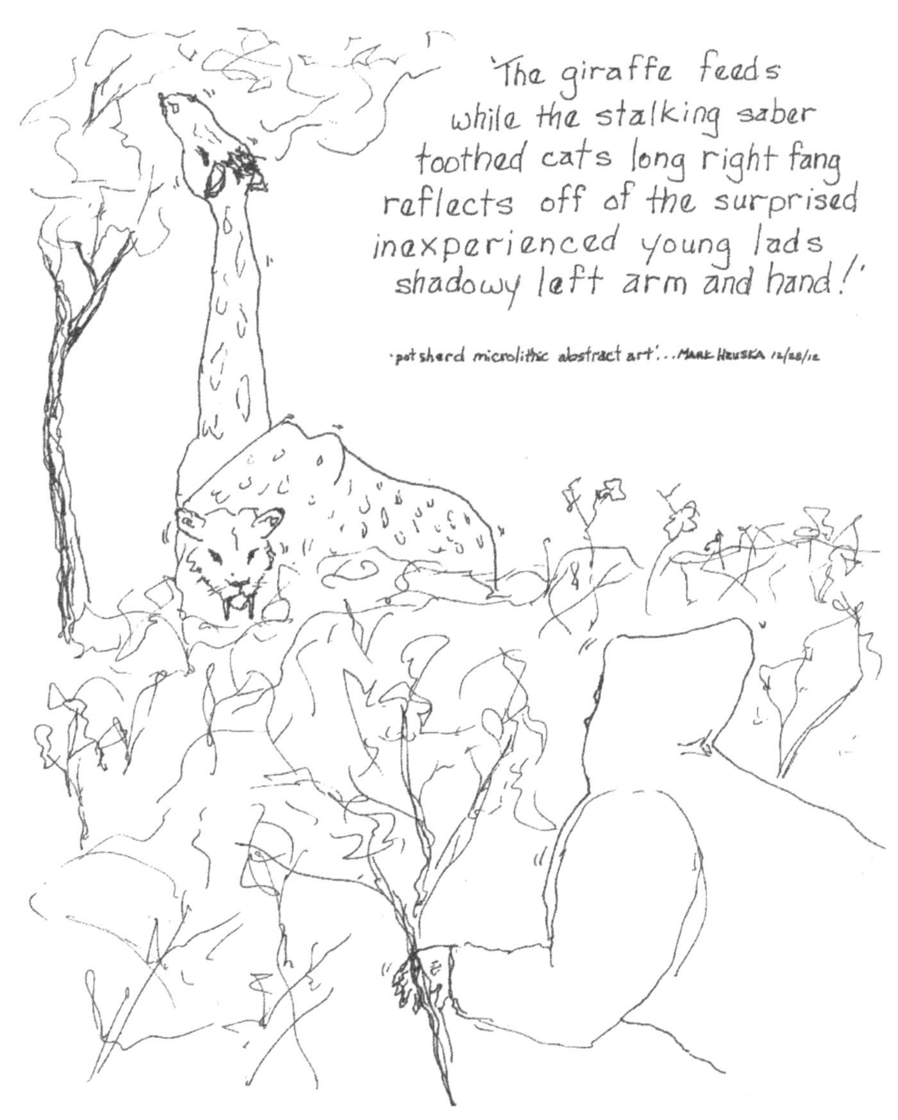

'potsherd microlithic abstract art'... 'The giraffe feeds
while the stalking saber toothed cats long right fang reflects off
of the surprised inexperienced young lads shadowy left arm and hand!'

176

159) First of all, you may be wondering how a potsherd can be called a microlith. Well... it's not the potsherd itself that's the microlith, rather it's the individual pieces of sand aggregate that are infused in it that are. They're actual individual rubbed and etched out combined optical and cognitive illusion reflection images of mostly heads and faces that are reflecting off of the whole piece which is usually a combined optical and cognitive illusion close-up image of a head and face. Secondly, you may be wondering how giraffes could have been in the middle of the North American continent, right? Well.... after seven years of research I'm convinced that they came with the Mammoth People trekkers in their long mammoth caravan. What verified that to me was when I repeatedly found them on the 'volcanic mass exodus' folklore tale. A pair of them is repeatedly seen trekking abreast of each other and when they pass up the fallen decrepit elderly herdswoman the one to the right lowers her long neck, her head and her sad looking face to view her in reverence.

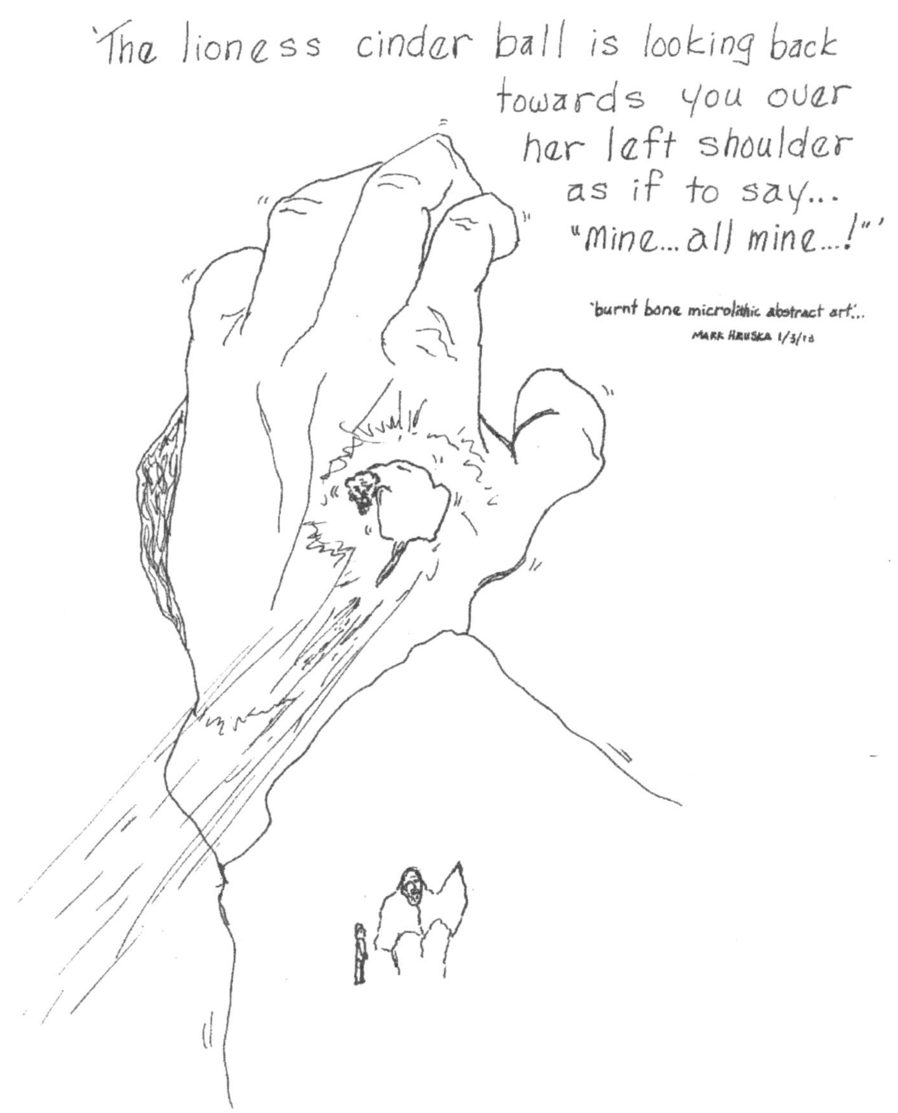

'burnt bone microlithic abstract art'... 'The lioness cinder ball is looking back towards you over her left shoulder as if to say... "mine...all mine!"'

160) This is a perfect illustration of what crotchety grandma sees when she looks down at her gnarled left hand that's being scorched by the smug lioness cinder ball.

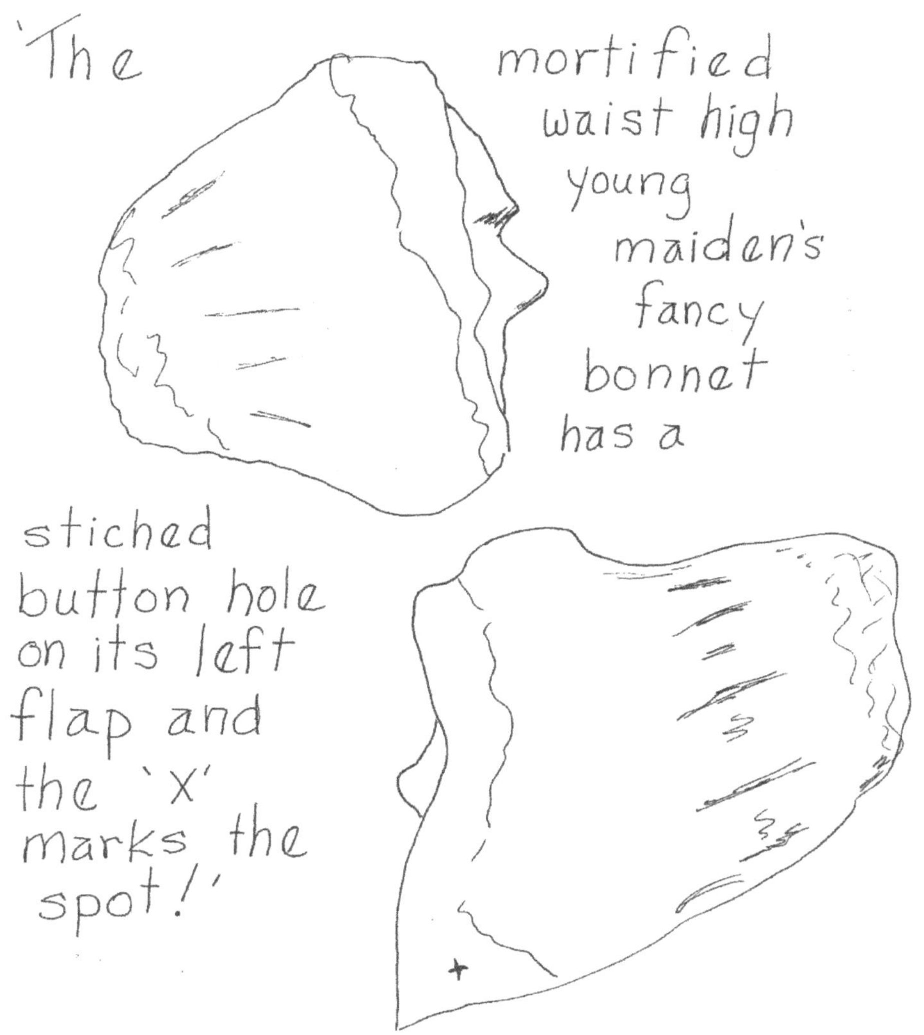

'potsherd microlithic abstract art'... 'The mortified waist high young maiden's fancy bonnet has a stitched button hole on its left flap and the 'x' marks the spot!'

161) This potsherd most likely has the 'opposing heads' of crotchety grandma and the mortified waist high young maiden's bonnet covered heads that are sharing one side of their heads. I remember being pretty excited when I realized that that left flap had a button hole in it.

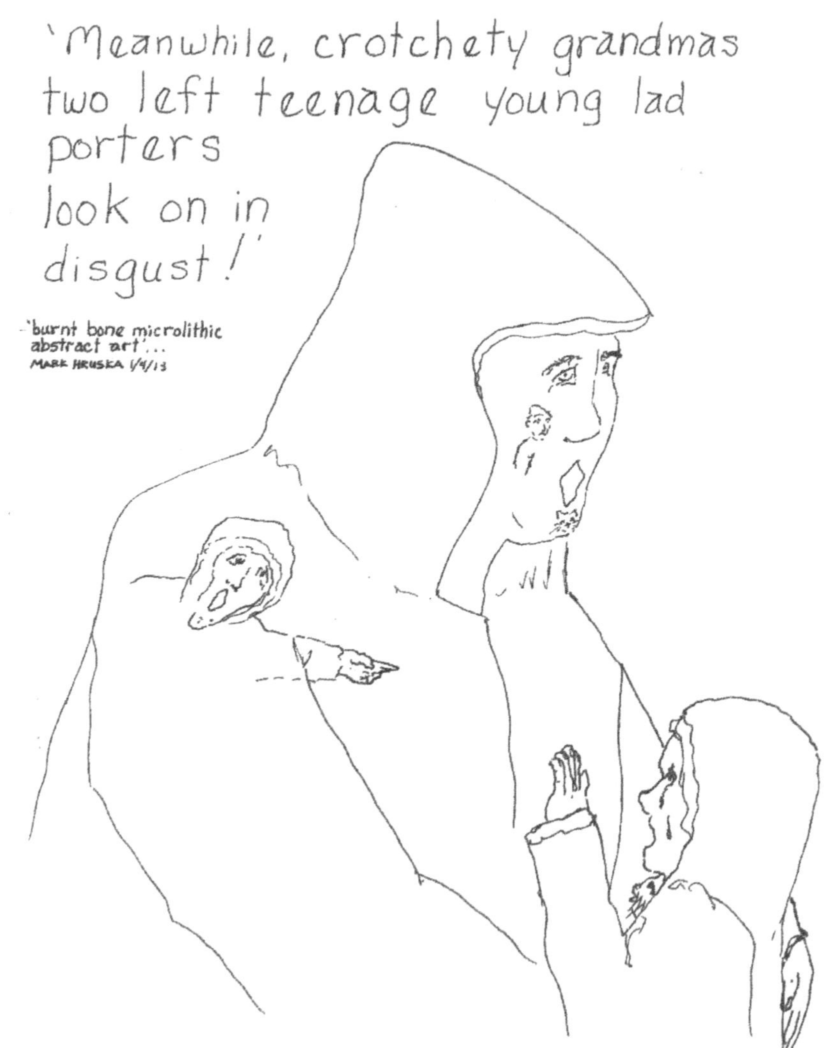

'burnt bone microlithic abstract art'... 'Meanwhile, crotchety
grandma's two teenage young lad left porters look on in disgust!'

162) You very seldom get to see the back porters, but I've seen enough repetition to know that the back left one was another teenage young lad just like crotchety grandma's teenage young lad grandson front left one who is trying to console his sobbing little sister.

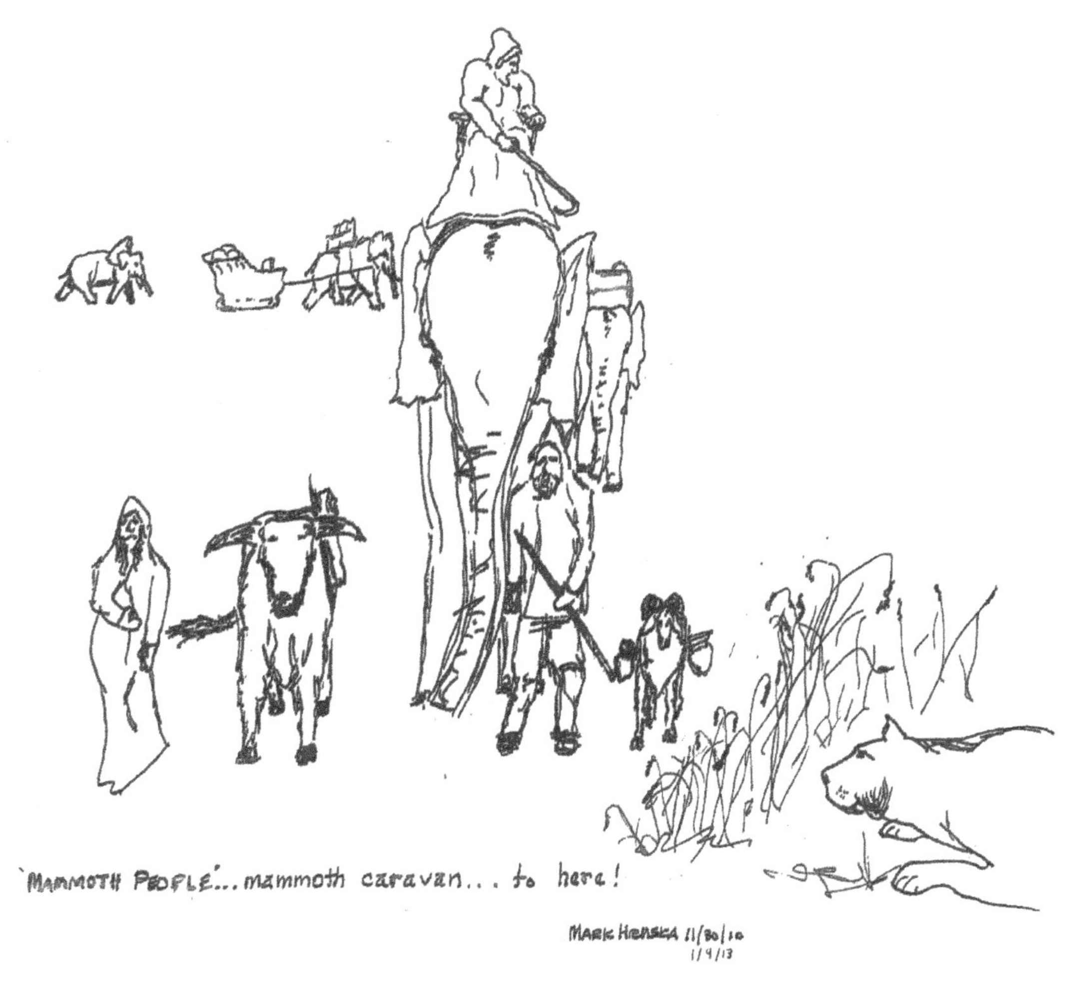

'1/9/13' 'MAMMOTH PEOPLE'...mammoth caravan...to here!'

163) On this previous illustration from 11/30/10 I decided to make an addendum by adding grandma sitting on her special armchair atop the lead mammoth where she had her bird's eye view of their surroundings and was able to spot the big cats that lurked out ahead of them in the tall swaying prairie grass.

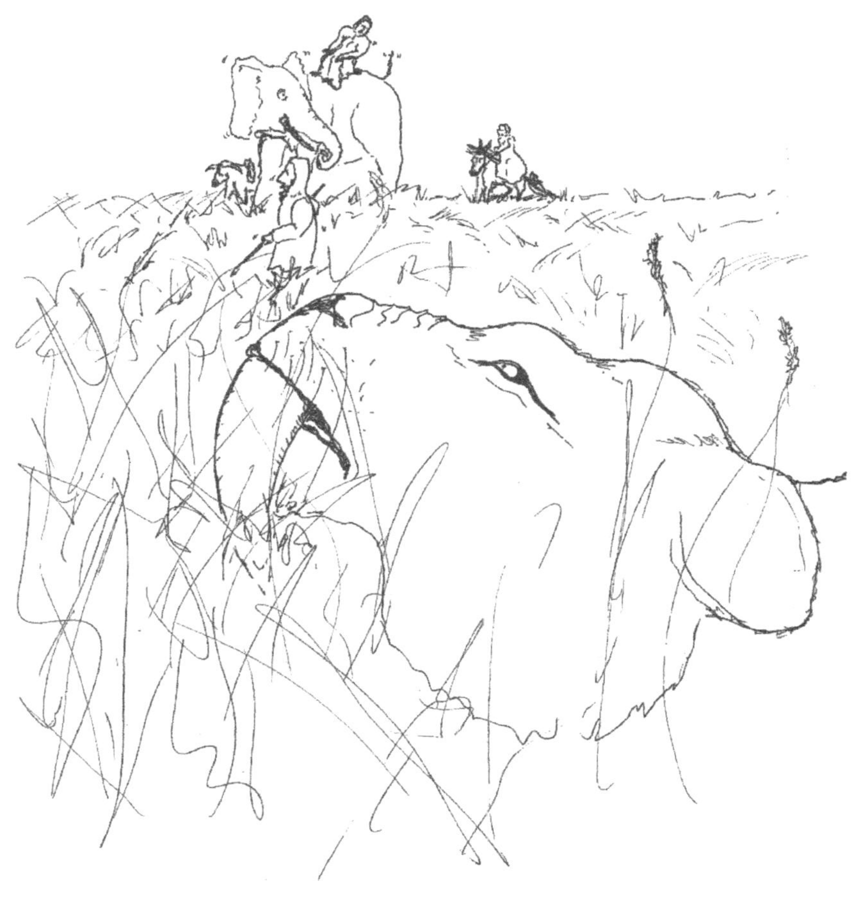

'stone microlithic abstract art'... '...well...if you see a saber
toothed cat's saber tooth fang this close up, you know what's coming next...'

164) This artworks illustration is awesome in that it shows the details of the scene clearly. The lead family is clearly searching for the lurking big cat that irate grandma swears that she saw out ahead of the lead mammoth and her lead hunter herder son. Shortly though, the overanxious fair young maiden will ride her nervous snorting horse 'too' far out ahead of her dad and easily find the lurking saber-toothed cat.

"The Mammoth People
hunter herder's
figurative microlithic
abstract art language
'is' the latch key that
unlocks the time portal
to the Pleistocene!"

.... "it just is what it is"....Mark Hruska 1/13/13

'What the Mammoth People Believed In'

The Mammoth People believed in the spirits of their ancestors that went thru epic trials and tribulations to get to 'here'! They didn't believe in a 'singular' god but they did believe that the flying 'submissive ewe spirit' would come swooping down during a crisis and simply suck up the dying Mammoth People persons last exhaled breath which was their 'spirit' and transport it into the heavens to be with their deceased ancestors.

.... "it just is what it is"....Mark Hruska 1/13/13

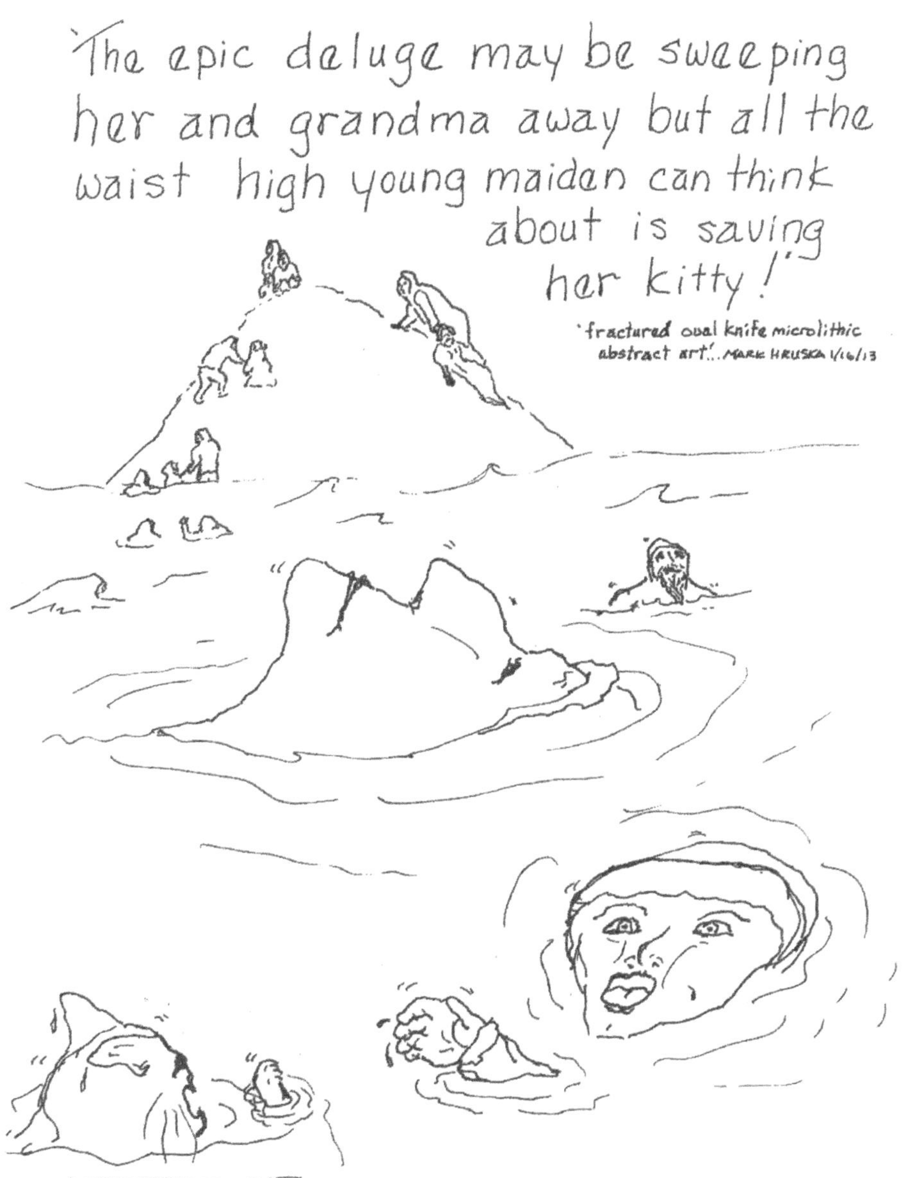

'fractured oval knife microlithic abstract art'... 'The epic deluge may be sweeping her and grandma away but all the waist high young maiden can think about is saving her kitty!'

165) This pieces illustration is self-explanatory.

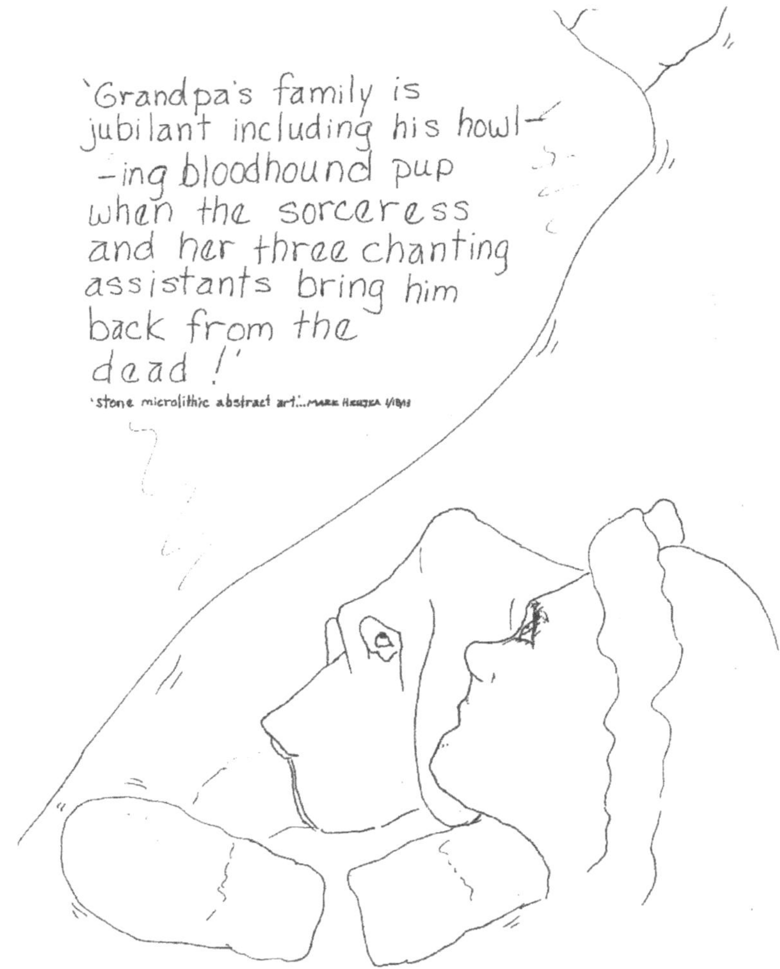

'stone microlithic abstract art'... 'Grandpa's family
is jubilant including his howling bloodhound pup when the
sorceress and her three chanting assistants bring him back from the dead!'

166) A pair of viper snakes bit grandpa when he laid down to take a nap while out walking his loyal bloodhound pup in the mountainous terrain of their beloved homeland. He fell into a deep slumber that could only be lifted during an exorcism ceremony in which the sorceress beckoned the stellar sea eagle spirit to lift the spell while she wafted thick smoke from the fireplace over his unconscious bearded face. Naturally the suffocating smoke brought the old coot sputtering back to life... and everyone celebrated.

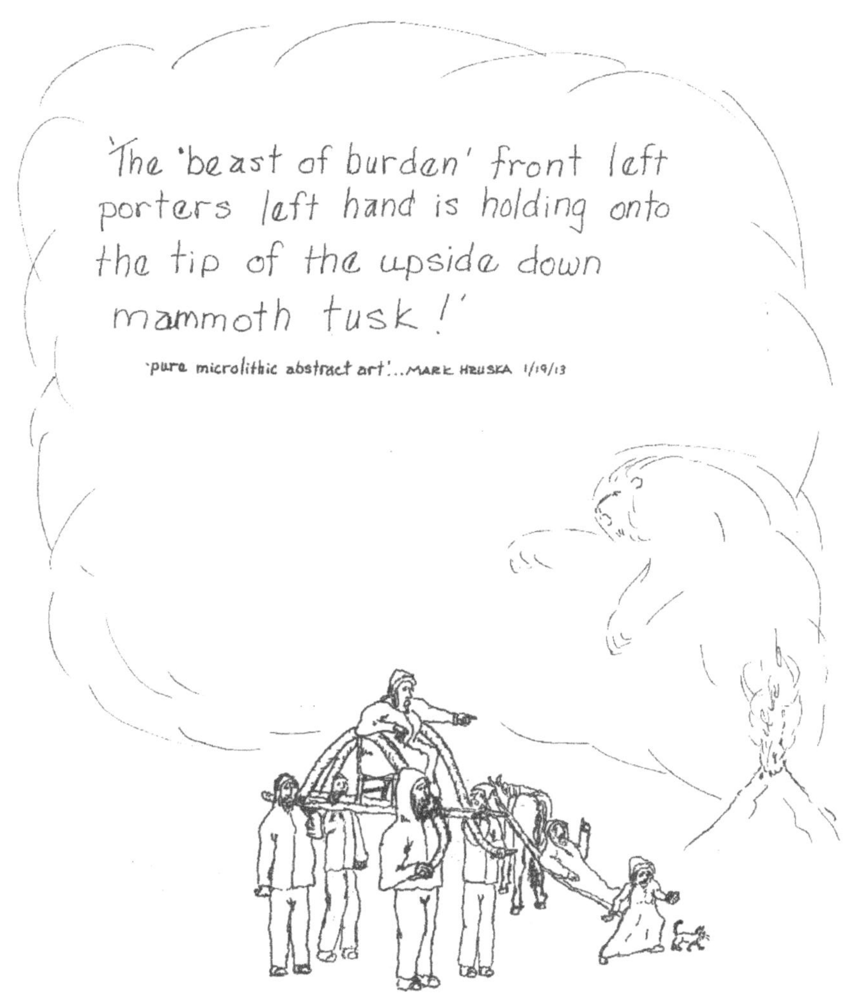

'pure microlithic abstract art'... 'The 'beast of burden' front left
porters left hand is holding onto the tip of the upside down mammoth tusk!'

167) This pieces illustration show's another image of how I envisioned the fleeing trekkers especially the front porters that carried crotchety grandma on her special armchair. The teenager's left hand would look like his stern dads right one as they grasped the end of the tusks. In most of the scenes from this folklore tale, they're simply carrying the special armchair that's attached to a stretcher on their shoulders or hanging from their hands depending on the steepness of the volcanic mountainous terrain. It's the steepness of the terrain that forces them to carry her instead of having her ride atop the lead mammoth.

'Bird head imagery'

Archaeologist's think that they're seeing 'bird head' imagery on stone made by Paleo man when in reality in most cases they're seeing the Mammoth People's 'submissive ewe spirits' head image that was created by the Caucasian Mammoth People hunter herder microlithic abstract artist's!

.... "it just is what it is"....Mark Hruska 1/19/13

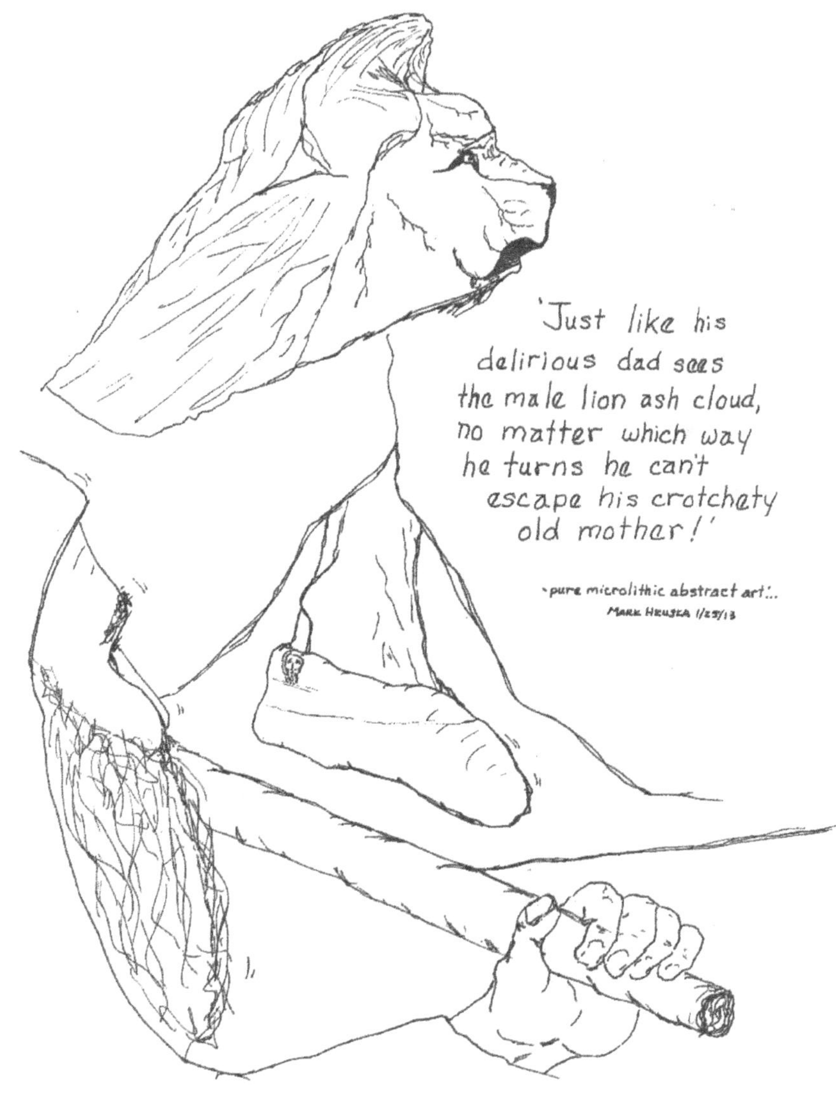

'pure microlithic abstract art'... 'Just like his delirious dad sees the male lion ash cloud, no matter which way he turns he can't escape his crotchety old mother!'

168) When stern dad looks back to his left over his sore left shoulder, he sees his reflection reflecting off of the outside side of his crotchety mother's old right foots shoe....near the heel.

'The Mammoth Peoples Religion'

The Mammoth Peoples religion was simply honoring their ancestors by recreating scenes of the epic trials and tribulations that they went thru to get to 'here' starting with the most important and common one of when they fled from the erupting volcano and its pursuing ash cloud. They created these scenes on 'every' tool that they made and then used which they felt somehow gave them a blessing from their ancestors.....while at the same time teaching their children valuable survival lessons and of their heritage..............

.... "it just is what it is"....Mark Hruska 1/21/13

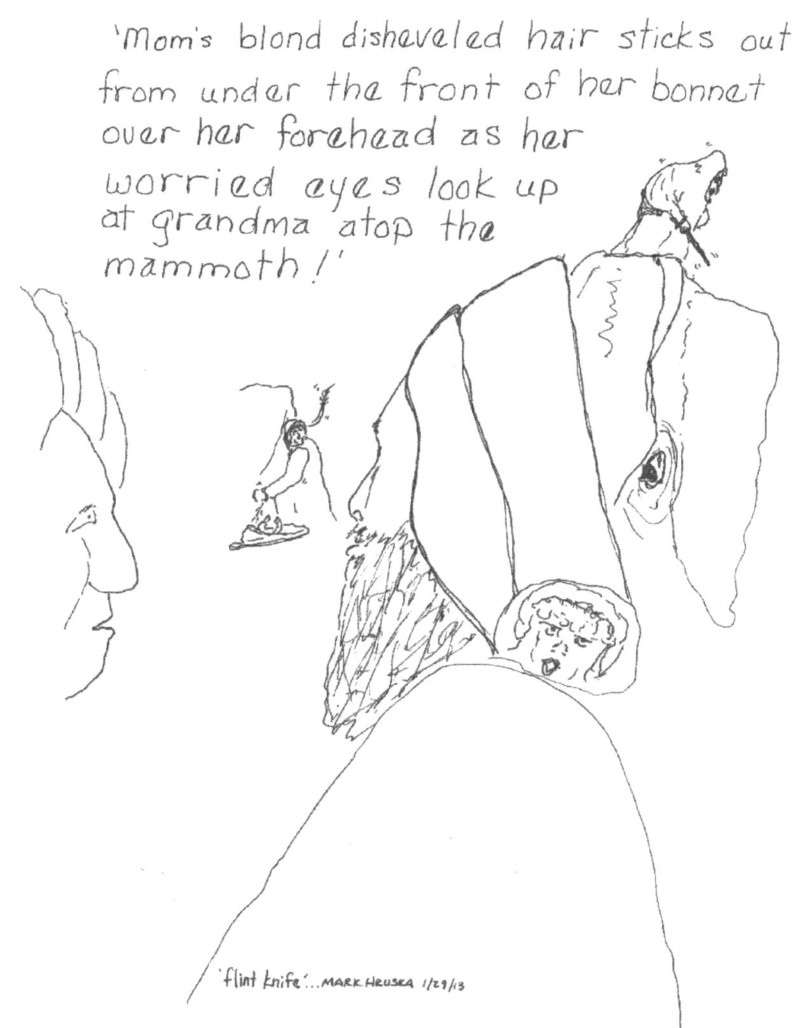

'flint knife'... 'Moms blond disheveled hair sticks out from under her bonnet
over her forehead as her worried eyes look up at grandma atop the mammoth!'

169) In this illustrations scene of the 'powwow', mom looks up and back over her left shoulder towards her yelling mother in law as she tries to silence her screaming infant. Meanwhile the screaming fair young maiden runs up to the powwow and her lead hunter herder dad who's standing face to face in front of the gruff chief. The front of her screaming childlike face is reflecting off of the left side of stern dad's vintage sailor style summertime hat. Irate grandma was barking out orders to everyone around her especially her two grandchildren who she loudly instructed to stand right next to their dad because he had a big spear.

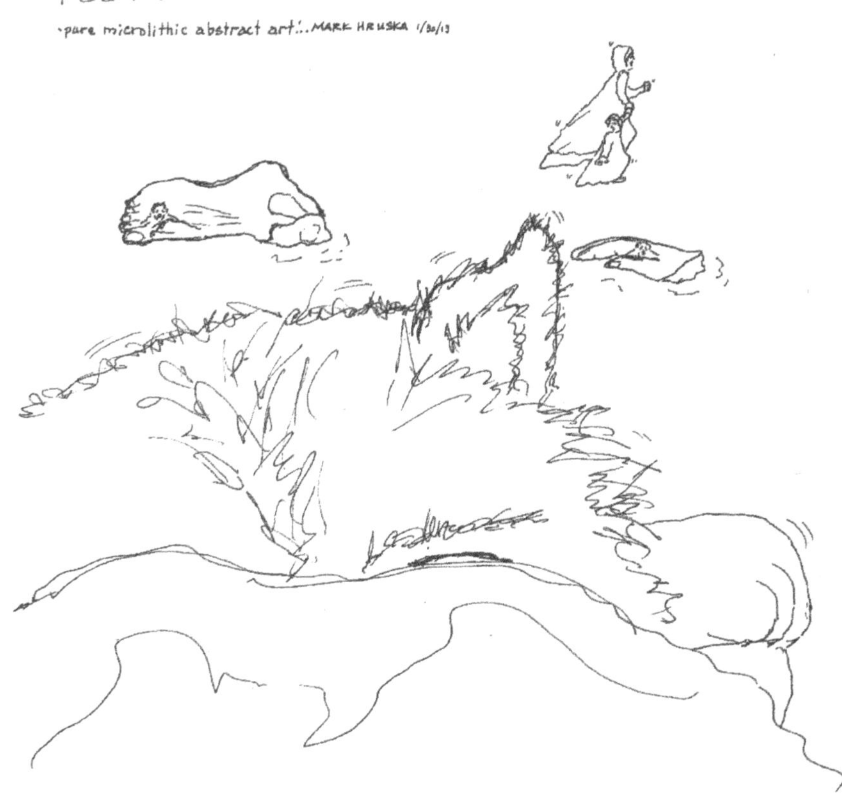

'pure microlithic abstract art'... 'The plump herdswoman's severed
right hand is an 'opposing severed body part' to her severed right foot!'

170) In this pieces illustration you are to imagine yourself in the position of the 'taken down' herdswoman prey. In other words what you perceive while you are lying supine and looking down towards your belly is the top front part of the ravenous dire wolf's head that's eating your entrails while all the other picnickers flee for their own lives. You can also see your horrified dead face that has wide opened glazed over eyes, reflecting off of your severed right foot and right hand! Yes... this is how the Mammoth People hunter herder's microlithic abstract art...works. It was definitely a different world....

192

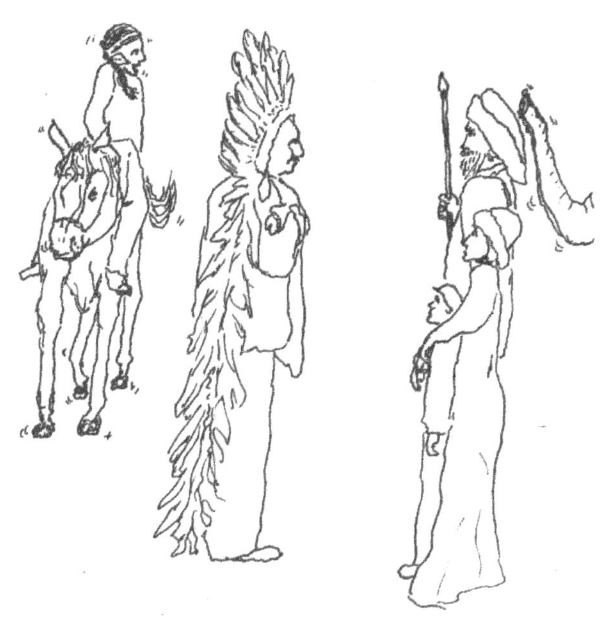

'pure microlithic abstract art'... 'The two youngsters are looking up over the gruff chief at the taunting and jeering warrior braves face. I bet his name is 'Twisted Feather'!'

171) In this pieces illustration I am continuing to piece together all aspects of the 'powwow' folklore tale but haven't gotten the whole story yet.

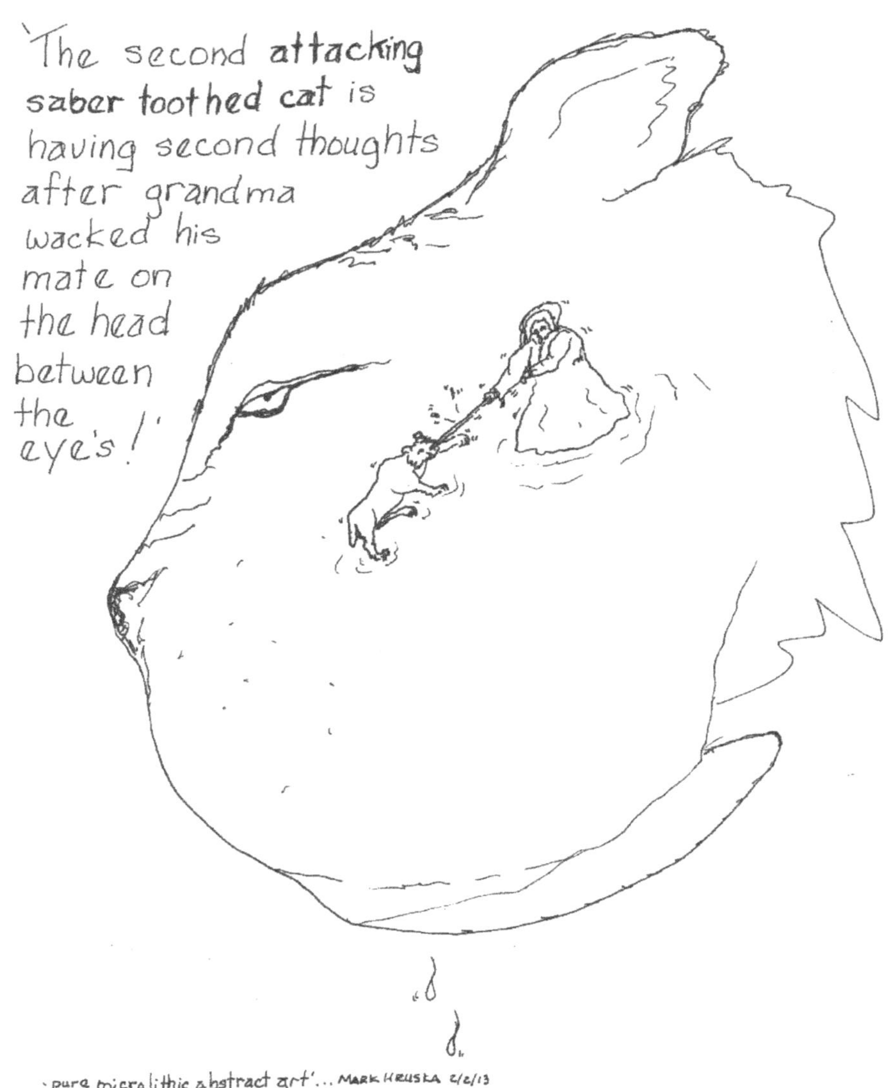

'The second attacking saber toothed cat is having second
thoughts after grandma whacked his mate on the head between the eyes!'

172) You can clearly see her whacking his mate over the head as they reflect off of the left side of his shying away face.

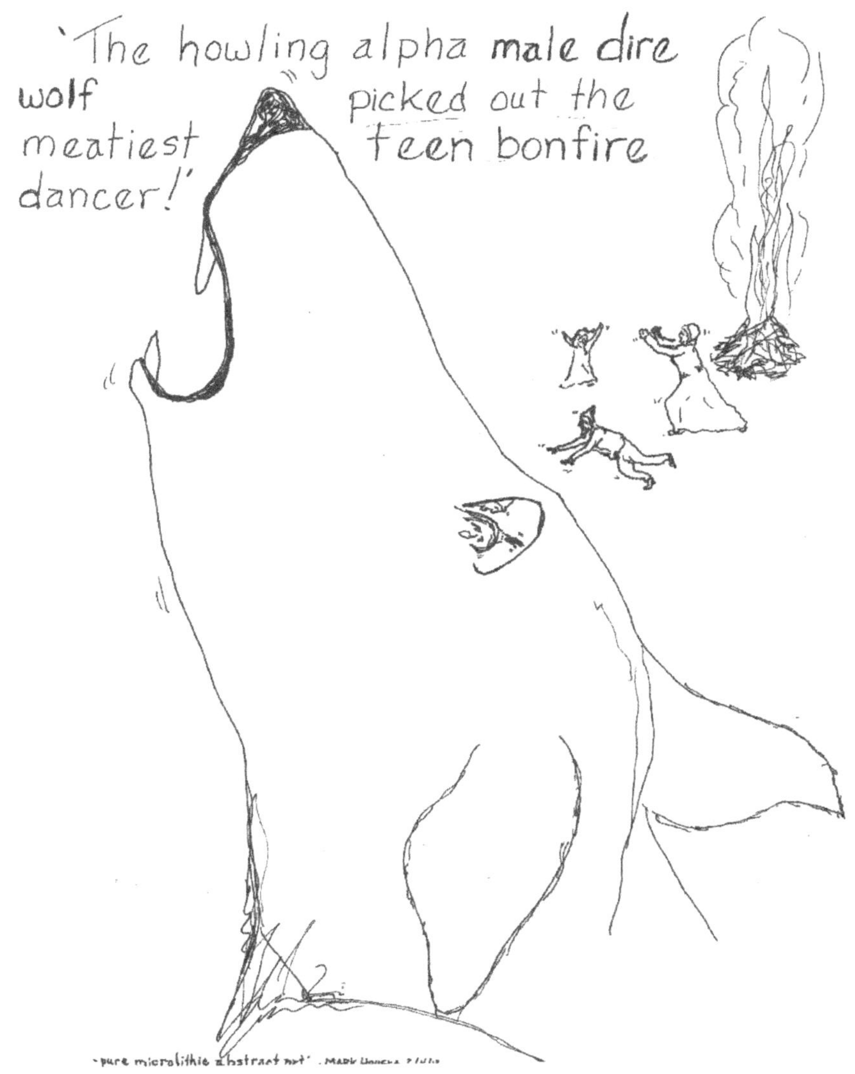

'pure microlithic abstract art'... 'The howling alpha
male dire wolf picked out the meatiest teen bonfire dancer!'

173) This pieces illustration should be fairly self-explanatory. The 'teenage bonfire' repetitive theme is not very common simply because the teenage hunter herder that was recreating it was more or less doodling and not creating the same boring folklore tales that venerated their ancestors.

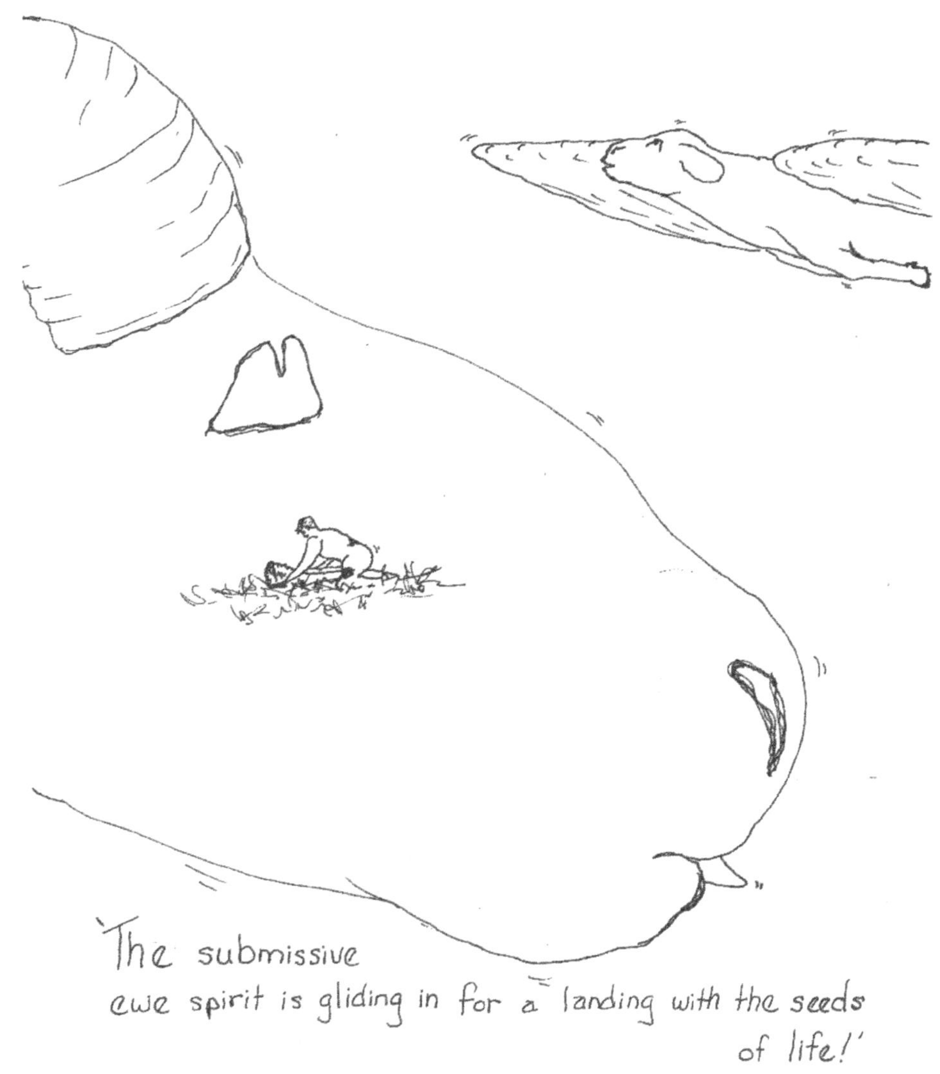

'mating stone knife'... 'The submissive ewe
spirit is gliding in for a landing with the seeds of life!'

196

174) I have to explain this pieces illustration beyond what appears so obvious and that is that the young couple is copulating out in the meadow where their domestic sheep and cattle are. It's also where the horny teenage hunter herders have to watch over their sheep and cattle to protect them from predators. In the springtime they had to have been constantly reminded of mating when they watched their mating cattle and sheep and there's one distinctive characteristic of mating rams that I learned from these Ice Age artist. That is that when a ram such as a black faced Shetland breed ram is riding the ewe and mating, the tip of his tongue will be seen sticking out of his mouth just like you see this ones that has the copulating couple reflecting off of the right side of his mating face!

Keep in mind that I'm not being disrespectful to the viewer, only respectful to the microlithic abstract artisan that created the artwork and planted this scene in my 'mind's eye'.

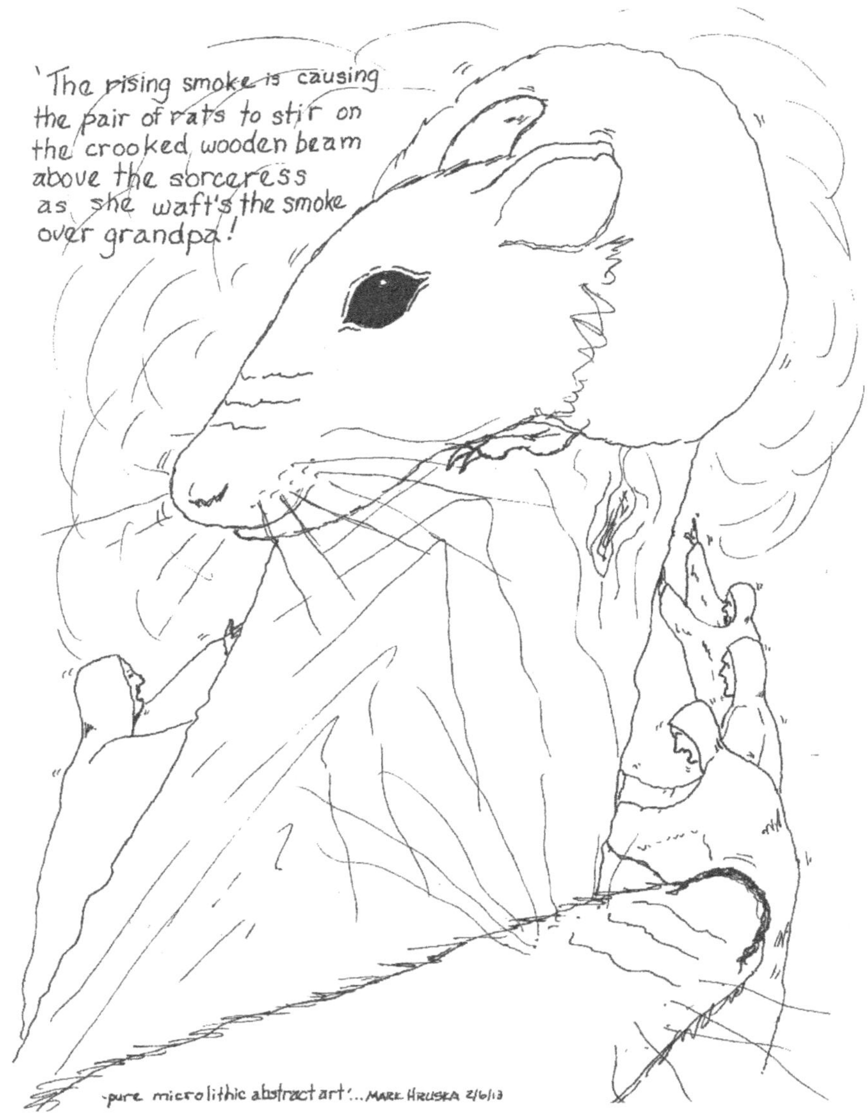

'pure microlithic abstract art'... 'The rising smoke is causing the pair of rats to stir on the crooked wooden beam above the sorceress as she wafts the smoke over grandpa!'

175) This is another one of those illustrations that I really like just because of the way that the hunter herder microlithic abstract artist made me see it in my 'mind's eye'. The sorceress is to your left raising her cloak covered arms or 'wing's' to the heavens while she recites incantations that are responded to by her three chanting assistants that can be seen bowing and then raising their heads back up to the heavens on the other side of the beam that the choking rats are hunkered down on. What's not seen are unconscious grandpa, his concerned bloodhound pup, his waist high young maiden granddaughter and her kitty that are all obviously directly under the wooden beam.

'prismatic knife'... 'The mammoth made her way towards the three survivors
and poor 'precious' was extremely concerned about being left to fend for himself!'

176) I later found out that this was a fairly popular version of the Mammoth People's folklore tale of the 'epic deluge'. The most important thing to the waist high young maiden's was their kitties and if the parents and grandparents wanted them to pay attention to the folklore tales nothing would make them pay more attention than to imagine having their kitty so violently taken away from them.

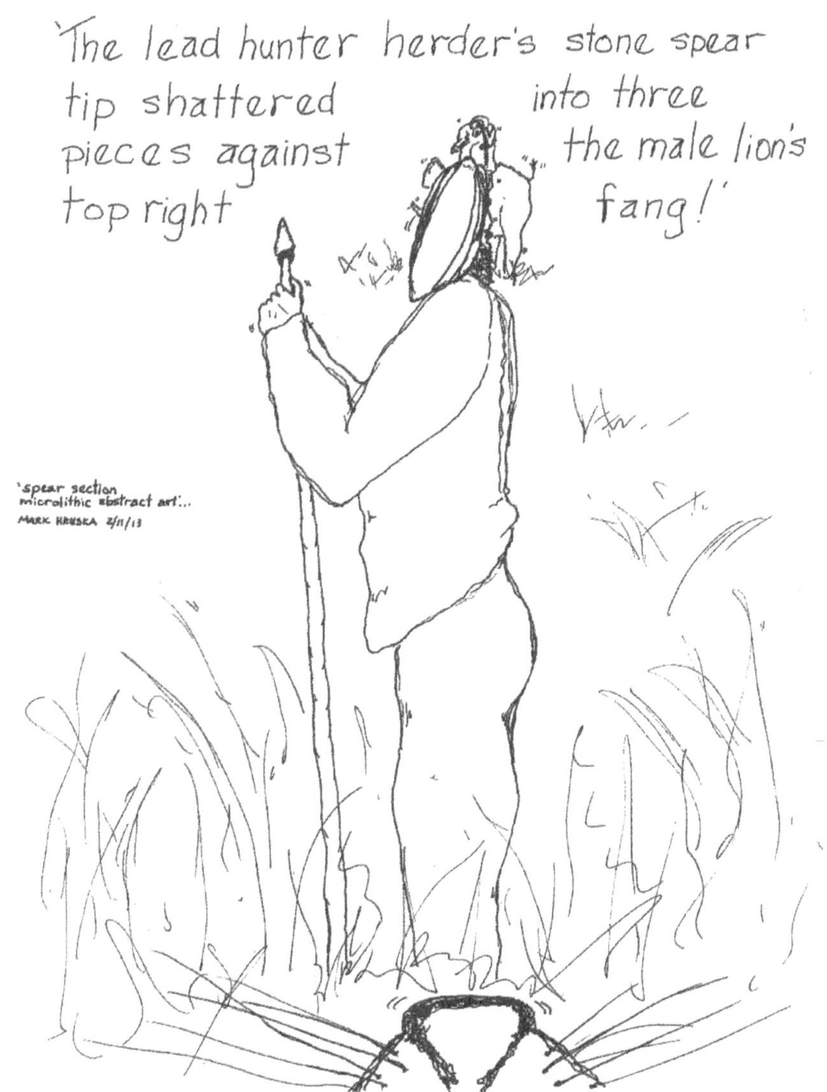

'spear section microlithic abstract art'... 'The lead hunter herder's
stone spear tip shattered into three pieces against the male lion's top right fang!'

177) The lead hunter herder is looking back over his right shoulder towards his elderly mother who's yelling back at him and pointing to exactly where she sees the lurking male lion.

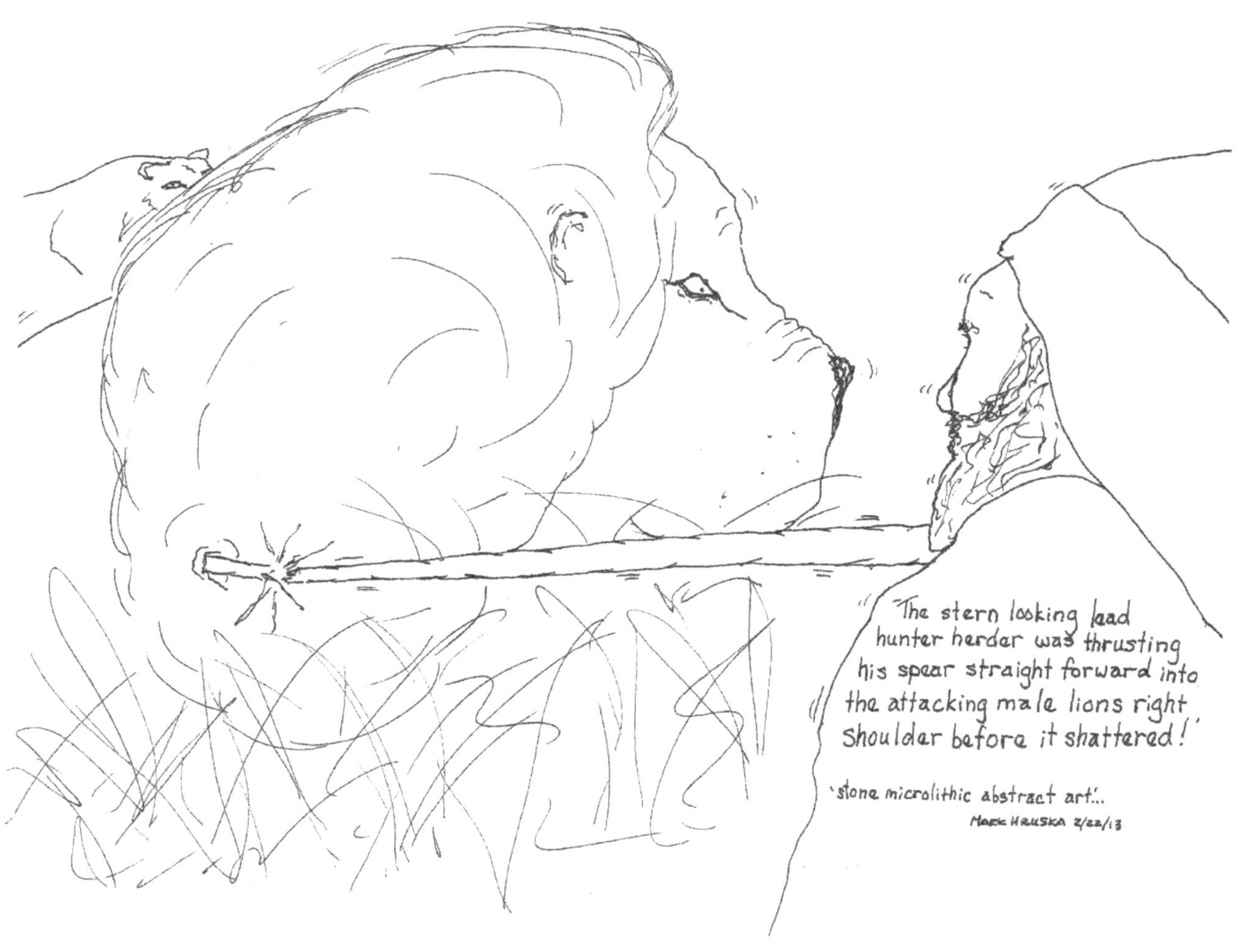

'stone microlithic abstract art'... 'The stern looking lead hunter herder was thrusting his spear straight forward into the attacking male lions right shoulder before it shattered!'

178) This could simply be the next scene as a continuation of the last pieces illustration, but it was interpreted on two entirely different artworks.

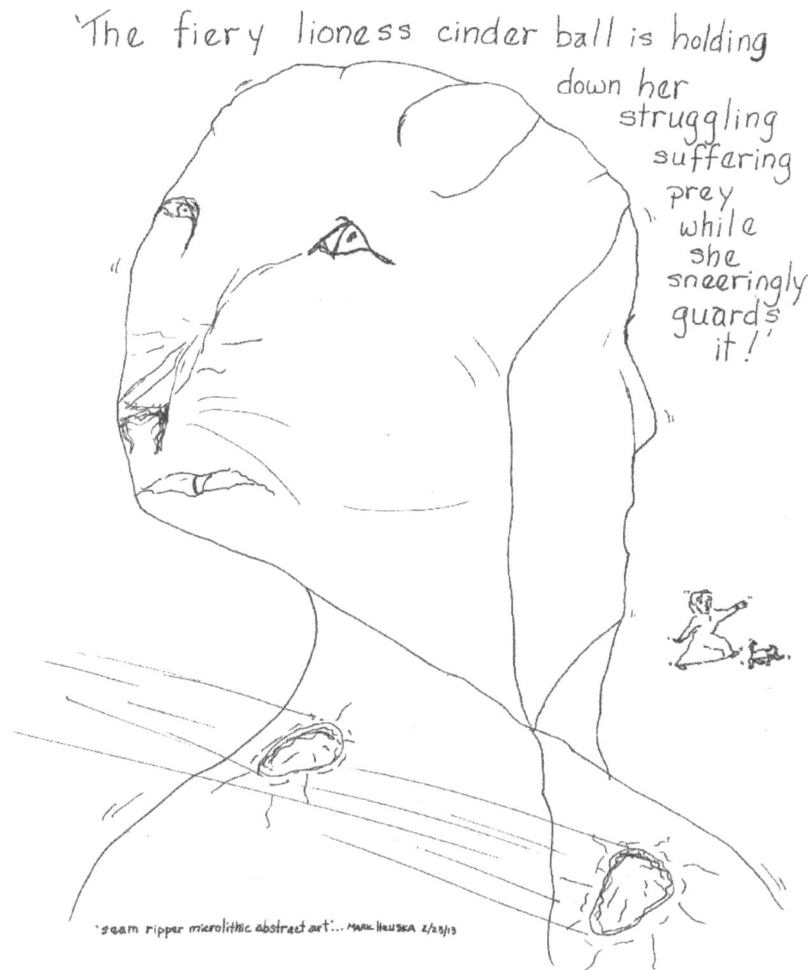

'seam ripper microlithic abstract art'... 'The fiery lioness cinder ball
is holding down the struggling suffering prey while she sneeringly guards it!'

179) You can clearly see that the close-up image of the sneering lioness cinder balls head is being seen as a close-up the way that crotchety grandma sees her when she looks down at the top of her scorched gnarled hand. The sneering lioness cinder ball is sitting on her haunches and looking back over her left shoulder towards crotchety grandma's painful looking face. They are 'opposing heads' sharing the backs of their heads which means that they are 'in' each other's heads thinking deeply of one another.

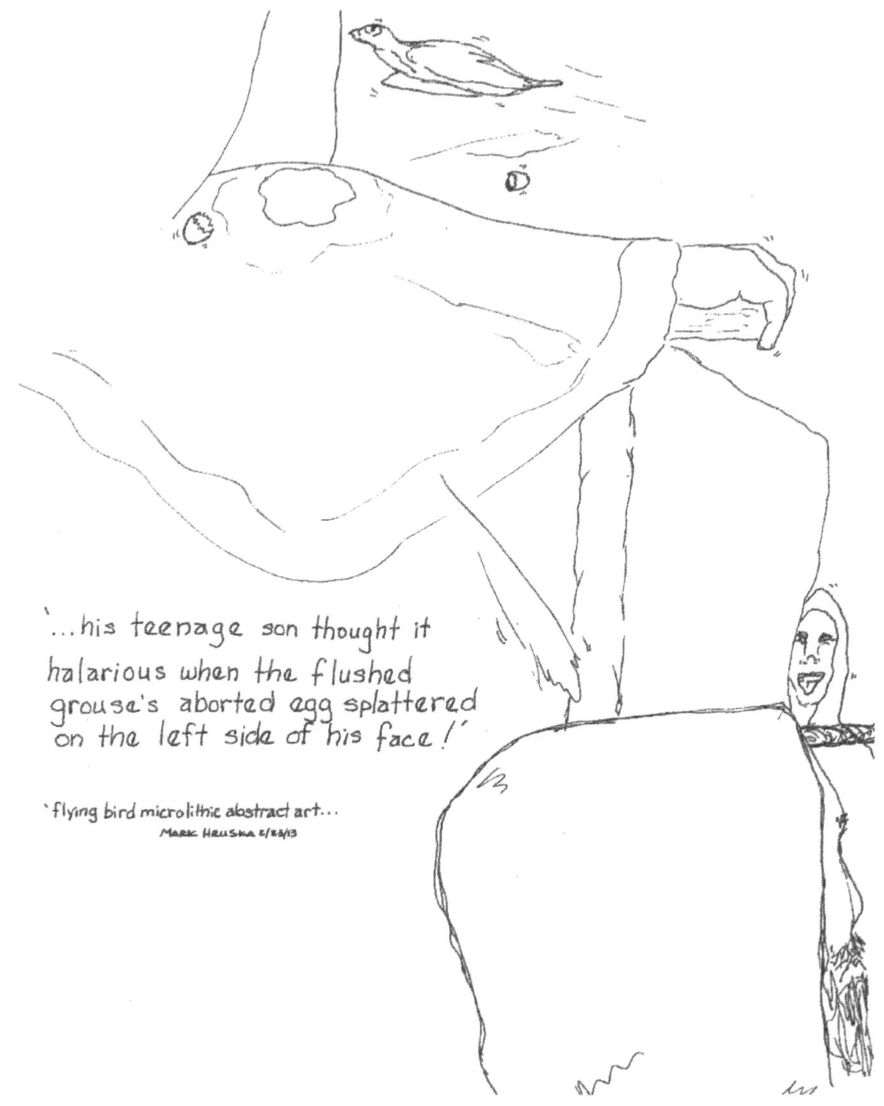

'flying bird microlithic abstract art'... '...his teenage son thought it hilarious when the flushed grouse's aborted egg splattered on the left side of his face!'

180) Once again, this pieces interpretations illustration is self-explanatory.

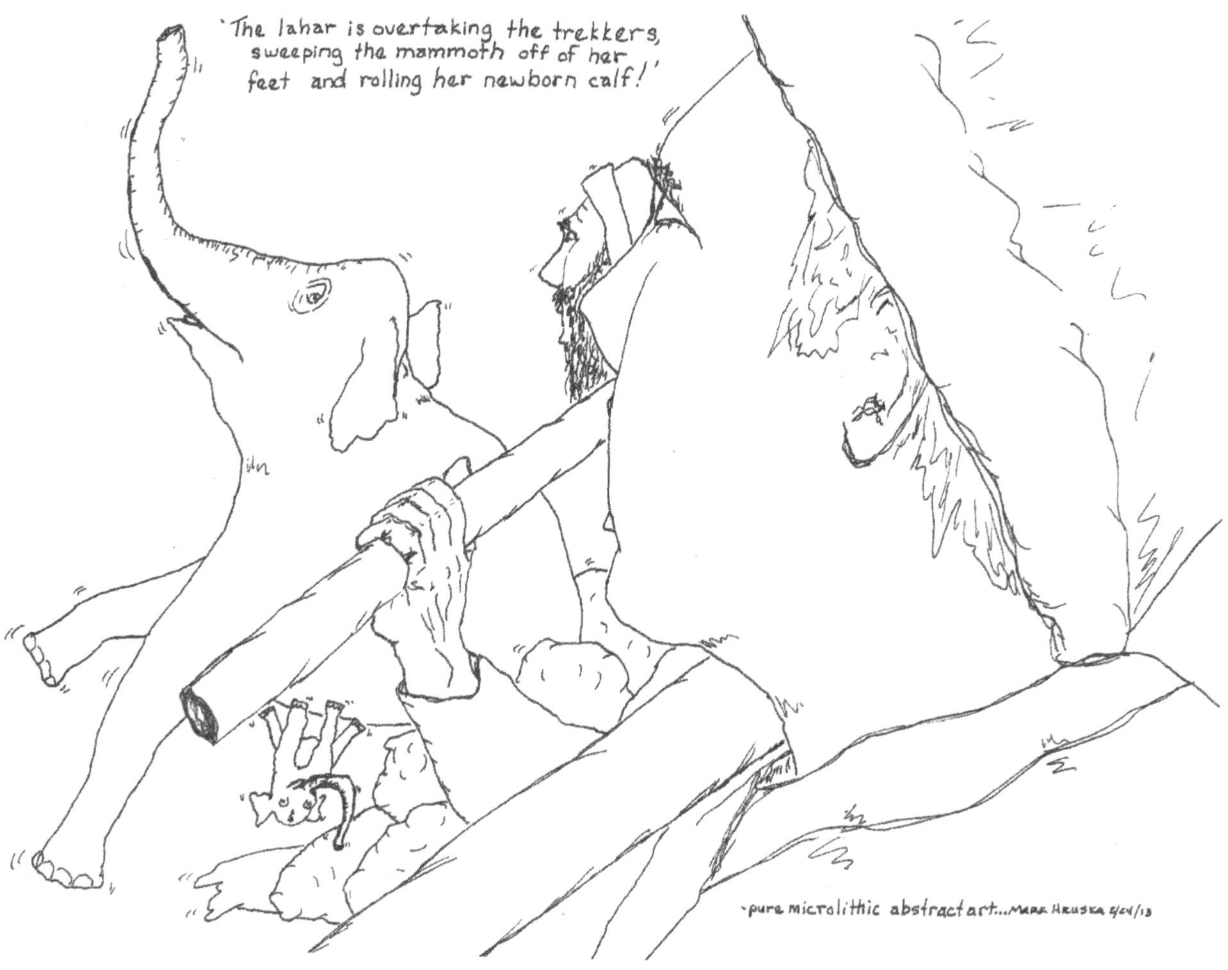

'pure microlithic abstract art'... 'The lahar is overtaking the trekkers sweeping the mammoth off of her feet and rolling her newborn calf!'

181) This is another one of my favorite illustrations that I couldn't possibly have made up unless the hunter herder that created the artwork planted it in my 'mind's eye'.

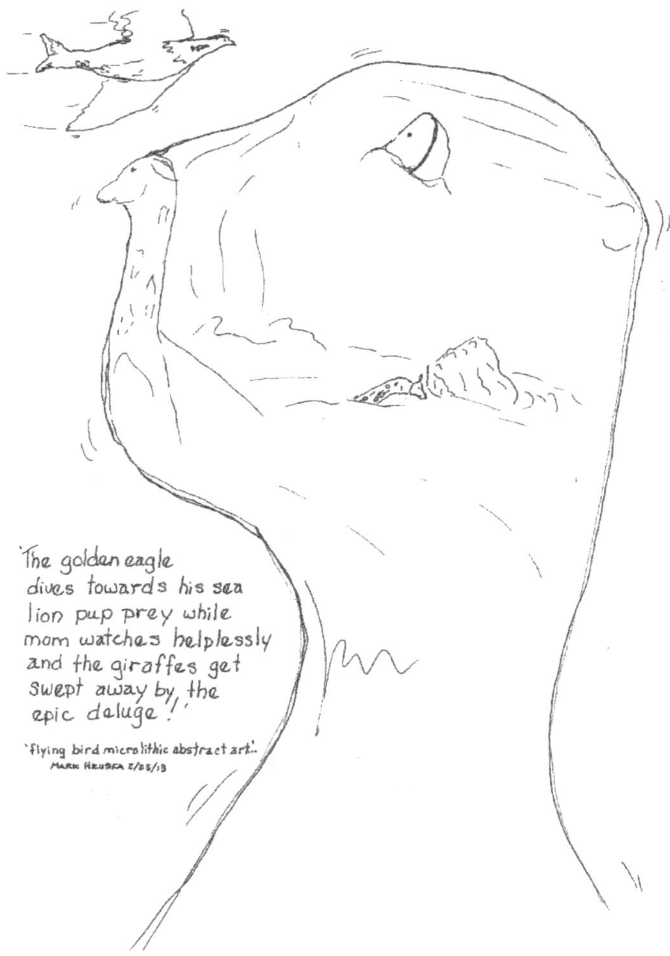

'flying bird microlithic abstract art'... 'The golden eagle dives towards his sea lion pup prey while mom watches helplessly and the giraffes get swept away by the epic deluge!'

182) Much of this pieces information must be reflecting off of the combined optical and cognitive illusion close-up image of the very concerned mother sea lion that can many times be seen floating on a big chunk of ice. It's also interesting to take note of how much the giraffes show up in so many of the trekking scenes which I can conclude had to have meant that they were always with the Mammoth People mammoth caravan of trekkers as they endured all of their epic trials and tribulations on their way to 'here'.

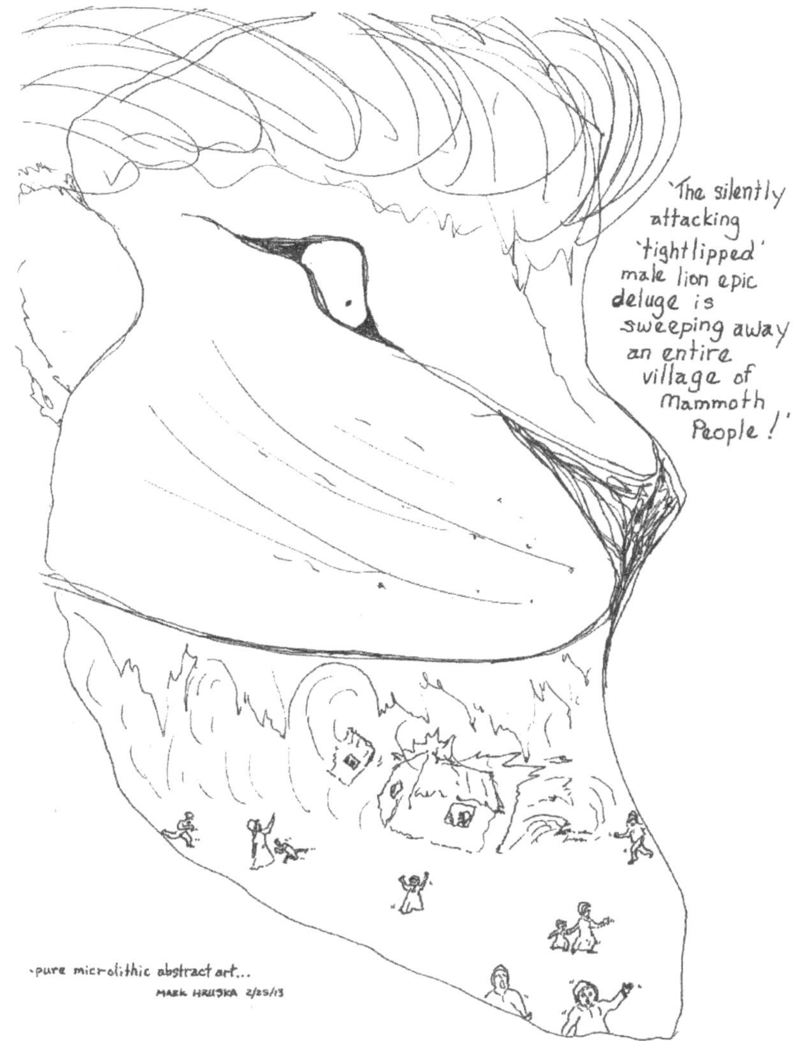

'pure microlithic abstract art'... 'The silently attacking 'tightlipped'
male lion epic deluge is sweeping away an entire village of Mammoth People!'

183) A picture is worth a thousand words and I see no reason why this illustration can't do the same. It's these artworks interpretations that cause me to believe that the Mammoth People actually became reestablished on the west coast of present day Washington State before the epic deluge swept them away and sent them trekking towards its source which was where lake Missoula's ice dam breached.

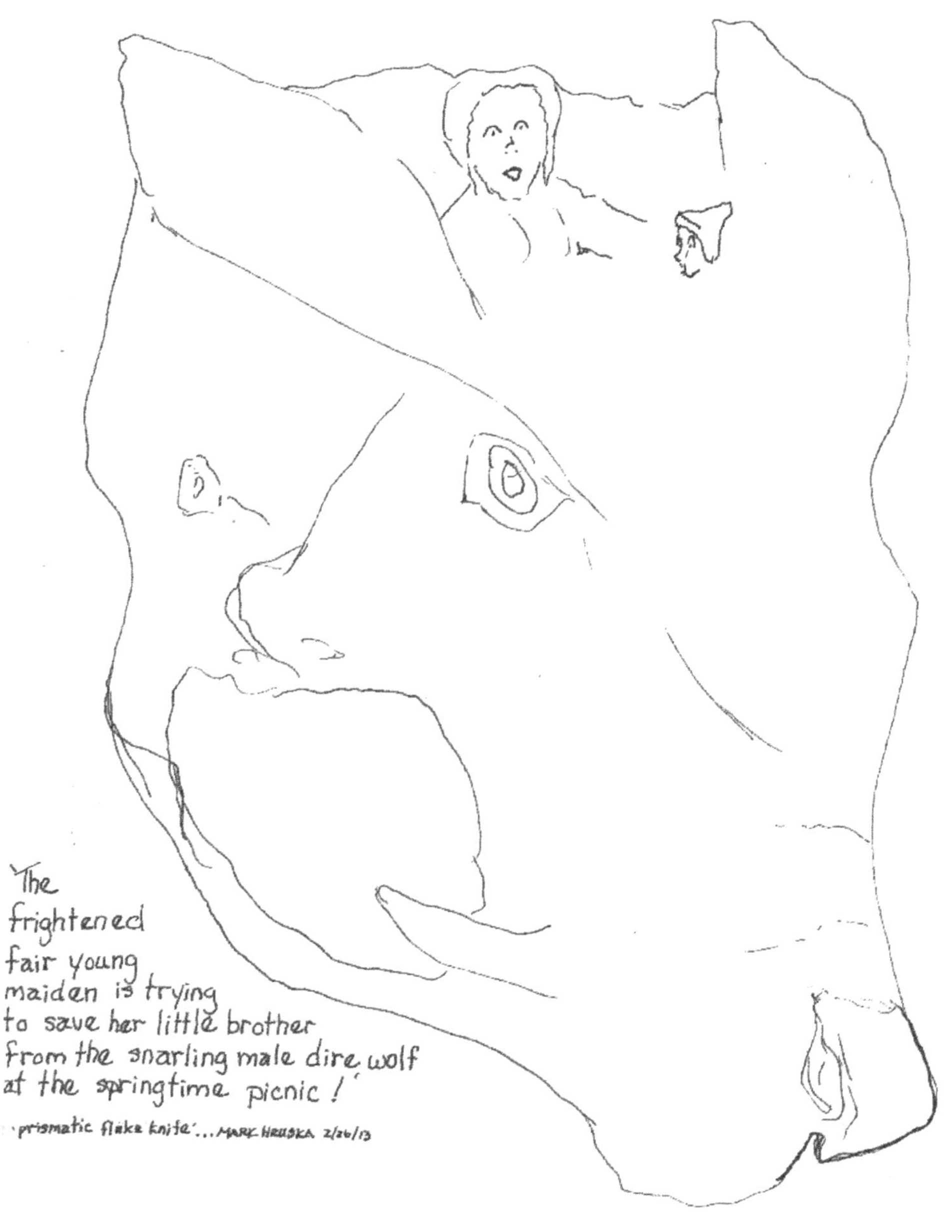

'prismatic flake knife'... 'The frightened fair young maiden is trying to save her little brother from the snarling dire wolf at the springtime picnic!'

184) As I view this illustration that describes the pieces interpretation, I see the close-up images of the front left side view of the horrified waist high young lad as an opposing head to the front right side view of the attacking snarling dire wolf's head that also has reflections reflecting off of his forehead. This means that since they're opposing heads they're actually face to face which means that grandma is coming up fast behind the petrified waist high young lad to knock the snarling dire wolf over the forehead with her cane as her petrified waist high young lad grandson stares on in shocked horror. When you zoom in and peer intently at his microlithic cognitive illusion reflection image, you'll see the same close-up view of him that you see when you take a step back and view the whole piece. What you'll also see many times on these close-up opposing head images is that the predator and the prey will be sharing one of their eyes. On this piece the petrified waist high young lad's left eye is also the snarling dire wolfs right one which always means that they are eye to eye in their predator prey confrontation.

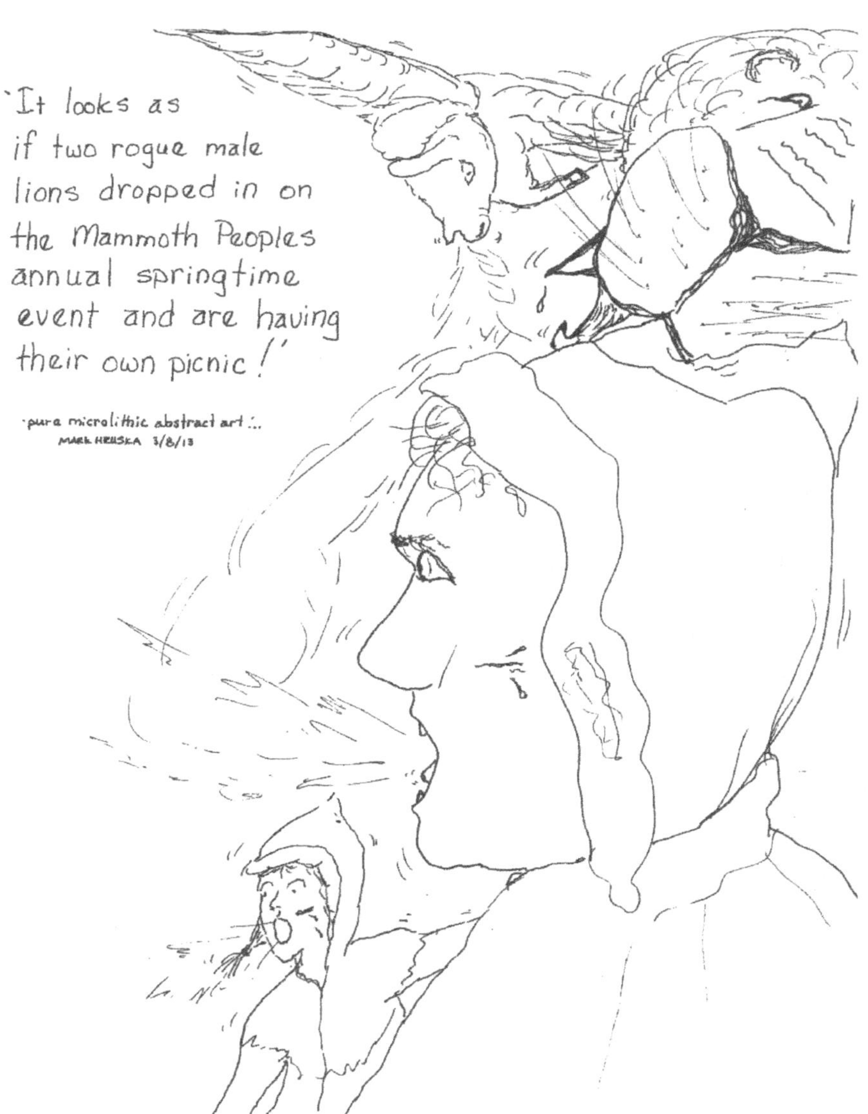

'pure microlithic abstract art'... 'It looks as if two rogue male lions dropped in on the Mammoth People's annual springtime event and are having their own picnic!'

185) If you look closely, you'll see the flying submissive ewe spirit's opened sucking mouth sucking up the exhaled last breaths of the fleeing picnickers as they get slaughtered by the pair of frolicking rogue male lions.

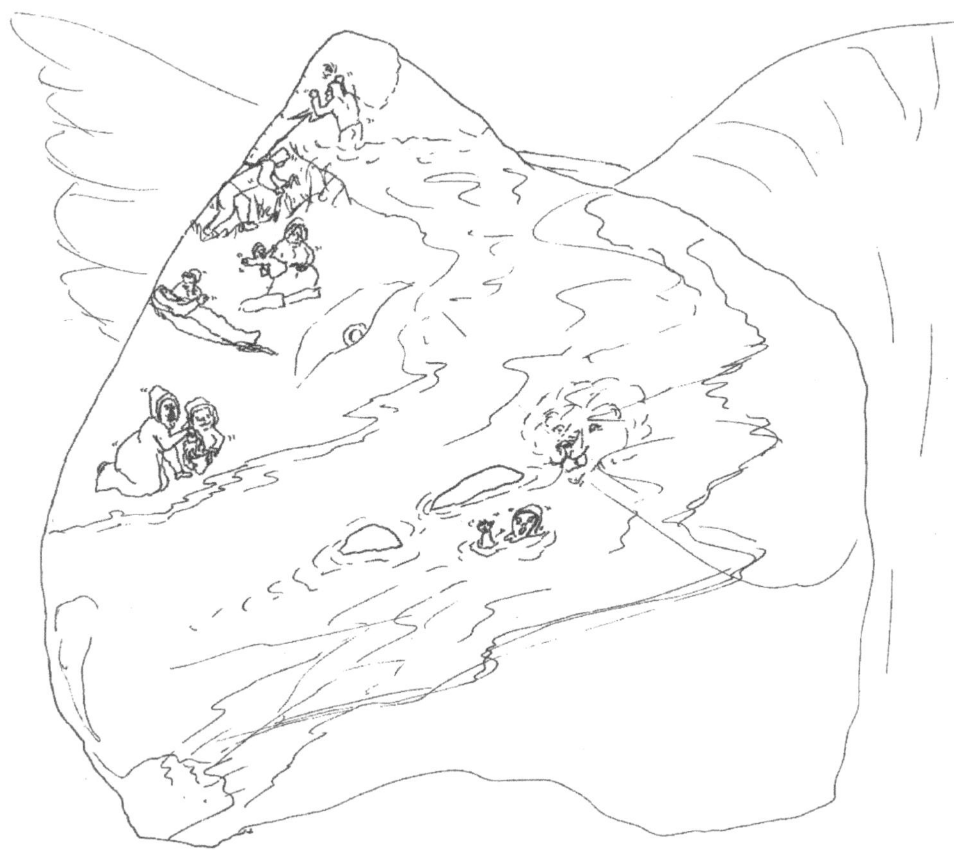

'pure microlithic abstract art'... 'The roaring male lion glacial ice melt water stream attacks the rambunctious waist high young lad while his busy family makes camp on its banks!'

186) This pieces interpretations illustration is clear, what isn't so clear is that the whole scene as is often the case, is reflecting off of some part of the incoming flying submissive ewe spirt. In this case it's reflecting off of the left side of her head. Look closely at the reflection images to see how everyone is busily doing their tasks including dad who's rubbing down the lead mammoth that's reflecting off of the top right side of the flying submissive ewes head.

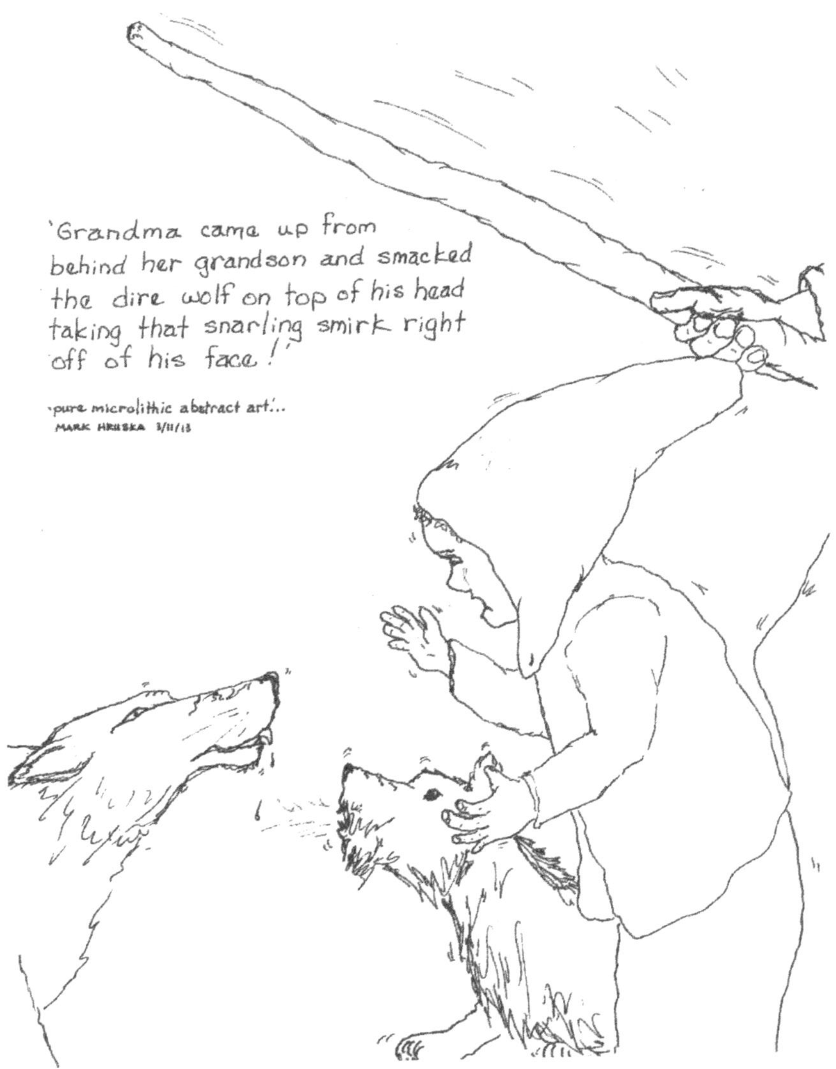

'pure microlithic abstract art'... 'Grandma came up from behind her grandson and smacked the dire wolf on top of his head taking that snarling smirk right off of his face!'

187) This is my favorite sketch that I've done to date. The hunter herder microlithic abstract artist did such a fantastic job of planting this imagery in my 'mind's eye' that I considered placing it on the cover of this 'Reflections From The Pleistocene'; The Sentient Mammoth People book of illustrations.

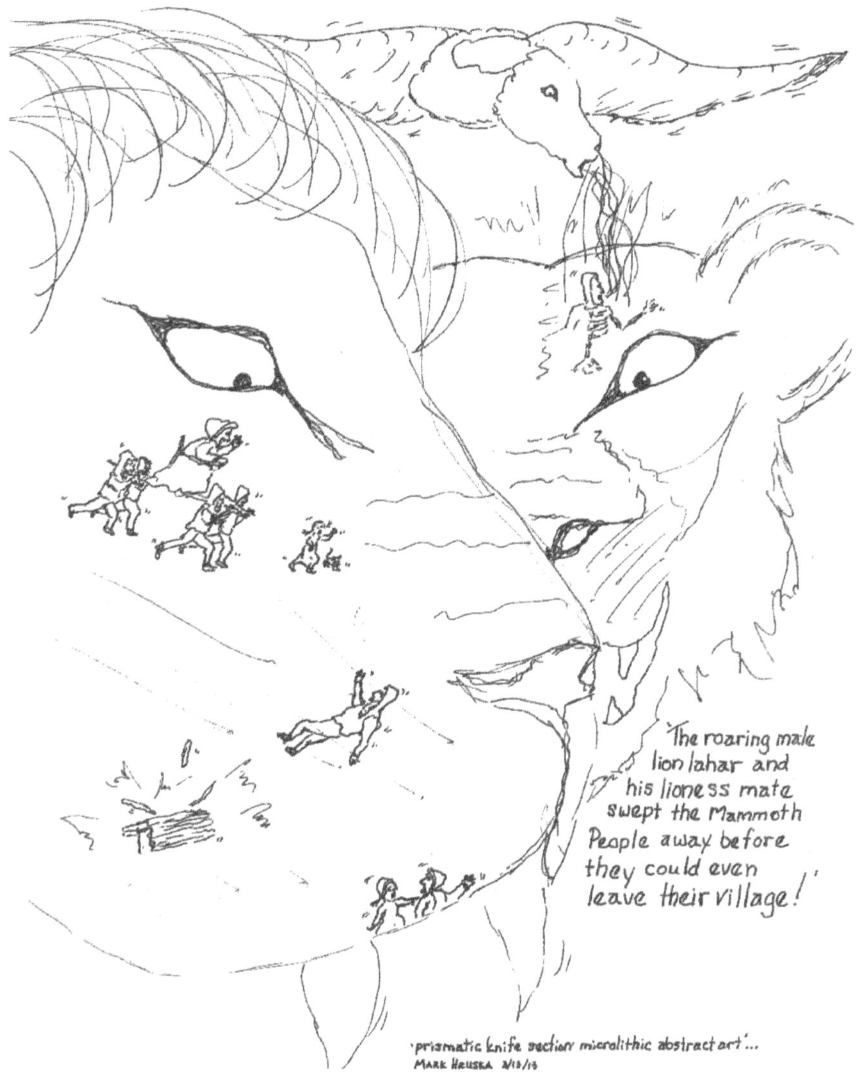

'prismatic knife section microlithic abstract art'... 'The roaring male lion lahar and his lioness mate swept the Mammoth People away before they could even leave their village!'

188) The overriding image that stuck in my 'mind's eye' from this pieces interpretation is that one of the microlithic cognitive illusion reflection images was of the front view of one of the fleeing villagers that was half skeleton as if he were dying on the run as he was overtaken by the roaring lahar. The flying submissive ewe spirit is sucking up his last exhaled breath which is his spirit.

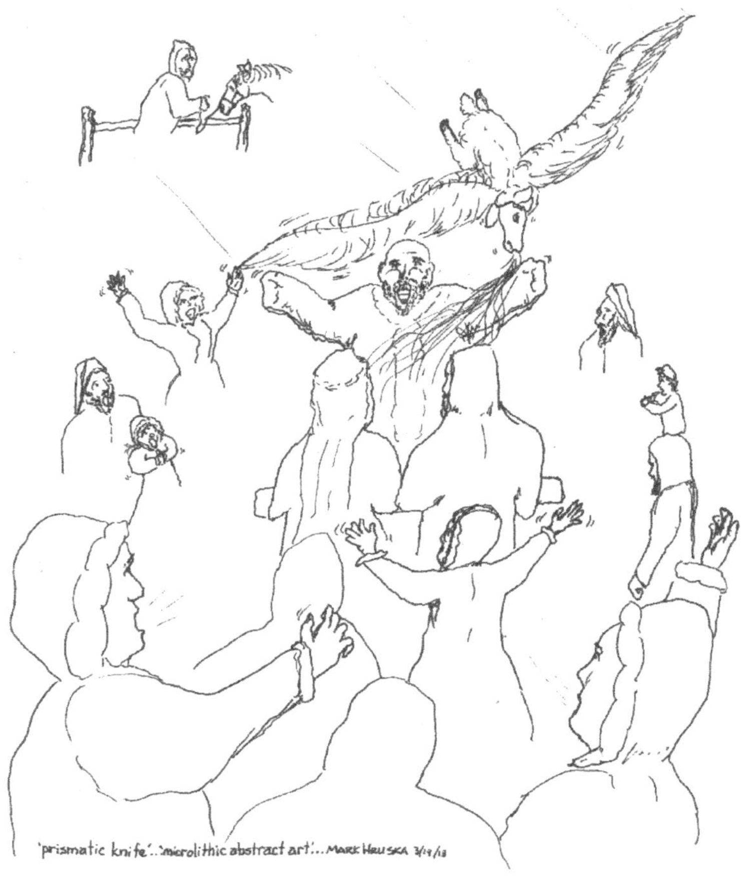

'prismatic knife'... 'microlithic abstract art'... 'Even though it was a joyous occasion for all of the other Mammoth People, the jilted forlorn lover was devastated!'

189) I always can't help but wonder when I interpret this folklore tale, if the term 'hitched' that we use to describe a wedded couple today, comes from the Mammoth People's folklore tale of the jilted forlorn lover who always heads towards the hitching post where his mare is tied when the pompous boisterous magistrate proclaims "I now pronounce you man and wife!". Take note too that the flying submissive ewe spirit is gliding down to deliver the 'unity blessing' by 'blowing' it into the bride and grooms 'I do' speaking mouths.

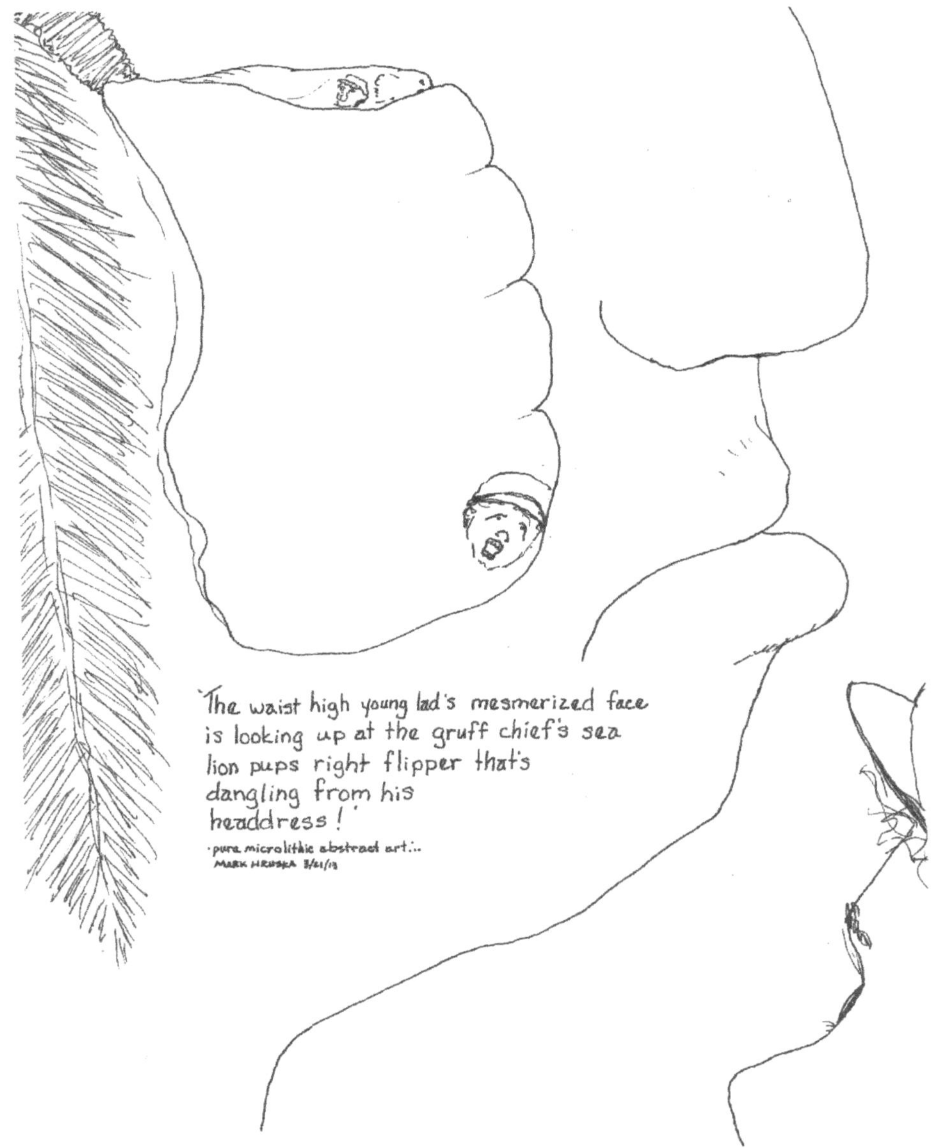

'pure microlithic abstract art'... 'The waist high young lads mesmerized face is looking up at the gruff chief's sea lion pups right flipper that's dangling from his headdress!'

190) His mesmerized childlike face is reflecting off of it to verify that.

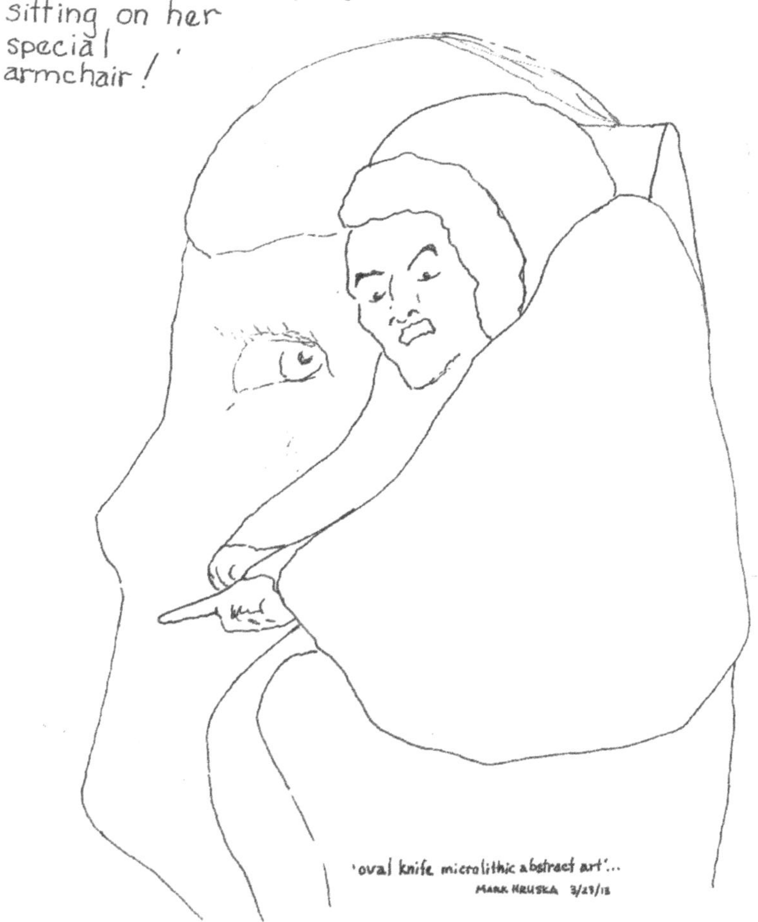

'oval knife microlithic abstract art'... 'You will never see
a bigger and clearer combined optical and cognitive illusion
close-up image of crotchety grandma sitting on her special armchair!'

191) It's most likely that if you'd get to see the actual artwork, that's exactly what you'd think.

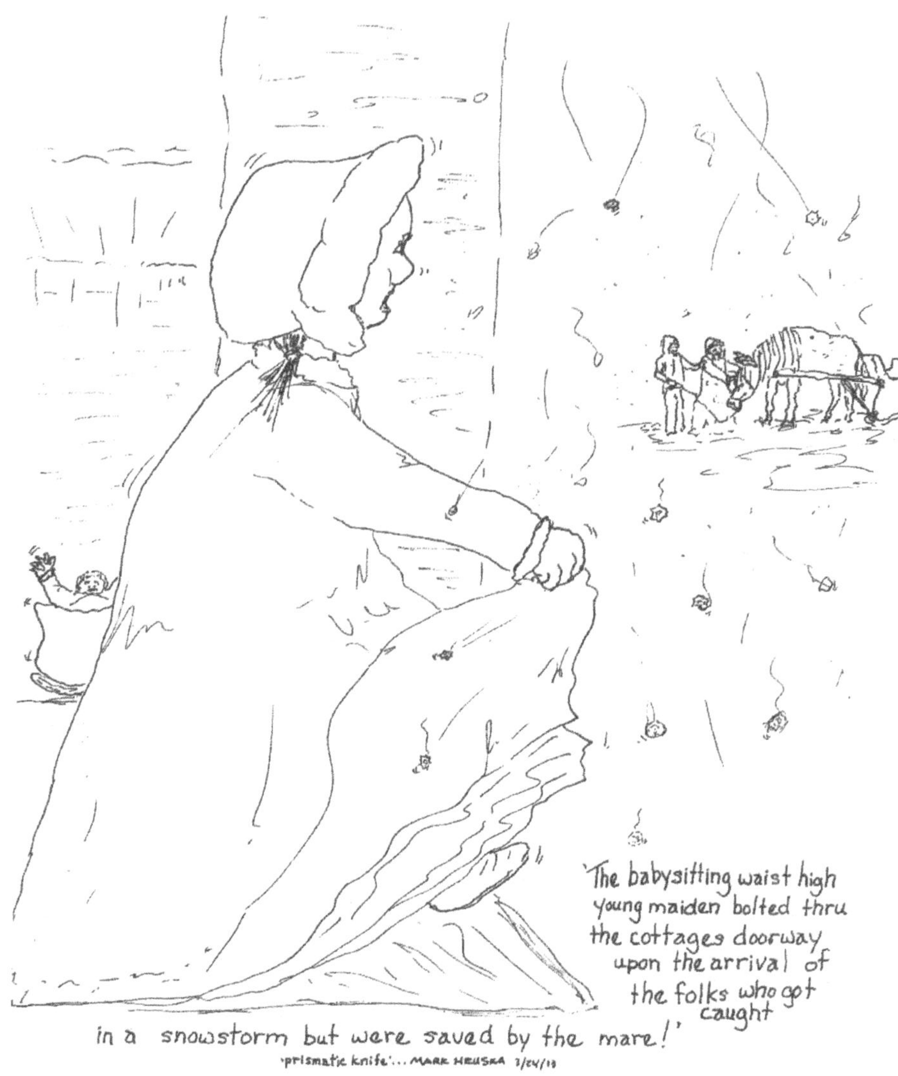

'prismatic knife'... 'The babysitting waist high
young maiden bolted thru the cottages doorway upon the arrival
of the folks who got caught in a snowstorm but were saved by the mare!'

192) This is a rare folklore tale but I know that I interpreted it at least three times. Its main theme centered on everyone praising the mare for getting mom and dad home in the blinding blizzard.

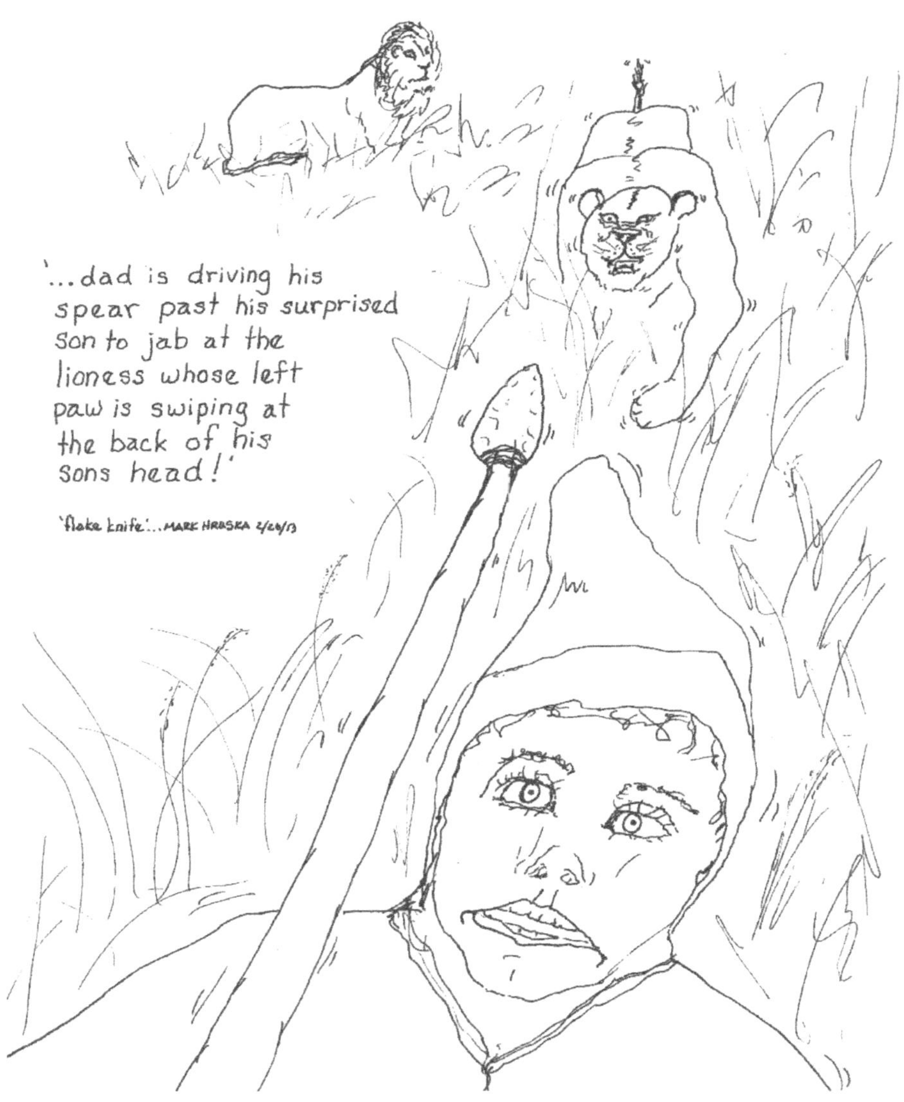

'flake knife'... '...dad is driving his spear past his surprised son to
jab at the lioness whose left paw is swiping at the back of his sons head!'

193) This piece's interpretations illustration simply shows what the lead hunter herder sees from his position in front of the nervous lead mammoth that he's leading.

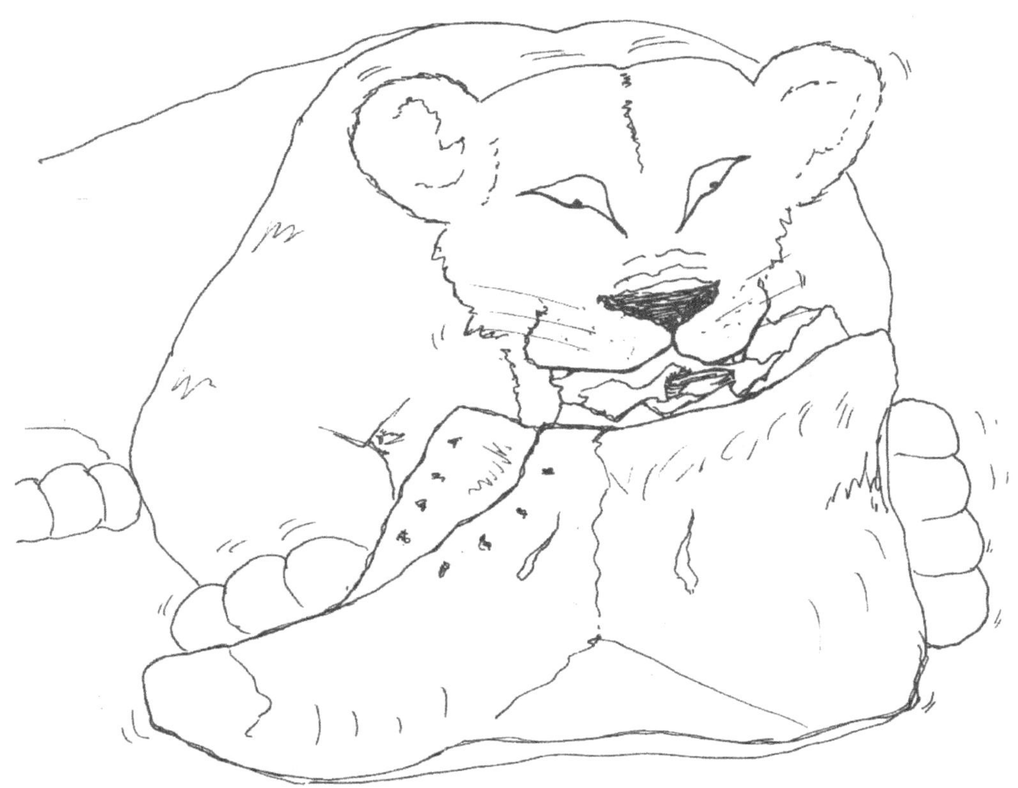

'pure microlithic abstract art'... 'The hungry lioness and her cubs ate everything but the toddler young maiden's left foot that's still inside of its left shoe!'

194) This pieces interpretation's illustration is self-explanatory.

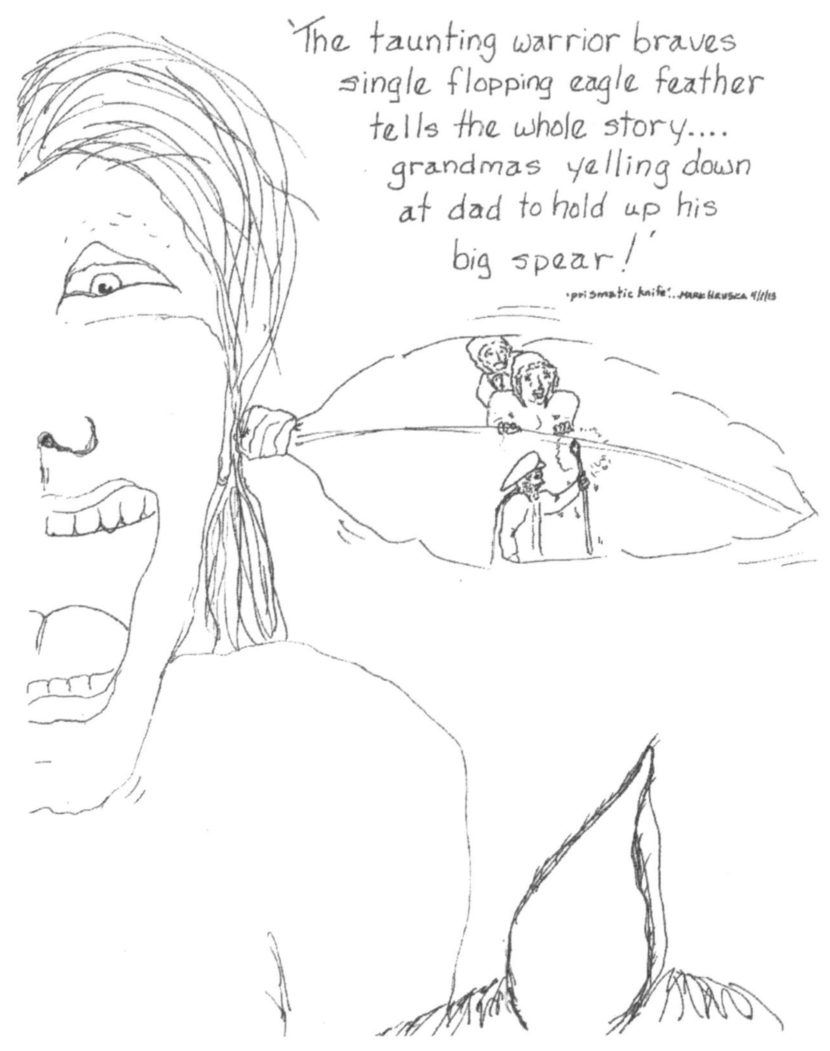

'prismatic knife'... 'The taunting warrior braves single flopping eagle feather
tells the whole story.... grandma's yelling down at dad to hold up his big spear!'

195) She's reflecting off of the one side of the quill of the flopping feather while the lead hunter herder who's below her is reflecting off of the other. She and the taunting warrior brave are across from each other because they're both up high on their rides. She's on her special armchair atop the nervous lead mammoth and he's up on his high horse behind the gruff chief.

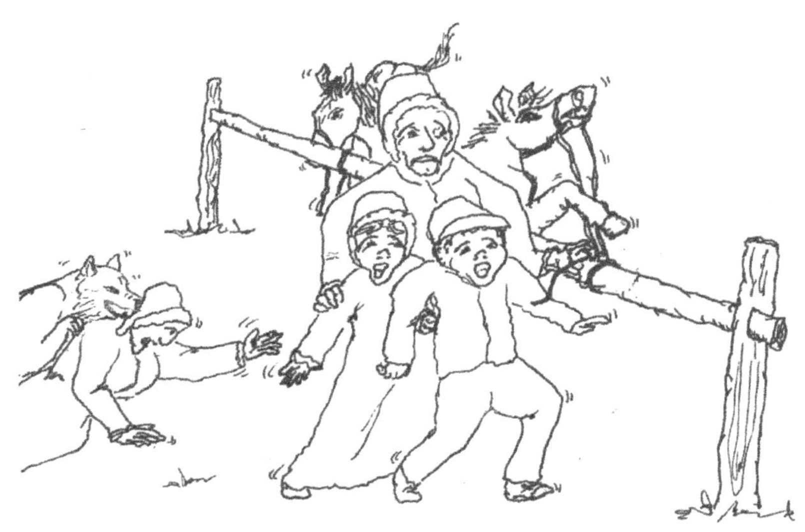

'pure microlithic abstract art'... 'The spooked horse is rearing while mom hurries to untie his reins from the hitching post when dire wolves attacked the summertime picnic!'

196) When that pack or pair of dire wolves attacked, everyone stampeded towards the hitching post causing the elderly and the children to get trampled and making their rides very agitated. It's worse when the lions attack because the agitated horses then know that they are on the dining list.

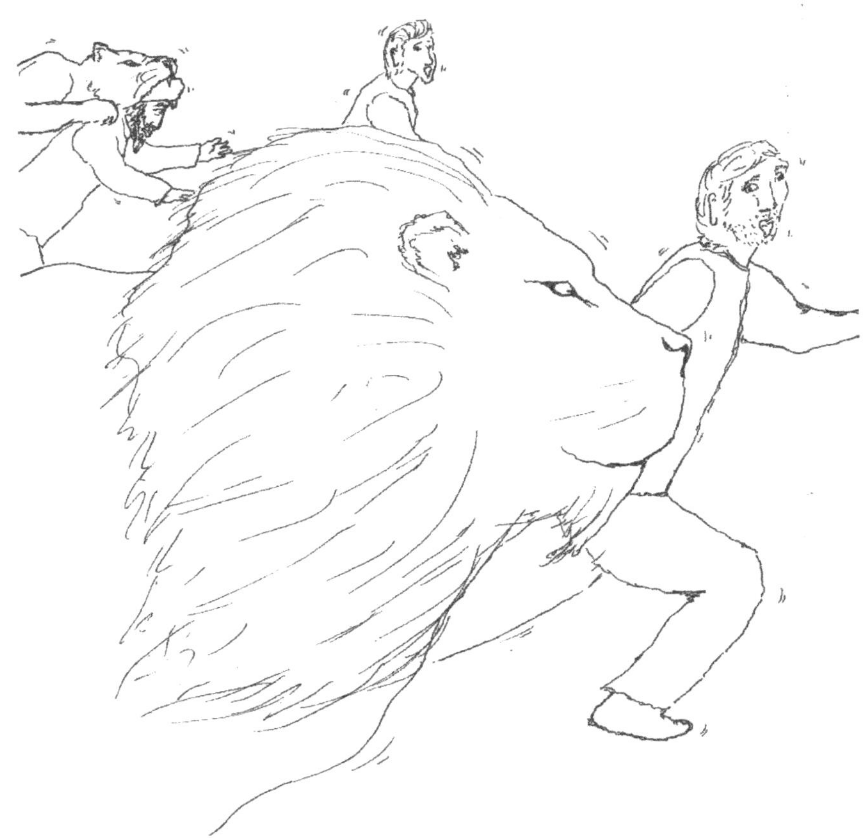

'prismatic knife'... '...a pair of lions raided the summertime event
slaughtering picnickers left and right which provided a feast for their cubs!'

197) This is one of my favorite line sketches that really seemed to record what I interpreted on the artwork. It's also a fairly common folklore tale that interchanges the predators. If it isn't the two rogue male lions it's a pair of lions, a pair of dire wolves, a pack of dire wolves or a single saber-toothed cat that attack and cause the frightened picnickers to stampede towards the hitching post.

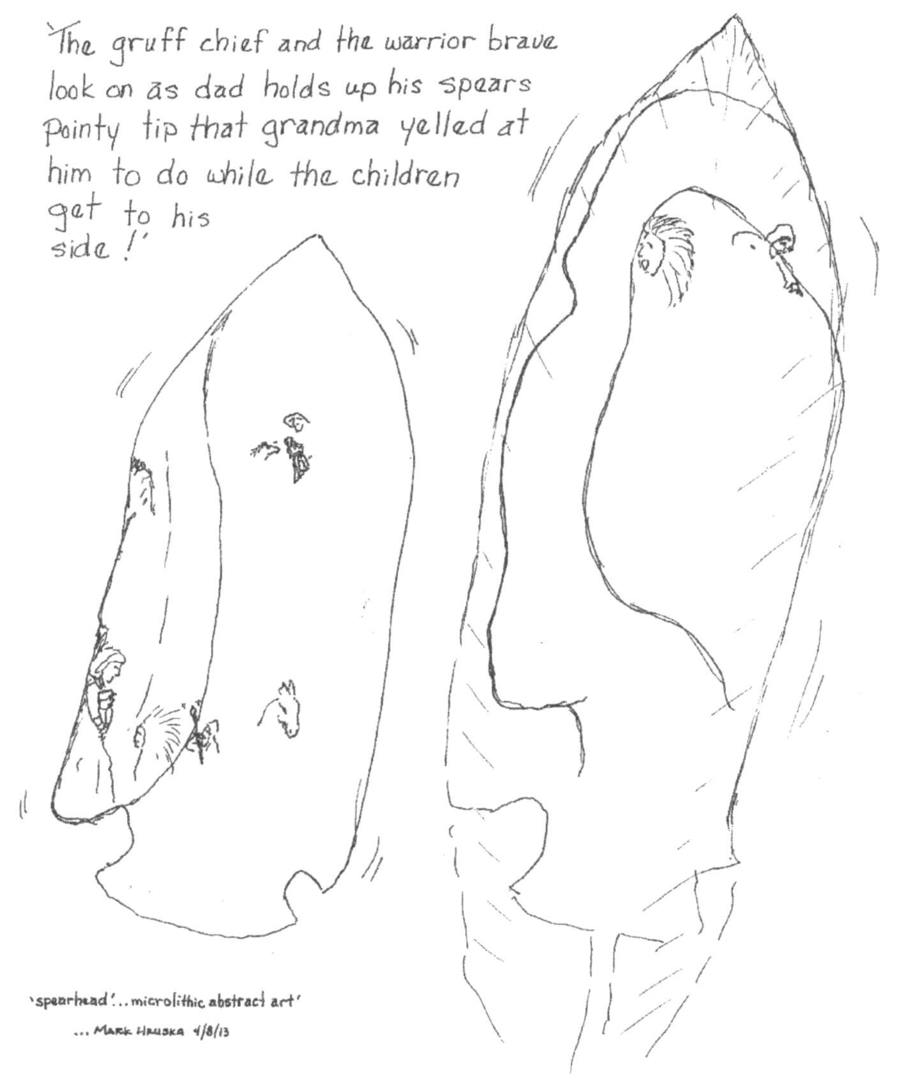

'spearhead'... 'microlithic abstract art'... 'The gruff chief
and the warrior brave look on as dad holds up his spears pointy
tip that grandma yelled at him to do while the children get to his side!'

198) Everything you see on this pieces' interpretations illustration is reflecting off of both sides of stern dad's stone spearhead which means that the close-up image 'is' the stone spearhead.... the 'actual' stone spearhead.

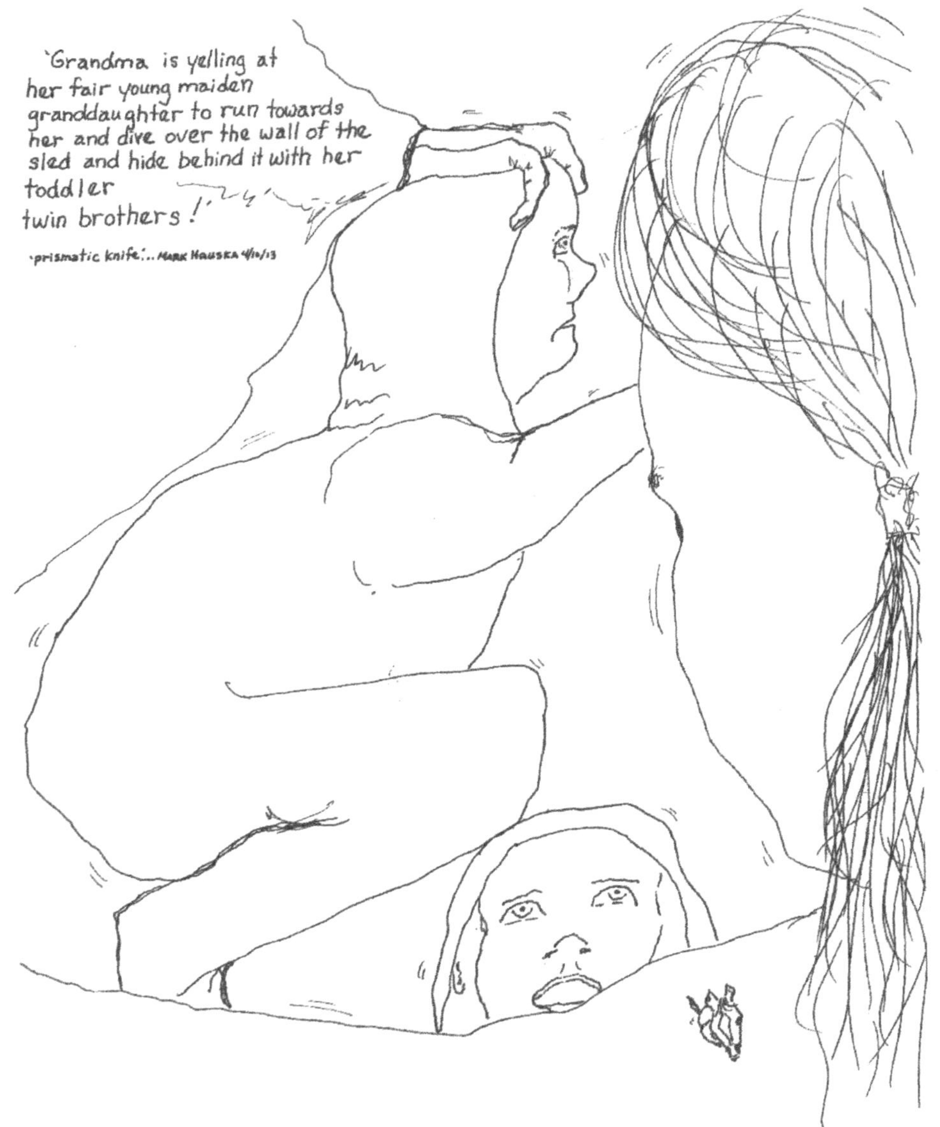

'prismatic knife'... 'Grandma is yelling at her fair young maiden granddaughter to run towards her and dive over the wall of the sled and hide behind it with her twin brothers!'

199) Grandma is sitting in the front seat of the sled and is sheltering the twins by hoovering over them covering them with her cape covered arms like a mother duck would shelter her ducklings with her spread out wings.

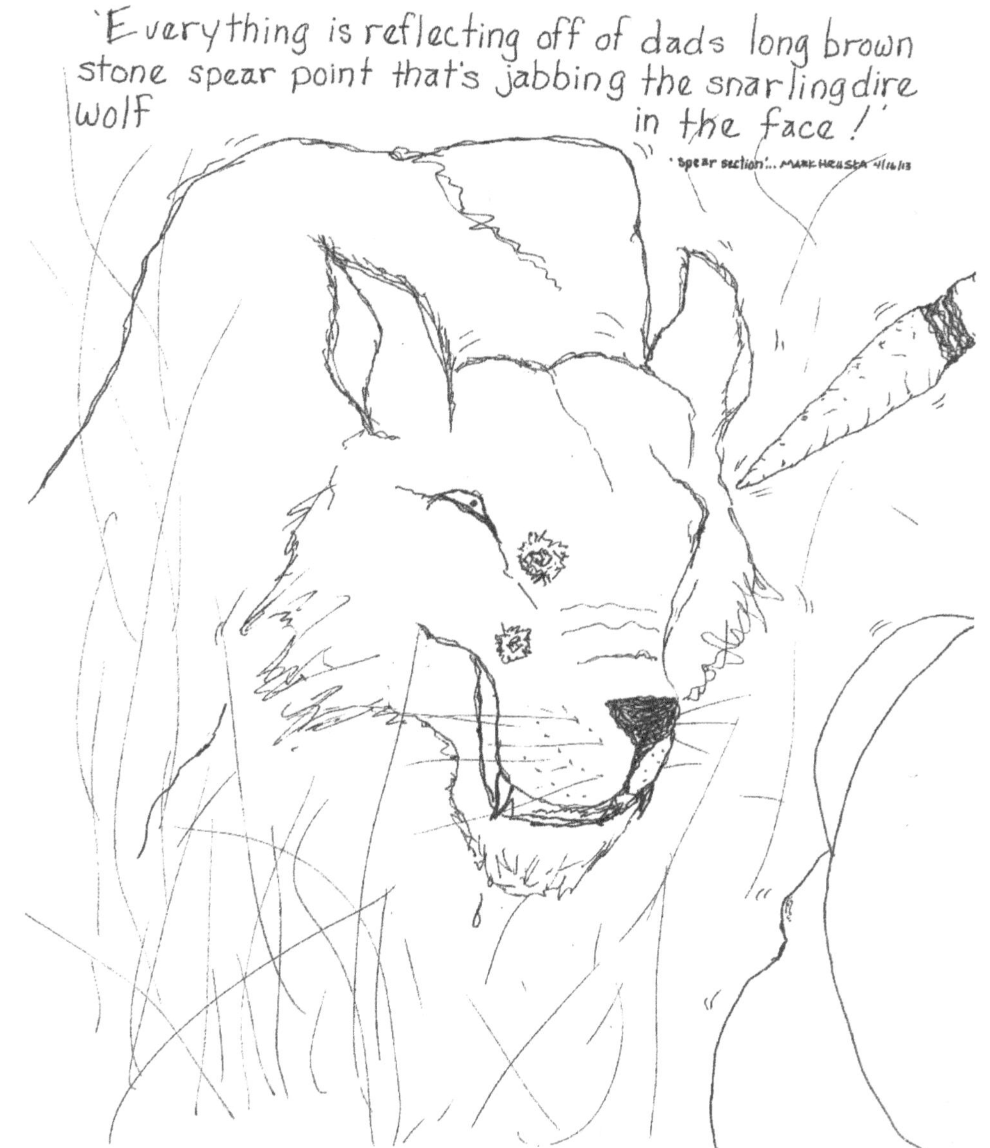

'spear section'... 'Everything is reflecting off of dads long
brown stone spear point that's jabbing the snarling dire wolf in the face!'

200) Once again, the exuberant waist high young lad must have gotten out ahead of dad as they trekked.

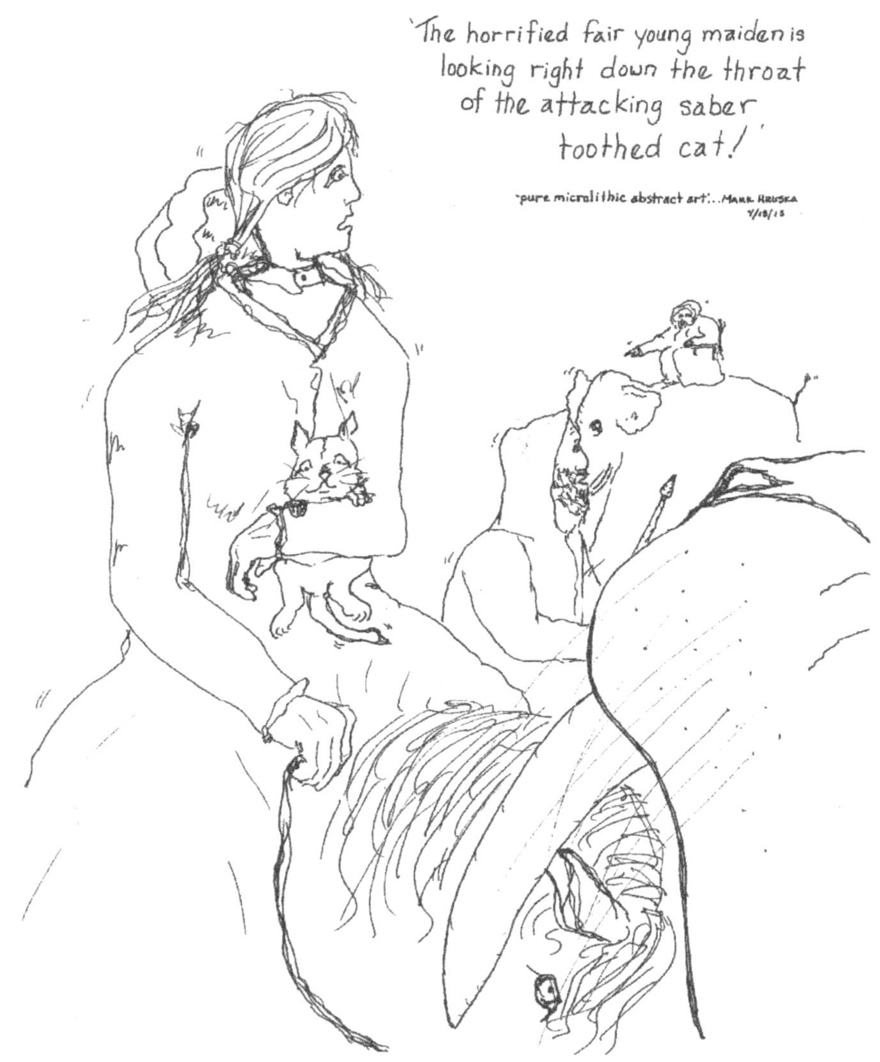

'pure microlithic abstract art'... 'The horrified fair young maiden
is looking right down the throat of the attacking saber toothed cat!'

201) She's even more exuberant than her little brother, you could say an over achiever...which in this case caused her demise. The lesson for the young maidens who were about to mature into fair young maidens and who the folklore tale was being told to, was to use your new found abilities and confidence...wisely.

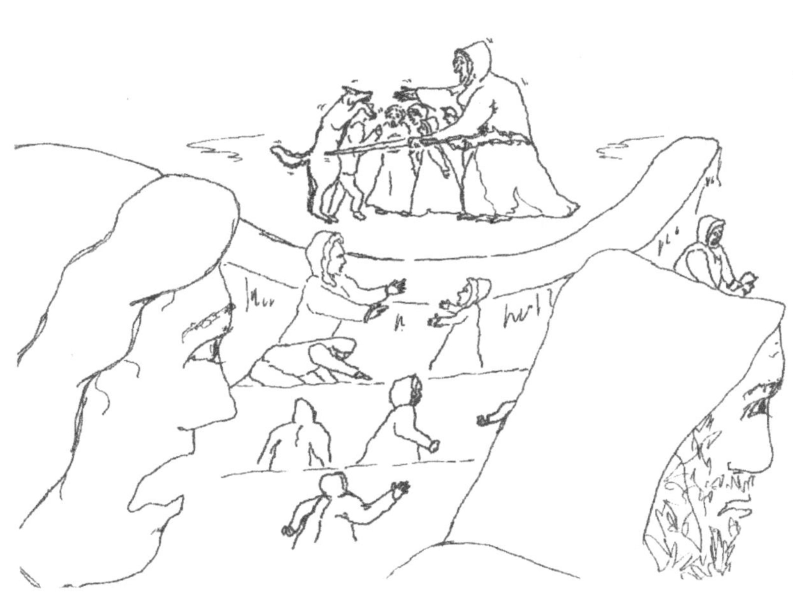

'prismatic flake knife microlithic abstract art'... 'The defiant elderly schoolmarm died defending her students from a dire wolf when they sang at the evening school program!'

202) This is another self-explanatory sketch from the interpretation of a prismatic flake knife eating utensil.

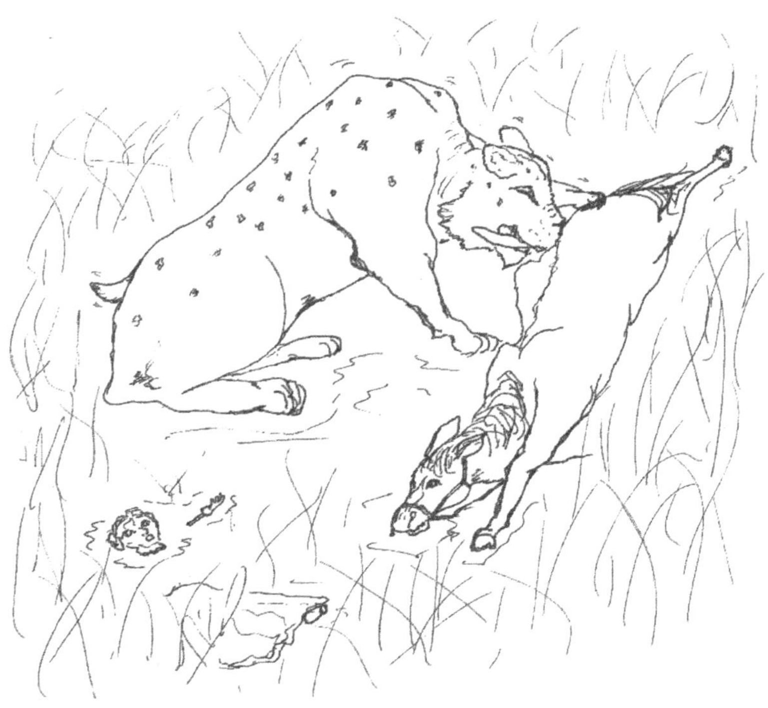

'pure microlithic abstract art'... 'The fair young maidens and her palomino
horses 'dead heads' eyes watched the saber toothed cat eat both of them alive!'

203) When you understand the 'rules' of the Mammoth People hunter herder microlithic abstract art figurative language, you'll also understand that anything's dead glazed over eyes can still see as long as they're open. So if you end up as prey, you would be watching the predator eat you... This adds a new dimension of horror to a child's innocent mind's eye and would surely make them 'more' aware then today's children who surely would never have to fear such a thing.

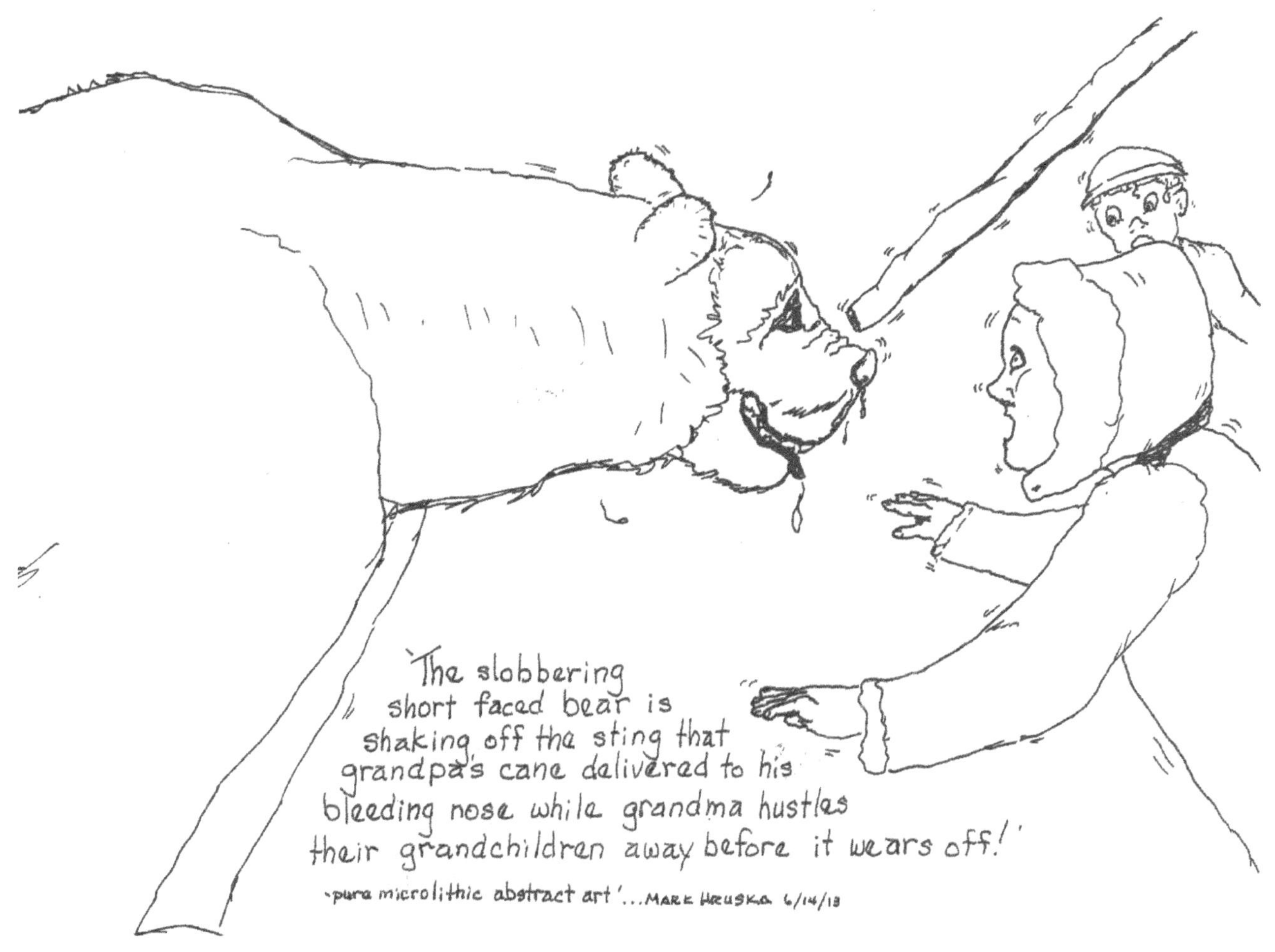

'pure microlithic abstract art'... 'The slobbering short faced
bear is shaking off the sting that grandpas cane delivered to his bleeding
nose while grandma hustles their grandchildren away before it wears off!'

204) This is another artwork interpretations line sketch that I really like simply because it captures the moment in Pleistocene time as good as I possibly could have.

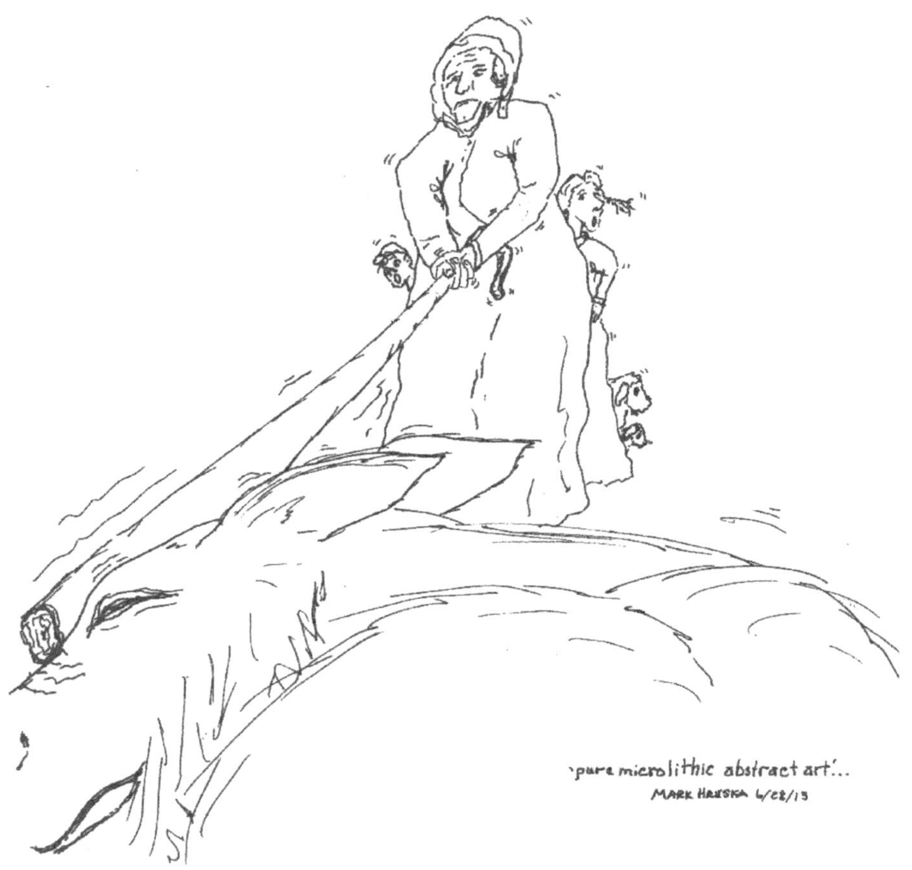

'pure microlithic abstract art'... 'Protective grandmas screaming grandchildren hid behind her while she whacked her shepherds crook over the attacking dire wolfs snout!'

205) I was getting better and better at expressing the complete scene that was fed to my 'mind's eye' one image at a time from the 'rotational change-up' artwork.

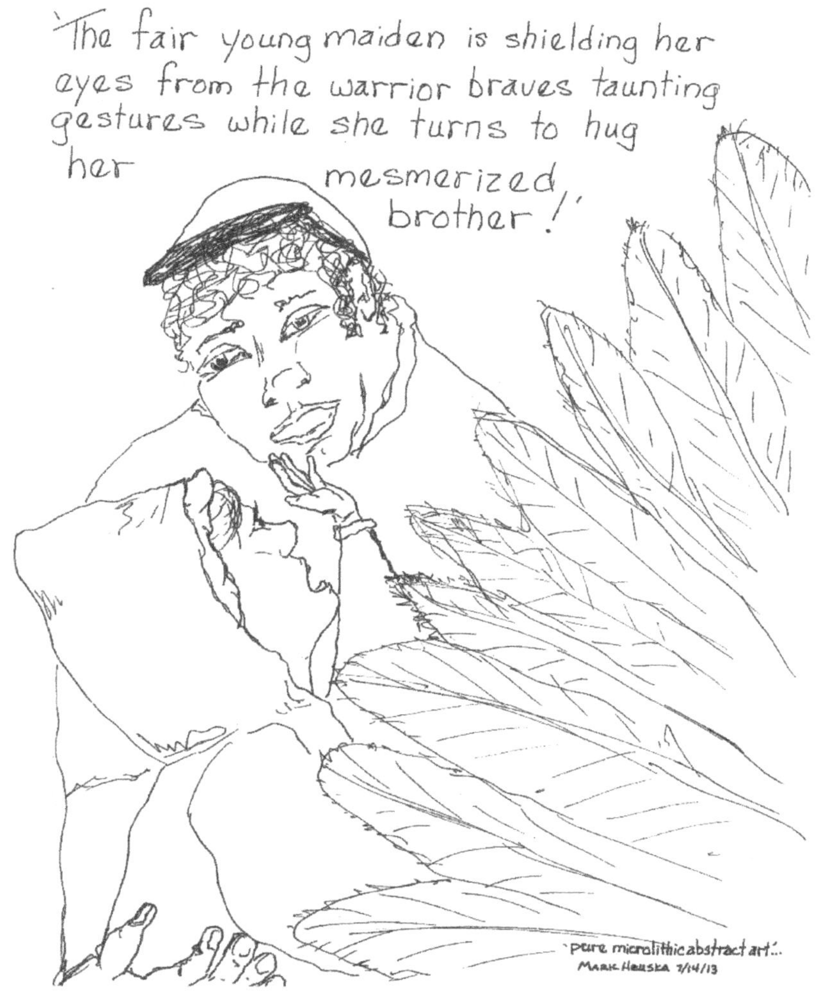

'pure microlithic abstract art'... 'The fair young maiden is shielding her eyes from the warrior braves taunting gestures while she turns to hug her mesmerized brother!'

206) I later realized that she was older than her mesmerized waist high young lad little brother and that when she ran up to the side of her stern lead hunter herder dad, she was instructed by her irate grandma to hold her mesmerized little brother close to the front of her because he was standing directly in front of the gruff chief and his agitated palomino horses head. While she did so, she had to witness the taunting warrior brave that had chased her up to the powwow and who was now sitting on his high horse behind and to the left of the gruff chief, make jeering gestures at her with his bright white toothy fake grin.

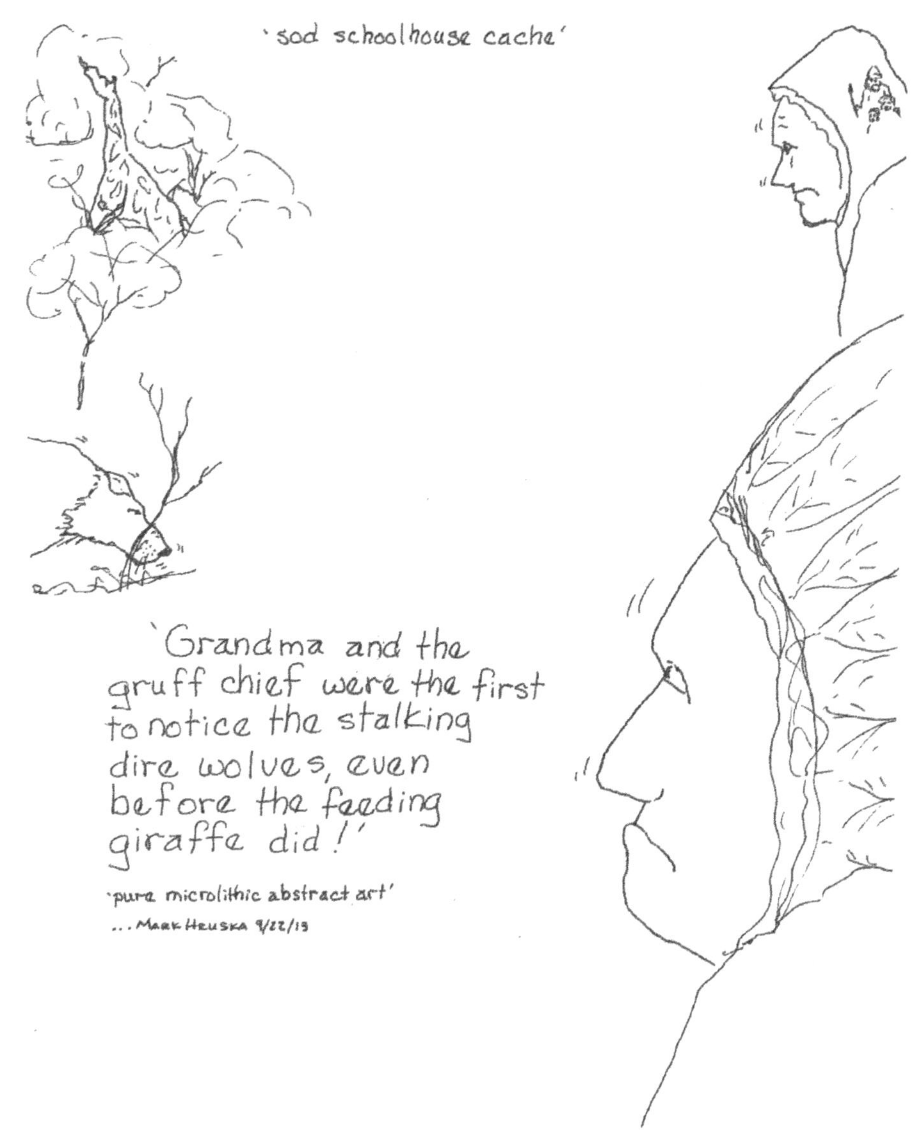

'pure microlithic abstract art'... 'Grandma and the gruff chief were
the first to notice the stalking dire wolves, even before the feeding giraffe did!'

207) Once again the giraffe is in a trekking scene and if there were no giraffes here on this North American continent thirteen millennia ago then they simply came along with the Mammoth People mammoth caravan of trekkers to 'here'.

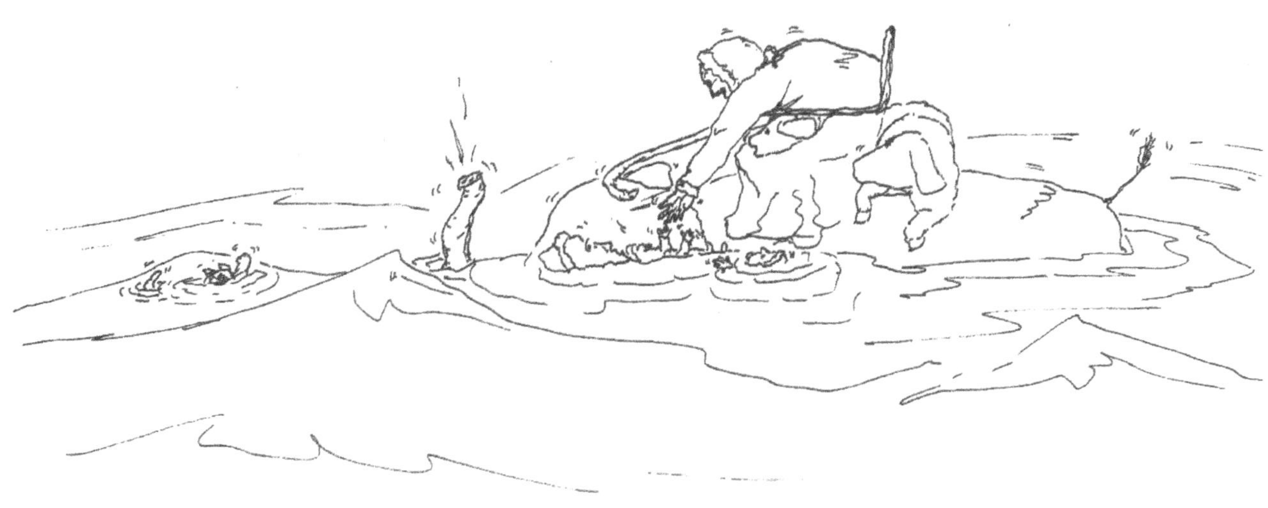

'predators bent foreleg microlithic abstract art'... 'Surrounded by
calamity, I can just hear grandma loudly say to mom... "Give me the baby..."'

208) Peer intently at the sketch to see mom and the infant and another one of her children next to the left side of the swimming mammoth. Grandma is trying to rescue the weakest lead family members first after the epic deluge swept them away. Off in the distance you'll see the swimming kitty trying to get her attention. What he doesn't know yet is that he'll be the last to be rescued.

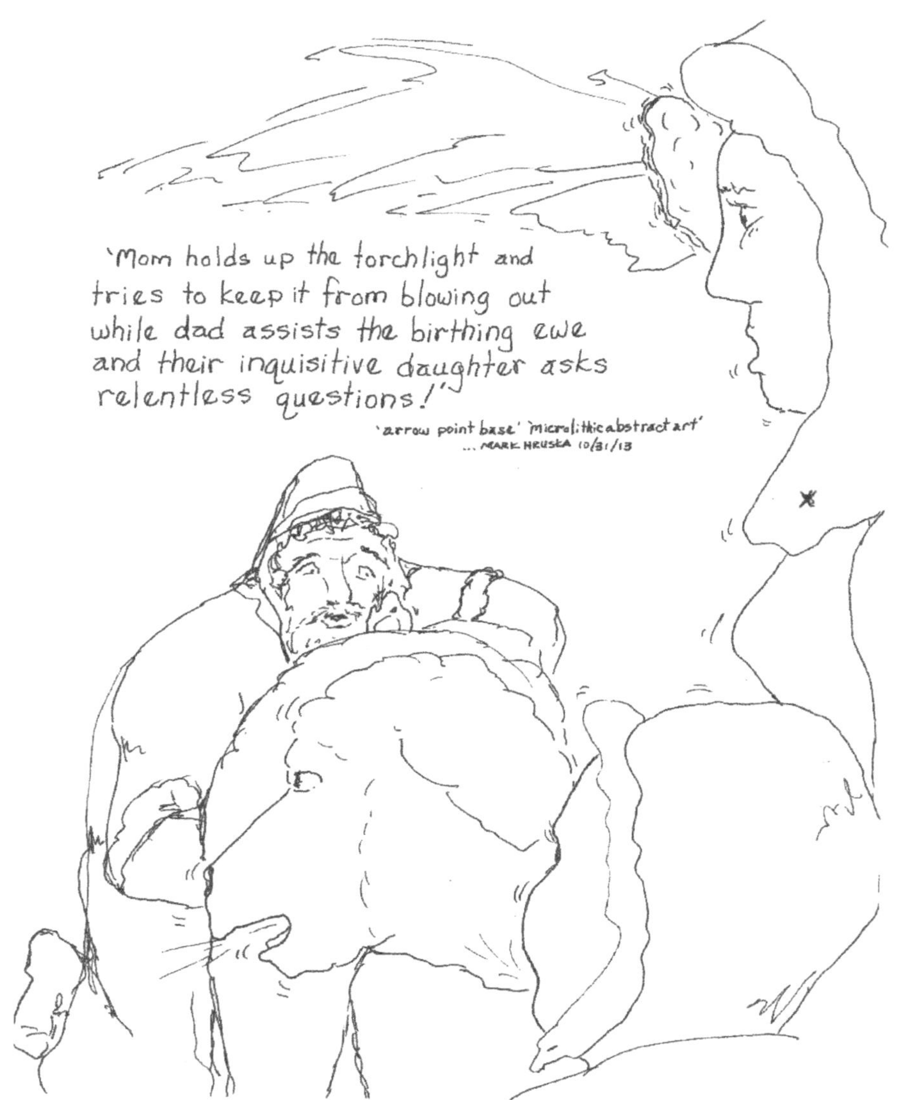

'arrow point base'... 'Mom holds up the torchlight and tries to keep it from blowing out while dad assists the birthing ewe and their inquisitive daughter asks relentless questions!'

209) If you look closely, you'll see the little newborns head making its newborn baa directly in front of dad's bearded face. He's the first thing that the newborn sees. This illustration really captures the important Pleistocene moment.

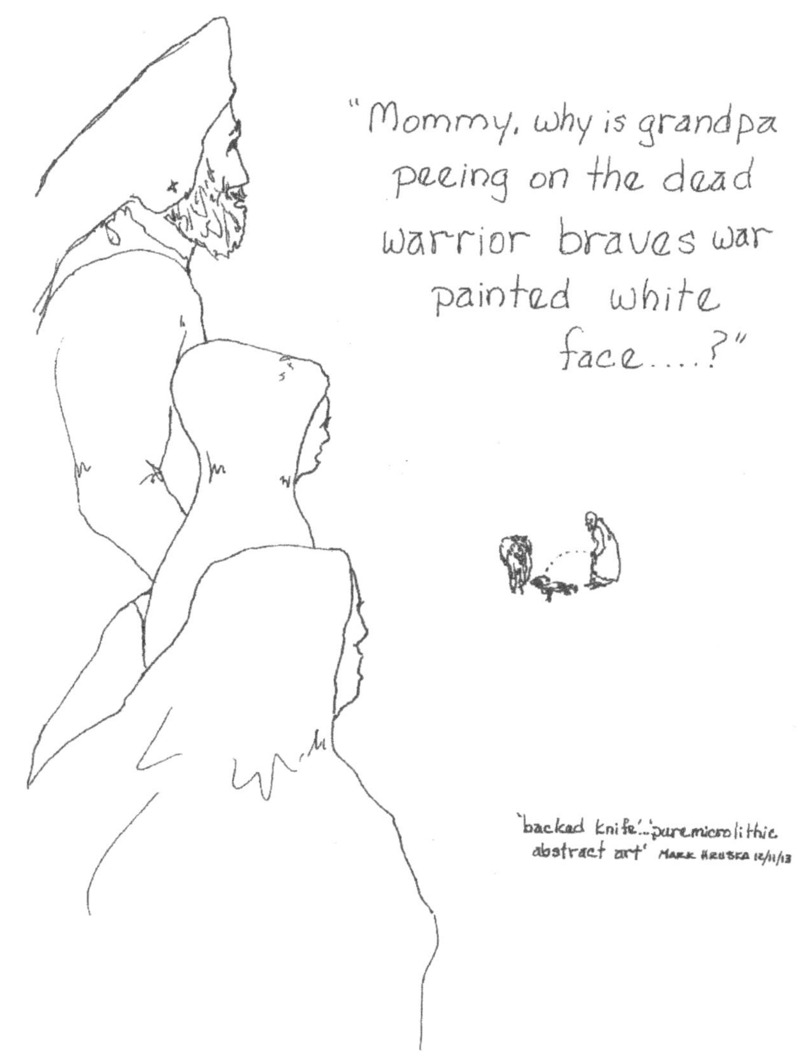

'backed knife' 'microlithic abstract art'... "Mommy, why is grandpa peeing on the dead warrior braves war painted white face...?"

210) I know that this line sketch may be offensive but I swore that I'd be true to the hunter herder microlithic abstract artist's artworks and show them the way that he intended. This is actually a popular version of the 'powwow' so offended or not you just have to get used to it, and trust me it gets worse because this scene is not showing irate grandma desecrating him too by spitting on his face.

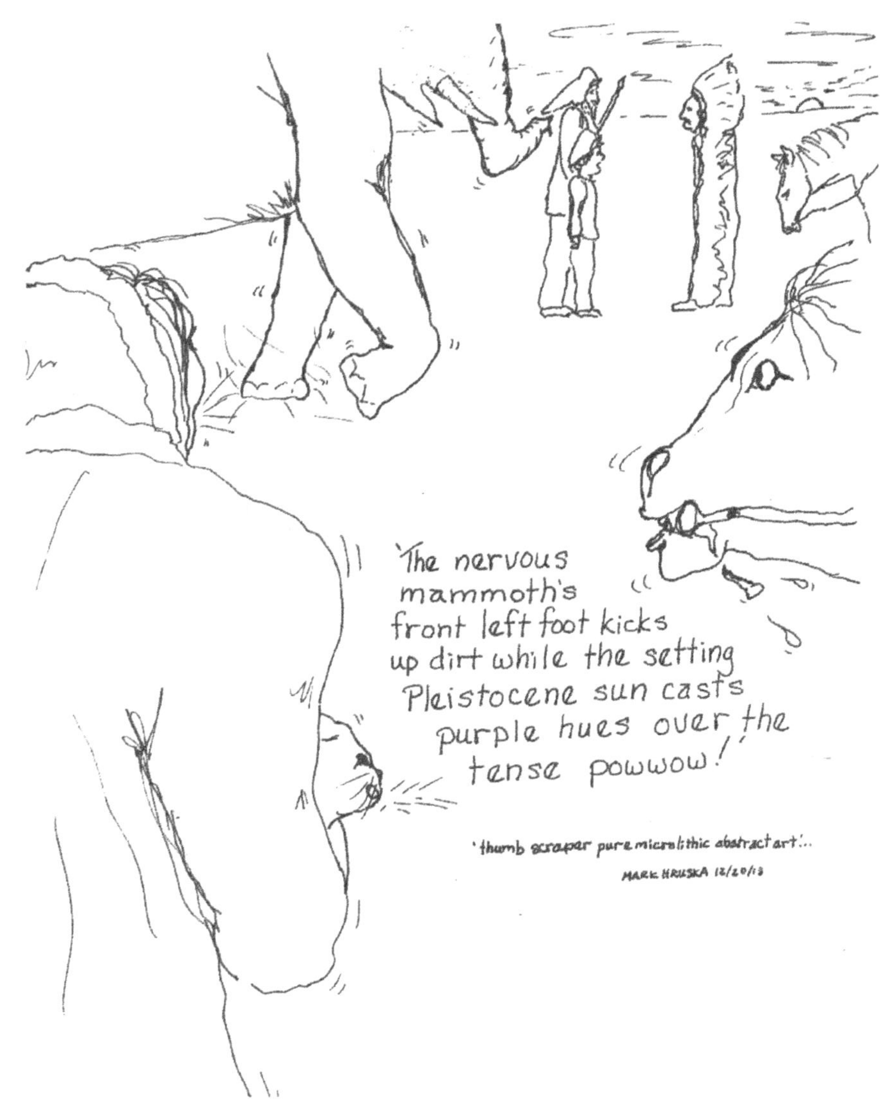

'Thumb scraper pure microlithic abstract art'... 'The nervous mammoth's front left foot kicks up dirt while the setting Pleistocene sun cast's purple hues over the tense powwow!'

211) You are seeing this entire scene from the perspective of the whooping and hollering warrior brave who's leaning way out to the left of his galloping palomino horse's neck so that he could whoop and holler in the running and screaming fair young maidens right ear over her right shoulder.

236

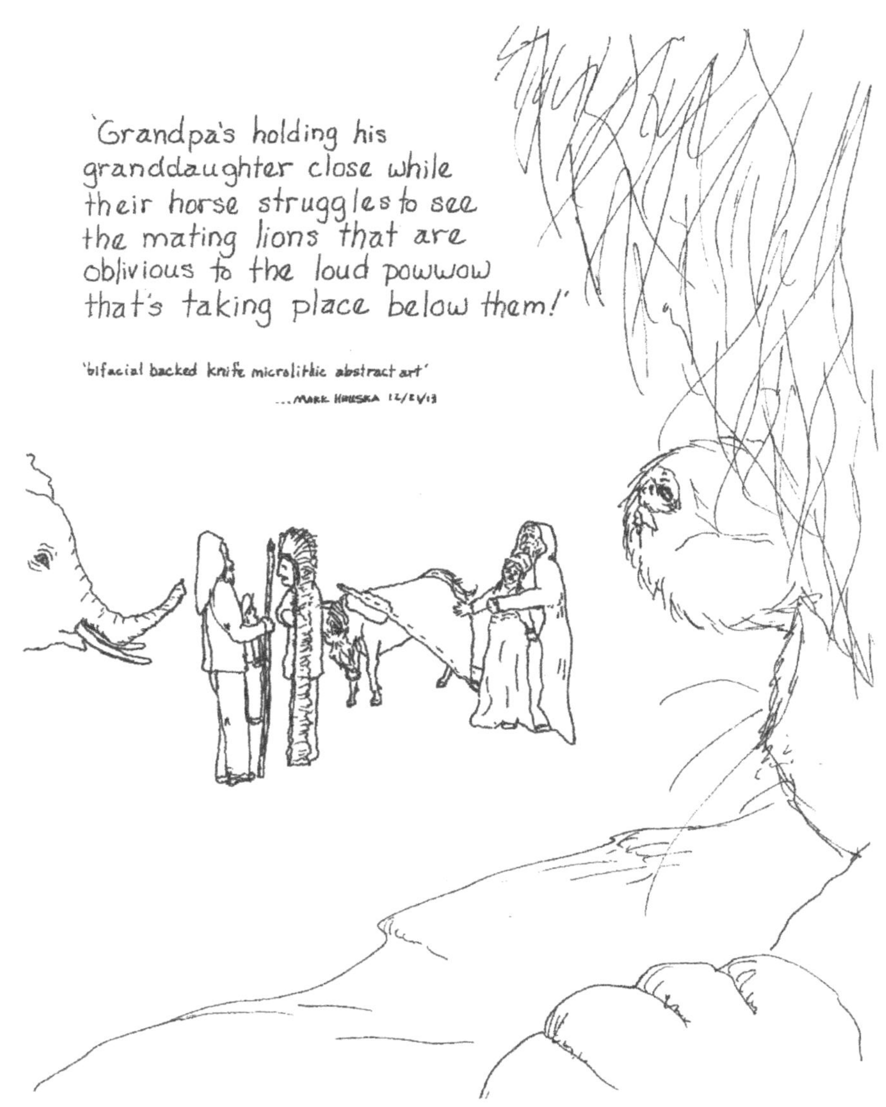

'bifacial backed knife microlithic abstract art'... 'Grandpa's
holding his granddaughter close while their horse struggles to see the
mating lions that are oblivious to the loud powwow that's taking place below them!'

238

212) Zoom in and peer intently at the back of the lioness's left ear to see the microlithic cognitive illusion reflection image of the front view of her mating male lions 'mating' face. To your lower left of it is the reflection of the left side view of the lead hunter herder who's down to the left of the mating lions that are up on a ledge to the right of the powwow. It's actually the reflection of the right side of the lead hunter herder because his reflection is a reverse image. You have to deal with this a lot when you interpret those clever hunter herder microlithic abstract artworks. The reflections always help give you the positions of the characters of the scene and in what positions they are to each other.

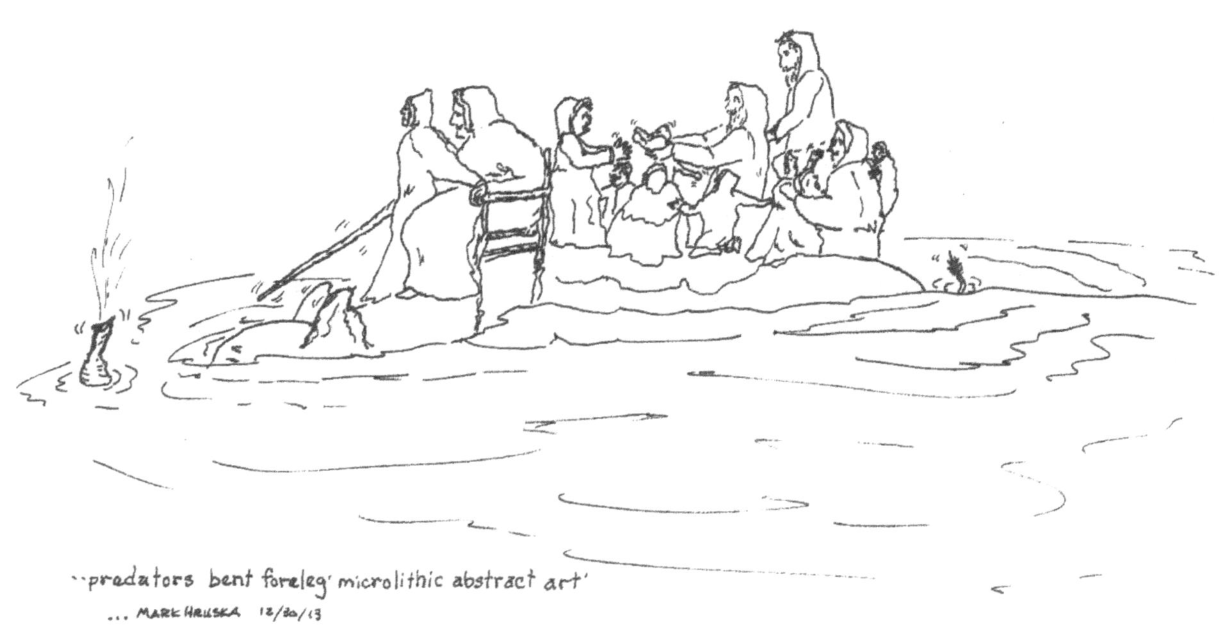

''predators bent foreleg' microlithic abstract art'... 'The waist high young maiden and her soaking wet kitty are lovingly reaching for each other and anticipating their embrace!'

213) Concentrating grandma is steering the submerged swimming lead mammoth after they rescued the entire lead family...after the 'epic deluge' swept them away.

240

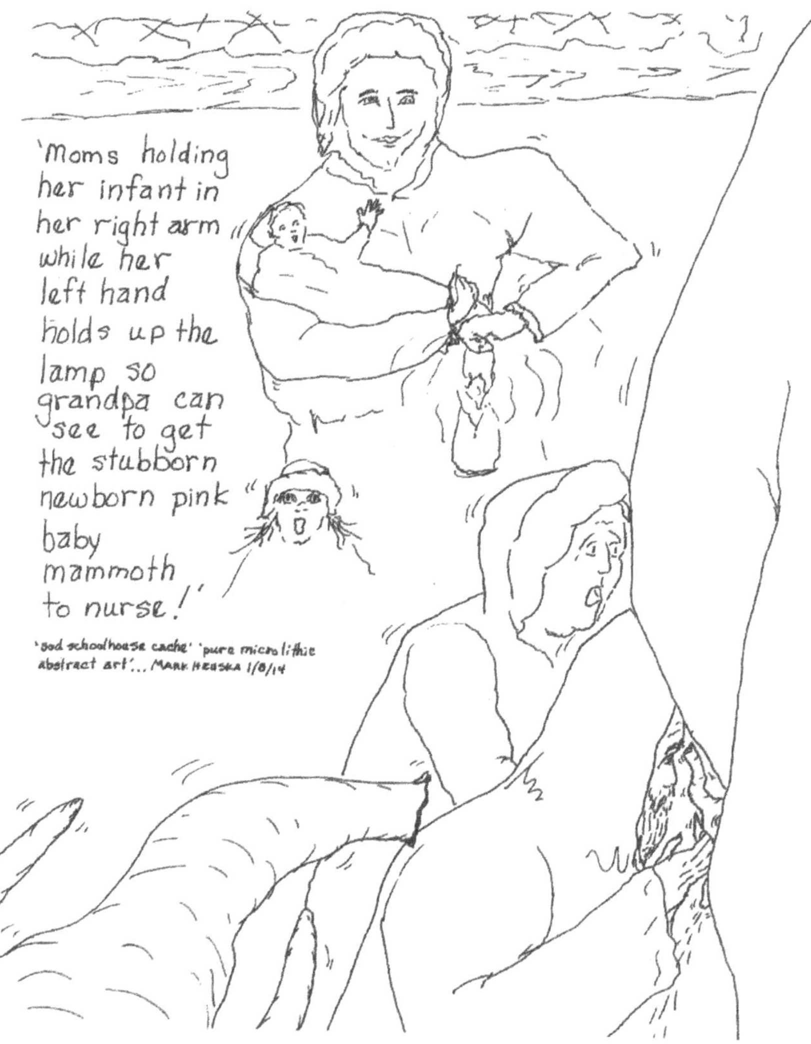

'sod schoolhouse' 'pure microlithic abstract art'... 'Moms
holding her infant in her right arm while her left hand holds up the lamp
so grandpa can see to get the stubborn newborn pink baby mammoth to nurse!'

214) The lamp could simply be a torchlight which definitely plays a big supporting role in this scene that always seems to take place during the Pleistocene nighttime and it's all being seen from the perspective of the mother mammoth.

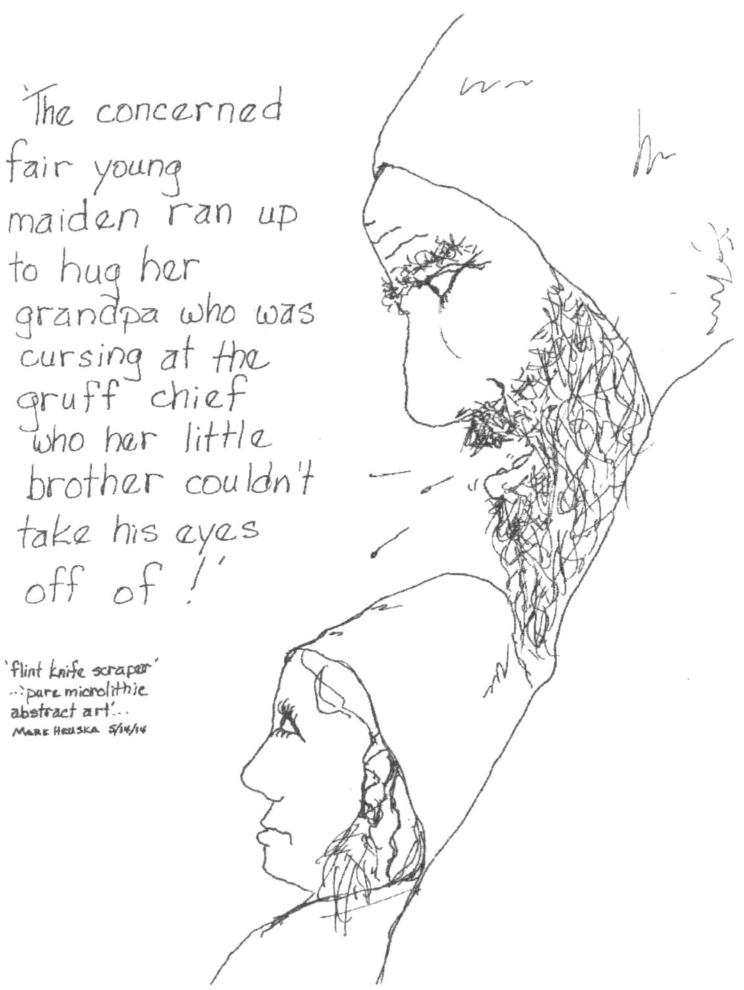

'flint knife scraper'... 'pure microlithic abstract art'...
'The concerned fair young maiden ran up to hug her grandpa who
was cursing at the gruff chief who her little brother couldn't take his eyes off of!'

215) This pieces interpretations illustration is a close up of the concerned fair young maiden and her injured cursing grandpa who just hobbled up to the powwow. Her irate grandma had shouted at her to leave the side of her lead hunter herder dad and go assist her injured hobbling grandpa.

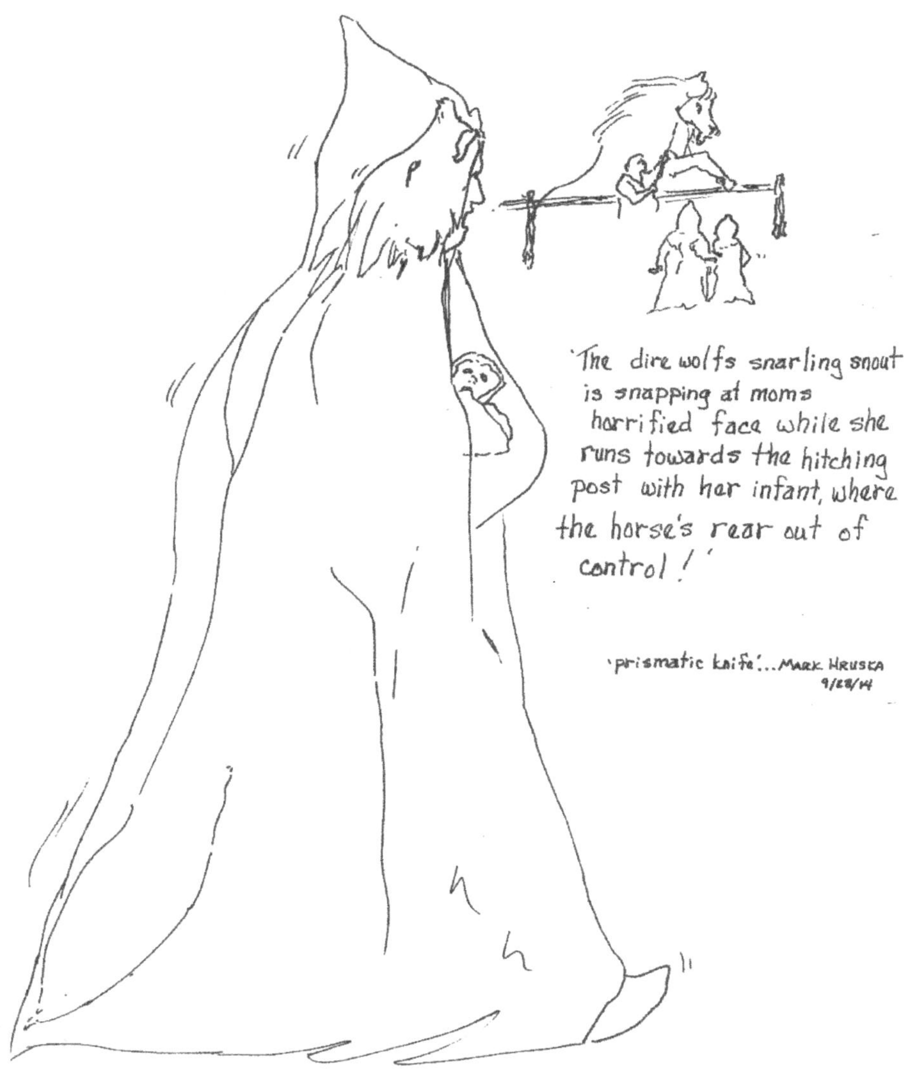

'prismatic knife'... 'The dire wolfs snarling snout is snapping at moms horrified face while she runs towards the hitching post with her infant, where the horses rear out of control!'

216) This pieces illustration is sketched to imitate the actual artworks shape which is why the attacking dire wolf seems to blend into the rear right side view of running mom herdswoman.

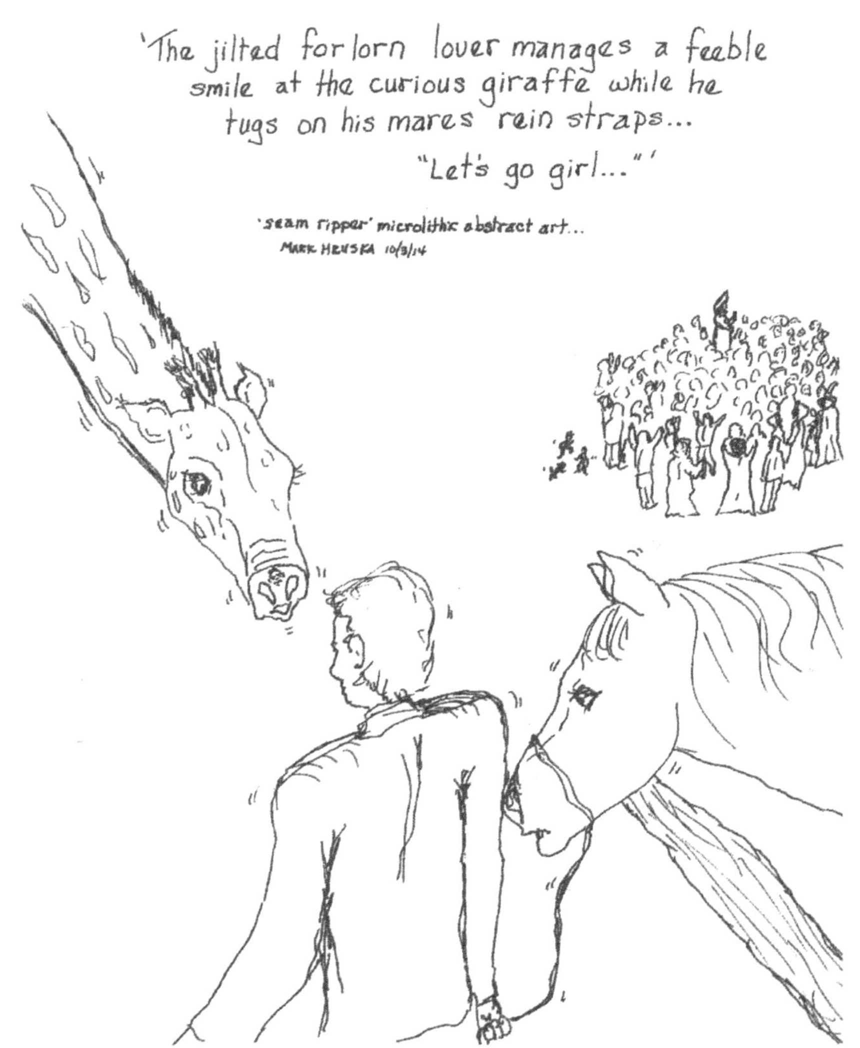

'seam ripper'...microlithic abstract art... 'The jilted forlorn lover manages a feeble smile at the curious giraffe while he tugs on his mares rein straps... "Let's go girl..."'

217) This is one popular folklore tale that regularly shows the feeding giraffe reaching for the highest most succulent leaves of the trees that are on the other side of the hitching post. You'll see her long purplish tongue reaching as high as she can possibly reach with it. It took me a long time to finally figure out that she wasn't just a giraffe that lived here all those millennia ago but that she was actually one of the Mammoth People's rides that was at the hitching post and most likely tied to it just like the horses.

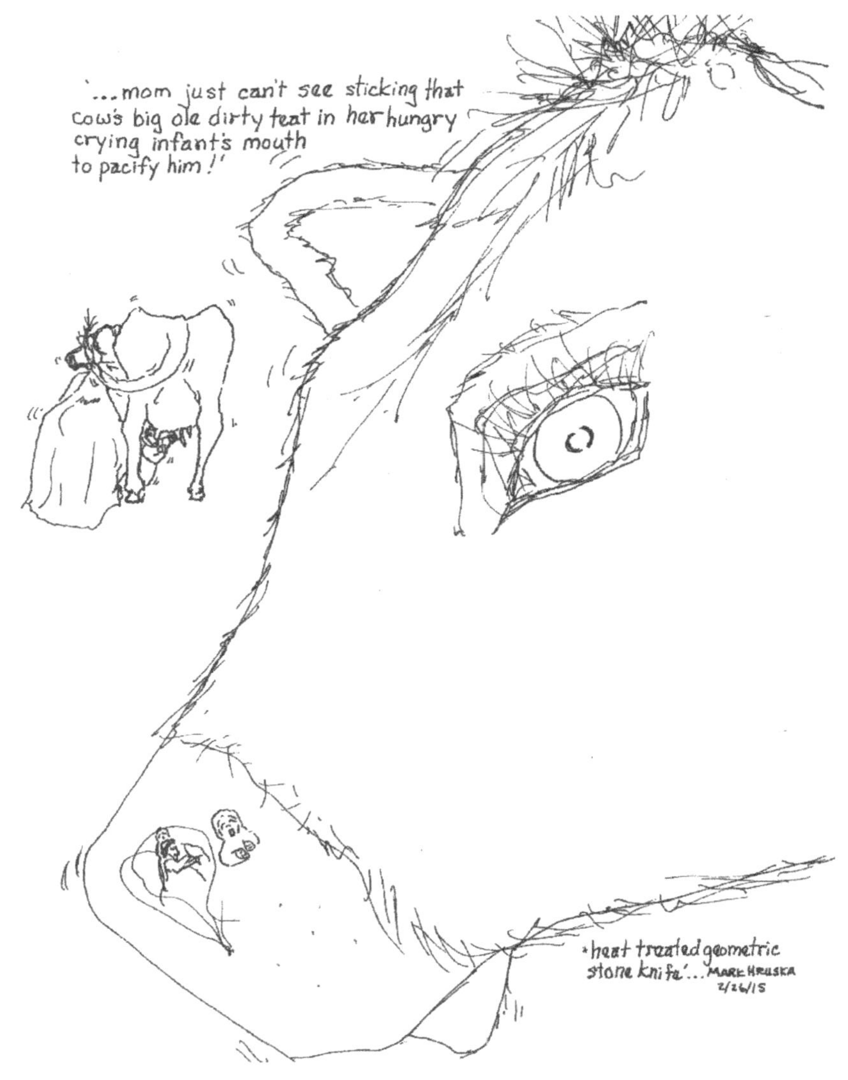

'heat treated geometric stone knife'... '...mom just can't see sticking
that cow's big ole dirty teat in her crying infant's mouth to pacify him!'

246

218) Zoom into the further away scene and you'll actually see mom holding up her infant's carrier under the milk cow. Then look at the part of the left side view of the milk cow's head that you can see on the other side of bent over mom herdswoman. Then if you take a step back and view the close-up image of the left side view of her head it's as if you could see that far away image of her by simply taking a step back and viewing the whole close-up scene. This is the way that mom herdswoman sees her as the mooing milk cow turns sharply to her left to look at what mom herdswoman is doing back there. To verify that, you'll see the reflection image of the left side view of bent over mom herdswoman and her screaming infant reflecting off of the left side of the milk cows mooing muzzle. This is the way that the Mammoth People microlithic abstract art figurative language works on the individual rotational change-up artworks.

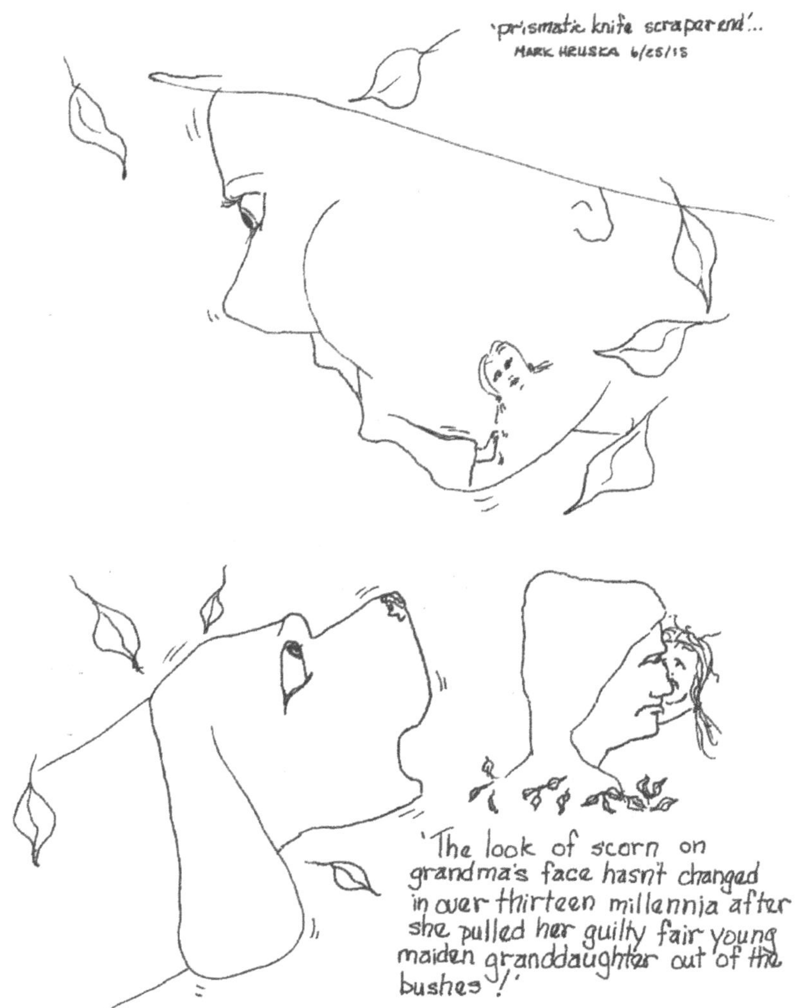

'prismatic knife scraper end'... 'The look of
scorn on grandma's face hasn't changed in over thirteen millennia
after she pulled her guilty fair young maiden granddaughter out of the bushes!'

219) This artworks interpretations illustration is showing the scene of when the fair young maiden's ornery little brother's bloodhound pup found her hiding in the bushes on the riverbank with her beau at the summertime picnic. The point of the folklore tale is to teach the fair young maidens to never attempt this at the risk of being immensely embarrassed in front of the entire Mammoth People community that's gathered at the annual event.

SIMULACRUM- a perceived image resulting from 'pareidolia', the mind's tendency to "recognize" common shapes (especially faces) in random patterns.

Pareidolia- the imagined perception of a pattern or meaning where it does not actually exist, as in considering the moon to have human features.

The Mammoth People hunter herder figurative microlithic abstract art is based on 'simulacrum' that are rubbed and etched out of heat treated stone, flint, chert, granite, limestone, sandstone or any other stone that they can see microlithic imagery in. They also did the same thing with pottery sherds and bone!

.... "it just is what it is"....Mark Hruska

"It simply comes down to this to describe the Mammoth Peoples microlithic abstract arts figurative language…. As the interpreter of it, you are in their heads imagining the telling of their repetitive epic folklore tales while you visually follow along, not by turning the pages of a two dimensional story book but by rotating the rubbed and etched out three dimensional combined optical and cognitive illusion close up almost 'statuesque' stone images that are seen from one distinct angle and that have microlithic cognitive or combined optical and cognitive illusion reflection images reflecting off of them, from one scene to the next!" "They did the same thing with potsherds but used the tiny pieces of embedded sand aggregate as the microlithic reflection images that reflected off of the combined optical and cognitive illusion close-up image that was the whole rubbed and etched out potsherd!" "Now, imagine that the combined optical and cognitive illusion images are rubbed and etched out 'PAREIDOLIA', the 'mind's tendency to "recognize" common shapes (especially faces) in random patterns." "I can't just call it 'pareidolia' because there's a difference between the optical, the cognitive and the combined optical and cognitive illusion images."

…………. "it just is what it is"……Mark Hruska 11/17/15

250

It appears that archaeologists have been looking at it from all the wrong angles.... literally and figuratively! You'll understand once you get it in your 'mind's eye' how the Mammoth People used the stone as rotational change ups to tell their folklore tales!

.... "it just is what it is"...Mark Hruska

12/20/15

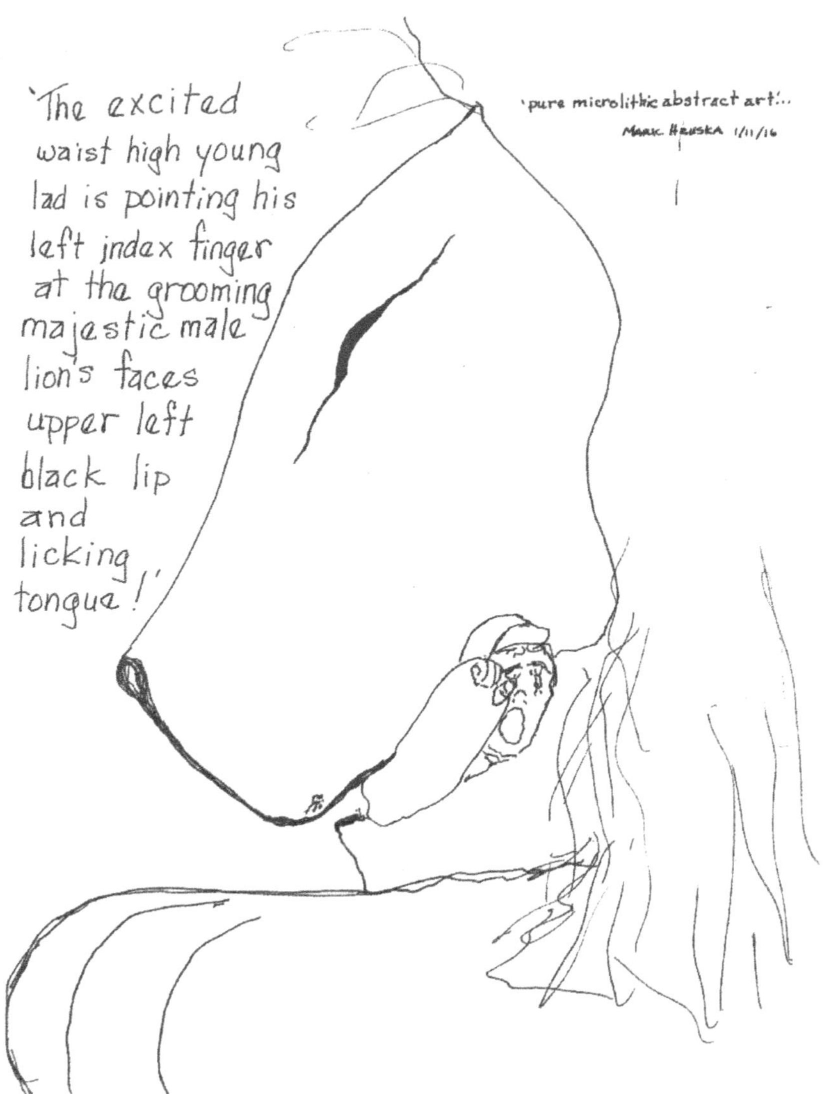

'pure microlithic abstract art'... 'The excited waist high young lad is pointing his left index finger at the grooming male lion's faces upper left black lip and licking tongue!'

220) This pieces illustration is of a popular variation of the 'powwow'. If you look closely, you'll see the microlithic cognitive illusion reflection image of the front view of the excited waist high young lad pointing towards the licking lip that he's reflecting off of.

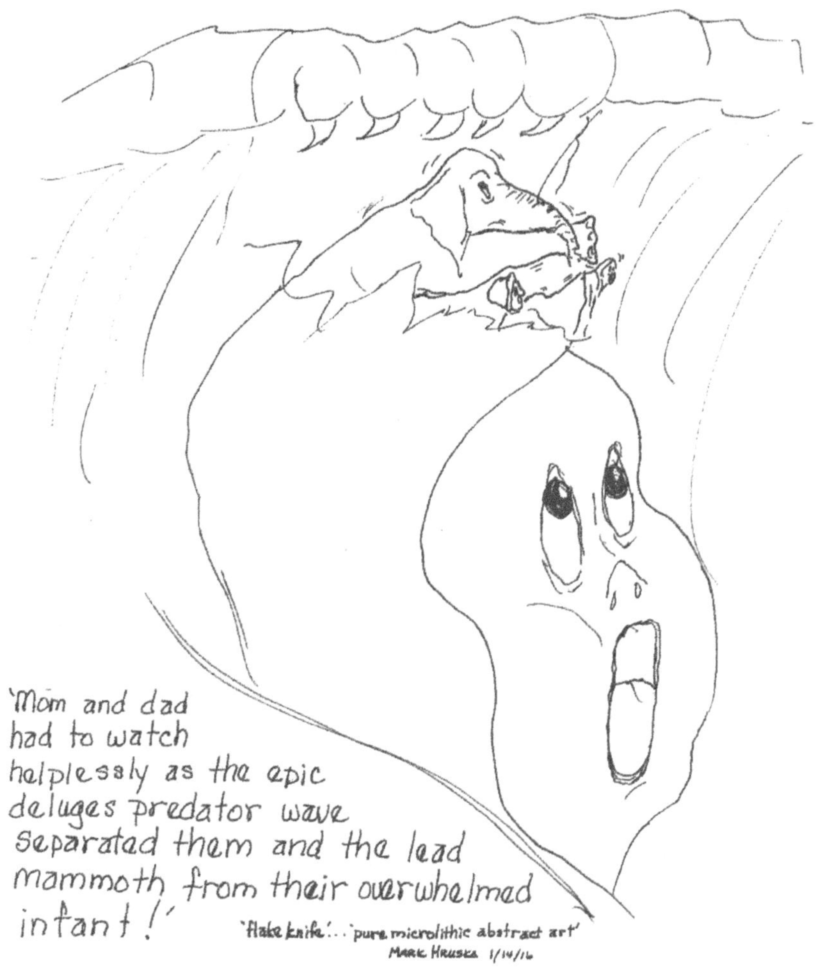

'flake knife'... 'pure microlithic abstract art'...
'Mom and dad had to watch helplessly as the epic deluges predator
wave separated them and the lead mammoth from their overwhelmed infant!'

221) This pieces interpretations illustration is self-explanatory. But it might help to know that the infant is strapped to his backboard that's slung over the milk cow's left shoulder and that mom was trekking between them and the lead mammoth before the immense roaring male lion epic deluge wave swept them away and separated them.

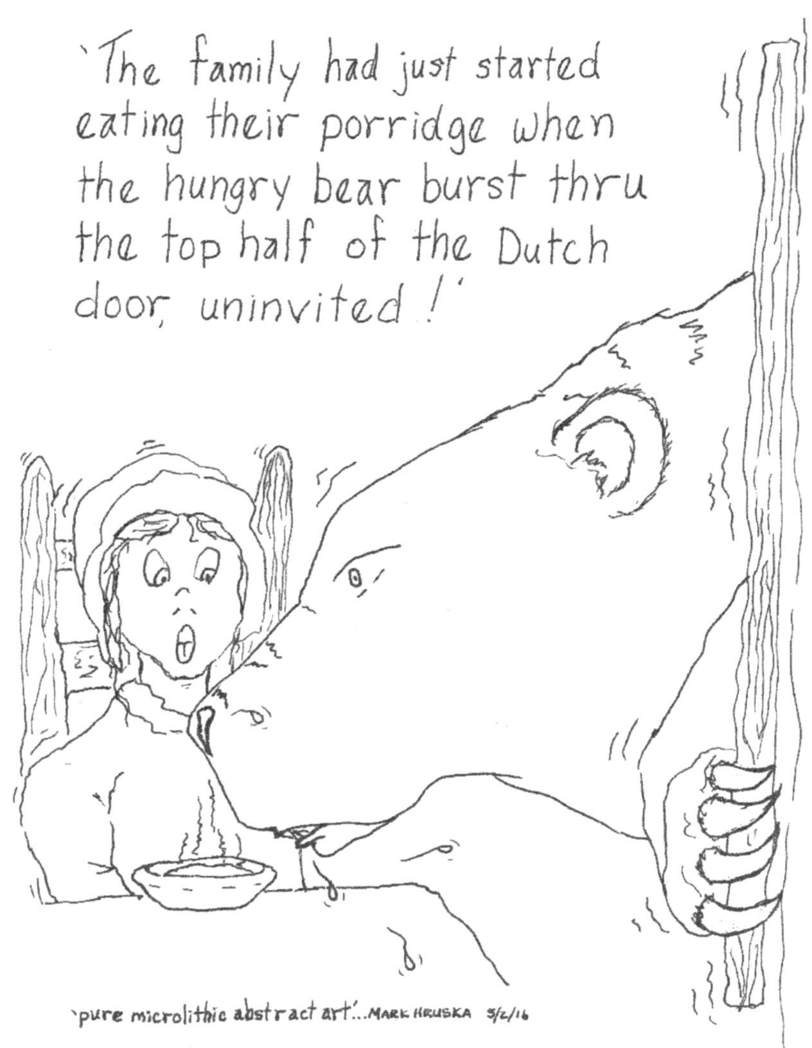

'pure microlithic abstract art'... 'The family had just started eating their porridge when the hungry bear burst thru the top half of the Dutch door, uninvited!'

222) I was absolutely blown away when I interpreted this piece. It was so easy to sketch it because this is exactly what the talented hunter herder microlithic abstract artist planted in my 'mind's eye'. Mind you, I never re-sketched an illustration.

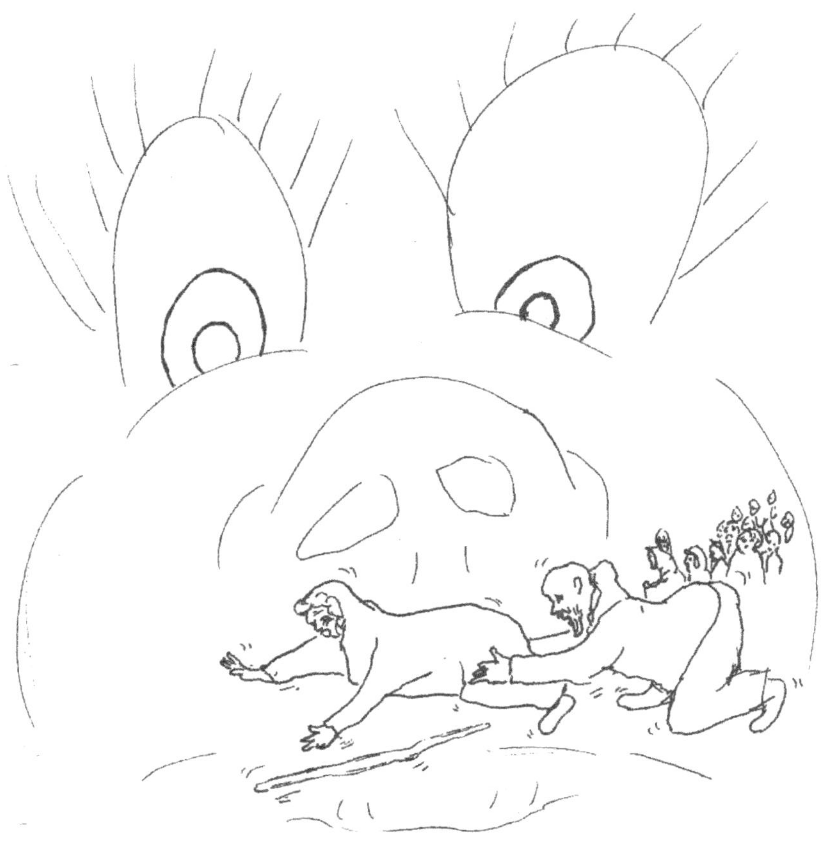

'flake knife pure microlithic abstract art'... 'The bewildered
expression on the waist high young maidens face is being created by
the reflections of the prostrate elderly herdswoman that she blindly ran into!'

223) This is another self-explanatory illustration.

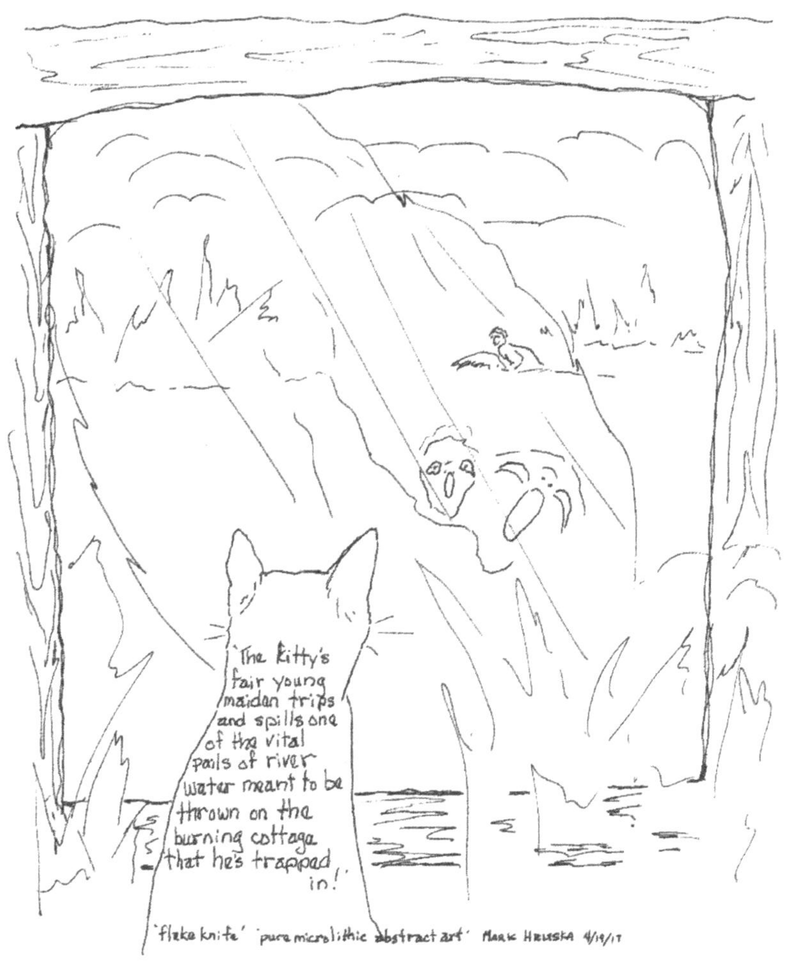

'flake knife' 'pure microlithic abstract art'...
'The kitty's fair young maiden trips and spills one of the vital pales
of river water meant to be thrown on the burning cottage that he's trapped in!'

224) You can see her back there tripping and spilling one of the pales of river water while moms shouting face is in front of the window between the further away fair young maiden's image and the closer up image of the front view of dads shouting face. He's superimposed on mom as he throws a pale of river water up towards the roof of the cottage. The water can be seen as a curtain of clear water that the kitty is looking through towards his fair young maiden who's tripping off in the distance. Behind her are the leaping flames of the windblown prairie fire with its billowing smoke cloud above it.

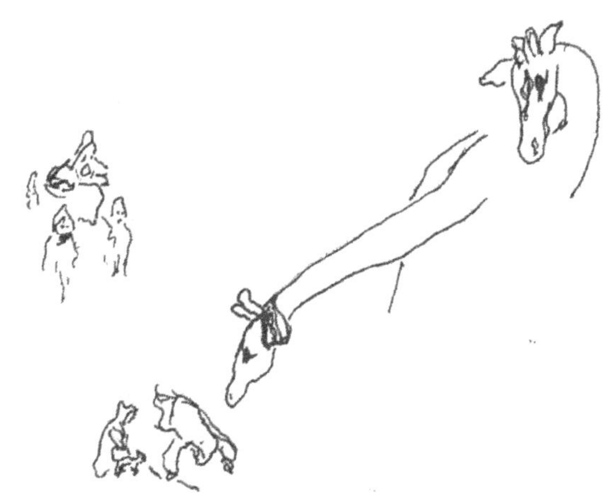

'pure microlithic abstract art'... 'The pair of curious sad giraffes is gazing down at the fallen decrepit elderly herdswoman as they trudge on by her in the narrow windy mountain pass!'

225) I distinctly interpreted this piece to reinforce what I had long expected which was that the giraffes trekked to 'here' with the rest of the Mammoth People mammoth caravan of trekkers. Their imagery on this artwork is unmistakable and you can see that I sketched it in a hurry because I was busy farming...which is supposed to be my main occupation...

Parting Thoughts

After having interpreted three flint and chert knife scraper tools from the West Central Sandhill's of Nebraska near Hyannis, I fully understand that I will be able to trace the route that the Mammoth People took to migrate to the center of this North American Continent from where I figured out their very existence. It will be obvious that if they trekked inland from the Washington State coastline then their folklore tales of everything that took place afterward or in their future, would be absent on their microlithic abstract artwork eating utensils and other tools as you worked backward along their route.

In other words, if I leave my local of Ulysses Nebraska from whence I figured out their very existence, and let's say go to the site of the breached lake Missoula in Montana that I suspect they traveled through, and interpret pieces of their microlithic abstract art, I shouldn't find any pieces that have the folklore tales of the 'powwow' or of when lurking saber-toothed cats and lions stalked the Mammoth People mammoth caravan of trekkers when they trekked through the tall swaying prairie grass that would obviously be further to their southeast and have taken place in the future of their epic trek. Then when I travel through the Columbia River Gorge and get to the West coast of Washington State, I shouldn't find any of their folklore tales of the previously mentioned folklore tales nor should I find any that include the 'epic deluge' that hadn't taken place yet. Consequently, if I could possibly find any of their microlithic abstract art at Kamchatka Russia which seems unlikely because sea levels were four hundred feet lower then, and they lived near the coast, then I shouldn't find any signs of the previously mentioned folklore tales nor should I find any that had the folklore tale of the 'predator ice' where the toddlers or the waist high young lad or the waist high young maiden fall through thinly iced over sea lion breathe holes. Neither should we see scenes of when the fair young maiden and the horse that she rode fall through the predator ice and eventually sink into the dark icy cold abyss that's beneath it. It seems totally plausible to me that I should be able to trace them all the way back across Eurasia to wherever Scottish terrier and Bloodhound dogs originated and where Shetland sheep, graylag and swan geese came from as well. This would seem to be somewhere in Europe but more exclusively, the British Isles which probably weren't Isles at all since the sea levels were four hundred feet lower and it might still have been a solid land mass with the whole of Eurasia.

Based on what the Mammoth People's microlithic abstract art figurative language has shown me, the current paradigm of our distant past that's widely accepted by present day archaeology is inadequate. This leaves me with an insatiable propensity to search for this enigmatic Caucasian cultures source and for where they ultimately migrated to

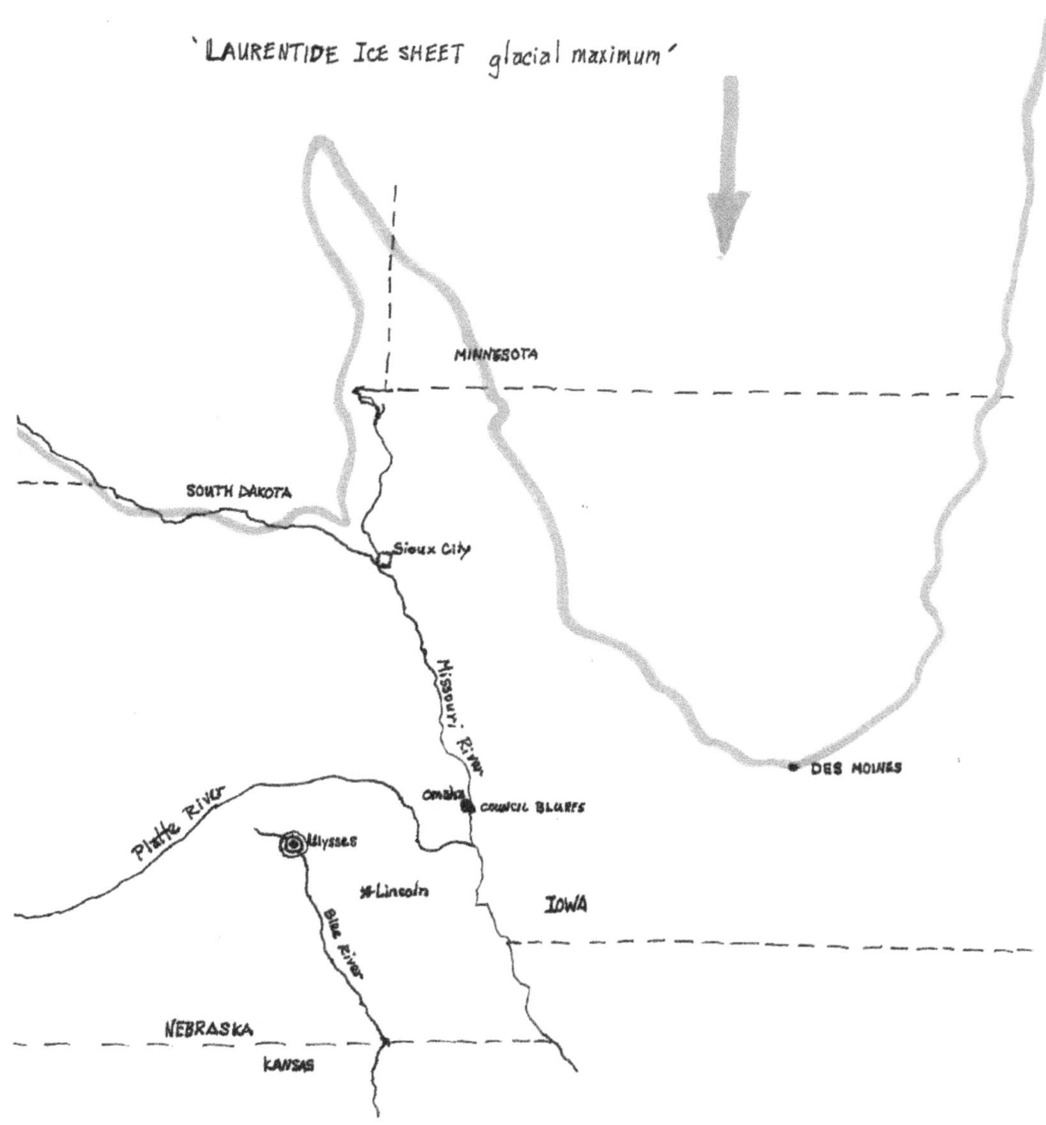

Index of Illustrations

26) "The predator ash is gaining on us!" "Shut that kid up and move those sheep!" pg. 30

27) "Leave me...son...get them out of here...", pg. 33

28) 'snapped lance base'... "Daddy!"... "Grandpa is trying to say something!", pg. 34

29) "I'm not going to make it son... save my grandchildren from the attacking 'male lion' volcanic predator ash cloud....", pg. 35

30) 'pure microlithic abstract art'... 'The frightened and burdened pony's 'snorting snot' is how the porters portray their 'order barking' crotchety old queen!', pg. 36

31) Line sketch dated 9/17/11, pg. 38

32) "Can you imagine standing right between them when the woolly rhino charged into the mammoth's long curvy white tusk?!", pg. 39

33) 'pure microlithic abstract art'... "Someday son....this will all be yours...", pg. 40

34) 'Backed prismatic knife'... 'Clearly, the roaring and attacking predator male lion prairie grass fire scared the 's _ _ t' out of the fleeing mammoth!', pg. 41

35) 'pure microlithic abstract art'... "If you stay too late to gab, the dire wolves will have a feast!", pg. 42

36) 'pure microlithic abstract art'... 'Mom and dad peer helplessly thru the predator ice as their beautiful vibrant and full of life young maiden daughter sinks into the depths below....', pg. 43

37) 'They're in each other's heads thinking the same thoughts, none of which her grandson wants to hear... "They're gaining on us!", pg. 44

38) 'pure microlithic abstract art'... 'It seems that the Scotties and Calico kitties have been fighting like cats and dogs for thirteen millennia!', pg. 45

39) 'stone knife'... 'The elderly shepherdess took a spear thru the chest to save her toddler grandson's lives while she was also trying to save her granddaughter!' pg. 46

40) Line sketch 10/15/11., pg. 47

41) 'pure microlithic abstract art'... 'Maybe the sorceress's incantations followed by the women's chanting in unison 'is' saving the dying old hunter herder 'spirits' life!', pg. 49

42) 'heat treated snapped prismatic knife'... "Oh quit your whining you stinky hairy mammoth or I'll use my dull flint knife that I used to sheer the sheep!", pg. 50

43) 'pure microlithic abstract art'.... 'You could feel her embarrassment when the copulating fair maiden looked up and saw the 'snickering' young lad above her!', pg. 51

44) 'backed flake knife'... 'Dad clearly saved her and mom is hollering at grandpa to hurry up and to bring that blanket to warm her up!', pg. 52

45) 'pure microlithic abstract art'... 'The women are cooking; the fair young milk maiden is milking, dad is pounding stone and grandpa is playing with his granddaughter!', pg. 53

46) 'pure microlithic abstract art'... 'Can you imagine the horror grandma felt as she watched the saber-toothed cat slice up her beautiful fair young maiden granddaughter?', pg. 55

47) 'prismatic knife'... '... "You can make it!" "It's just a few more steps!" followed by the Scotties own encouragement "Arf!-Arf!",pg. 56

48) 'prismatic knife'... 'The male lion waits patiently for his dinner while his lioness's rustle something up for him!', pg. 57

49) 'heat treated prismatic knife'... "Here's something else that my grandma gave me.... her shepherds crook!" "Do you want to see how pretty it is?!", pg. 58

50) 'pure microlithic abstract art'... "Watch out for your fingers... dads in an all fiery hurry!", pg. 59

51) 'heat treated flake knife'... 'Then the jilted forlorn lover mounted his pony and rode off into the Pleistocene sun... Oh... it's so sad...', pg. 60

52) 'heat treated backed knife'... '...the erupting volcano and approaching pyroclastic flow were reflecting off of the bottom of her right foot thru her quaint cottages bedroom window!', pg. 61

53) 'pure microlithic abstract art'...'The laboring herdswoman is looking down in front of her towards the head of the bed as she pushes!', pg. 63

54) 'backed finger knife'... 'The brown woolly mammoth battled the predator ice until her rear end finally sank with her head going down last like a sinking battle ship!', pg. 64

55) 'backed knife'... 'The red blood running down the ox's sweaty neck makes it obvious that he's 'bucking' to get the saber-toothed cat off his back!', pg. 66

56) 'Mammoth People mammoth caravan trekking to here!', pg. 67

57) 'flake knife'...'The snarling male lion's head is above the fleeing Mammoth People's heads as a pyroclastic flow that's pouncing on them!', pg. 68

58) 'prismatic knife midsection'... 'Grandma has such a stern resolve look on her face because she knows what her son and granddaughter must endure having already lost a wife and a mother...', pg. 69

59) 'rotational change-up'... "Good girl!" "You are the most awesome mammoth ever...yes you are!", pg. 70

60) 'pure microlithic abstract art'... 'Dad pulled mom and his fair young maiden daughter up out of the lahar and grandma came to pick them up with the mammoth!', pg. 71

61) 'polished stone'... 'Grandpa's telling a tall tale to his terrified grandkids around the campfire about how he speared the saber-toothed cat right in the nose!', pg. 72

62) 'snapped knife section'... 'The fair young maiden's right white hand is clutching the rein strap and slapping it as she kicks her pony into high gear!', pg. 73

63) 'prismatic knife'...'The snarling saber-toothed cat has chosen the plump slow moving herdswoman and is about to bite into her!', pg. 74

64) 'oval knife section'... 'There's a white lightning bolt coming out of the lioness's left paw!', pg. 75

65) 'predators bent foreleg'... 'Dad sent the rambunctious waist high young lad to the earth lodge to show grandma the hole in his muddy left mitten that she made for him!', pg. 76

66) 'alternately flaked knife'... 'The fair young maiden is asking her grandmother how much longer it will take to squirt cow's milk into her infant brother's mouth!', pg. 77

67) 'pure microlithic abstract art'... 'Grandma's looking down to her right from her armchair perch atop the mammoth and screaming, "Get that kid out of his carrier!"', pg. 78

68) 'awesome prismatic knife'... 'That's when the freezing waist high young maiden yells, "Blow harder Daddy!" "Blow harder!"', pg. 79

69) 'snapped oval knife'... "Mom and dad's cottage has been hit by white hot lightning, girl!", pg. 80

70) 'pure microlithic abstract art'... 'The milk cow is bucking wildly to get the pair of lions off her back!', pg. 81

71) 'predators bent foreleg'... 'The fair young maiden has a stare down with the male lion from a respectable distance knowing that he has no intention of relinquishing his kill!', pg. 82

72) 'oval knife'... 'Grandma's shepherds crook saved the fair young maiden's life because she could hook her neck and pull her to the edge of the predator ice!', pg. 83

73) 'oval knife'... '"Daddy.... grandpa's hollering something about the roaring male lion catching us!"', pg. 84

74) 'pure microlithic abstract art'... 'The toddler is crawling on his hands and knees towards his hollering grandpa's travois!', pg. 85

75) 'heat treated flake knife'... '"Na, na, na, na...na!" "You can't catch me!"', pg. 87

76) 'pure microlithic abstract art'... 'The pair of oxen was driven home hard so that the young

lad could show the rest of his family his first kill!', pg. 88

77) 'prismatic knife'... 'The elderly herdsman and herdswoman see the erupting volcanoes dark ominous ash cloud coming fast and they're both sensing that the end is near!', pg. 89

78) 'pure microlithic abstract art'... '"Put the un-hatched goose eggs down sweetheart... or we'll both smell like rotten eggs!"', pg. 90

79) 'prismatic knife'... '...when the dire wolves killed and ate his beloved wife and waist high young maiden daughter they ripped his heart right out of his chest too!', pg. 91

80) 'oval knife'... 'Mom and her fair young maiden daughter could be seen clinging to each other thru the cottages rectangular window as the deluge swept them away!', pg. 92

81) 'pure microlithic abstract art'... 'The roaring male lion and his stalking lioness mate breached the glacial ice damn wall and unleashed an epic deluge on the trekking Mammoth People!', pg. 93

82) 'pure microlithic abstract art'... 'The roaring male lion deluge swept the entire caravan away but the orange fat kitty managed to pull himself onto the ox's back and save himself....again!', pg. 94

83) 'bladelet knife'... 'Dad took his inexperienced young lad son out in the kayak to hunt humpback whales but only one of them returned!', pg. 95

84) 'heat treated flake knife'... 'The attacking roaring male lion ash cloud is swiping at all of the weary trekkers including the alerted grouse family!', pg. 96

85) 'snapped prismatic knife'... 'The alpha male dire wolfs front left paw is pushing the waist high young maidens head forward while he bites her grandmothers neck!', pg. 97

86) 'pure microlithic abstract art'... 'The extremely sad dad is watching his extremely happy fair young maiden daughter bride wave goodbye over the back of the 'just married' sled!', pg. 98

87) 'flake knife'... 'The snarling saber-toothed cat turned completely around in front of his prey before he took his first juicy bite!', pg. 99

88) 'pure microlithic abstract art'... 'The ox is turning his head sharply to his left to hear the mortified waist high young maiden scold her naughty fat kitty!', pg. 100

89) 'pure microlithic abstract art'... 'The sorceress is wafting smoke over grandpa's white face that's sputtering to life while her three canting assistants chant an incantation!' pg. 101

90) 'pure microlithic abstract art'... 'If grandpa's ranting hadn't stopped them the volcanoes ejected cottage size white hot cinder ball would have killed them all!', pg. 102

91) 'pottery shard'... 'The majestic male lion takes a catnap while the lioness and the cubs feed on grandma's leftovers!', pg. 103

92) 'pottery shard'... "Good girl... what's that dog howling about....?", pg. 104

93) 'hammer stone'... 'The cute little kitties won't stay hidden from the persistent waist high young maiden for long!', pg. 105

94) 'pure stone microlithic abstract art'... 'The sneaky rat snuck in the cottages opened door while grandma herdswoman went out to milk the milk cow in the meadow!', pg. 106

95) 'micro flake knife'... 'Mom's squirting cow's milk into her screaming infant's mouth to help lower tensions during the powwow that nobody can understand each other at!', pg. 107

96) 'pure microlithic abstract art'... 'The sharp predator ice slowly separated the inseparable Pleistocene twins while the submissive ewe spirit waited patiently!', pg. 108

97) 'backed knife'... 'The 'feeding' cub looks startled as the three screaming herdswomen charge towards him and his male lion dad in a unified assault!', pg. 109

98) 'flake knife'... 'Grandma is so upset with these warrior braves that chase her fair young maiden granddaughter that she's spitting on this one's dead grey face!', pg. 110

99) 'pure microlithic abstract art'... 'The mortified waist high young maiden would never do anything to intentionally hurt her already delirious grandfather!', pg. 111

100) 'snapped spear point'... 'The fair young maiden's brave 'hissing' and 'clawing' kitty caused the 'proud' warrior braves Pleistocene dust eating demise!', pg. 113

101) 'pure microlithic abstract art'... 'Amongst all of the commotion, grandma's yelling back at her struggling granddaughter.... "Grab the end of my crook sweetheart.... grab it now!"', pg. 115

102) 'pure microlithic abstract art'... 'A gift of wildflowers for her delirious grandfather turned ugly when her kitty scratched his face and grandma's evil eye made her feel mortified!', pg. 116

103) 'pure microlithic abstract art'... 'Once again, the dire wolves culled the weakest and most feeble prey while the healthy young ones fled for their Pleistocene lives!', pg. 117

104) 'triple notched 'snapped' arrow base, pure microlithic abstract art'... 'The descending male lion ash cloud is in grandpa's delirious face and they're reflecting off of the alerted stag-moose's antler rack!', pg. 118

105) 'pure microlithic abstract art'... 'The 'cud chewing' milk cow looks back when grandma squeezes her big front left teat and says in a whispery voice...ho bossy....', pg. 119

106) 'pure microlithic abstract art'... 'It's a race against Pleistocene time, is grandpa's fair young maiden granddaughter going to get to him before the roaring male lion epic deluge swallows him up?', pg. 120

107) 'pure microlithic abstract art'... 'Looking down over the forehead of her mammoth at the powwow below, grandma speaks in her crotchety old voice... "Use your spear to convince him...son..."', pg. 121

108) 'pure microlithic abstract art'... 'Her frightened kitty's rear left paw scratched grandpa's delirious white face while grandma's white eyeballs glared at her mortified granddaughter...', pg. 122

109) 'prismatic flake knife'... '"Ho Bossy!" The tired hunter herder looks relieved as the newborn baby mammoth takes off and sucks on his own...', pg. 123

110) 'obsidian pure microlithic abstract art'... 'The mortified waist high young maiden is reaching up towards her older brothers consoling face on her way to march in front of her grandma's front porters...', pg. 124

111) 'backed flake knife'... 'As grandma removes the pillow from under her deceased husband's head she mumbles... "You won't need this anymore 'love'..."', pg. 125

112) 'pure microlithic abstract art'... 'Grandmas clinging to her Scottie while her right index finger reaches up and touches the pointy tip of the attacking roaring male lion ash clouds lower left fang!', pg. 126

113) 'predators bent foreleg'... 'The predator chief had grandma speared thru the chest in front of her son's and her waist high young lad grandson's four disbelieving eyes!', pg. 127

114) 'pure microlithic abstract art'... 'After the mammoth rescued the trekkers from the epic deluge she pulls herself up on dryland and looks both ways!', pg. 128

115) 'pure microlithic abstract art'... 'After the mortified waist high young maiden's frightened kitty scratched grandpas delirious face, grandma made her march in front of the tan mammoth so that she could keep a glaring eyeball on her!', pg. 129

116) '6/14/12'.... 'This is what the 'roaring' male lion volcanic ash cloud sees as he descends on the Mammoth People trekkers.....and grandpa's delirious eyes see him about to pounce on them!', pg. 130

117) 'heat treated stone microlithic abstract art'... 'That left side close-up view of grandma's bonnet covered head and crotchety face with her 'glaring' left eyeball 'Rocks'!', pg. 132

118) 'prismatic knife'... 'The submissive ewe spirit has taken her last exhaled breath into the heavens because the mammoth can't smell her presence anymore!', pg. 133

119) 'snapped oval knife'... 'All of the surviving trekkers including the baby mammoth are swimming towards grandma and the mother mammoth that she's sitting atop!', pg. 134

120) 'heat treated stone'... 'The horse is turning his head from right to left to try to get it either over or under the travois poles to see what's going on behind him!', pg. 135

121) 'pure microlithic abstract art'... '...now you know that grandma's crotchety face is reflecting off of her 'kicked off' left shoe!, pg. 136

122) 'heat treated flake knife'... 'Grandma and her fair young maiden granddaughter were conversing as they trekked when the predator ice swallowed her and her palomino pony whole!, pg. 137

123) 'huge backed knife'... 'The front of the male lions 'attacking' face is about to 'slice' into the dumbfounded ewe's neck!', pg. 138

124) 'micro prismatic knife'... 'It's quite possible that crotchety grandma kicked her shoe at the frightened kitty to keep him away from grandpa!', pg. 139

125) 'pure microlithic abstract art'... 'The only reason that the pack of ravenous dire wolves didn't eat mom's head or clenched left hand is because they were covered in cow shit!', pg. 140

126) 'pure microlithic abstract art'... 'Grandma's leaning forward over dads head from atop her special armchair that's attached to a stretcher that has its poles made from mammoth tusks!', pg. 141

127) 'snapped prismatic knife microlithic abstract art'... 'In fact, grandpa's hooked pointy nose is a drip of the 'straining' palomino pony's slobber!', pg. 142

128) 'pure microlithic abstract art'... 'Both of the mortified waist high young maiden's grandparents are extremely irritated!', pg. 143

129) 'pure microlithic abstract art'... 'The family of Mammoth People trekkers are all grieving inconsolably along with the mammoth and the fair young maiden's pony!', 144

130) 'prismatic knife microlithic abstract art'... 'Dad just finished saying... "I wonder where the lioness is?..."', pg. 145

131) 'backed knife microlithic abstract art'... 'The submissive ewe spirit is 'gliding' in for a landing to collect the Mammoth Peoples exhaled last breaths!', pg. 146

132) 'backed knife microlithic abstract art'... 'Besides...only saber-toothed cats sliced off its preys ears...and trunks!', pg. 147

133) 'pure microlithic abstract art'... 'Grandma looked the 'diving' submissive ewe spirit in the left eye as she dived past her submerged head...', pg. 148

134) 'pure microlithic abstract art'... 'Mom and dad are looking on in horror as the attacking male lion clings on to the bucking ox's back!', pg. 149

135) 'flake knife'... 'The 'jeering' warrior brave is sitting atop his pony behind the chief's raised purple arm with the amber setting Pleistocene sun setting on the horizon to the right of him!', pg. 150

136) 'stone prismatic knife'... 'The angry charging mother sea lion has the 'predators bent foreleg featuring the prey that it's stalking'...it's her right flipper... and she's gaining on them!', pg. 151

137) 'pure microlithic abstract art'... 'I'm sure that mom's doing her best to answer all of the waist high young maidens perplexing questions!', pg. 152

138) 'prismatic knife microlithic abstract art'... 'The hungry bear is so close that the waist high young maiden's bonnet covered head and pug nosed face is reflecting off of its quivering upper lip and shiny nose!', pg. 153

139) 'pure microlithic abstract art'... '...you'll see that the waist high young maiden's face is reflecting off of the back of the kitty's 'swiping' left paw!', pg. 154

140) 'pure microlithic abstract art'... 'The entire Mammoth People family of trekkers is watching in horror as dad and the mammoth that he was leading sink into the icy cold abyss!', pg. 155

141) 'prismatic flake knife'... 'The prey was killed and eaten out in the tall prairie grass by a pair of rogue male lions!', pg. 156

142) 'pure microlithic abstract art'... 'The young lad is giving the matriarchal mammoth's trunk a big hug for saving his life!', pg. 157

143) 'baked stone lancet microlithic abstract art'... 'The inexperienced young lad had no idea how 'messy' bludgeoning baby sea lion pups could be!' , pg. 158

144) 'polished stone microlithic abstract art'... 'The watchful bloodhound pup won't leave his loving old masters side while the sorceress flaps her wings over him!', pg. 159

145) 'predators bent foreleg microlithic abstract art'... 'The erupting volcanoes male lion ash cloud is descending on the trekkers making everyone miserable!', pg. 160

146) 'predators stalking body microlithic abstract art'... '"It's the biggest stalking saber-toothed cat that you've ever seen and it's less than an ox length in front of you!"', pg. 161

147) 12/6/12... 'The waist high young lad looks cross-eyed as he peers intently at the 'predators bent foreleg featuring the prey its stalking' microlithic abstract art form that his dad made for him to use as an eating utensil

and that has one of the repetitive themes on it of the trials and tribulations that their ancestors went thru to get to here!', pg. 162

148) 'pure microlithic abstract art'... 'Grandma was trying to warn her fair young maiden granddaughter of the incoming fiery cinder ball that barely missed them!', pg. 163

149) ''boot' microlithic abstract art'... 'Grandpa's cursing at the poor performance after the bucking bull jerked his grandson cleanly out of his sea lion pup pelt boots!', pg. 164

150) 'pure microlithic abstract art'... 'Mom doesn't realize that they're just getting started on their epic journey... "Honey...we can't go much further like this!"', pg. 165

151) 'pure microlithic abstract art'... 'Grandma knew that the epic deluge would drown grandpa before any of the other healthy females that could tread water longer!', pg. 166

152) 'pure microlithic abstract art'... 'When the teenage front porter looks back over his left shoulder he sees his crotchety grandmothers glaring left eye as that of a vicious lioness!', pg. 167

153) 'pure microlithic abstract art'... 'This extremely close-up image of crotchety grandma leaning forward and squishing her Scotty that's on her lap...is priceless!', pg. 168

154) 'prismatic flake knife' 'microlithic abstract art'... 'Grandma and grandpa are so disappointed in their grandson's bull riding performance that they're getting up to go home!', pg. 169

155) 'pure microlithic abstract art'... 'Grandma and grandpa slept soundly thru the severe thunderstorm while mom worriedly awaited the return of dad and their mammoth!', pg. 170

156) 'pure microlithic abstract art'... 'The youngsters bonnet is slipping down over her eyes as she flees but the saber toothed cat clearly has his eyes on the stumbling plump herdswoman!', pg. 172

157) 'fossiliferous stone microlithic abstract art'... 'The screaming waist high young maiden that has the ribbon on her bonnet is being past up by the slaughtering male lions bloodied face!', pg. 174

158) 'pure microlithic abstract art'... 'The 'smug' looking lioness glacial ice melt water rushing stream appears content as if she's standing over her kill of rambunctious waist high young lad that will feed her cubs!', pg. 175

159) 'potsherd microlithic abstract art'... 'The giraffe feeds while the stalking saber toothed cats long right fang reflects off of the surprised inexperienced young lads shadowy left arm and hand!', pg. 176

160) 'burnt bone microlithic abstract art'... 'The lioness cinder ball is looking back towards you over her left shoulder as if to say... "mine...all mine!"', pg. 178

161) 'potsherd microlithic abstract art'... 'The mortified waist high young maiden's fancy bonnet has a stitched button hole on its left flap and the 'x' marks the spot!', pg. 179

162) 'burnt bone microlithic abstract art'... 'Meanwhile, crotchety grandma's two teenage young lad left porters look on in disgust!', pg. 180

163) '1/9/13' 'MAMMOTH PEOPLE'...mammoth caravan...to here!', pg. 181

164) 'stone microlithic abstract art'... '...well...if you see a saber toothed cat's saber tooth fang this close up, you know what's coming next...', pg. 182

165) 'fractured oval knife microlithic abstract art'... 'The epic deluge may be sweeping her and grandma away but all the waist high young maiden can think about is saving her kitty!', pg. 185

166) 'stone microlithic abstract art'... 'Grandpa's family is jubilant including his howling bloodhound pup when the sorceress and her three chanting assistants bring him back from the dead!', pg. 186

167) 'pure microlithic abstract art'... 'The 'beast of burden' front left porters left hand is holding onto the tip of the upside down mammoth tusk!', pg. 187

168) 'pure microlithic abstract art'... 'Just like his delirious dad sees the male lion ash cloud, no matter which way he turns he can't escape his crotchety old mother!', pg. 189

169) 'flint knife'... 'Moms blond disheveled hair sticks out from under her bonnet over her forehead as her worried eyes look up at grandma atop the mammoth!', pg. 191

170) 'pure microlithic abstract art'... 'The plump herdswoman's severed right hand is an 'opposing severed body part' to her severed right foot!', pg. 192

171) 'pure microlithic abstract art'... 'The two youngsters are looking up over the gruff chief at the taunting and jeering warrior braves face. I bet his name is 'Twisted Feather'!', pg. 193

172) 'The second attacking saber toothed cat is having second thoughts after grandma whacked his mate on the head between the eyes!', pg. 194

173) 'pure microlithic abstract art'... 'The howling alpha male dire wolf picked out the meatiest teen bonfire dancer!', pg. 195

174) 'mating stone knife'... 'The submissive ewe spirit is gliding in for a landing with the seeds of life!', pg. 196

175) 'pure microlithic abstract art'... 'The rising smoke is causing the pair of rats to stir on the crooked wooden beam above the sorceress as she wafts the smoke over grandpa!', pg. 198

176) 'prismatic knife'... 'The mammoth made her way towards the three survivors and poor 'precious' was extremely concerned about being left to fend for himself!', pg. 200

177) 'spear section microlithic abstract art'... 'The lead hunter herder's stone spear tip shattered into three pieces against the male lion's top right fang!', pg. 201

178) 'stone microlithic abstract art'... 'The stern looking lead hunter herder was thrusting his spear straight forward into the attacking male lions right shoulder before it shattered!', pg. 202

179) 'seam ripper microlithic abstract art'... 'The fiery lioness cinder ball is holding down the struggling suffering prey while she sneeringly guards it!', pg. 203

180) 'flying bird microlithic abstract art'... '...his teenage son thought it hilarious when the flushed grouse's aborted egg splattered on the left side of his face!', pg. 204

181) 'pure microlithic abstract art'... 'The lahar is overtaking the trekkers sweeping the mammoth off of her feet and rolling her newborn calf!', pg. 205

182) 'flying bird microlithic abstract art'... 'The golden eagle dives towards his sea lion pup prey while mom watches helplessly and the giraffes get swept away by the epic deluge!', pg. 206

183) 'pure microlithic abstract art'... 'The silently attacking 'tightlipped' male lion epic deluge is sweeping away an entire village of Mammoth People!', pg. 207

184) 'prismatic flake knife'... 'The frightened fair young maiden is trying to save her little brother from the snarling dire wolf at the springtime picnic!', pg. 208

185) 'pure microlithic abstract art'... 'It looks as if two rogue male lions dropped in on the Mammoth People's annual springtime event and are having their own picnic!', pg. 210

186) 'pure microlithic abstract art'... 'The roaring male lion glacial ice melt water stream attacks the rambunctious waist high young lad while his busy family makes camp on its banks!', pg. 211

187) 'pure microlithic abstract art'... 'Grandma came up from behind her grandson and smacked the dire wolf on top of his head taking that snarling smirk right off of his face!', pg. 212

188) 'prismatic knife section microlithic abstract art'... 'The roaring male lion lahar and his lioness mate swept the Mammoth People away before they could even leave their village!', pg. 213

189) 'prismatic knife'... 'microlithic abstract art'... 'Even though it was a joyous occasion for all of the other Mammoth People, the jilted forlorn lover was devastated!', pg. 214

190) 'pure microlithic abstract art'... 'The waist high young lads mesmerized face is looking up at the gruff chief's sea lion pups right flipper that's dangling from his headdress!', pg. 215

191) 'oval knife microlithic abstract art'... 'You will never see a bigger and clearer combined optical and cognitive illusion close-up image of crotchety grandma sitting on her special armchair!', pg. 216

192) 'prismatic knife'... 'The babysitting waist high young maiden bolted thru the cottages doorway upon the arrival of the folks who got caught in a snowstorm but were saved by the mare!', pg. 217

193) 'flake knife'... '...dad is driving his spear past his surprised son to jab at the lioness whose left paw is swiping at the back of his sons head!', pg. 218

194) 'pure microlithic abstract art'... 'The hungry lioness and her cubs ate everything but the toddler young maiden's left foot that's still inside of its left shoe!', pg. 219

195) 'prismatic knife'... 'The taunting warrior braves single flopping eagle feather tells the whole story.... grandma's yelling down at dad to hold up his big spear!', pg. 220

196) 'pure microlithic abstract art'... 'The spooked horse is rearing while mom hurries to untie his reins from the hitching post when dire wolves attacked the summertime picnic!', pg. 221

197) 'prismatic knife'... '...a pair of lions raided the summertime event slaughtering picnickers left and right which provided a feast for their cubs!', pg. 222

198) 'spearhead'... 'microlithic abstract art'... 'The gruff chief and the warrior brave look on as dad holds up his spears pointy tip that grandma yelled at him to do while the children get to his side!', pg. 223

199) 'prismatic knife'... 'Grandma is yelling at her fair young maiden granddaughter to run towards her and dive over the wall of the sled and hide behind it with her twin brothers!', pg. 224

200) 'spear section'... 'Everything is reflecting off of dads long brown stone spear point that's jabbing the snarling dire wolf in the face!', pg. 225

201) 'pure microlithic abstract art'... 'The horrified fair young maiden is looking right down the throat of the attacking saber toothed cat!', pg. 226

202) 'prismatic flake knife microlithic abstract art'... 'The defiant elderly schoolmarm died defending her students from a dire wolf when they sang at the evening school program!', pg. 227

203) 'pure microlithic abstract art'... 'The fair young maidens and her palomino horses 'dead heads' eyes watched the saber toothed cat eat both of them alive!', pg. 228

204) 'pure microlithic abstract art'... 'The slobbering short faced bear is shaking off the sting that grandpas cane delivered to his bleeding nose while grandma hustles their grandchildren away before it wears off!', pg. 229

205) 'pure microlithic abstract art'... 'Protective grandmas screaming grandchildren hid behind her while she whacked her shepherds crook over the attacking dire wolfs snout!', pg. 230

206) 'pure microlithic abstract art'... 'The fair young maiden is shielding her eyes from the warrior braves taunting gestures while she turns to hug her mesmerized brother!', pg. 231

207) 'pure microlithic abstract art'... 'Grandma and the gruff chief were the first to notice the stalking dire wolves, even before the feeding giraffe did!', pg. 232

208) 'predators bent foreleg microlithic abstract art'... 'Surrounded by calamity, I can just hear grandma loudly say to mom... "Give me the baby..."', pg. 233

209) 'arrow point base'... 'Mom holds up the torchlight and tries to keep it from blowing out while dad assists the birthing ewe and their inquisitive daughter asks relentless questions!', pg. 234

210) 'backed knife' 'microlithic abstract art'... "Mommy, why is grandpa peeing on the dead warrior braves war painted white face...?", pg. 235

211) 'Thumb scraper pure microlithic abstract art'... 'The nervous mammoth's front left foot kicks up dirt while the setting Pleistocene sun cast's purple hues over the tense powwow!', pg. 236

212) 'bifacial backed knife microlithic abstract art'... 'Grandpa's holding his granddaughter close while their horse struggles to see the mating lions that are oblivious to the loud powwow that's taking place below them!', pg. 238

213) ''predators bent foreleg' microlithic abstract art'... 'The waist high young maiden and her soaking wet kitty are lovingly reaching for each other and anticipating their embrace!', pg. 240

214) 'sod schoolhouse' 'pure microlithic abstract art'... 'Moms holding her infant in her right arm while her left hand holds up the lamp so grandpa can see to get the stubborn newborn pink baby mammoth to nurse!', pg. 241

215) 'flint knife scraper'... 'pure microlithic abstract art'... 'The concerned fair young maiden ran up to hug her grandpa who was cursing at the gruff chief who her little brother couldn't take his eyes off of!', pg. 242

216) 'prismatic knife'... 'The dire wolfs snarling snout is snapping at moms horrified face while she runs towards the hitching post with her infant, where the horses rear out of control!', pg. 243

217) 'seam ripper'...microlithic abstract art... 'The jilted forlorn lover manages a feeble smile at the curious giraffe while he tugs on his mares rein straps... "Let's go girl..."', pg. 244

218) 'heat treated geometric stone knife'... '...mom just can't see sticking that cow's big ole dirty teat in her crying infant's mouth to pacify him!', pg. 246

219) 'prismatic knife scraper end'... 'The look of scorn on grandma's face hasn't changed in over thirteen millennia after she pulled her guilty fair young maiden granddaughter out of the bushes!', pg. 248

220) 'pure microlithic abstract art'... 'The excited waist high young lad is pointing his left index finger at the grooming male lion's faces upper left black lip and licking tongue!', pg. 252

221) 'flake knife'... 'pure microlithic abstract art'... 'Mom and dad had to watch helplessly as the epic deluges predator wave separated them and the lead mammoth from their overwhelmed infant!', pg. 253

222) 'pure microlithic abstract art'... 'The family had just started eating their porridge when the hungry bear burst thru the top half of the Dutch door, uninvited!', pg. 254

223) 'flake knife pure microlithic abstract art'... 'The bewildered expression on the waist high young maidens face is being created by the reflections of the prostrate elderly herdswoman that she blindly ran into!', pg. 255

224) 'flake knife' 'pure microlithic abstract art'... 'The kitty's fair young maiden trips and spills one of the vital pales of river water meant to be thrown on the burning cottage that he's trapped in!', pg. 256

225) 'pure microlithic abstract art'... 'The pair of curious sad giraffes is gazing down at the fallen decrepit elderly herdswoman as they trudge on by her in the narrow windy mountain pass!', pg. 257

226) 'Laurentide Ice Sheet glacial maximum', pg. 261

Index of Quotes

9 780692 081433